UNITED STATES ARMY IN WORLD WAR II

China—Burma—India Theater

TIME RUNS OUT IN CBI

by

Charles F. Romanus

and

Riley Sunderland

MILITARY INSTRVCTION

OFFICE OF THE CHIEF OF MILITARY HISTORY

UNITED STATES ARMY

WASHINGTON, D.C., 1959

Library of Congress Catalog Card Number: 59–60003

Reprinted 1970

UNITED STATES ARMY IN WORLD WAR II
Kent Roberts Greenfield, General Editor

Advisory Committee
(As of 30 April 1958)

Elmer Ellis
University of Missouri

Brig. Gen. John D. Sullivan
U.S. Continental Army Command

Samuel Flagg Bemis
Yale University

Brig. Gen. Edgar C. Doleman
Army War College

Gordon A. Craig
Princeton University

Brig. Gen. Frederick R. Zierath
Command and General Staff College

Oron J. Hale
University of Virginia

Brig. Gen. Kenneth F. Zitzman
Industrial College of the Armed Forces

W. Stull Holt
University of Washington

Col. Vincent J. Esposito
United States Military Academy

T. Harry Williams
Louisiana State University

Office of the Chief of Military History
Maj. Gen. Richard W. Stephens, Chief

Chief Historian	Kent Roberts Greenfield
Chief, Histories Division	Col. Seneca W. Foote
Chief, Editorial and Publication Division	Lt. Col. E. E. Steck
Editor in Chief	Joseph R. Friedman
Chief, Cartographic Branch	Elliot Dunay
Chief, Photographic Branch	Margaret E. Tackley

The History of

THE CHINA–BURMA–INDIA THEATER

Stilwell's Mission to China
Stilwell's Command Problems
Time Runs Out in CBI

This volume, one of the series UNITED STATES ARMY IN WORLD WAR II, is the third and last to be published in the subseries THE CHINA–BURMA–INDIA THEATER.

The volumes in the over-all series will be closely related and will present a comprehensive account of the activities of the Military Establishment during World War II. A tentative list of subseries is appended at the end of this volume.

. . . to Those Who Served

Foreword

This volume, third of a subseries, carries the story of the Army's anomalous mission in China–Burma–India from the recall of General Stilwell in October 1944 to V-J Day. It deals with problems at all levels from platoon to theater, from tactics to diplomacy. The postwar concern of the Army with military assistance gives a special interest to the military advisory system that General Wedemeyer developed in the China theater to strengthen and guide the forces of Chiang Kai-shek. Stopping with the end of the war against Japan, *Time Runs Out in CBI* necessarily leaves the Wedemeyer story incomplete. But the authors' utilization of hitherto unused Army sources throws a light on the China tangle that should make this book useful to makers of policy, as well as interesting to readers of the history of our times.

Washington, D. C.
25 April 1958

RICHARD W. STEPHENS
Maj. Gen., U.S.A.
Chief of Military History

The Authors

From 1946 to 1953 the authors formed the CBI Section of the staff engaged in writing the history of the U.S. Army in World War II.

Charles F. Romanus received the degree of Master of Arts in History at the University of Illinois in 1937 and pursued his work for the doctorate at Louisiana State University, where he was a teaching fellow in history. Entering the Army in 1943 he was commissioned in March 1945 and became a historical officer in the headquarters of the China Theater. He is now Chief of the Organizational History and Honors Branch of the Office, Chief of Military History.

Riley Sunderland graduated from the University of Chicago in 1937. In April 1942 he was called to active duty as a second lieutenant in the Field Artillery, and from July 1945 to May 1946 was in the Historical Section, Headquarters, India–Burma Theater, in New Delhi. After leaving OCMH in 1955, he entered the field of operations research and is now studying mathematics at The George Washington University, Washington, D. C.

Preface

The history of China, Burma, and India, as U.S. theaters of operations in World War II, ended as it began. As in 1942, so in 1945 the Americans in China were still attempting to improve the Chinese Army so that China might be a more effective partner in the United Nations war against Japan. Other Americans in India and Burma were making an effort to fly supplies to their American and Chinese comrades and to help drive the Japanese from North Burma so that still more supplies might go to China by road and pipeline.

The volume begins with the division of the China–Burma–India Theater into the India–Burma and China Theaters in October 1944 and ends with a Japanese surrender that cut across the accelerating Sino-American preparations in China. The scope of this subseries has required covering both of the successor theaters of CBI in a single volume. Though an effort has been made to do justice to the India–Burma Theater, its mission of supporting the China Theater dictated subordinating the account of its activities to the story of the latter theater. Perhaps the most significant story told in this volume describes the efforts of Lt. Gen. Albert C. Wedemeyer and his staff to create an effective system for Sino-American co-operation in building a better Chinese Army.

This volume is the last of a three-volume subseries that describes a continuing flow of events and the space given to the several topics treated within reflects that fact. The authors have tried to make the volume reasonably complete within itself, yet the perspective in which events have appeared to them will emerge more clearly if viewed in the light of the first two volumes.

Like its predecessors, the present volume is written at the level of theater headquarters in the India–Burma and China Theaters. The emphasis is on the over-all roles of the organizations comprised in the Army Ground Forces and the Army Service Forces. The authors have not attempted to duplicate the efforts of the U.S. Air Force in presenting its own story of air operations in China, Burma, and India, or of the several technical services in telling their histories. Moreover, the other nations that took part in the closing phases of World War II in the Pacific must perforce be left to tell their own stories from their own records.

The authors were greatly aided by the privilege of examining that portion of the papers of Maj. Gen. Patrick J. Hurley, U.S.A., Ret., which relates to his services in China. Since General Hurley was Presidential representative and then Ambassador to China in 1944 and 1945, his papers are essential to any serious study of the period. The personal notebook and private papers of Brig. Gen. Ernest F. Easterbrook gave an interesting and helpful glimpse of Burma operations through the eyes of an infantry regimental commander.

General Wedemeyer, with Brig. Gen. Paul Caraway, Col. B. F. Taylor, and Mr. William MacAfee, offered their recollections in the form of detailed critiques of the draft manuscript. The critiques are valuable, representing as they do the reactions of the sometime China Theater commander, one of his principal planners, the secretary of his general staff, and his aide. The former Chief of Staff, China Theater, Maj. Gen. Robert B. McClure, also commented at considerable length on the draft manuscript. The comments of other participants who read the manuscript formed a rich and varied source of material.

Among the authors' professional colleagues, grateful acknowledgment is due Brigadier Michael R. Roberts, D.S.O., of the Cabinet Office Historical Section. Brigadier Roberts examined the account of British operations from the standpoint of a skilled soldier and accomplished author. Our task would have been impossible without the generous help of many archivists in the Departmental Records Branch, The Adjutant General's Office, and in the General Reference Office of the Office, Chief of Military History.

The distinguished maps in all three volumes of the subseries were prepared under the supervision of Mr. Wsevolod Aglaimoff, Deputy Chief Historian for Cartography.

We wish to record our appreciation of the pains taken by our editor and copy editor to bring this book to print. Miss Ruth Stout, who edited the first and second volumes of this subseries and who over the years has become identified as much with the entire subseries as have the authors, is due our special thanks and gratitude. We also acknowledge a particular debt of gratitude to Mrs. Gay Morenus Hammerman, the copy editor. Mrs. Norma B. Sherris selected and captioned the photographs for this volume. The index was prepared by Mrs. Michael Burdett Miller. Mrs. Mitzi Bucan Rusmisel, our stenographer, gave us invaluable aid in the preparation of the manuscript.

The authors assume sole responsibility for the use made of the comments and criticism offered by participants and for any errors of fact or interpretation of the sources open to them.

Washington, D. C.   CHARLES F. ROMANUS
25 April 1958   RILEY SUNDERLAND

Contents

PART ONE

Opening the Road to China

PART TWO

Plans and Preparations for Opening a Port in China

Charts

Tables

Maps

Illustrations

Illustrations are from
Department of Defense files.

PART ONE

OPENING THE ROAD TO CHINA

CHAPTER I

New Commanders in a Split Theater

As in January 1942, so again in October 1944, the United States of America ordered one of its general officers to act as a chief of staff to Generalissimo Chiang Kai-shek, then Supreme Commander of the China Theater in the war between the United Nations and Germany, Italy, and Japan. On both occasions, Japanese successes in the field alarmed the U.S. Government and preceded the step. But events had not been static during the intervening thirty-four months, and so the two officers concerned, Lt. Gen. Joseph W. Stilwell in 1942–1944, and Lt. Gen. Albert C. Wedemeyer in 1944–1946, faced situations whose differences are as enlightening as their similarities.

The Japanese in December 1941 and January 1942 had overrun American and British possessions in the Far East with a speed that appeared to the United States to spread gloom and despondency in China and aroused anxiety that China might make peace with Japan. On the positive side, the U.S. War Department hoped that a revitalized Chinese Army might offer a defense of China effective enough to ease pressure on the United States and the British Commonwealth in the Pacific. So General Stilwell was sent to China to be chief of staff to the Generalissimo in the latter's role as Supreme Commander, China Theater; to reassure the Generalissimo of United Nations' interest in and support for China; and to carry out the specific added mission of improving the combat efficiency of the Chinese Army.

After he took up his mission, Stilwell found it difficult to persuade the Chinese Government to undertake those steps which he thought essential to create a potent Chinese force, such as reducing the number of divisions to a total within China's ability to support, bringing the remainder to strength, providing them with professionally qualified officers, and giving them the bulk of China's arms. Stilwell's task of persuading the Chinese—for he could not order them—was complicated by the Japanese seizure of Burma, which lent force to the argument that China could do nothing for itself until its Allies broke the Japanese blockade. Among those who opposed Stilwell's plans was Maj. Gen. Claire L. Chennault, the senior American air officer in China, who believed that by stressing reform of the Chinese Army, and devoting his meager resources to it, Stilwell—with his superiors in the War Department—was missing the chance to defeat Japan from the air.   Winning the support of President Franklin D. Roosevelt and of the Generalissimo, Chennault received priority on supplies flown into China by the U.S. Air Transport Command.   This greatly hindered Stilwell in his efforts to rearm and reform 60 Chinese divisions—5 in India–Burma, 25 in Yunnan (Y–Force), and a projected 30 in east China (Z–Force).   (*Map 1—inside back cover.*)

In the winter of 1943–44 the Japanese grew concerned lest the Americans base their newly developed long-range bombers in east China and resolved to take the airfields there, from which Chennault operated.[1]   The Japanese offensive opened in April 1944, and as it drove ahead revealed grave weaknesses in the Allied command structure in China.   The Generalissimo refused to give arms to the Chinese commanders in east China, while some of them sought Japanese and American support for a revolt against him. General Chennault threw his every resource into supporting the east China commanders and later charged Stilwell with ulterior motives when the latter would not ship arms to them, in part because of the Generalissimo's injunction, in part because of a developing crisis over command.

Since the U.S. Joint Chiefs of Staff wanted to give land-based air support from east China's airfields to American operations in the western Pacific, they were anxious to hold those bases.   They believed that if Stilwell took command of all forces in China Theater, both Nationalist and Communist, he might be able to keep the Japanese from seizing the American airfields in China.   The President agreed, and from July to September, through his special representative, Maj. Gen. Patrick J. Hurley, tried to persuade the Generalissimo to make Stilwell the field commander in China Theater. First in principle agreeing to accept Stilwell, the Generalissimo later reversed himself, charged that Stilwell had shown himself unqualified, and asked that he be recalled.   The President acknowledged Chinese sovereignty in the matter and recalled Stilwell, but he refused to accept the Generalissimo's request that another American take command of the Chinese forces in China.

During the last phases of these negotiations, the strategic situation in the Pacific altered in a manner that greatly lessened the dependence of the United States on Chinese co-operation in the Pacific war.   The U.S. Navy decisively defeated the Imperial Japanese Navy in the Battle of Leyte Gulf, and General Douglas MacArthur firmly re-established U.S. power in the Philippines. Meanwhile, on 15 October, Marshal Joseph V. Stalin told the American Military Mission to Russia and Prime Minister Winston S. Churchill that the Soviet Union would employ sixty divisions against Japan beginning about

---

[1] For a discussion of the Japanese offensive plan (Operation *ICHIGO*), see the second volume of this subseries, Charles F. Romanus and Riley Sunderland, *Stilwell's Command Problems,* UNITED STATES ARMY IN WORLD WAR II (Washington, 1956), pp. 316ff.

MAJ. GEN. ALBERT C. WEDEMEYER ARRIVING AT CHUNGKING, *31 October 1944.*
At the airfield to greet him are, from left: Lt. Gen. Adrian Carton de Wiart, His
Majesty's Special Representative in Chungking; Mr. T. V. Soong, Chinese Minister of
Foreign Affairs; Maj. Gen. Patrick J. Hurley, President Roosevelt's Special Representa-
tive to Generalissimo Chiang Kai-shek; Maj. Gen. Thomas G. Hearn, Chief of Staff,
U.S. Army Forces, China Theater; General Wedemeyer, new Commanding General,
U.S. Army Forces, China Theater, and Chief of Staff to Generalissimo Chiang Kai-shek;
and General Ho Ying-chin, Chief of Staff, Chinese General Staff.

three months after Germany's defeat. Two days later he described the
projected operations of those forces as involving a thrust from Lake Baikal
to Tientsin, thus separating the Japanese forces in Manchuria from those in
China. Thenceforth, the Joint Chiefs of Staff were aware that whatever
might happen in China sixty Russian divisions were promised for operations
against Japan, and these operations would sweep south and east below the
Great Wall.[2]

Chinese bases were no longer considered essential in the war against
Japan, but there remained the problems that would be created if the General-

---

[2] Maj. Gen. John R. Deane, USA, Ret., *The Strange Alliance: The Story of Our Efforts at
Wartime Co-operation with Russia* (New York: The Viking Press, 1947), pp. 246–49.

issimo's government signed a separate peace, or if Chiang himself were to be removed through a coup by pro-Japanese elements that might choose to ignore the signs of accelerating disaster in Germany and Japan. Either event would raise the possibility that substantial Japanese forces, given a peace in China, might be withdrawn to reinforce the Japanese homeland garrison.

General Wedemeyer, then a major general, was nominated by the President and accepted by the Generalissimo to be the senior U.S. officer in the China Theater, and a chief of staff to the Generalissimo. His orders from the War Department and the resources at his disposal were very different from those given Stilwell in January 1942, yet his problems as he himself saw them were very similar to those which faced Stilwell: "A. Create conditions for the effective employment of maximum U.S. resources in the area. . . . B. The Chinese must be required to play an active role in this war. . . ."[3]

In late summer of 1944 the War Department, in planning for the new situation that would result were General Stilwell to become field commander of the Chinese armed forces under Generalissimo Chiang Kai-shek, had contemplated splitting the China, Burma and India (CBI) Theater in two. Though Stilwell was recalled, such a move still seemed advisable, and Wedemeyer assumed command in a separate China Theater on 31 October 1944, Lt. Gen. Daniel I. Sultan in India-Burma on 24 October 1944.[4] (*Map 2*) For a few days, General Chennault, senior American officer in China Theater, acted as the first U.S. theater commander.

While Deputy Chief of Staff, Southeast Asia Command, Wedemeyer had had ample opportunity since October 1943 to observe the workings of the United Nations effort in Asia from behind the scenes. Before taking up his post in Southeast Asia, Wedemeyer had been in the Operations Division, War Department General Staff, and so was intimately familiar with the wartime plans and policies of the United States. On 29 October 1944, two days after his predecessor flew from Karachi to the United States, Wedemeyer left the headquarters in Ceylon and flew to Chungking, arriving there 31 October.[5]

Nor was Dan Sultan, as the U.S. Army knew him, a stranger to the Asiatic scene, for he had been Stilwell's deputy theater commander. In his various peacetime assignments, Sultan had made a name for himself as an engineer and administrator, developing talents that would be eminently serviceable in his new post.

---

[3] RAD CFB 36841, Wedemeyer to Brig Gen Douglas L. Weart, DCofS Rr Ech USFCT, 5 May 45. Item 645, Bks 3 and 4, ACW Personal File. (See Bibliographical Note.)
[4] (1) CM–OUT 51593, JCS to Sultan, 25 Oct 44. (2) History of Services of Supply in India–Burma Theater, 1944–45, Vol. I, p. 4. OCMH. (Hereafter, SOS in IBT.)
[5] (1) The Wedemeyer letters in the OPD Exec Files (see Bibliographical Note) describe the general's reactions during the time he was Deputy Chief of Staff, Southeast Asia Command. (2) History of China Theater, 20–31 Oct 44. OCMH. Initialed by Wedemeyer, 12 Nov 44.

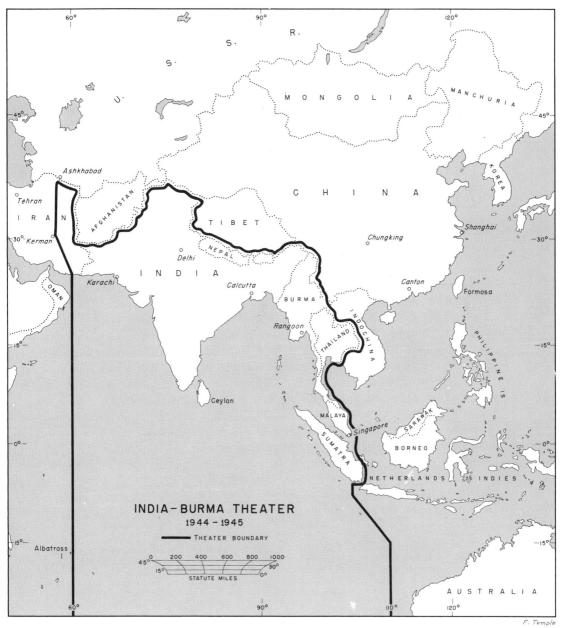

INDIA-BURMA THEATER
1944-1945
━━━━━ THEATER BOUNDARY

200   400   600   800   1000
STATUTE MILES

F. Temple

MAP 2

The Political and Economic Scene in China

The political and economic scene that Wedemeyer faced in China Theater placed as many obstacles in his path as did the Japanese themselves. Dissension among the Chinese sharply limited the strength that China would devote to facing the Japanese. In north China, the Chinese Communists had set up a state within a state that controlled its own territory and had its own forces. Its boundaries were indeterminate, its relations with the Japanese ambiguous, its finances in part sustained by taxes levied on trade with the enemy. But the embryonic Communist state controlled a considerable body of troops, and the Chinese Nationalists feared both its present power and its future intentions.[6] Nor were the Nationalists united among themselves. When the Japanese drove south from Hankow in the spring of 1944, the Chinese troops they faced were those of the local commanders. The Generalissimo refused to let arms of any sort, Chinese or U.S. lend-lease, be sent to the Chinese defending the airfields.[7] There were many and detailed reports that the east China commanders bitterly resented the Generalissimo's failure to support them. When Heng-yang fell on 8 August, Chinese claiming to be emissaries of these men presented to American authority a plan for a separatist regime and pleaded for American support. Unknown to the Americans, Chinese making identical representations had been negotiating with the Japanese since the winter of 1943–44. Intelligence reports were received at U.S. headquarters to the effect that the Generalissimo's attitude toward the east China campaign reflected an understanding between him and the Japanese under which they would leave him undisturbed in southwest China if he in turn would not interfere while they took the airfields that presented so obvious a menace to the Japanese homeland.[8]

These were grave charges. Supporting them were three relevant circumstances: (1) the Japanese garrisoned their great Hankow supply base, which

---

[6] (1) Hurley Papers. (2) Capt. Robert L. Bodell, History of DIXIE Mission. OCMH. (Hereafter, History of DIXIE Mission.) (3) The Japanese troop movements which preceded the east China campaign of 1944 seem to have been made without Communist interference.

[7] (1) On 4 December 1944 Wedemeyer criticized the poor performance of the Chinese forces that had tried to defend the U.S. bases in east China. Unless the interpreter erred badly, the Generalissimo replied that those were provincial troops but that now Nationalist divisions were going to fight to save Kunming. Min, Mtg 12, Wedemeyer with Generalissimo, 4 Dec 44. Bk 1, Generalissimo Minutes, 1–69, 13 Nov 44–15 Jul 45, Job T–49–20 CBI. (Hereafter, Generalissimo Minutes.) (See Bibliographical Note.) (2) For a discussion of the Generalissimo's refusal to let arms be sent to the east China commanders, see *Stilwell's Command Problems,* Ch. XI. The ban stayed in effect until February 1945. See Rad CAK 6126. Brig Gen Edgar E. Glenn, CofS Fourteenth AF, to Chennault, 22 Feb 45. Item 439, Bks 1 and 2, ACW Personal File.

[8] (1) Min, Mtg 27, Wedemeyer with Generalissimo, 10 Jan 45. Item 7, Bk 1, Generalissimo Minutes. (2) For an account of the separatist movement in east China to October 1944, see *Stilwell's Command Problems.*

supported their drive in east China, with the equivalent of two divisions, though sixty Chinese divisions lay within striking distance; (2) Nationalist officers close to the Generalissimo objected to shipment of arms to the Chinese forces defending the east China airfields; and (3) the Generalissimo himself embargoed shipment of arms to General Hsueh Yueh, principal defender of east China, and kept the embargo until February 1945.[9]

In 1951 a group of senior Japanese staff officers of *China Expeditionary Army* were interrogated on the question of Sino-Japanese relations in 1944. They denied that there had been any understanding between the Japanese and the Chinese Central Government. Two of them, Lt. Cols. Yoshimasa Okada and Yoshio Fukuyama, stated that an agreement was reached between the Japanese *23d Army* at Canton and the local Chinese commander, General Yu Han-mou, in February 1944 under which General Yu agreed not to disturb Canton when the Japanese marched north from it. Yu kept his word, according to Okada, even though the Generalissimo was ordering him to attack Canton.

The Japanese officers agreed among themselves that there had been extensive contact with dissident Nationalist commanders in southeast China, and stated that through many channels they had sought to inform the Chinese that the east China drive offered no threat to them, but only to the U.S. airfields.[10]

It may be that the truth of this complicated matter lies in the Generalissimo's appreciating that the Japanese drive was directed toward the east China airfields, rather than on Kunming and Chungking, as can be seen by a glance at the map. These airfields lay within the domain of Chinese leaders whose loyalty to him he doubted. The Generalissimo may not have been sorry to see their power diminished and may have felt that there was no need to weaken his regime by rushing to their support, the more so since, very plainly against his will, he had recently, in April 1944, joined in the North Burma Campaign. The reports that reached American headquarters may well have been echoes of these matters.[11]

When Wedemeyer took command these issues had yet to be settled. The Generalissimo still would not permit shipment of arms to the east China commanders, who seemed to at least one senior U.S. officer to be contemplating revolt, and it was impossible to tell where the Chinese would make their

---

[9] (1) For a discussion of the Japanese-Chinese dispositions in 1944, see *Stilwell's Command Problems*. The problem of shipping arms to the east China commanders is also discussed there. The lifting of the embargo is discussed below, Ch. II.

[10] (1) Ltr and Incls, Lt Col James M. Miller, Exec Officer Mil Hist Sec FECOM, 13 Mar 52, to Maj Gen Orlando Ward, Chief of Mil Hist. (2) Ltr and Incls, Col Allison R. Hartman, Chief Mil Hist Sec FECOM, to Ward, 19 Dec 51. OCMH.

[11] The comments of Maj Gen Claire L. Chennault and of former Japanese officers on the draft manuscript of this volume tend to support this hypothesis, OCMH.

stand or where the Japanese would stop. As of late October their leading
elements were before Kweilin and Liuchow. It would be no mean achievement if Wedemeyer could stop the centrifugal tendencies of the Chinese and
thus deprive the Japanese of the diplomatic triumph that would be theirs
if China fell into a group of openly warring factions. As for the Generalissimo, he faced a domestic situation requiring the fullest exercise of his
diplomatic talents.

Economic distress within China limited the resources that could be devoted
to war, put still further strain on the Generalissimo's internal political arrangements, and placed increasing demands on tonnage flown into China.
Very simply stated, by fall 1944 the Central Government was growing weaker
because the Chinese dollar was losing value faster than Chinese fiscal agencies
could accumulate currency from either the tax gatherer or the printing press.
In concrete terms, in 1944 the Central Government was buying only one third
of the goods and services that it bought in 1937. One Chinese authority estimated that the national budget was but 3 percent of the national income. At
the same time, the United States was able to devote 47 percent of its national
income to war.[12] It was therefore advisable that Free China have an army no
larger than it could support, for every man taken from productive labor meant
added inflationary pressure, while poverty of the resources at the disposal of the
Central Government suggested that they should be used with the greatest attention to thrift and efficiency. However, the Central Government budget did
not represent the ceiling on China's war-making capacity. The decentralized
system of command, under which war area commanders acted as semi-independent provincial governors, plus the lack of internal transport facilities
suited to the movement of quantities of goods and masses of troops, meant
that the local resources of Kwangsi Province, say, stood behind Kwangsi
Province divisions, supplemented by whatever subsidies the local authorities
could obtain from the Central Government. Nevertheless, the national
budget reflected the resources at the direct command of the Generalissimo
and limited his power to govern.

The transportation situation in that part of China unoccupied by the
Japanese made it very difficult to move goods and people. The U.S. Foreign
Economic Administration estimated that at most 10,000 trucks were on hand,
the number in operation at any one time limited by poor maintenance and
bad fuel. Water transport was the classic resort in China, but unfortunately
a mountain range lay between the Hump terminus at Kunming and the east

---

[12] (1) Economic Conditions in Free China and Their Effect on Army Procurement, Jan 45,
pp. 2–3, prep by Resources Sec. Central Purchasing and Procurement Authority, Hq SOS
USFCT. OCMH. (Hereafter, Economic Conditions in China.) (2) *Statistical Abstract of the
United States: 1950* states that the U.S. national income in 1944 and 1945 was at a level of
over $180,000,000,000 (page 265) and that national defense, expenditures in fiscal 1944 were
$83,766,000,000 and in fiscal 1945, $84,569,000,000 (page 312).

TERRAIN IN THE KUNMING AREA

China front.   On the east side of the range use was made of water transport, but at a high monetary cost which the U.S. Services of Supply headquarters attributed in part to the steady rise in the boatmen's wages and in part to the "squeeze" the boatmen paid to officials at the numerous inspection points in order to get their cargoes through.

The weakness of Chinese internal transport greatly affected the military situation.   The Chinese divisions, national and provincial, were spread out all over unoccupied China.   Each Chinese war area contained a fair number of divisions that lived off the local countryside; great quantities of supplies simply could not be moved in Free China, for the Japanese had seized, in 1937, most of what rail net existed.   The difficulty was further compounded by the fact that the Chinese had not set up an efficient services of supply. Consequently, troop movements could not be supported by a steady flow of rations.   As a result of all these factors, even if Chinese domestic politics had permitted it, moving large numbers of divisions from one province to another was not within Chinese capabilities, while feeding them after their arrival in a province already strained to support the troops at hand would offer more and possibly insoluble problems, both economic and political.

The accelerating inflation in China directly affected the U.S. forces there, for the Japanese blockade of China forced them to depend upon local procurement for the necessities of everyday life since Hump tonnage had to be reserved for gasoline, oil, ammunition, ordnance, spare parts, and the like. Food, clothing, construction materials, all had to be obtained in China. The prices of these items in Chinese currency rose much faster than did the exchange rate for the U.S. dollar on the open market, so much so that in December 1944 the purchasing power of the U.S. dollar in China was but one sixth of what it had been in 1937. Plainly, the mere expenditure of U.S. currency in China would not provide resources for Wedemeyer's command, and would only aggravate an already bad inflation. Supplies would have to be brought in from the outside.

After allowance was made for the steady rise in prices and the high costs in transporting goods, the Services of Supply (SOS) still had to recognize the steady drain of commodities to the Japanese-held portion of China. Trade between occupied and unoccupied China was legal save for a limited number of items that could not be exported to Japanese-held areas without permit from Chungking. As a result, rice, tung oil, wolfram, timber, paper, sugar, hemp, vegetable tallow, hides and leather, resin, tea, and alum were exported in quantity to Japanese-held China. Moreover, SOS learned from intelligence reports that medicines available in unoccupied China through Red Cross and International Relief grants were shipped by parcel post from Chungking to villages near the China coast, where the writ of the Central Government did not hold, and were then shipped to the Shanghai market.[13]

The major constructive elements in the scene that confronted Wedemeyer were two—first, the Air Transport Command and China National Aviation Corporation were carrying supplies into China at a rate never approached before, and, second, on 15 October 1944 the Allied forces in north Burma opened an offensive with six divisions to clear the last Japanese from north Burma and open a new supply route to China. In October 1944, 35,131 tons were flown into China, four times the tonnage which entered China to support Stilwell in October 1943.[14] (*Chart 1*) When Wedemeyer assumed command on 31 October, the Chinese 38th Division, Chinese Army in India, was probing the outer defenses of Bhamo in Burma, and was thus about seventy miles from the old Burma Road. Such was Allied power in north Burma and so battered were the Japanese that the end was a matter

---

[13] Economic Conditions in China, pp. 14, 17–18, 19–20.
[14] See Charles F. Romanus and Riley Sunderland, *Stilwell's Mission to China,* UNITED STATES ARMY IN WORLD WAR II (Washington, 1953), Chart 6, p. 284, and *Stilwell's Command Problems,* Chart 5, p. 112.

C-46 OF THE AIR TRANSPORT COMMAND *over the Himalaya Mountains.*

of weeks. Time was on Wedemeyer's side, for every day that China remained a belligerent Wedemeyer's hand would be strengthened by the ever-nearing prospect that American supplies on a considerable scale would soon be ready for distribution in China.[15]

To sum up, when Wedemeyer took command of the U.S. forces in China Theater, there was extensive evidence of serious dissension among the Nationalist commanders, in addition to the highly publicized and generally known state of latent civil war between Nationalists and Communists, while the economic situation was an adverse factor that would weigh heavily against any American effort exerted in China. Under these circumstances, preventing the dissolution of China into a group of warring factions—some supported by the Japanese, some by the Soviet Union, some by the United States and the British Commonwealth—in order for the nation to reach the end of the war as a state rather than a geographic expression would be a major achievement.

[15] History of India–Burma Theater, 25 Oct 44–23 June 45, I, 106. OCMH. (Hereafter, History of IBT.)

CHART 1—TONNAGE SUPPLIED TO CHINA FROM INDIA–BURMA:
OCTOBER 1944–SEPTEMBER 1945

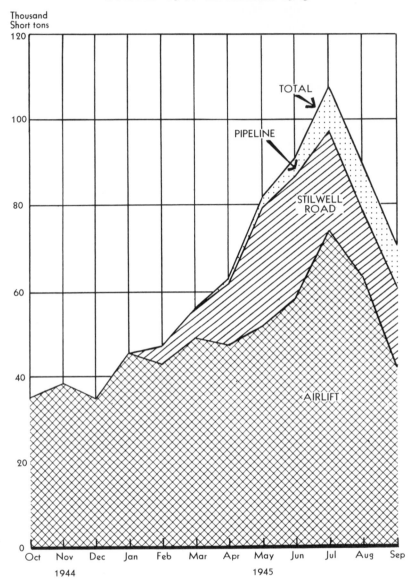

Source: Statistics, Transportation Section, prepared by George M. Adams, under the direction of Theodore E. Whiting. Draft in files of OCMH.

Gradually, the appreciation of these circumstances molded Wedemeyer's interpretation of his mission.

Wedemeyer's Missions and Roles

On 24 October 1944 the Joint Chiefs of Staff told Wedemeyer:

a. Your primary mission with respect to Chinese Forces is to advise and assist the Generalissimo in the conduct of military operations against the Japanese.

b. Your primary mission as to U.S. Combat Forces under your command is to carry out air operations from China. In addition you will continue to assist the Chinese air and ground forces in operations, training and in logistical support.

c. You will not employ United States resources for suppression of civil strife except insofar as necessary to protect United States lives and property.

This directive stood unchanged until August 1945.[16]

The problem that confronted Wedemeyer from the beginning was that of the content and the goal of the advice he was to give the Generalissimo. On 3 November, his G-3, Col. Thomas F. Taylor, suggested that the first mission of China Theater was "To aid and support the main effort which is being made in the Pacific," then listed the missions given above. In practice, Colonel Taylor advised, this meant securing the line of communications that led from the India base to Kunming and containing as much of the Japanese strength within China as possible. Taylor's concepts appear frequently in later studies, and were a step along the way of China Theater's continuing appraisal of its mission.[17]

The directive to Wedemeyer was significantly different from that given to his predecessor, which had been "to increase the effectiveness of United States assistance to the Chinese Government for the prosecution of the war and to assist in improving the combat efficiency of the Chinese Army." The old hope of reforming the Chinese Army was not suggested in the directive to Wedemeyer, possibly because the Operations Division of the War Department had come to doubt that it could be accomplished in time to assist in Japan's defeat; Wedemeyer was simply to assist the Chinese.[18]

The Joint Chiefs, in establishing Wedemeyer's position in China, told him that he was Commanding General, United State Forces, China Theater, which made him the U.S. theater commander, and they then "authorized [him] to accept the position of Chief of Staff to the Generalissimo." In so doing, the Joint Chiefs did not refer to the Generalissimo in his role as Supreme Commander, China Theater, and make Wedemeyer Chief of Staff to

---

[16] (1) Rad cited n. 4(1). (2) The mission as quoted above is closely paraphrased in History of China Theater, 20–31 Oct 44, which Wedemeyer initialed 12 November 1944.

[17] Memo, Col Thomas F. Taylor, G-3, for Wedemeyer, 3 Nov 44, sub: Reorientation of Chinese-American Effort in China. OCMH.

[18] (1) The increasing tendency of the War Department to minimize China's role in the war is described in *Stilwell's Command Problems*. (2) *Stilwell's Mission to China*, Ch. II.

him in that capacity alone, which would have limited Wedemeyer, as it had Stilwell, to assisting the Generalissimo in the conduct of combined operations in China.[19]   Rather, they made Wedemeyer's potential sphere of activity coextensive with the Generalissimo's, and left Wedemeyer free to advise the Generalissimo on any topic of interest to the Chinese leader, whether as Allied Supreme Commander or Chinese Generalissimo.   The role of a chief of staff is what the commander chooses to make it.   As matters developed, Wedemeyer found himself advising the Generalissimo on such Chinese domestic concerns as daylight-saving time, traffic regulations, the treatment of collaborators, and policy toward foreign holdings in Shanghai. But these aspects took some months to evolve, and in December 1944 Wedemeyer's personal summary of data on his theater described the relationship as not clearly defined.[20]

An intangible but constructive influence in the relationship may be found in the impression, shared by several members of Wedemeyer's staff, that Wedemeyer and Chiang Kai-shek quickly established an easy and pleasant personal relationship.   Wedemeyer's tact, his disarming personality, and his regard for the amenities made his advice palatable; the Generalissimo, as will be seen, was able to consider Wedemeyer's proposals on their merits.[21]

The Generalissimo's other chief of staff was General Ho Ying-chin, who was chief of the Chinese General Staff, which limited Ho's role to the Chinese Army as against Wedemeyer's concern with all regular forces present in China.   In practice, Ho proved co-operative, and in retrospect the relationship between the two men seems to have been easy and amicable.

Wedemeyer's relationship to his American superiors was different from Stilwell's.   Because General Hurley was now in China as the President's personal representative, Wedemeyer was not called upon to deliver messages from the President to the Generalissimo, a task which had sometimes embarrassed Stilwell in his relationship with the Generalissimo and ultimately precipitated his recall.   From November 1944 until his death the President rarely addressed the Generalissimo, in contrast with the twenty-three messages of 1944 and the twenty-two of 1943 that were sent through Army channels, to which must be added the unknown number sent through the Chinese Embassy or the Navy.[22]

---

[19] Stilwell's position as chief of the Generalissimo's (projected) Allied staff is discussed in *Stilwell's Mission to China*, Chapter II.

[20] (1) CM-OUT 51593, JCS to Wedemeyer, 24 Oct 44.   (2) Memos 513, 605, 909–7, Wedemeyer for Generalissimo, 17 Apr 45, 9 Jun 45, 2 Apr 45, Bks 9, 8, and 3, ACW Corresp with Chinese, Corresp File, Off CG Hq China Sv Comd. Box 45519, KCRC.   (Hereafter, ACW Corresp with Chinese.)   (See Bibliographical Note.)   (3) Item 2, Wedemeyer Data Book. OPD Copy, OCMH.

[21] See, for example, comments of Brig. Gen. Paul W. Caraway (former Chief, Planning Section, China Theater) on draft manuscript of this volume.   OCMH.

[22] Presidential messages of 1943–44 sent through Army channels to the Generalissimo are in the nine books of JWS Personal File.   (See Bibliographical Note.)

ANCIENT CHINESE VILLAGER *posing with General Wedemeyer in Kweichow Province during the latter's inspection trip through southeastern China.*

Wedemeyer's relationship to the Secretary of War, Henry L. Stimson, was not that of Stilwell to Stimson. Writing his memoirs in 1947, Stimson spoke of the "Stimson-Marshall-Stilwell" policy, noting that with Stilwell's recall he had "surrendered for good his bright hopes for a real rejuvenation of the Chinese forces," and wrote that he had had "no important part" in Wedemeyer's activities.[23]

A certain liaison between Wedemeyer and the President was created by General George C. Marshall's practice of sending portions of Wedemeyer's correspondence to the President. This was consistent with the Army Chief of Staff's policy; he had done the same with Stilwell's radios.[24]

An interesting aspect of the command structure in China Theater was the large number of American organizations in China which were completely or partly independent of the U.S. theater commander. The press and public would hold him responsible for sunshine or rain alike, yet his authority was greatly diminished by special arrangements which press and public would ignore as being dull military details not worthy of note. Thus, the XX Bomber Command was directly under the Joint Chiefs of Staff (JCS). The Air Transport Command was independent of control either by India–Burma or China Theater. Navy Group, China, reported to the Navy Department. The Office of Strategic Services (OSS) reported to its headquarters in Washington. The Joint Intelligence Collection Agency was under the JCS. In addition to these American organizations there were the large number of Allied missions and clandestine organizations, the bulk of them British. As one of the Generalissimo's chiefs of staff, Wedemeyer could with Chiang's consent assert authority over these latter in the name of the Generalissimo as Supreme Commander, China Theater, yet each Allied organization might claim that the original agreement under which it entered China freed it from any attempts at control by a third party.[25]

Thanks to the presence in Chungking of Maj. Gen. Adrian Carton de Wiart as the personal representative of Prime Minister Churchill, British agencies enjoyed the same sort of part military, part diplomatic representation

[23] (1) Henry L. Stimson and McGeorge Bundy, *On Active Service in Peace and War* (New York: Harper & Brothers, 1948), quotation on page 539. (2) But Stimson may have abandoned hope when Stilwell did, in October 1943, for there was not the collaboration and correspondence between them in 1944 that there had been in 1943. See *Stilwell's Mission to China*. Chapter X.

[24] (1) See the Wedemeyer correspondence in WDCSA 091 China, DRB AGO. (2) *Stilwell's Mission to China*, p. 246.

[25] (1) The status of the Fourteenth Air Force and the Air Transport Command is discussed in *Stilwell's Mission to China*. (2) The XX Bomber Command relationship is treated in *Stilwell's Command Problems*. (3) The problems Wedemeyer faced in attempting to assert authority over approximately twenty U. S. and Allied intelligence agencies operating in China are described in History of China Theater, Chapter III. OCMH.

that the Americans did.   Their diplomatic position and their resources were important; Wedemeyer was to find their co-operation valuable.[26]

To place Wedemeyer's various missions in their proper perspective against the myriad problems of China it may be helpful to note the number of U.S. troops in China as of 30 November 1944:

Organization	Number
Total	[a] 27,739
Army Air Forces (less XX Bomber Command and Air Transport Command	17,723
Air Transport Command	[b] 2,257
Theater troops	5,349
Services of Supply	2,410

[a] STM–30, *Strength of the Army.*   TAG, for 30 Nov 44, reports only 24,216 in China.

[b] STM–30 reports 23,713 ATC troops in CBI: India Headquarters, 482; India Wing, 7,550; Assam Wing, 15,681; none in China Wing.

The immediate logistical support of Wedemeyer's theater was to be given by General Sultan's India–Burma Theater; his requirements on the zone of interior for units, supplies, equipment, and personnel were to be submitted through Sultan's headquarters, which thus could screen them for items that could be supplied from India–Burma Theater.   In November 1944, Sultan had a total of 183,920 men.[27]

The U.S. Command Structure in China Theater

On assuming command, Wedemeyer found in China U.S. personnel from the Army, the Navy, and the Army Air Forces.   (*Chart 2*)   Some were engaged in aerial combat against the Japanese; some were giving logistical support to the U.S. air force units and to the other Americans; some were trying to train and advise the Chinese armies; some were gathering intelligence. There were no U.S. ground combat units, for the U.S. effort in China had always been intended by the War Department to help the Chinese defend themselves, to which end the War Department and the Joint Chiefs had been willing to give advice plus technical and air support.   Moreover, since every American flown into China meant that .62 of a ton of supplies had to be flown to China every month for his support, Stilwell had kept the number of U.S. ground force and service personnel in China to a minimum hence there were few indeed in that category.   Most of them were intended to act as technicians or instructors, and so the number of higher commissioned

[26] Sir Adrian Carton de Wiart, *Happy Odyssey: The Memoirs of Lt. Gen. Sir Adrian Carton de Wiart* (London: Cape, 1950).

[27] (1) Item 2, Wedemeyer Data Book.   (2) STM–30, *Strength of the Army,* TAG, for 30 Nov. 44, reports 23,713 ATC troops in CBI, 15,469 in XX Bomber Command, and 141,750 in India, Burma, and Ceylon—a total of 180,932.

CHART 2—ORGANIZATION OF U.S. FORCES, CHINA THEATER: JANUARY 1945

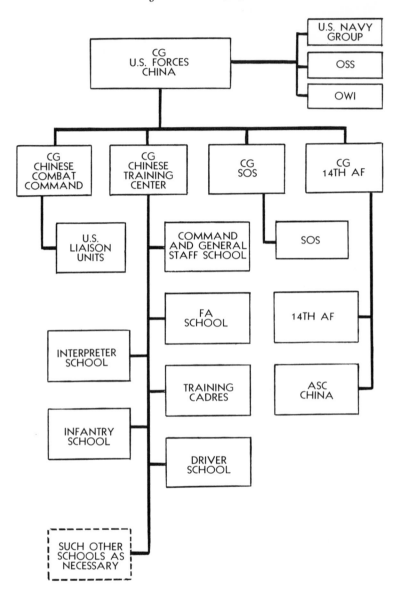

Source: Wedemeyer Data Book.

ranks and enlisted grades made China Theater relatively top-heavy in rank, while shifting plans made it often hard to give them suitable assignments.[28]

These Americans were divided by their missions into five major categories. Perhaps first in importance, in that they included the only U.S. combat forces in China, were the several Army Air Forces units: the Fourteenth Air Force under General Chennault; the XX Bomber Command, under Maj. Gen. Curtis E. LeMay; and the China Wing, India–China Division, Air Transport Command, under Brig. Gen William H. Tunner. The logistical effort was being made by the Air Service Command under the command of the Fourteenth and by Advance Section No. 1, SOS in CBI, Col. Robert R. Neyland, Jr., commanding. The SOS kept the designation "Advance Section No. 1" until 10 November 1944.

Those ground force men who had been training and advising the Chinese had been divided among the operational staff working with the American-sponsored divisions in Yunnan Province (Y–Force Operations Staff or Y–FOS), and those doing similar work in east China with the Z–Force divisions. The Japanese occupation of east China disrupted the Z–Force; a rearrangement of the U.S. troops on Z–Force Operations Staff (Z–FOS) was clearly necessary. The officers and enlisted men assigned or attached to theater headquarters were easily identified as a fourth functional group.[29]

Almost as soon as he heard of his new position, Wedemeyer asked the Army's Chief of Staff, General Marshall, to define his relationship to these several organizations and commanders and to General Hurley in the latter's role as the President's personal representative. The wording of Wedemeyer's queries made plain his belief that reports to Washington, by whomever sent, should be channeled through him and that clandestine, quasi-military, and intelligence activities should be under his control. His queries also indicated that personnel matters caused him some concern. And, having had ample opportunity during his nineteen months' previous service in Asia to become aware of some of the less-publicized problems of that area, Wedemeyer requested a clear definition of his duties in regard to lend-lease, Hump allocations, smuggling over the Hump, and black marketing.

In planning to create his own team in China, Wedemeyer asked that Maj. Gen. Thomas G. Hearn, who had been Stilwell's Chief of Staff, and Brig. Gen. Benjamin G. Ferris, who had been Deputy Chief of Staff, be replaced by Maj. Gen. Robert B. McClure and Brig. Gen. Thomas S. Timberman,

---

[28] (1) Ltr, Col Eugene B. Ely, Pres Boards of Investigation USFCT, to CG USFCT, 7 Dec 45, with Incl, A Reconsideration of Report, "The Strength, Distribution and Orgn of American Personnel in the China Theater." Exhibit 16, CT 41, Dr 1, KCRC. (2) Memo, Col Edward H. Young et al for Actg CofS, 7 Jan 46, sub: Recommendations Pertaining to Reconsideration of Report on Strength, Distribution, and Organization of American Personnel in China Theater. Tabs 5, 6, 8, 14, same file.
[29] Wedemeyer Data Book.

MAJ. GEN. CLAIRE L. CHENNAULT *(left)*, *Commanding General, Fourteenth Air Force, welcomes General Wedemeyer to the China Theater, October 1944.*

respectively. Of Chennault, Wedemeyer wrote: "I fully appreciate his abilities and recognize in him an intrepid and inspirational leader; however, I am not sure that he will cooperate in the premises." He requested the War Department to order Brig. Gen. Eugene H. Beebe to China to be Chennault's deputy and ultimately his successor. If it were true that, as Wedemeyer had heard, Chennault's health was failing, then he asked that advantage be taken of that circumstance to relieve the airman at once without prejudice to his splendid combat record.[30]

As drafted by Brig. Gen. John E. Hull, Assistant Chief of Staff, Operations Division, the War Department's initial response was largely noncommittal. Wedemeyer was told that his directive (discussed above) would answer many of his queries. Since Hurley was the President's personal representative, it appeared to the War Department that he could radio the President directly. Hurley's mission was described simply as having been to harmonize the Chiang-Stilwell relationship. In regard to Chennault, Wedemeyer was told to observe the situation in China, then send further recom-

[30] CM–IN 23448, CM–IN 23602, Wedemeyer to Marshall, 25 Oct 44.

mendations.   More specific answers were promised later, but he was also told to study existing instructions.[31]

Wedemeyer, in compliance with this suggestion, studied the situation on the scene in China before moving to set up his command through the issuance of directives to his principal subordinates.   In November 1944 his operational activity was directed toward the Chinese, in urging them to make a co-ordinated and effective use of their existing resources to stop the Japanese short of the Hump airline terminus of Kunming, while he began drafting directives to his air force, Services of Supply, and field commanders.

General Hearn, who had been in China since March 1942, asked to be relieved after Stilwell's recall.   The War Department, believing that his presence in Chungking if continued for a while would give an element of continuity, directed that Hearn confer with Wedemeyer to arrange the time of his leaving.   China Theater was authorized to issue orders for Hearn's relief "when his services could be spared." [32]

The XX Bomber Command, though it was a major burden on the logistical and air resources of China Theater, was, as previously observed, not under Wedemeyer's command.   It was part of the Twentieth Air Force, whose commanding general was the executive agent of the Joint Chiefs of Staff in carrying out their directives for its employment.   Subject to contingencies set forth in JCS directives, Wedemeyer could divert the B–29's from their primary mission if a tactical or strategic emergency arose.   In practice, the provision had meant little, for the JCS defined emergency with the utmost rigidity.[33]   Though in the early days of his command in China, Wedemeyer did not recommend that the B–29's be withdrawn from China, he did advise that he should be authorized to make recommendations as to their most profitable use.[34]

The China Wing of the India-China Division, Air Transport Command, also was not under Wedemeyer's command though the India-China Division had assigned it missions that supported Wedemeyer.   The China Wing operated regular scheduled flights between such cities as Wedemeyer might desire; it flew supplies from Kunming to Cheng-tu; it operated missions that Wedemeyer might want, such as movement of Chinese troops from Burma to east China; and when not required for any such missions it flew the Hump from China to India.[35]

---

[31] CM–OUT 53093, Marshall to Wedemeyer, 27 Oct 44.

[32] History of China Theater, 20–31 Oct 44, p. 23.

[33] (1) Item 9, Wedemeyer Data Book.   (2) For Stilwell's attempt to use the B–29's, see *Stilwell's Command Problems,* Chapter X.

[34] Rad CFB 25886, Wedemeyer to Marshall, 10 Nov 44.   Item 58, Bk 1, ACW Personal File.

[35] Memo, Gen Tunner, CG ICD ATC, for Wedemeyer, 17 Dec 44.   Item 10, Wedemeyer Data Book.

KUNMING AIRFIELD. *The Air Transport Command flew supplies to Chennault's forward fields from the Kunming bases.*

On 10 November Wedemeyer issued the first interim directive to the SOS in China. Maj. Gen. Gilbert X. Cheves became SOS commander, vice Colonel Neyland, who became commanding officer of the Base General Depot No. 2 at Calcutta (and ultimately commanding general of that base section). General Cheves was simply told that existing directives would remain in force as far as applicable. Under them, the SOS in China had been virtually independent, for Neyland had acted as a deputy in China for Maj. Gen. William E. R. Covell, commanding the SOS in CBI.[36]

As for the various intelligence agencies, Wedemeyer did not move to integrate them into a harmonious team until late December 1944. Then he began by questioning them as to their missions and authority to operate in China.[37]

The U.S. Projects in China

The long-standing intent of the War Department to help the Chinese to help themselves and Roosevelt's and the Generalissimo's desire that U.S. air

---

[36] (1) Opnl Dir 2, Wedemeyer to Cheves, 1 Dec 44. Item 4, Wedemeyer Data Book. (2) SOS in IBT, p. 15.

[37] History of China Theater, Ch. III, p. 1.

INDIA-BASED B-29's *of the XX Bomber Command staging at Cheng-tu for a strike against Japan.*

power play the stellar role in China interacted to produce a number of air, supply, and training projects whose sum defined the theater's sphere of operations. Of all these, the Fourteenth Air Force currently seemed the most important; Wedemeyer's initial judgment of the importance of the air element in his operations was suggested by his writing to General Henry H. Arnold, who commanded the Army Air Forces: "[General Marshall] has given me a task which is almost wholly dependent upon proper employment of air and I must have adequate air representation to accomplish this task. . . . I should have over 50% air officers on the China Theater staff."[38]

The Fourteenth Air Force had, in November 1944, an average strength of 398 fighters, 97 medium bombers, and 47 heavy bombers. In that same month the Fourteenth received 13,578 tons of supplies flown in over the Hump, of which 9,357 tons were gas and oil.[39] From the Kunming airfields, the China Wing of the ATC flew these supplies to Chennault's forward fields, this intratheater transport being of course a charge on Hump tonnage. The apparent crisis in east China made it seem advisable to use all available

[38] Rad CFB 25485, Wedemeyer to Arnold, info Stratemeyer, Chennault, Tunner, and Sultan, 4 Nov 44. Item 45, Bk 1, ACW Personal File.
[39] Item 8, Wedemeyer Data Book.

Chinese trucks for concentrating the Chinese for the defense of Kunming; the quartermaster truck companies of the SOS were not by themselves enough to support the Fourteenth Air Force.

These resources of air power, unimpressive in contrast to what Allied commanders had in Europe or the Pacific, but a good deal more than the Japanese had in China, were divided among two composite wings—the 68th and 69th—the 312th Fighter Wing, the Chinese-American Composite Wing (CACW), and the 308th Bombardment Group (H). An example of Chennault's flexibility, the 68th Wing had three fighter squadrons assigned, with bombers attached as the mission required. The 69th had four fighter squadrons and three medium squadrons. With headquarters at Kunming, it was shifting its attention from the campaign in Burma to the defense of Kunming against a Japanese attack from the south or southeast. The Chinese-American Composite Wing, headquarters at Peishiyi, had two fighter groups and one bombardment group. The 312th had two fighter groups (50 P–47's, 60 P–51's, and 6 P–61's), a total of five squadrons, protecting the B–29 fields at Cheng-tu.[40]

The B–29's of the XX Bomber Command were based on India, but staged through the Cheng-tu complex of air bases to attack their targets in Formosa, Manchuria, and Japan. The Cheng-tu fields, an expansion of existing Chinese facilities, were a major installation. There were four airfields, each with a runway about 2,600 yards long, and storage for 168,000 gallons of gasoline. Three fields had hardstandings for fifty-two B–29's each, and the fourth, for forty-three. There was housing for 7,078 airmen. Providing these facilities was the responsibility of China Theater, though the power the B–29's represented was not at Wedemeyer's command.[41] Hobbled though the B–29's were by the logistic problems of accumulating supplies at Cheng-tu, they were still capable of a few massive blows within a given time period, for experience proved they could mount raids of from 84 to 91 aircraft, with bomb loads of from two tons per plane on maximum-range missions to four tons over-all, that is, 5,901 tons of bombs on 1,576 combat sorties from China in seven months of operations.[42]

The major effort of the Services of Supply in October–November 1944 was devoted to operations on the line of communications from Kunming to east China, the eastern line of communications (or ELOC). The line had been forcibly shortened by the Japanese who overran its eastern termini, while the lack of resources at the SOS's command made its efforts necessarily

---

[40] (1) Item 8, Wedemeyer Data Book. (2) Chennault comments on draft MS of this volume. OCMH.

[41] Item 9, Wedemeyer Data Book.

[42] United States Strategic Bombing Survey [USSBS], *Air Operations in China, Burma, India, World War II* (Washington, 1947).

on a small scale. So the 3732 and 3843d Quartermaster Truck Companies, making extensive use of rather unsatisfactory Chinese drivers and supported by the 857th Ordnance Heavy Automotive Maintenance Company, brought forward what they could to the Chanyi truckhead, and later to northern fields of the Fourteenth Air Force. The bulk of tonnage to east China was carried by Chinese agencies.

The major engineering projects were highway construction, maintenance, and repair. The Engineer Section of SOS used Chinese contractors and Chinese Government funds on the Kutsing–Tushan section of the ELOC. On the other side of China, men of the Burma Road Engineers, attached to the SOS and commanded by Col. Robert F. Seedlock, were charged with maintaining and improving the Chinese end of the Burma Road, roughly from Kunming to the Salween, against the day when the Ledo Road would connect with it. Essentially they were a task force of engineers and heavy equipment operators, numbering about 180 all told. Airfield construction, so important to the Fourteenth Air Force, was a Chinese responsibility, for the SOS did not have the necessary facilities.

In addition to these major efforts, the SOS performed its housekeeping tasks for the U.S. forces in China, operating a station hospital in Kunming, providing 3d and 4th echelon motor maintenance facilities in the same city, purchasing subsistence in the open market, maintaining signal communications, and the like. All this was on a small scale, for the Hump restricted everything that might be flown in and often the SOS received nothing it had requisitioned; the Fourteenth Air Force was until October 1944 responsible for its own supply through the Air Service Command in that great area east of the 108th meridian; and lastly, the Chinese Government, through the War Area Service Command, supplied food and shelter to the U.S. forces in China through its hostels.[43]

After the air effort and the attempts to move tonnage to the airfields and to the troops, the remaining U.S. project in China was liaison with and training and observing of Chinese troops. On the Salween front, liaison and technical advice was given in the forward areas, while troop training continued in the rear. In east China, the reluctance of the Chinese to attempt a stand after Heng-yang's fall on 8 August led to the withdrawal of almost all the Americans who had tried since 1 January 1944 to train a second Thirty Divisions in east China. The so-called Z–Force Operations Staff that remained comprised an observer group with the headquarters of the Chinese IX War Area and a liaison team of twenty-eight under Col. Harwood C. Bowman in the city of Liuchow. This handful of Americans, in the first

---

[43] History of Services of Supply, China, India, Burma Theater, 28 February 1942–24 October 1944, Apps. A–I. OCMH. (Hereafter, SOS in CBI.) Despite the title, the manuscript carries the story through 31 December 1944.

months of Wedemeyer's command, sought to give technical aid to the Chinese defenders of Kwangsi while sending a flow of information back to theater headquarters in Chungking. They provided air-ground liaison, supervised demolitions, helped distribute the 500 tons of munitions flown in to east China in late October 1944, and helped with administrative and logistical matters. The rest of the Z–FOS men, including the headquarters, were in Kunming, their future mission dependent on Wedemeyer's estimate of the situation. They numbered 625.[44]

Near Kunming there were a Field Artillery Training Center, a Command and General Staff School, and a Chinese Ordnance Training Center. American officers and enlisted men acted as instructors while the Chinese provided the administrative staff and school troops. The Field Artillery Training Center had opened its doors 1 April 1943 and had trained individual students, trained and equipped artillery battalions, and repaired Chinese ordnance.[45] Activated 15 May 1944, the Command and General Staff School used the plant of the old Infantry Training Center and gave instruction to 100-man classes of Chinese field-grade and general officers.

Farther west, on and behind the Salween front itself, a much larger group of Americans, the Y–Force Operations Staff, was giving close support to the Chinese attempt to clear the Japanese from the Chinese end of the Burma Road. Infantry, artillery, veterinary, engineer, signal, medical, and air personnel were attached to Chinese armies and divisions.[46] American portable and field hospitals gave medical care to Chinese troops of a sort hitherto unknown in Chinese wars. A chain of liaison teams, reporting to Brig. Gen. Frank Dorn, Chief of Staff, Y–FOS, observed the Chinese, and checked on their compliance with the orders of General Wei Li-huang, the Chinese commander on the Salween. The whole attempt to clear out the Japanese was made possible by air support and air supply from the Fourteenth Air Force. At the Chinese Communist headquarters, Yenan, there was the small American Observer Group under Col. David D. Barrett. In terms of American troops working directly with the Chinese the effort was small, some 4,800 officers and enlisted men. To provide supplies for the projects just described was one of the most important missions of General Sultan's India–Burma Theater.[47]

---

[44] (1) Rpt, Hq CT&CC USFCT to The Adjutant General, 1 Jan 45, sub: Hist Rpt of CT&CC, 25 Oct 44–31 Dec 44. OCMH. (2) Bowman comments on draft MS. (3) Z–FOS Morning Rpt, 31 Oct 44, KCRC.

[45] See *Stilwell's Mission to China*, Ch. VIII.

[46] (1) See *Stilwell's Command Problems*, Pt. III. (2) History of C&GS School, 1944–45. OCMH.

[47] (1) History of DIXIE Mission. (2) *Stilwell's Command Problems*, Ch X.

Y-FORCE OFFICERS *observing a Chinese artillery attack on the walled city of Teng-chung. From left: Col. John H. Stodter, Commander, Liaison Group, Chinese 53d Army; Brig. Gen. Frank Dorn, Chief of Staff, Y-FOS; Lt. Col. Frank Sherman, Liaison Officer, Chinese 2d Division; and Lt. Col. John Darrah, Executive Officer, Y-FOS.*

Sultan's Task

The situation in India and Burma contrasted sharply with the darkling scene in China. If in May and August of 1942 and April and May of 1944 Japanese victories in Burma had threatened to inflame nationalist sentiment to the point of large-scale revolt, by the end of October 1944 Japanese defeat was so apparent a prospect that only those Indians who, like Subhas Chandra Bose, had joined the Japanese camp acted as though they thought they had picked the winner; Indian nationalism waited on Allied victory for the satisfaction of its claims. The military outlook was bright. The Japanese attempt to invade India in 1944 with three divisions had been a debacle, no less; the plans, the commanders, the divisions were all ruined. The Japanese hoped to hold Burma as long as possible to keep China blockaded to the last minute, but never again could it be a springboard to conquest. In the north of Burma General Sultan had one British and five Chinese divisions plus an American brigade, all supported by India–Burma Theater, concentrated in the Myitkyina–Mogaung area of north Burma, the Bhamo–Namhkan–Wanting area, ready to pry open the last Japanese grip on the Burma Road. Their unbroken series of past successes against the Japanese *18th* and *53d Divisions*

CHART 3—ALLIED CHAIN OF COMMAND: NOVEMBER 1944

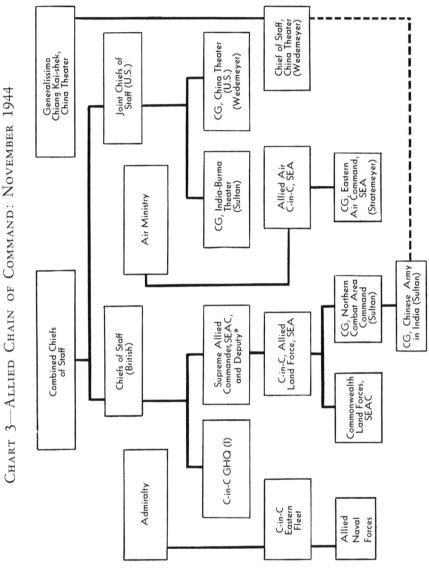

Combined Chiefs of Staff

Generalissimo Chiang Kai-shek, China Theater

Joint Chiefs of Staff (U.S.)

CG, China Theater (U.S.) (Wedemeyer)

Chief of Staff, China Theater (Wedemeyer)

Air Ministry

CG, India-Burma Theater (Sultan)

Allied Air C-in-C, SEA

CG, Eastern Air Command, SEA (Stratemeyer)

Chiefs of Staff (British)

Supreme Allied Commander, SEAC, and Deputy*

C-in-C, Allied Land Force, SEA

CG, Northern Combat Area Command (Sultan)

CG, Chinese Army in India (Sultan)

Commonwealth Land Forces, SEAC

Admiralty

C-in-C GHQ (I)

C-in-C Eastern Fleet

Allied Naval Forces

*Lt. Gen. Raymond A. Wheeler, U.S. Army, was Deputy SAC, SEA.

LT. GEN. DANIEL I. SULTAN *(left)*, *Commanding General, India–Burma Theater, with Admiral Lord Louis Mountbatten (center), Supreme Allied Commander, Southeast Asia, and Brig. Gen. John P. Willey, Commanding General, 5332d Provisional Brigade.*

plus regiments from the *2d* and *49th* indicated they were well able to do so. Opposite central Burma, on the Indian border, the British 4 and 33 Corps were drawing close to the Chindwin River. In the Arakan, the British 15 Corps was preparing to move down the coast of Burma in order to secure bases from which air supply could reach deep into central Burma to sustain the 4 and 33 Corps when they should return the British flag to Mandalay and Meiktila.[48]

When he had been deputy commander of the old China–Burma–India Theater, General Sultan had had his office in theater headquarters in New Delhi, with India and Burma as his area of responsibility. Supervision of the U.S. effort in India–Burma and liaison between the New Delhi headquarters and the field headquarters in Burma had been his major tasks. *(Chart 3)* When he took command of the new India–Burma Theater, his

[48] Report and Supplement for the Combined Chiefs of Staff by the Supreme Allied Commander, South-East Asia, 1943–1946, Vice Admiral Viscount Mountbatten of Burma, New Delhi, India, July 30, 1947, pars. 268, 299, 300, and 345. (Hereafter, Mountbatten Report.)

directive in effect required him to continue with his administrative responsibilities in India and Burma, adding to them the command of India-based U.S.
and Chinese operations in Burma. The JCS directive made clear that Sultan's
was a supporting role:

> Your primary mission is to support the China Theater in carrying out its mis-
> sion. . . . This includes the establishment, maintenance, operation, and security of the
> land line of communication to China, and the security of the air route to China. . . . you
> will participate in and support the operations of the Southeast Asia Command. For this
> purpose, forces involved under your command will be under the operational control of
> SACSEA [Supreme Allied Commander, Southeast Asia]. . . . you will be responsible
> for the logistic and administrative support of all U.S. Army Forces in the India–Burma
> theater. . . . Requirements of the China Theater which cannot be met from resources
> available to you will be submitted by you to the War Department. . . . You will co-
> ordinate directly with the Commanding General of the China Theater and with the
> Supreme Allied Commander, Southeast Asia Command and with the Commander-in-Chief,
> India, to the extent necessary to carry out the mission. The India–Burma Theater must
> serve as a communications zone for the China Theater and requisitions will be made
> accordingly by the Commanding General of India–Burma Theater.[49]

The directive meant that the installations and troops in India and Burma
would continue at their familiar tasks. It also defined the relationship between Sultan and Admiral Lord Louis Mountbatten, Supreme Allied Commander, Southeast Asia Command.

In China, the major problems of inter-Allied command relations revolved
around Wedemeyer's relation to the Generalissimo. In India–Burma, they
arose between India–Burma Theater (IBT) and Southeast Asia Command
(SEAC), which had operational control of Allied forces in Burma. Stilwell
had acted as Deputy Supreme Allied Commander, SEAC. This post was now
given to Lt. Gen. Raymond A. Wheeler, onetime Commanding General,
SOS, CBI, who had been promoted to Principal Administrative Officer,
SEAC. But Sultan did inherit Stilwell's duties of field commander in Burma
by succeeding him as Commanding General, Northern Combat Area Command (NCAC), and Commanding General, Chinese Army in India.

The Northern Combat Area Command had originally been created in
early 1944 to provide a headquarters that would be legally and actually
American to command American, British, and Indian service and combat
troops in north Burma. Its personnel were concurrently the American staff
of a Sino-American headquarters, Chih Hui Pu, which commanded the
Chinese in north Burma. By summer 1944, through common and informal
consent of Chinese and Americans, the term Northern Combat Area Command had quietly superseded Chih Hui Pu and all concerned were content to
refer to NCAC as the senior Allied headquarters in north Burma.

In addition to U.S. service troops, there were two Chinese armies, the

---

[49] (1) History of IBT, I, 37. (2) Quotation from Rad cited n. 4(1).

New Sixth and the New First, and the 1st Chinese Separate Regiment under NCAC. Together, they formed the Chinese Army in India (CAI). The New First Army, under General Sun Li-jen, included the 30th and 38th Divisions. The 38th Division had been engaged since 30 October 1943, and had previously taken a creditable part in the First Burma Campaign of 1942. The division had been trained, re-equipped, and brought up to strength at Ramgarh Training Center in Bihar Province, India. Its sister division, the 30th, was also Ramgarh-trained. Its 88th and 89th Regiments had fought at Myitkyina. The New Sixth Army included the 14th, 22d, and 50th Divisions, commanded by General Liao Yao-shiang. The 22d Division had fought in the First Burma Campaign, then been rebuilt at Ramgarh. It had been in action since January 1944.

As a field commander and as a theater commander, Sultan found that SEAC had the ultimate operational control of all U.S. and Chinese combat troops under his command, though he himself, through General Covell, the SOS commander, controlled the U.S. logistic effort in India, for India lay outside SEAC's boundaries. As a theater commander, Sultan was independent of SEAC, but as commander of the Northern Combat Area Command, he was one of two Army commanders under SEAC. In his capacity as theater commander, Sultan had under him the U.S. Tenth Air Force, Maj. Gen. Howard C. Davidson, but operational control of the Tenth had been yielded to SEAC's Eastern Air Command, an integrated organization with Royal Air Force (RAF) and Army Air Forces (AAF) units. Eastern Air Command was commanded by Maj. Gen. George E. Stratemeyer of the AAF. So, even as Wedemeyer had two superiors, the Joint Chiefs and the Generalissimo, Sultan had two, the Joint Chiefs and the Supreme Allied Commander, SEAC, Admiral Mountbatten. As a chief of staff to the Generalissimo, Wedemeyer had a more elevated position in the hierarchy of China Theater than did Sultan in Southeast Asia Command, for between Mountbatten and Sultan lay still another echelon of command, Allied Land Forces, Southeast Asia.[50]

The American Effort in India and Burma

To carry out his tasks, Sultan in November 1944 had a U.S. force many times the size of Wedemeyer's:[51]

Total	[a] 183,920
Theater troops	21,230
SOS	60,223
AAF	79,946
ATC	[a] 22,521

[a] See note 27(2), above.

[50] (1) History of IBT, I, 1, 2, 60–64. (2) *Stilwell's Mission to China,* Ch. X. (3) *Stilwell's Command Problems,* Ch. III. (4) Since Sultan's combat forces were part of the much larger SEAC command, they will be described below in Chapter III.

[51] History of IBT, II, chart facing p. 269.

As the table above indicates, the missions of these troops—one cannot say "men" because nurses and members of the Women's Army Corps were also present—were principally in the fields of logistics and air war.

Their tasks were to give logistical support to the Hump and Tenth Air Force airfields; operate the Assam line of communications which sustained the six Allied divisions in north Burma; provide air supply to British, Indian, and Chinese divisions in Burma; build the Ledo Road; and operate both the communications and combat zones of the Chinese divisions in north Burma.

As he took up his new tasks, General Sultan was spared a duty which in China had absorbed Wedemeyer and his staff for many days; he did not have to frame new directives for his subordinate commands. The SOS could continue as it had, operational directives to the Tenth Air Force would come from Eastern Air Command, and the Chinese Army in India and Northern Combat Area Command were going concerns, with plans complete for the fall campaign.

The basic mission of the SOS was to construct, operate, and maintain a ground line of communications that would in its initial phases support the airlift to China and the North Burma Campaign and when complete stretch to China to support the U.S. effort there.

The India-based air effort comprised the B–29's, which from their home bases around Calcutta were staged through China to attack Japan; the Air Transport Command, which from bases in Assam and later Bengal as well flew supplies over the Japanese lines into China; the Tenth Air Force, which flew strategical and tactical missions in Burma; and the Combat Cargo Task Force, which furnished air supply.

Training Chinese troops at Ramgarh, Bihar Province, was still one of the major American activities in India, but the days of maximum effort there passed with the completion of preparations for taking north Burma. As of 24 October 1944, when the CBI Theater was split, 5,368 Chinese officers and 48,124 Chinese enlisted men had been trained at Ramgarh. Still present were 1,309 Chinese officers and 7,951 Chinese enlisted men. Training of artillery, armor, and corps and army troops was the major task in fall 1944. Ramgarh's facilities were also used to train the only U.S. regiment to be sent as such from the United States to China, Burma, and India, the 124th Cavalry Regiment of the Texas National Guard, now a dismounted unit.[52]

The SOS in India, Fall 1944

There was very little immediate effect on Covell's SOS in India and Burma from the division of the China–Burma–India Theater. The SOS in China had been substantially independent, as far as command went, and as

[52] History of IBT, I, 22–23.

it had but a few weeks before received a substantial increase in its personnel allotment, there was no immediate impact on the personnel situation. Then, as Wedemeyer's plans jelled, personnel requisitions began to arrive from China, including one for the commander of the Calcutta base, General Cheves. As they arrived, a survey showed that attempts to fill them from the SOS organization in India–Burma were the principal effect of the split on SOS in India–Burma. Immediately after the split, the SOS was organized as:

Headquarters, New Delhi

Base Section No. 1, with headquarters at Karachi

Base Section No. 2, with headquarters at Calcutta

Intermediate Section No. 2, with headquarters at Chabua, Assam

Advance Section No. 3, with headquarters at Ledo, Assam

Each section commander was responsible for all SOS installations in his area.[53]

The principal task of the SOS was operating the terrestrial elements of the long line of communications that stretched, ultimately, from dockside at Calcutta to the unloading stands on the Chinese airfields. (*Map 3*) The major components of the line were the port facilities of Calcutta; the rail, barge, road, and pipe lines of the Assam line of communications; the Air Transport Command fields in Bengal, Assam, and Burma; the transport aircraft themselves; and, finally, the airfields in China. The Air Transport Command was autonomous, but its support was one of the greatest single problems of the SOS.

In India and Burma, construction and transportation were no longer a major puzzle but were routine operating problems. The depot system and local procurement were well established so that the intratheater supply problem was in hand. Indeed, the major problem remaining was that of the backlog of water-borne supply tonnage which had been built up between Los Angeles and Calcutta because shipping was not available in quantity to satisfy every overseas command.

Calcutta, the heart of Base Section No. 2, was the principal seaport in India–Burma, for Karachi, in Base Section No. 1, regarded as the only secure port in the days of Japanese victories, was now too far from the front and received very few vessels to unload. In the winter of 1943–44, Base Section No. 2 had received two more port battalions, the 497th and 508th, modern dock and barge equipment, and full use of a section of the King George Docks. This plus dynamic leadership had broken the port bottleneck at Calcutta. In October Calcutta handled 61,591 long tons, a figure that though large in comparison with past performance was shortly estimated by General Covell to be but one fifteenth of Calcutta's potential capacity.[54]

---

[53] (1) SOS in IBT, pp. 16–17, 19. (2) Wedemeyer comments on draft MS of this volume. OCMH.

[54] (1) SOS in IBT, pp. 130–32. (2) *Stilwell's Command Problems*, Ch. VII.

LOADING RIVER BOATS *at Calcutta with rations for the fighting front. U.S. port battalion men trained and supervised the Indian dock workers.*

In November 1944 Brig. Gen. Robert R. Neyland, Jr., took command of Base Section No. 2, in General Covell's opinion greatly increasing the port's efficiency by improving the morale and performance of duty of the American port battalions and the Indian dock workers and stevedores supplied by the Government of India under reciprocal aid.   During 1944 the United States adopted the system of paying for tonnage unloaded rather than for man-hours of Indian labor expended.   This, together with the introduction of labor-saving devices and training of Indian labor by the men of the port battalions, resulted in a substantial reduction of Indian man-hours and Indian labor costs. Between September and December 1944 Indian man-hours were cut from 647,929 per month to 357,390, handling costs per ton from $2.87 to $1.36.

Nor did supplies accumulate in warehouses or at dockside, for the Assam line of communcations from Calcutta north and east had, if General Covell was correctly informed, a capacity 15 percent above anticipated military requirements.   The major factor in this happy situation, a considerable change from that in 1942, 1943, and early 1944, was that American railway troops

LOADING BOXCARS. *Soldiers of the 748th Railway Operating Battalion oversee the transfer of supplies from river boat to boxcar, India, November 1944.*

managing the line of communications were now under Allied military control which extended along key sections of the Bengal and Assam Railway. Completion of several major construction projects had eliminated some major bottlenecks.[55] The unbridged and turbulent Brahmaputra River had been a problem, for the two ferries crossing it had been unable to meet traffic demands. Two more ferries were completed by fall 1944 and drastically changed procedures greatly increased the traffic flow at each of the four. A steep section of single track had limited train lengths and speeds, for long trains on it were apt to break apart. Double-tracking met one problem, vacuum brakes and American engineers the other, so that from February 1944 to November 1944 traffic over the stretch jumped from 75,110 tons to 138,393 tons a month.[56]

There were both broad and meter-gauge railways in the line of communications, and the transshipment points that linked them restricted traffic. On

[55] *Stilwell's Command Problems,* Ch. VII.
[56] History of IBT, I, 10.

6 October SOS took over one such major point which had remained under Indian civil control long after the rest of the system had passed under Allied military control.   This point had threatened to hold back the whole line of communications.   Out went the antiquated steam gantry cranes, and in came new electric models from the United States.   A new railroad yard was built to handle more cars.   Floodlights were erected and operations went on a twenty-four-hour basis.   Other transshipment points were similarly treated, and such modern techniques promptly brought results; by November 1944, rail-to-river traffic at one point had increased 224 percent over February, and at a river-to-rail point traffic was up 204 percent for the same period.   Malaria and dysentery in the Military Railway Service area, which had in the past helped make Indian rail traffic even more of a hazard, were directly attacked in September by converting some boxcars into diners and mobile dispensaries to serve troop trains on long runs through Assam.   Thanks to these improvements, the Military Railway Service carried its all-time peak load of troops in October, when it moved 92,800 troops plus matériel into place for the fall offensive.[57]

The steady progress of the pipeline program directed by the Quebec Conference of August 1943 was shifting attention from the problem of transporting fuel to that of procuring it.   From the port of Budge-Budge, near Calcutta, one six-inch line ran to the Tinsukia tank farm in Assam while another of six-inch and four-inch combined served the B–29 fields outside Calcutta.   From Tinsukia, two four-inch lines went on into Burma alongside the Ledo Road.   One had reached Myitkyina by the time the CBI Theater was split, the other by 31 October 1944 was complete to mile 219 from Ledo, near Warazup.   The neat black line that these arteries made on a map looked rather different in the field—years later, an officer recalled seeing a working party laying pipe in flood water chin high.   "One, two, three," the leader would count, and at "three" all would take a deep breath and duck below to connect the pipe under water.[58]

In Assam, there were now enough airfields to accommodate the Air Transport Command's Hump operations and permit the fullest degree of air support and air supply to the forthcoming campaign in Burma.   In the spring and summer of 1943 the condition of the airfields had greatly hindered supply of the Fourteenth Air Force in China; that was now a thing of the past.[59]

Though the Air Transport Command was in no sense part of the SOS, its role as the vital link in the line of communications to China requires its

---

[57] History of IBT, I, 11, 12.

[58] (1) History of IBT, I, 17–18.   (2) Interv with Col Rothwell M. Brown, 10 Jun 52. OCMH.   (3) *Stilwell's Command Problems.*   Ch. I.

[59] SOS in IBT, p. 6.

BULLDOZER IN OPERATION SOUTH OF MYITKYINA

mention here. The Ledo Road and the pipelines were hopes for the future, but after its early struggles the ATC had become a present reality and was delivering supplies to China at a pace that increased daily. Its successes in 1944 and 1945 must be regarded as the indispensable foundation for Wedemeyer's achievements in China; the steady increase in tonnage delivered to China merits a departure from chronology.[60]

In October 1944 the India-China Division of the ATC had an average strength of 297.8 operationally assigned aircraft. They were manned and maintained by 22,423 service troops and 23,812 locally hired civilians. By June 1945 the India-China Division had an average of 622.4 operationally assigned aircraft. Service troops then totaled 33,938, their numbers augmented by 47,009 civilians.[61] Table 1 shows tonnages delivered.

The Ledo Road was nearing completion. The ground was drying in north Burma, the rivers returning to their channels, and the soldiers begin-

[60] The two earlier volumes of this series, *Stilwell's Mission to China* and *Stilwell's Command Problems,* offer a brief account of the early days of the ATC in CBI. A detailed account may be found in the manuscript histories of the ATC. On file with Hist Div, ATC. See also Wesley Frank Craven and James Lea Cate, eds., The *Army Air Forces in World War II, IV, The Pacific: Guadalcanal to Saipan, August 1942 to July 1944* (Chicago: Univ. of Chicago Press, 1950) and *V, The Pacific: MATTERHORN to Nagasaki, June 1944 to August 1945* (1953).

[61] History of IBT, II, 383–86.

TABLE 1—TONNAGES DELIVERED BY INDIA-CHINA DIVISION, ATC

Year and Month	To China [a]	Intra-India
1944		
October	24,715	12,224
November	34,914	15,553
December	31,935	16,249
1945		
January	44,099	17,112
February	40,677	17,118
March	46,545	19,424
April	44,254	19,569
May	46,394	15,015
June	55,387	14,269

[a] Tonnages shown on Chart 1, p. 14, above, include hauls by other carriers than ATC, such as Chinese National Airways.

Source: History of IBT, II, 383–86.

ning to get the mud and mildew in their camps reduced to less than nightmare proportions. The lead bulldozer was about eighty miles away from the Myitkyina–Bhamo Road. Maj. Gen. Lewis A. Pick, commanding Advance Section No. 3, the builder of the Ledo Road and so closely connected with it that the soldiers called it "Pick's Pike," thought that another ninety days would see it joined to the Burma Road.[62] Breaking the blockade of China was now a problem of tactics rather than of engineering.

Surveying their command in October 1944, Sultan and his principal subordinates—General Stratemeyer, the airman; General Covell, of the SOS; General Tunner, of the ATC; General Davidson, of the Tenth Air Force; Maj. Gen. Thomas J. Hanley, Jr., of the India-Burma Air Service Command; General Cheves, of Base Section No. 2 (Calcutta); Brig. Gen. John A. Warden, of Base Section No. 1 (Karachi); Brig. Gen. Joseph A. Cranston, of Intermediate Section No. 2 (Chabua); and General Pick, of Advance Section No. 3 (Ledo)—could feel that the work of the past two years was approaching fruition. The power accumulated in and based on India could pump supplies into China Theater on a scale equal to the boldest planning of the past.

Supply Activities in India

Though in October 1944 the supply situation in India gave cause for quiet satisfaction, it would not stay that way without effort and attention. Perhaps indicative of the difficulties of the past, as of October 1944 CBI had

[62] SOS in IBT, pp. 6, 160.

been authorized the highest levels of supply of any overseas command; the War Department might soon direct a reduction.[63]

There were also stirrings within the Government of India, upon whose generosity via reciprocal aid (or reverse lend-lease) SOS depended heavily. In 1942 the War Department had directed that, in view of the shipping shortage, the Americans in India should rely on local sources to the utmost, and by late 1942 the SOS reported that CBI was living off the land. India had co-operated. Now, in late 1944, it appeared to the SOS that reciprocal aid was leveling off and more apt to decline than rise.[64] The Government of India was becoming increasingly aware of inflationary pressures, and the U.S. forces and U.S.-sponsored Chinese divisions in Burma were heavy users of consumer goods. Thus, to take but one clothing item, in 1944 the SOS received 557,087 pairs of shoes. Among subsistence items—in a country which in 1943 had suffered one of the great famines of all time—in 1944 SOS drew from Indian sources 24,472,293 pounds of meat, fish, and fowl.[65]

In addition to objective physical and financial factors, there were subjective and political factors. The cinema had long ago convinced the Indian public that the United States was incomparably the richest nation in the world; it was difficult to persuade Indian legislators and editors that India should share its stocks of food, cloth, and construction materials with the Americans, whose rate of pay, munificient by local standards, was making them the joy and the salvation of local shopkeepers.[66]

So there were numerous hints from official Indian sources in the summer of 1944 that the supply of food and cloth was about to be cut back, and the SOS, as the theaters split, was engaged in diplomatically trying to keep the flow of reciprocal aid at past levels.[67] Receipts of clothing and subsistence were beginning to fall, how far and how fast remained to be seen. In the negotiations on reciprocal aid, SOS had one advantage. Beginning October 1944 the War Department directed that the theater commander screen all requests for lend-lease from India Command and SEAC. This responsibility was delegated to the SOS, and SOS believed its hand was strengthened accordingly in dealings with its British and Indian colleagues.[68]

---

[63] SOS in IBT, p. 88.

[64] See *Stilwell's Mission to China,* Chapter VI, for a discussion of reciprocal aid in 1942 and 1943.

[65] History of IBT, II, chart facing p. 218.

[66] (1) History of IBT, I, 24. (2) During his service in India, Sunderland observed this attitude in many forms, some most amusing: "So I thought I would borrow your jeep. . . . . What! I thought every American had a jeep!"

[67] See *Stilwell's Command Problems,* Ch. VII.

[68] SOS in IBT, pp. 287–90, 272, 285. British and Indian forces in India proper were under India Command.

JORHAT AIRFIELD, *one of the U.S.-built airfields in Assam.*

Supplies from the United States were distributed to the several parts of the theater through the general depots.   High priority items, flown from the United States and landed at Karachi, were an ATC responsibility and were airlifted by that agency direct to the general depot to which the item was consigned.   For water-borne supplies, the Calcutta Base General Depot acted as a clearing point.   Some supplies went from Calcutta to another general depot at New Delhi, but most went to the Intermediate General Depot at Chabua, Assam.   Chabua in turn sent supplies to China Theater via the Hump and to north Burma via the Advance General Depot at Ledo.   With minor exceptions, all SOS, theater, and Chinese troops in India were served by the depot of the section in which they were stationed.   This system seemed too decentralized for effective control of supply stocks, so on 1 November the depot commanders were placed directly under SOS.[69]

With the split of the CBI Theater, the fact that China Theater was still dependent of India–Burma Theater for supplies led to a certain amount of confusion, for some individual units in China such as the Burma Road Engineers were requisitioning direct on the Chabua depot, while China Theater itself was simply forwarding requisitions made on it without consolidating or screening them.   In effect, this meant that the clerical staff at Chabua was handling much of the paper work for supply of China Theater.

[69] (1) SOS in IBT, p. 98.   (2) History of IBT, II, 231.

Ultimately, this had to be brought to the attention of China Theater for remedial action.[70]

But even as the scanty American resources in Asia were being marshaled to halt what seemed a grave threat to China, the War Department's planning looked ahead to the day when these same resources would be surplus and in September 1944 theater commanders were ordered to begin disposing of all surplus property except aircraft and items peculiar to aircraft. These surpluses were to be reported to the Foreign Economic Administration. The Chinese and Indian economies had long been starved for goods, and the two U.S. theaters had supplies and installations that ranged from emergency rations to fully equipped modern hospitals. Both the Government of India and the Republic of China would have the liveliest concern in the disposition of such surpluses, and would seize on any wartime action as a precedent. Indeed, India set up its own India Disposals Board in September 1944, six days before the War Department issued its own circular. This board immediately asked the U.S. diplomatic mission to India for authority to dispose of all U.S. surpluses.

Disposal of U.S. surplus property, though promising a number of complicated problems for India–Burma Theater, appeared simplicity itself compared to disposal of surplus lend-lease, for there were several varieties of lend-lease, some of it involving four governments. There was reciprocal aid to the United States from India; there was British aid to China, e. g., vehicles at Ramgarh Training Center; there were U.S.-built airfields in India; there was Indian reciprocal aid to China, and U.S. lend-lease to China. In the winter of 1944–45 questions about how items in such categories were to be set aside for disposition, by whom, and for whose account began to arise; theater headquarters followed them closely, either as a party or as an interested observer to negotiations between the SOS and Indian and British authority.[71]

Lend-Lease to China

With the opening of the Stilwell Road appearing to be a certainty, an event that would enable vehicles and artillery to be moved into China in quantities, India–Burma Theater's role as the present custodian and eventual delivering agent began to assume current operational importance. Originally, in 1941 and 1942, lend-lease had been requisitioned on the basis of filling the gaps in the equipment of thirty Chinese divisions. In the fall of 1942 Stilwell had asked War Department approval of a sixty-division program. Initially the Department had concurred; then what seemed a lack of Chinese interest in the program plus the difficulty of delivering arms led the Depart-

[70] SOS in IBT, pp. 102–03.
[71] History of IBT, II, 242–57.

ment in July 1943 to cut the program back to arms for the first thirty divisions plus 10 percent of the requirements of the second thirty for training purposes. When the CBI Theater split, this was the current program approved by the War Department.[72]

During the command crisis that preceded the split of CBI Theater, there had been a series of changes in lend-lease procedure, all in the direction of putting certain Chinese divisions squarely in U.S. supply channels. If this trend continued, if certain of the Generalissimo's best divisions were to enjoy the full support of the theater SOS and Army Service Forces, the political implications could be great. However, a considerable portion of these developments took place in the period July–September 1944 when it appeared probable to the War Department and the President that Stilwell would have command of a considerable Chinese force in China; it remained to be seen if the end of that prospect meant the end of this trend.

In the spring of 1944 the circumstance that a considerable tonnage of lend-lease for China was in Indian stockpiles with no prospect of immediate delivery suggested some new approaches to the storage, issue, and delivery of lend-lease to Chinese divisions. One was the idea of pooling stocks, with both lend-lease and U.S. Army supplies being treated as one stockpile and supplies being issued to U.S. and U.S.-sponsored Chinese units as required.

Another new approach was the "six-months rule," under which lend-lease for China could not be requisitioned from depots in the United States unless it could be delivered to China within six months. One objection raised by theater headquarters to the six-months rule was that the stockpiles in India were unbalanced, that there were items needed by the U.S.-sponsored Chinese divisions which were not at hand in India and which could not be requisitioned under the six-months rule, although a sudden and unpredictable victory in north Burma might open the way for immediate and substantial deliveries to China. But the rule remained in effect and the steady improvement in the Assam line of communications, which greatly reduced the transit time through India, made it appear that the six-months rule would not be too great a limiting factor.

By September 1944 it seemed so obvious the Japanese would soon be driven from north Burma and a road opened to the Chinese forces in Yunnan that a new and speedier process for requisitioning lend-lease seemed necessary. Existing procedure called for clearing bids through the Munitions Assignments Board. Requisitioning on the Los Angeles Port of Embarkation brought supplies to India far more quickly. If lend-lease arms could be requisitioned rather than bid for, the rearming of U.S.-sponsored divisions would be greatly speeded. Therefore in September 1944 the War Depart-

---

[72] Tables of Organization and Equipment for the Chinese thirty-three-dvision programs are attached to a letter from Stilwell to Covell, 8 September 1944. OCMH.

ment permitted drawing replacement and maintenance equipment plus ammunition for the Chinese Army in India by requisition on the Los Angeles Port of Embarkation.   Arms for initial issue would still be bid for through the International Division of Army Service Forces in Washington for presentation to the Munitions Assignments Board.   But the precedent for requisition as against bidding was strongly indicated.   A month later, on 6 October, the Munitions Assignments Board approved supply through the SOS of medical replacement and maintenance equipment of all U.S.-sponsored Chinese divisions with which U.S. medical personnel were working.   Supplies for control of malaria could be drawn from the SOS even by units that did not have direct U.S. medical supervision.

In preparation for the opening of the road to China, the SOS sought to have on hand, as of 1 February 1945, for immediate shipment, equipment for five divisions plus army troops.   SOS planned to deliver this matériel in February and to follow with delivery of matériel for two and one-half divisions every month thereafter, until the current thirty-three-division program was complete, and advised China Theater accordingly on 20 November.[73]

[73] SOS in IBT, pp. 307–09, 314.

CHAPTER II

Wedemeyer Begins His Work in China

After assuming command on 31 October 1944, General Wedemeyer proceeded to estimate the situation that faced him in China. The Japanese menace was an immediate one. Considering that he had to hold the Kunming area, Wedemeyer tried to gauge the intentions of the Japanese from their strengths, disposition, and capabilities. Since Wedemeyer had no U.S. ground combat forces, any renewed Japanese drive would have to be met by the Chinese Army and the Fourteenth Air Force.

Japanese Plans in American Eyes

On arriving in Chungking, Wedemeyer began a series of conferences with senior Chinese military officials, his principal subordinates, such as General Chennault, and his own staff. From these meetings emerged a series of recommendations to the Generalissimo for strengthening the Chinese Army, an estimate of Japanese plans and intentions, and a plan to hold the vital Kunming area. Since the Japanese held the initiative in east China, the first reports from China Theater headquarters to General Marshall for the Joint Chiefs of Staff began with surveys of the Japanese position vis-à-vis the Chinese and the American forces in the Pacific. The intelligence reports used by theater headquarters, many of which come from the Forward Echelon, Z–Force, placed ten well-equipped Japanese divisions in the area between Heng-Yang and Liuchow. It seemed obvious to the Americans that such a force had been concentrated with further offensive intent in mind.[1]

A Japanese drive on Kunming from the Kweilin–Liuchow–Nanning area did not at first appear imminent to China Theater headquarters but the results if the Japanese should take Kunming appeared so grave that such a

---

[1] Rad CFB 26558, Wedemeyer to Marshall for JCS, 17 Nov 44. Item 6, Wedemeyer Data Book. (2) Bowman comments on draft MS of this volume.

move by the Japanese was an object of "urgent concern" on 6 November. Eleven days later the Japanese advance had intensified and Wedemeyer felt that he had to "move fast" to stabilize the situation in the Kweilin–Liuchow area and prepare the defense of Kunming.   If Kunming fell, Wedemeyer believed it would mean the end of the Allied effort to save China and to maintain air bases in that nation.   Wedemeyer warned that the loss of China would release twenty-five Japanese divisions for service elsewhere.   So pessimistic an estimate necessarily assumed that the Japanese would not feel the need of more than a token occupation force in China to control a population of 400,000,000 and protect the Japanese position in North China from the USSR.[2]

Though Wedemeyer considered a Japanese drive on Kunming his most immediate concern, he did not believe that the Japanese were seeking to end the war in China by military pressure on the Generalissimo's regime.   He thought rather that the Japanese were seeking to prepare a "continental inner-zone defense" to compensate for the loss of their island positions in the Pacific.   Such a position would comprise the Japanese home islands, Formosa, and Hainan, backed by a wide belt of Asiatic mainland running from north Korea to Indochina.   Within China proper, the Japanese would seek to control everything east of the line Peiping–Hankow–Nanning, inclusive, by holding the key rail lines, airfields, waterways, and highways.   Within such a zone, the Japanese could in the opinion of China Theater headquarters organize a withdrawal route in coastal waters and another over the mainland of China whereby troops and matériel could be evacuated from the south, e. g., Malaya and Burma, for a final stand in the inner zone.

Effective possession of this great band of Chinese territory appeared to open many opportunities whereby the Japanese might increase their capabilities against the forces of Admiral Nimitz and General MacArthur as more and more of them approached the Japanese homeland.   From safe airfields deep in the interior of China, Japanese bombers could stage through coastal airfields, attack U.S. task forces, then retire again to fields beyond the range of U.S. carrier aircraft.   This belt of Japanese airfields would also interpose a barrier of fighters against Chennault's aircraft if, from bases in west China, they tried to attack Japanese shipping.   Japanese divisions could be shifted up and down the coastal corridor to meet any developing American invasion threat.[3]

---

[2] (1) Rad CFB 25612, Wedemeyer to Marshall info Sultan, 6 Nov 44.   Item 6, Wedemeyer Data Book.   (2) Rad cited n. 1.   (3) Rad CFB 25545, Wedemeyer to Chennault, 5 Nov 44.   Item 29, Bk 1, ACW Personal File.

[3] (1) Rad cited n. 2(1).   (2) Commenting on the passage above, a group of senior Japanese officers said that Chennault's operations made it impossible for them to shift divisions about as feared by China Theater.   And they planned to reinforce the south, not to evacuate it.   Japanese Officers' Comments on draft MS of this volume.

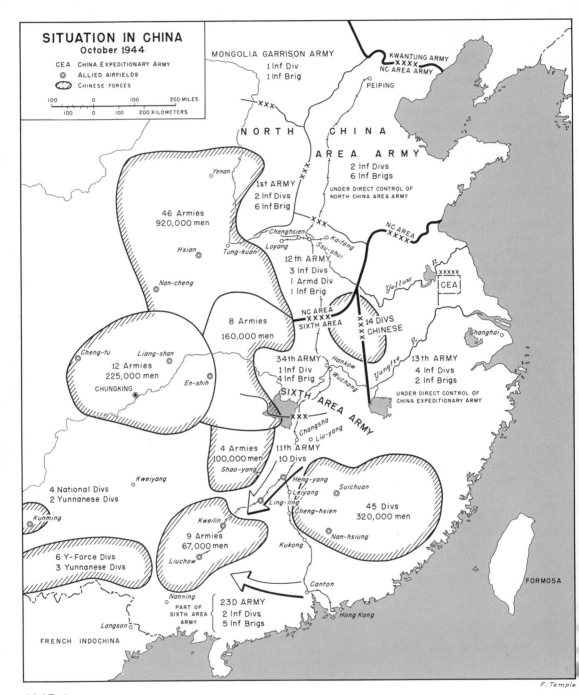

SITUATION IN CHINA
October 1944

CEA ⊚ CHINA EXPEDITIONARY ARMY
⊚ ALLIED AIRFIELDS
◯ CHINESE FORCES

100   0   100   200 MILES
100   0   100   200 KILOMETERS

MONGOLIA GARRISON ARMY
1 Inf Div
1 Inf Brig

KWANTUNG ARMY
XXXX
NC AREA ARMY

PEIPING

NORTH   CHINA

AREA   ARMY
2 Inf Divs
6 Inf Brigs
UNDER DIRECT CONTROL OF
NORTH CHINA AREA ARMY

Yenan

1st ARMY
2 Inf Divs
6 Inf Brig

46 Armies
920,000 men

Hsian

Chenghsien   Kaifeng
Loyang   Ssu-shui

Tung-kuan

NC AREA
XXXX

Nan-cheng

12th ARMY
3 Inf Divs
1 Armd Div
1 Inf Brig

Yellow   R.

XXXXX
[CEA]

8 Armies
160,000 men

NC AREA
XXXX
SIXTH AREA

XXX 14 DIVS
CHINESE

Shanghai

Cheng-tu   Liang-shan

12 Armies
225,000 men

CHUNGKING

En-shih

34th ARMY
1 Inf Div
4 Inf Brig

Hankow
Wuchang

Yangtze   R.

13th ARMY
4 Inf Divs
2 Inf Brigs

UNDER DIRECT CONTROL OF
CHINA EXPEDITIONARY ARMY

SIXTH   AREA   ARMY

XXX
Changsha
Liu-yang

4 Armies
100,000 men

11th ARMY
10 Divs

Shao-yang

Kweiyang

4 National Divs
2 Yunnanese Divs

Heng-yang   Suichuan
Leiyang
Ling-ling
Cheng-hsien

45 Divs
320,000 men

Kunming

Kweilin

9 Armies
67,000 men

Nan-hsiung

6 Y-Force Divs
3 Yunnanese Divs

Liuchow

Kukong

Canton

FORMOSA

Nanning

PART OF
SIXTH AREA
ARMY

23D ARMY
2 Inf Divs
5 Inf Brigs

Hong Kong

Langson

FRENCH INDOCHINA

F. Temple

MAP 4

Lending confirmation to this belief that Japan was staking out such a continental belt was the opinion in China Theater headquarters that more Japanese divisions had arrived in east China.[4]

The Japanese Side of the Hill

The Japanese forces whose future plans China Theater sought to discern were organized as *China Expeditionary Army,* General Yasuji Okamura commanding. They numbered about 820,000 in November 1944 and were organized into 25 infantry divisions of very uneven quality, 1 armored division, 11 independent infantry brigades, 1 cavalry brigade, and 10 independent mixed brigades. Under General Okamura were three principal formations, *North China Area Army,* holding the north China plain from the Yellow River to the Great Wall; the *6th Area Army,* which was conducting the operations against the Chinese and Americans in east China; and the *13th Army,* which held the lower Yangtze valley and the great port city of Shanghai. (*Map 4*)

North China Area Army had three missions: training, occupying the north China plain, and watching the Soviet forces in the Far East. It had three subordinate army headquarters, the *1st, 12th,* and *Mongolian,* and 8 infantry divisions, 1 armored division, 1 cavalry brigade, 4 independent infantry brigades, and 6 independent mixed brigades. The 8 infantry divisions were "Class C," with no artillery.

The *13th Army,* with 4 divisions and 2 brigades, trained itself, occupied the Shanghai area, and prepared for the day when the Americans might try to land in the Yangtze valley.

The *6th Area Army,* under Okamura himself, comprised the *11th, 20th, 23d* and *34th Armies,* with 13 divisions, 6 independent infantry brigades, and 3 independent mixed brigades. Here was the Japanese elite force, 3 "Class A" divisions with 36 cannon each, 5 "Class B," with 24 cannon each. This was the force whose intentions so disturbed China Theater headquarters. The *23d Army,* considering itself relieved of garrison duties by an arrangement with the local Chinese commander, General Yu Han-mou, was driving north and west from the Canton–Hong Kong area with 2 divisions. The *11th Army* controlled the stretch of rail and river south of Hsin-shih and Yueh-yang with 7 divisions, and was approaching Kweilin. The *34th Army,* a garrison force, with 1 division and 4 brigades, held the vital Hankow area, supply base and headquarters for Okamura, against the 55 Chinese divisions of the Generalissimo's V and VI War Areas.[5]

---

[4] Rad cited n. 1.
[5] (1) Japanese Studies in World War II (hereafter, Japanese Study—), 129. OCMH. (2) Chinese Order of Battle. Item 13, Wedemeyer Data Book. The Order of Battle is dated I January 1945, but the divisions stayed where they were in 1944. (3) Ltr, Col Preston J. C. Murphy, Chief Mil Hist Soc FECOM, to Ward, 18 Nov 52. OCMH.

The basic plan under which the Japanese now fought their war was denominated by the Japanese character *SHŌ*, meaning "to conquer." When, in the summer of 1944, the situation Japan faced appeared grave in the extreme, Japan's leaders resolved to launch every available resource in a great counterattack by sea, land, and air that would hit the American forces as they were engaged in the complicated and hazardous task of establishing themselves ashore somewhere in Japan's inner defense zone of the western Pacific. They called their riposte the *SHŌ* Operation. The Japanese estimated that any one of four different areas might be struck by the American forces, and as many variants of *SHŌ* were prepared. It was the supreme operation, and *Imperial General Headquarters* gave it first priority. Therefore, Okamura had to detach two divisions for *SHŌ*, while the Japanese forces in Manchuria were drawn on heavily indeed. If the Soviet Union entered the war, *China Expeditionary Army* would have to release from 10 to 20 more divisions.[6]

When *SHŌ* was framed, *China Expeditionary Army* had been engaged in occupying the east China airfields, the *ICHIGO* Operation. Visiting Okamura's headquarters in September 1944, Col. Takushiro Hattori of *Imperial General Headquarters* stated that, far from lessening *ICHIGO*'s importance, the imminent prospect of beginning the *SHŌ* Operation made it ever more important to complete *ICHIGO*. In Hattori's opinion, which was taken by his auditors as echoing that of higher realms in Tokyo, the success of *ICHIGO* would—by taking the east China fields—force U.S. aircraft from China bases to confine their operations to the west until such time as *SHŌ*'s outcome was apparent. So the *6th Area Army* made detailed plans to complete *ICHIGO* by taking Kweilin and Liuchow, tentative date early November 1944, and hoped in the process to cut off some of the Chinese defenders. After Kweilin and Liuchow were taken, the Canton–Hankow railway would be cleared of all barriers, and the Suichuan group of airfields destroyed. This latter piece of territory was not to be held.[7]

In mid-October, Okamura directed that the Suichuan airfields be taken as soon as possible after occupation of Liuchow and Kweilin, though this was in compliance with Tokyo's orders rather than with local Japanese military opinion. Then the American task forces were sighted heading for Leyte, and

---

[6] (1) The brief summary above does far less than justice to the complicated and detailed *SHŌ* Operation. The connection between *SHŌ* and Japanese operations in China in summer 1944 is outlined in *Stilwell's Command Problems,* Chapter XI. (2) For a longer account see Japanese Study 72, Part V. (3) For the naval side, see James A. Field, *The Japanese at Leyte Gulf: the SHŌ Operation* (Princeton, N. J.: Princeton University Press, 1947) and C. Vann Woodward, *The Battle for Leyte Gulf* (New York: The Macmillan Company, 1947). (4) The strategy of the Pacific war will be more fully treated by Louis Morton, in Command, Strategy, and Logistics, a Pacific subseries volume in preparation in the series UNITED STATES ARMY IN WORLD WAR II.

[7] Japanese Study 129, pp. 53–56.

on 18 October Tokyo ordered the $SH\bar{O}$ Operation to begin.[8]   When Wedemeyer assumed command on 31 October, $SH\bar{O}$ was under way.   The naval
part of $SH\bar{O}$ had failed; the air part was failing, but the Japanese were doing
their utmost to reinforce and support their Philippine garrison, and continued
their efforts for many weeks.

The Japanese in Manchuria and Korea were being used as a troop pool
from which to reinforce garrisons in the central and south Pacific.   In the
latter half of 1944, 6 infantry divisions, 1 armored division, 2 independent
mixed brigades, and most of the stock of reserve matériel were shipped out
and only partially replaced by 5 newly activated divisions.[9]

As for China, *Imperial General Headquarters* had no intent to take Kunming or end the war, nor was it trying to create a continental fortress.
Chinese territory did not attract the Japanese leaders.   Their orders to Okamura showed that his armies would be used aggressively in a mobile role:
if possible, to forestall Allied moves, as they now sought, by occupying the
east China airfields, to prevent interference with $SH\bar{O}$ or the bombing of
Japan from Chinese bases; if necessary, to counter Allied moves, as shown
by the warning to Okamura that if the Soviet Union entered the war from
10 to 20 of his divisions would have to be moved to Manchuria.   Therefore,
the strategy of *Imperial General Headquarters* in November 1944 was not quite
what China Theater headquarters concluded from the menacing Japanese
dispositions in south China.   The Japanese forces on the mainland of Asia
had missions rather more limited than those with which the Americans
credited them.

Wedemeyer's Reactions to the Chinese Scene

There were two points requiring Wedemeyer's immediate attention—the
defense of the Kweilin airfield, if possible, and the absolutely vital holding
of Kunming.   On taking command, Wedemeyer lost no time in becoming
acquainted with his Chinese superior, the Generalissimo, and with the Generalissimo's staff.   Could Kweilin be held, Wedemeyer asked the Generalissimo and his staff.   What resources could be mustered by the Chinese to
stop the Japanese short of a major victory?   In discussions with his staff,
Chennault, and the Chinese, Wedemeyer also sought to learn why the east
China fields had been lost.   And he made his appraisal of China's leaders,
which he reported to Marshall and the War Department.

---

[8] (1) Col Takushiro Hattori, *Imperial General Headquarters*, Army Department, Operations
Section, 1 June 1948.   Statements of Japanese Officials, I, p. 324.   OCMH.   (See Bibliographical Note.)   (2) Japanese Study 129, p. 59.

[9] Japanese Study 72, p. 148.

Wedemeyer found no air of alarm or urgency in the Chinese Government. Initially, he reported the Chinese to be "apathetic and unintelligent." [10] Three weeks later, he found his Chinese colleagues still in a state of apathy with regard to the Japanese. If the Chinese had more accurate information regarding Japanese intentions, they either kept it to themselves or failed to convince Wedemeyer that it was valid. He judged their apathy to be an indication of inward impotence and of confusion on the part of the Generalissimo and his advisers:

. . . .

3. In previous radios I have suggested that the Chinese attitude was apathetic. This remains true; however, I have now concluded that the Generalissimo and his adherents realize seriousness of situation but they are impotent and confounded. They are not organized, equipped, and trained for modern war. Psychologically they are not prepared to cope with the situation because of political intrigue, false pride, and mistrust of leaders' honesty and motives. . . . Frankly, I think that the Chinese officials surrounding the Generalissimo are actually afraid to report accurately conditions for two reasons, their stupidity and inefficiency are revealed, and further the Generalissimo might order them to take positive action and they are incompetent to issue directives, make plans, and fail completely in obtaining execution by field commanders.[11]

The Chinese methods of making war appeared ineffective to Wedemeyer. He found that the Chinese had no one commander responsible for the conduct of operations in east China. Instead, the Chinese staff at Chungking tried to control everything. In many cases, he believed they simply assumed a situation and issued orders accordingly, even though there might be little connection between their imaginings and the actual state of affairs. And so the Chinese armies marched and countermarched futilely. The orders from Chungking were not part of any plan; indeed, to Wedemeyer it seemed that "the disorganization and muddled planning of the Chinese is beyond comprehension." Every commitment of Chinese troops to battle was made piecemeal. There was neither co-operation nor co-ordination between Chinese senior commanders in adjacent areas. As for the Chinese divisions themselves, Wedemeyer, like Stilwell, believed that at best their leadership was mediocre. Unit training appeared to be of a low standard. There was no effective replacement system. The men often lacked equipment and food.[12]

A few days later, Wedemeyer stated that a "sound replacement program simply does not exist for there are so many officials involved with their nar-

[10] Quotation from radio cited n. 1.

[11] Rad CFB 28167, Wedemeyer to Marshall for JCS, 4 Dec 44. Item 6, Wedemeyer Data Book.

[12] (1) Wedemeyer's first analysis of the Chinese ideas of war is in radio cited n. 2(1). It reflects a study by Colonel Taylor, G–3, 3 November 1944, sub: Reorientation of Chinese-American Effort in China. OCMH. (2) Quotation from Rad CFB 25886, Wedemeyer to Marshall, 10 Nov 44. Item 58, Bk 1, ACW Personal File.

NATIONALIST CHINESE SOLDIERS *marching to the front, Kwangsi Province, November 1944.*

row and unscrupulous self-interest that it has not been possible to mobilize [the Chinese] forces in an efficient manner." [13]

In talking to the Generalissimo and the Chinese staff, Wedemeyer found it hard to learn just what the Chinese could or would do to defend any one position or to venture attacks on limited local objectives. When Wedemeyer arrived in Chungking, the Japanese offered an imminent threat to Kweilin. It appeared possible the Chinese could hold that city with its vital airfield. The newly arrived Chinese 97th Army held what seemed strong positions above Kweilin. They were reported to be well fed and well equipped. There was plenty of time for them to dig in, and Wedemeyer on his arrival had rushed U.S. officers to the 97th Army to assist them in preparing their positions. The Generalissimo and his staff were positive that the Kweilin-Liuchow area would be held for two months if the Japanese

[13] Rad cited n. 12(2).

attacked and the Generalissimo so assured Wedemeyer "categorically." U.S. observers on the scene may have been less confident, for many years later one of them recalled having noted very bad feeling between the 97th Army and General Chang Fa-kwei, as well as faulty dispositions at Kweilin.[14]

While conferring with his own staff and the Chinese, Wedemeyer made his estimate of the situation within the American organization. The long-continued differences between Chennault and Stilwell had left their mark in bad feelings among their subordinates. Therefore the situation Wedemeyer found in his headquarters seemed to be "rife with dissension and disorganization." He later concluded that many members of Stilwell's old staff had had "a defeatist attitude, non-cooperative spirit and ideas of suspicion in their relations with other headquarters." In remodeling his organization, Wedemeyer attached importance to having more airmen assist him as staff officers, a clear indication of his sympathetic approach to the air force.[15]

Though on the eve of his assuming command Wedemeyer had expressed forebodings over the co-operation he might receive from Chennault, he lost no time in approaching the latter with a request for a conference.[16] The prospects for co-operation between the two men were excellent, for the passage of time had removed many of the issues that had tended to divide Stilwell and Chennault. It was no longer possible to argue that Japan could be defeated by 137 China-based tactical aircraft.[17] Nor could the Generalissimo now have such faith in his Army as to renew his promises of April 1943 that the "existing Chinese Forces" could defend the east China fields, for those airfields had fallen into Japanese hands after one battle.[18] The bitter debates over who should receive what share of Hump tonnage were becoming just an unpleasant memory, for the Air Transport Command was delivering tonnage in impressive and increasing quantities.

There were also favorable factors on the personal side. For whatever reason, perhaps his customary reticence, perhaps his sharp differentiation among his many command posts in CBI, Stilwell did not take Chennault into his confidence as to what he would have liked to do in China. In such a situation, rumor and the personal interest of subordinates and outsiders seem to have flourished. Wedemeyer, making no distinction between his several roles in China, brought Chennault into many of his conferences with

[14] (1) Rad cited n. 11. (2) Bowman comments on draft MS.

[15] (1) Wedemeyer's comments on the staff he inherited are in a letter, Wedemeyer to Marshall, 13 April 1945. Case 45, OPD 319.1 TS, Sec. I. (2) Rad CFB 25485, Wedemeyer to Arnold, 4 Nov 44. Item 45, Bk 1, ACW Personal File.

[16] Rad CFB 25545, Wedemeyer to Chennault, 5 Nov 44. Item 29, Bk 1, ACW Personal File.

[17] Maj. Gen. Claire L. Chennault, USA, Ret., *Way of a Fighter: The Memoirs of Claire Lee Chennault* (New York: G. P. Putnam's Sons, 1949), p. 212.

[18] The Generalissimo's personal assurances to the President were in an inclosure to a letter, T. V. Soong to Harry L. Hopkins, 29 April 1943. *Stilwell's Mission to China*, Ch. IX.

CHINESE REFUGEES EVACUATING LIUCHOW

the Generalissimo and kept both Chennault and Chennault's staff fully informed of what he was recommending to the Chinese.

The Japanese Begin To Threaten

The Japanese headquarters immediately responsible for operations in east China was the *6th Area Army*. It in turn ordered the *11th* and *23d Armies* to converge on the Kweilin–Liuchow area from north and south. The *11th Army* requested and obtained permission to secure the area around Kweilin, and *China Expeditionary Army* approved, providing "only short advances were to be made." However, *11th Army* had ambitious schemes of its own.[19]

Japanese operations resumed over 27 and 28 October. The *11th Army,* using four divisions and a company of tanks, made steady progress, and was swinging its left flank toward the south in order to cut off Kweilin from that

[19] Japanese Study 130, pp. 2–3.

direction. The *23d Army,* with two divisions, was coming up toward Liuchow from the south. The Japanese believed Kweilin to be defended by
two armies, Liuchow, only by the 62d. After considering his situation, the
aggressive commander of the *11th Army* decided to take Kweilin and Liuchow simultaneously, though he had been repeatedly told that for reasons of
prestige the *23d Army* would take Liuchow. The Japanese were plagued
with communications problems and *6th Area Army* could not restrain the
impetuous *11th.* So, even as the Generalissimo was assuring Wedemeyer
that Kweilin and Liuchow would hold two months, *11th Army* was preparing to take the conduct of ICHIGO into its own hands.[20]

   With the approach of the Japanese, the Chinese evacuated the garrisons
of Kweilin and Liuchow on 10 November. Little resistance was offered,
according to Wedemeyer's information, which he promptly passed to the
Generalissimo.[21] So much was still within the frame of *ICHIGO,* and within
the propaganda with which the Japanese had preceded and accompanied that
operation to the effect that *ICHIGO* was aimed only at the U.S. airfields in
east China, and not at the Chinese forces.[22] Taking both Kweilin and Liuchow, and leaving Lt. Gen. Shinichi Tanaka of the *23d Army* to think of the
glories he might have won by a more speedy advance, the *11th Army* now
took matters into its own hands and began a rapid advance north and west
towards Kweichow Province.[23]

ALPHA: Beginning an Attempt To Save

   Three days after the Japanese took Kweilin and Liuchow Wedemeyer
had his first formal meeting with the Generalissimo and the latter's senior
assistants. The approach Wedemeyer took to the formalities, the mechanics
of the meeting, was characteristic, and different from Stilwell's. Stilwell had
rigidly separated his post of Chief of Staff to the Supreme Commander,
China Theater, from his post of Commanding General, China, Burma and
India Theater. The minutes of his meetings with the Generalissimo Stilwell kept to himself; usually not until the last was his U.S. staff aware of his
plans for China. Wedemeyer, on the contrary, normally had his own chief
of staff attend his meetings with the Generalissimo and he was always attended by other American officers. Minutes of the meetings were kept with
care and instead of being isolated were filed in with the other top secret

[20] Japanese Study 130, pp. 24, 27, and 28.
[21] Rad cited n. 11.
[22] Ltr, Col Miller, Exec Officer Mil Hist Sec FECOM, to Gen Ward, 29 Apr 52, with attached papers of ex-Maj Gen Kitaru Togo, former Chief, Intel Sec, Gen Hq, *China Expeditionary Army.* OCMH.
[23] Japanese Study 130, pp. 26 and 30.

documents of U.S. theater headquarters.[24]   Therefore, whatever might happen, Wedemeyer would have witnesses and records aplenty in his own headquarters to document his every word in conference with the Generalissimo, and these records would be easily accessible to every qualified seeker after information.   For his part, the Generalissimo often brought T. V. Soong, who in the fall of 1944 and 1945 was Prime Minister, to attend the meetings. Often General Hurley attended on the U.S. side.

Plans and staff studies from the old CBI Theater headquarters offered the material from which Wedemeyer's staff could prepare his proposals to the Generalissimo.   The geography and the contending forces were not changed by Stilwell's recall; ideas worked out by the CBI planners in the summer of 1944 were still applicable.   Cols. William M. Creasy, Thomas F. Taylor, Harold C. Donnelly, and Dean Rusk, in New Delhi and Chungking, had spent many months on plans to establish a secure base in the Kunming area, then for a drive to the coast to open a port in the Canton–Hong Kong area.

Approving their suggestions, Stilwell on 18 September had urged the Generalissimo to concentrate the defeated east China divisions in the Kweiyang area for reorganization, rearming, and training, and on 22 September warned his staff and principal subordinates that he contemplated moving the victorious Chinese forces from north Burma and the Salween front to Kweiyang.   Once this concentration was completed, Stilwell, assuming that he would then be field commander of the Chinese forces, had contemplated massing 63,000 redeployed Chinese troops plus 183,000 more Chinese in 30 divisions, stiffening them with a reinforced U.S. army corps and two long-range penetration groups, and driving for the coast.

Colonel Taylor, who was familiar with these plans, was Wedemeyer's G–3 in the early days of China Theater.   Colonel Creasy gave copies of the old CBI plans to Wedemeyer as the latter was preparing to leave Ceylon for his new assignment in China.[25]

The speediest possible planning and organizing appeared necessary to theater headquarters if Kunming was to be secure against the Japanese.

---

[24] In addition to keeping minutes of his conferences with the Generalissimo and other Chinese officers, Wedemeyer contined Stillwell's system of preparing, numbering, and dispatching memorandums to the Chinese on items of mutual concern.   Wedemeyer, during the time he served as Chief of Staff to the Generalissimo, presented over a thousand such papers.   For details on Wedemeyer's file of memorandums to the Chinese, including many Chinese replies, see the Bibliographical Note.

[25] (1) *Stilwell's Command Problems,* Chs. XI and XII.   (2) Memo, Stilwell for Generalissimo, 18 Sep 44.   Stilwell Documents, Hoover Library.   (See Bibliographical Note.)   (3) Memo, Stilwell for Stratemeyer, sub: Outline of Proposed Future Opns in China, 22 Sep 44. Folder 10, Hq AAF IBT, USAF CBI, Stratemeyer Files, KCRC.   (4) Ltr, Maj Gen William M. Creasy, Chief Chemical Officer, to Col George G. O'Connor, Chief, War Histories Div, OCMH, 16 Jun 54.   OCMH.   (5) Ltrs, Col Taylor to Maj Gen Albert C. Smith, Chief Mil Hist, 1, 9 Jun 54.   OCMH.

Theater headquarters, in close co-operation with the President's representative, General Hurley, began drafting a series of proposals which if adopted by the Chinese would offer the chance of a more effective defense. The suggestions called for a rapid concentration of Chinese troops south and east of Kunming and for a command structure that would permit a co-ordinated defense. The code name for the operations comprised in the plan was ALPHA.[26] In addition, Wedemeyer and his staff spent many hours assisting Hurley in the latter's efforts to bring about co-operation between the Chinese Government and the Communists, for they believed Communist military aid could assist materially in stopping the Japanese advance.[27]

Basically, the old CBI plan which had been drafted in August and September 1944 called for first priority to defense of the Kunming area, since its loss, entailing as it would loss of the Hump air terminals, would be decisive, while loss of Chungking, seat of the Generalissimo's wartime government, though deplorable and distastrous, would not be fatal.[28] It was now time for General Wedemeyer, as Chief of Staff to Chiang Kai-shek, to present a tactical plan to the Chinese for their consideration. Having adopted the code name ALPHA—a term which had been applied in the CBI plan to the defense of Kunming—Wedemeyer first presented a detailed plan to the Generalissimo on 21 November 1944.[29] This plan was divided into several phases. The period to 31 December 1944 was set for Phase I of ALPHA, in which the Chinese forces in contact with the Japanese in south and southeast China would try to slow their advance. The Americans would assist in demolitions, help plan prepared positions, and give the maximum of air support. American officers would fill liaison and advisory roles with the Chinese Army down through division level. Other Americans would work closely with the operations, intelligence, and supply officers of higher Chinese headquarters. Plainly, the mission of Phase I was to win time within which to complete a concentration for defense of Kunming.

In Phase II, Chinese forces would be placed across the principal avenues of approach to Kunming while a central reserve would be built up around Kunming itself. To guarantee the availability of dependable Chinese troops two divisions of the Chinese Army in India would be flown in from Burma, together with the 53d Army from the Salween front. About 87,500 troops would be brought to the Kunming area from less menaced sectors of China.

---

[26] ALPHA, as the term was used at the time and is here used, refers not only to a series of tactical plans, so designated, but to the preparatory measures adopted to support, in its successive phases, theater planning to take a major port on the China coast.

[27] (1) History of China Theater, Ch. VI.   (2) Gen McClure, Memo for Record.   Communist File, 06104-M, 3 Nov-10 Dec 44, T-49-20 CBI, DRB AGO.

[28] Memo and Ltrs cited n. 25(3), (4), (5).

[29] (1) Min, Mtg 1, Wedemeyer with Generalissimo, 13 Nov 44.   (2) Min, Mtg 3, Wedemeyer with Generalissimo, 21 Nov 44.   Bk 1, Generalissimo Minutes.

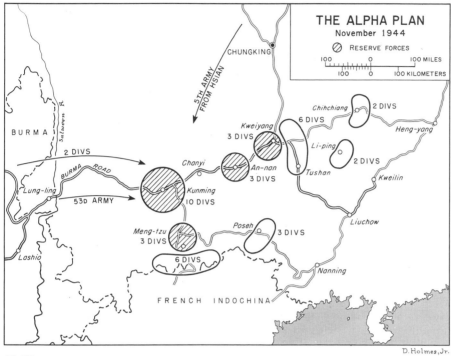

MAP 5

The planners sought to place a Chinese force capable of meeting the most likely Japanese threat across each avenue of approach. In the Chihkiang area there would be two divisions. There would be two more at Li-ping to block the Japanese threat from Kweilin. The vital Tushan–Kweiyang area, whose possession would give the Japanese the option of attacks on Kunming or Chungking, would receive six divisions. Three divisions at Poseh (Pai-se) would have the mission of stopping a Japanese drive west from Nanning. Six divisions in southern Yunnan would complete the ring and bar any Japanese drive north from Indochina.[30] Reserve forces, each of three divisions, would be placed in the Kweiyang, An-nan (Ching-lung), and Meng-tzu areas. A ten-division reserve would be built up around Kunming. (*Map 5*)

The prospect of a favorable outcome of these recommendations was probably increased by the fact that a Chinese general of good reputation, General Tang En-po, was en route to the Kweiyang area. As a result of a series of

[30] (1) Rad cited n. 11.   (2) Ltr, cited n. 25(4).

conferences in east China in September and October between Stilwell, Chennault, Brig. Gens. Thomas S. Timberman and Malcolm D. Lindsey, Colonel Bowman of Z–Force, Brig. Gen. Casey Vincent of the Fourteenth Air Force, and Generals Chang Fa-kwei and Pai Chung-hsi, General Pai had visited Chungking to present the consensus of the Allied field commanders to the Generalissimo. Bowman later concluded that as a result of General Pai's good offices General Tang was sent to the front.[31]

The command provisions of ALPHA reflected the belief long held by the staff of theater headquarters that the Chinese would benefit immeasurably if their operations were conducted by a responsible commander in the field rather than by telephone, letter, telegram, and radio from Chungking.[32] ALPHA provided for a Chinese Supreme Commander and staff to command the assigned Chinese troops. U.S. officers were to act as deputies to the Supreme Commander, to the commander of each sector, and to the commander of the general reserve. Each of the American deputies would have a complete U.S. staff whose members would work with their Chinese opposite numbers. Training would be conducted by the Americans.

To provide an organization for the American liaison and training personnel who were to assist the Chinese, Wedemeyer grouped the Y–FOS and Z–FOS staffs, training groups, liaison teams, and the existing service schools into the Chinese Training and Combat Command, activated 17 November 1944, General Dorn, commanding. Dorn had been Stilwell's aide in the First Burma Campaign; his last major post had been Chief of Staff, Y–FOS, so he was the senior American staff officer on the Salween front.[33]

Supply and transport received careful attention, for theater headquarters believed the Chinese Army in China had suffered from Chinese neglect of such prosaic but necessary aspects of war. A Chinese was to be supply officer to the Supreme Commander, assisted by a deputy from the U.S. Services of Supply. This latter officer would control transport. In the lower echelons of command, supply problems would be handled by the Chinese commanders assisted by their American deputies.[34]

Having accepted ALPHA as the first step in carrying out his directive to advise and assist the Chinese, Wedemeyer turned to his next tasks—persuading the Chinese to adopt ALPHA and, once they had, persuading them to carry it out.

---

[31] Bowman comments on draft MS.

[32] *Stilwell's Mission to China*, Ch. V, and *Stilwell's Command Problems*, Part Three.

[33] (1) Rpt, Gen Dorn, CG CT&CC, to Wedemeyer, 1 Jan 45, sub: Hist Rpt of CT&CC (Y–FOS and Z–Force). 25 Oct 44–31 Dec 44. OCMH. (2) Information on Dorn's role in CBI is given in *Stilwell's Mission to China* and *Stilwell's Command Problems*.

[34] Rad cited n. 2(1). (2) Memo, Marshall for President, 20 Dec 44. Item 20, WDCSA 091, China (20 Dec 44). (3) Min, Mtgs 3, 5, Wedemeyer with Generalissimo, 21, 27 Nov 44. Bk 1, Generalissimo Minutes. (4) Rad CFB 27895, Wedemeyer to Marshall, 5 Dec 44. (5) History of China Theater, Ch. VI, p. 14.

GENERAL DORN, *commanding the new Chinese Training and Combat Command, with General Wei Li-huang (left), Commanding General, Chinese Expeditionary Forces, and General Ho Ying-chin, Commanding General, ALPHA Forces, 27 November 1944.*

Chinese Reactions to ALPHA

The Chinese reaction of November–December to the complicated ALPHA plan was equally complex; some parts of it appeared to be accepted, some the Chinese modified to suit themselves, and some received formal approval only to be quietly disregarded later. That the Chinese did not accept ALPHA as a whole had its effect on operations, because the plan was as integrated as a piece of machinery; the discard or alteration of any part had its effect on the workings of the whole. So it was a mixed picture that unfolded before Wedemeyer and his staff, a blend of progress, passive acceptance, inertia, and outright rejection.

The initial discussions of 13 and 16 November, before the formal presentation of ALPHA, concerned issues of deployment and command, which had their place in ALPHA but which were also measures to meet the immediate threat to Kunming. Toward the issue of rushing troops south from the Hsian front, where considerable Nationalist forces watched the Chinese Communists, the Generalissimo showed a certain coolness. He remarked that since Kweilin and Liuchow had fallen, and since these troops were originally intended to reinforce the garrisons of the two cities, there was no need for haste. The Kweiyang airfield, their destination, should be repaired, which he thought would take thirty days, and the men could then be flown direct to their destination rather than by way of Chanyi or Peishiyi.

Successful execution of ALPHA depended completely on whether the Chinese forces to confront the Japanese would resist. Wedemeyer regarded this as an unknown factor; "We can throw in great numbers of troops at tremendous cost logistically, but we do not know whether the Chinese will stick and fight." So Wedemeyer concluded that two of the Chinese divisions Stilwell had trained and equipped would have to be flown from Burma. He decided that nothing but what he thought the best would serve, the 22d and 38th Divisions, and requested the Generalissimo to approve their recall. The Generalissimo agreed, adding that he himself had thought of recalling two divisions. The next step was to arrange co-ordination of the transfer with Admiral Mountbatten's Southeast Asia Command, which would be affected by removing these troops.[35]

As for the creation of an effective command structure for China Theater, the Generalissimo agreed to the most important points, for which Stilwell had so long argued, that there should be a single responsible field commander and a combined Sino-American staff for the ALPHA troops.[36]

If the Generalissimo was willing to give what the Americans regarded as normal command responsibilities to whoever became field commander, that would end the Chinese practice of attempting to conduct campaigns in minutest detail from Chungking. A Sino-American staff for the ALPHA plan would mean that the Generalissimo, through his U.S. chief of staff, General Wedemeyer, would have a suitable instrument through which to exercise his responsibilities as Supreme Commander, China Theater, and that Wedemeyer, unlike Stilwell, would be permitted a Sino-American staff to help him.[37] In practice, what followed were conferences, much like those of the Anglo-American Combined Chiefs of Staff, which decided what agency would take action. Not for many months were staff sections created.

[35] (1) Quotation from Memo cited n. 34(2). (2) Min of Mtgs 1, 2, 4, Wedemeyer with Generalissimo, 13, 16, 24 Nov 44. Bk 1, Generalissimo Minutes. (3) Rad cited n. 34(4)

[36] (1) For the Soong-Stimson accord of January 1942 on a Sino-American staff for China Theater, see *Stilwell's Mission to China*, Chapter II. (2) For Stilwell's views on the need for a responsible field commander and a Sino-American staff, see *Stilwell's Mission to China*, Chapter V.

[37] (1) The Generalissimo's permission to set up a combined staff for ALPHA was given at his second formal meeting with Wedemeyer, 16 November 1944. On 24 November Wedemeyer limited its role to ALPHA. Min, Mtgs 1, 2, 4, Wedemeyer with Generalissimo, 13, 16, 24 Nov 44. Bk 1, Generalissimo Minutes. (2) Min. Combined Staff Mtgs 84, 85, on 20. 22 Jan 45. DRB AGO.

The Generalissimo's reaction to ALPHA's command proposals, that a most highly qualified Chinese officer be placed in charge of operations in the field and that he be responsible for their conduct, had its effect on the movements of Chinese troops, an effect some weeks in appearing. Wedemeyer had been impressed by General Chen Cheng, and suggested to the Generalissimo that he be chosen to execute the ALPHA plan. The Generalissimo told Wedemeyer he would consider appointing Chen to this vital position though he would prefer to make him Minister of War. A few days later, on 21 November, when Wedemeyer formally presented ALPHA to the Generalissimo he stressed the importance of having China's best general to execute ALPHA. In reply, the Generalissimo said he would appoint General Ho Ying-chin, the current Chief of Staff, to the post. "Asked if he realized that this was the most important job in China today and . . . if General Ho Ying-chin was his best choice, the Generalissimo said that an able United States deputy would help." Twice more the Americans asked the Generalissimo if Ho was his best choice, and each time the Chinese leader said yes.[38]

To Wedemeyer, the appointment was "a decided blow." Raising the matter again with the Generalissimo "as forcefully as [he] could to the Head of a State," he received the answer that Ho had been appointed because he was China's outstanding general. So Wedemeyer did what he could to bolster Ho. General McClure, Wedemeyer's new chief of staff, became Ho's deputy. The appointment of a competent Chinese, General Hsiao I-hsu, formerly chief of staff to the Chinese Salween forces, as Ho's chief of staff was arranged. General Dorn, who had worked closely with General Hsiao on the Salween, was detailed as Hsiao's adviser. Other Americans were detailed to work with Ho's projected staff, in the intelligence, operations, supply, medical, engineer, and signal sections.[39]

Therefore, the suggestion of China Theater headquarters that General Chen Cheng be field commander was not accepted by the Generalissimo, but the latter was willing to create the post of field commander. The significance of this step would lie in the Generalissimo's willingness to permit General Ho actually to exercise command in the field. In the past, the Generalissimo had on two occasions granted field command to an American officer, General Stilwell, then sent to the latter's Chinese subordinates a number of letters and radios countermanding Stilwell's orders, of which Stilwell learned only as his orders were disregarded. If the Generalissimo followed his past practice the result would be substantially to nullify Ho's new appointment. So the Generalissimo's actions immediately after 21

---

[38] Min, Mtg 3, Wedemeyer with Generalissimo, 21 Nov 44. Bk 1, Generalissimo Minutes.
[39] (1) Rad cited n. 34(4). (2) Wedemeyer comments on draft MS.

November would indicate his thoughts about ALPHA much more accurately than would his oral expression.[40]

Meanwhile, the Japanese supplied arguments for the speedy execution of ALPHA. Their propaganda had stressed that theirs was a limited campaign, aimed only at the east China airfields and, as has been noted, the Generalissimo himself thought that the loss of Kweilin and Liuchow ended any urgency of moving up reinforcements. Moreover, Japanese higher headquarters had specified that pursuit should not go far beyond the Kweilin–Liuchow area. Then the *11th Army* began to act independently. In late November 1944 elements of its *3d* and *13th Divisions* drove rapidly and steadily in a northwesterly direction. About 28 November they crossed the provincial border, where they had been ordered by higher authority to halt, and kept right on into Kweichow.[41]

Strengthening the Chinese Forces

After proposing ALPHA to provide an effective command system for and deployment of the Chinese forces, theater headquarters suggested a number of steps to increase the resistance that the Chinese might offer a Japanese offensive aimed at Kunming or Chungking. These included the provision of replacements to bring the Chinese divisions in Kwangsi and Kweichow Provinces back to strength, better rations to end the malnutrition that so severely affected the physical capacity of the Chinese soldier to march and fight, efficient use of existing transport facilities, returning Chinese troops from Burma, suggestions to arm the Chinese Communists, and suggestions to fly a task force of Chinese Communists into Kweichow.[42]

The question of properly feeding the Chinese soldier arose when moving divisions into place for ALPHA was discussed with the Chinese. Showing an appreciation of the state of the Chinese Army, the Generalissimo remarked on 24 November that it would not do to attempt to march troops all the way from Hsian to Nan-cheng for there would be many desertions. In Wedemeyer's opinion, given to the Chinese a few days later, this was because the men were not being fed. If they were being well fed, he thought they would not desert.[43] In a few weeks, as Wedemeyer spent more time studying the state of the Chinese Army, he became increasingly convinced

---

[40] *Stilwell's Command Problems*, Ch. VI.

[41] Japanese Study 130, pp. 26, 30.

[42] (1) Memo, Barrett for Wedemeyer, 30 Nov 44, sub: Organization of Special Units of Communist Forces, Incl to Min, Mtg 11, Wedemeyer with Generalissimo; (2) Min, Mtg 11, Wedemeyer with Generalissimo. Bk 1, Generalissimo Minutes.

[43] Min, Mtgs 4, 5, Wedemeyer with Generalissimo, 24, 27 Nov 44. Bk 1, Generalissimo Minutes.

that simple failure to feed the Chinese soldier underlay most of China's military problems and that the Chinese armies needed food even more than they needed guns.   Long-continued malnutrition made many Chinese soldiers too weak to march; they died along the roads.   Semistarvation had to be eliminated before effective combat formations could be put into the field.

In November the conversations with Chiang had been mostly about troop movements; by mid-December Wedemeyer was spending much of his time with the Generalissimo pleading with the Chinese to improve the diet of their troops.   Indeed, on one occasion, his chief of staff, then acting for Wedemeyer, said that to the U.S. theater commander food seemed to be the most important Chinese military problem.[44]

Wedemeyer recognized four reasons for the extensive malnutrition of the Chinese forces.   He thought that full responsibility had not been given to the commanders involved; that many agencies were concerned, thus diffusing responsibility; that adequate storage and transport facilities were lacking; that there was no prior planning and there were too many administrative details.[45]

In the immediate present, Wedemeyer believed it imperative that for the six months' period beginning 15 December all Chinese armies employed against Japan should have the best food that could be provided.   In addition to his rice rations each man should have fifteen pounds of beef or pork products every month.   Wedemeyer suggested to the Generalissimo that in the future, instead of collecting taxes in kind, the government pay for all rice, pork, and food furnished.   He recommended further that these foodstuffs be delivered by the farmer to the Chinese SOS at roadside, these victuals then to be shipped to food subdepots.   From there supplies would go by truck to divisions and armies.   He suggested that two general supply bases be set up, one at Kunming and one at Chungking.   So that transport for the food would be at hand, Wedemeyer proposed that the American SOS commander control all Chinese military and commercials trucks not essential to the Chinese war effort, plus all emergency air supply.[46]

The Generalissimo was willing to consider suggestions that the Chinese present a plan for proper feeding, a plan supported by staff studies.   He agreed to consider proposals that there should be one responsible agency,

---

[44] (1) Min, Mtg 15, Wedemeyer with Generalissimo, 8 Dec 44.   Bk 1, Generalissimo Minutes.   (2) Memo 277, Wedemeyer for Generalissimo, 11 Dec 44, sub: Rations, Feeding Stations, and Supplemental Rations for Chinese Troops in Defense of Chungking Area.   Bk 16, ACW Corresp with Chinese.   (3) Min, Mtg 3, Wedemeyer with Generalissimo, 21 Nov 44. Bk 1, Generalissimo Minutes.   (4) Memo 267, Wedemeyer for Generalissimo, 7 Dec 44.   Bk 16, ACW Corresp with Chinese.
[45] Memo cited n. 44(2).
[46] Memo 264, Wedemeyer for Generalissimo, 6 Dec 44.   Bk 16, ACW Corresp with Chinese.

that commanders should be indoctrinated with the idea that they were responsible for the proper feeding of their troops, that feeding stations should be set up, and that there should be Sino-American supervision of the whole process.[47]

In retrospect, General McClure, who as chief of staff to Wedemeyer and deputy chief of staff to the Generalissimo had ample opportunity for observation, summed up the program for reform of the Chinese Army in five steps: [48]

1. Feed
2. Arm and equip
3. Train
4. Lead well
5. Indoctrinate

Filling the Gaps in the Chinese Divisions

Information at the disposal of China Theater headquarters strongly indicated that the divisions on the Chinese order of battle were far understrength, and that when divisions engaged the enemy and took casualties the resulting gaps in their ranks were seldom if ever replaced. One reason for this was that commanders were given lump sums in cash for pay and rations based on the paper strength of their units; it was profitable to be understrength.[49] Another reason lay in the functioning of the Chinese replacement system. The Chinese Government allotted quotas to the several provinces, whose governors in turn divided them among the local magistrates. The officials procured conscripts from among the lowest classes by methods that Wedemeyer, after many months of observing the system, described to the Generalissimo as follows: "Conscription comes to the Chinese peasant like famine or flood, only more regularly—every year twice—and claims more victims. Famine, flood, and drought compare with conscription like chicken pox with plague." Wedemeyer made it quite clear that by victims were meant those who died as a result of the abuses and inefficiencies attending the conscription process.[50]

Those conscripts who survived induction were examined by the local governor who selected the best for his own forces. The rest were turned over to the local war area representative of the National Military Council. The numbers he received were of course far short of the provincial quota.

---

[47] Min, Mtg 17, Wedemeyer with Generalissimo, 11 Dec 44. Bk 1, Generalissimo Minutes.
[48] McClure comments on draft MS. OCMH.
[49] (1) Item 13, Wedemeyer Data Book. (2) McClure comments on draft MS.
[50] Memo 678-7, Wedemeyer for Generalissimo, 5 Aug 45. Bk 8, ACW Corresp with Chinese. For an extended quotation from this memorandum, see pages 368–73, below.

Then came the process of transporting conscripts to their destination, which meant still further attrition of the sort described in the Wedemeyer memorandum. On arrival the survivors "were ready for a General Hospital rather than the General Reserve."

The fighting strength of the Chinese divisions suffered still more by the numerous exemptions permitted by the draft laws. The system was very like that in vogue in the United States in 1861–65 in that the prosperous could hire substitutes. Graduates of high schools and colleges easily arranged permanent exemption. Only sons were automatically exempt. Physical weakness was not a disqualifying factor. Therefore, those elements in the populace who should have furnished noncommissioned and junior officers, who had the education and background that would most readily enable them to learn modern techniques of warfare, were exempt.[51]

If the ALPHA plan was to be carried out, a number of full-strength Chinese divisions would have to be provided. So on 30 November 1944 the Generalissimo was asked to provide a grand total of 270,000 replacements by 1 April 1945. The priority with which different armies were to receive replacements was carefully worked out.

To meet the transport problem, the proposals provided for requisitioning replacements from areas near their final destinations. The Ministry of Conscription was to be notified well in advance of the number of men it was to supply, thus easing its problems. The Generalissimo approved the plan and ordered that the Ministry of Conscription plan to obtain replacements within two months.[52]

Plans To Break the Transport Bottleneck

The Chinese forces badly needed food, shoes, clothing, drugs, small arms ammunition, spare parts, and artillery shells, roughly in that priority.[53] Priority of necessity went to the Chinese divisions facing the most imminent Japanese threat, in east China. So supplies had to be moved from the Kunming base area to east China. Any improvement in the line of communications to east China would also benefit the Fourteenth Air Force, for it too depended on the same artery. Though the traditional carrier of most Chinese goods was water transport, the pattern of the rivers and canals was not well adapted to movement of goods from west to east. Trucks had to bridge many of the gaps in the water routes.

As noted above, there were perhaps 10,000 trucks in Nationalist China,

---

[51] (1) History of China Theater, Ch. VII, pp. 10 and 11. (2) Quotation from McClure comments on draft MS.

[52] History of China Theater, Ch. VII, p. 13.

[53] Wedemeyer's November and December 1944 memorandums for and conferences with the Generalissimo are the source of this conclusion.

many of them inoperable through lack of spares, inadequate or bad maintenance, overloading, the unavoidable use of alcohol instead of gasoline for
fuel, the impact of poor roads on the structure of the vehicles, and accidents.
Those vehicles which were in operating condition numbered perhaps 2,000.
Their operational efficiency was further limited by the primitive road net,
and by their dispersal among a number of Chinese agencies and private
individuals.[54]

Some improvement in the resources available was promised by the operation of two projects approved by Stilwell's headquarters some months before.
One had called for flying in 700 trucks to carry supplies east from Kunming
to Chennault's airfields.[55]   With the gradual loss of the airfields in 1944, the
supply situation was altering accordingly.   The trucks were being flown in
steadily and would be a welcome addition.   Between April 1944 and 31
December 1944, 544 trucks arrived in China.   Another project, which called
for driving 500 5-ton truck-trailer combinations across the Soviet Union to
China, was canceled by the Soviets on the plea of uprisings across the route
of march in Sinkiang Province, and the trucks and personnel (LUX Convoy)
were rerouted to India.[56]

On 4 December 1944 Wedemeyer in conference suggested to the Generalissimo that the Chinese SOS operate a great motor pool in which would be
placed all Chinese motor vehicles.   Confiscation of the trucks was not being
suggested, Wedemeyer observed, but rather registering the vehicles, so that
the Chinese Army would receive priority in their use.[57]   The Generalissimo
approved the proposal in principle, so Wedemeyer a few days later submitted
detailed proposals to operate Chinese motor transport.

On 8 December Wedemeyer requested the Generalissimo to place all
transport and maintenance facilities directly under the control of the Commanding General, Chinese SOS, to place all the stations which checked the
movement of trucks under control of the same officer, and to direct that U.S.
Army personnel in conjunction with the Transportation Section, Chinese
SOS, jointly control and direct the operation of all vehicles.[58]   In effect,
Chinese and Americans would work together as members of the same transportation team.

Priorities for movements were to be determined in accordance with the
directives of the combined Sino-American staff of the Generalissimo's China
Theater.   The motor routes were divided into four sections, of which Sec-

---

[54] History of China Theater, Ch. IV, pp. 15–17.
[55] *Stilwell's Command Problems,* Ch. VII.
[56] (1) *Stilwell's Command Problems,* Ch. VII.   (2) Joseph Bykofsky, U.S. Army Transportation in China, Burma, India During World War II, p. 304.   OCMH.   (Hereafter, Bykofsky MS.)
[57] Min, Mtg 13, Wedemeyer with Generalissimo, 4 Dec 44.   Bk 1, Generalissimo Minutes.
[58] Memo 270, Wedemeyer for Generalissimo, 8 Dec 44.   Bk 16, ACW Corresp with Chinese.

LUX CONVOY *ascending the famous twenty-one curves of the Kunming–Kweilin road.*

tions 1 and 2 to east China would be operated under control of a combined Sino-American SOS staff at Kunming. Sections 3 and 4, which linked with the north, toward the Yellow River, would be controlled by the Sino-American Combined Staff at Chungking. Co-ordination between the different operations would be maintained over U.S. communications.

All the checking stations which Chinese governmental agencies had set up on the roads to control the vehicle flow would be placed under the Commanding General, Chinese SOS. An American enlisted man would be attached to the staff of the control station and would tabulate all traffic. His reports would be sent to a central control station.

Transportation personnel would reconnoiter areas in the communications zone and combat zone, and determine the availability of vehicles. Requests for use of these vehicles would be made in the name of the Generalissimo. No trucks would be confiscated unless the owners refused to co-operate. All maintenance and supply facilities would be placed at the disposal of the Commanding General, Chinese SOS. All stocks of fuels and lubricants were to be pooled.[59]

This plan, the initial recommendation of China Theater headquarters to the Generalissimo, was rejected by the Chinese. In effect, the plan would have placed Americans at every level of the operation, and this may have made it unacceptable. On 15 December another plan was presented to the Chinese. This paper suggested that the Chinese War Transport Board control and operate all Chinese Government and commercial trucks. China Theater headquarters understood that acceptance of the plan by the Chinese would give the War Transport Board complete control of trucks in both categories. SOS did not control even Chinese Army trucks, for many truck regiments were on detached service with Chinese Government agencies.[60]

This proposal met with partial Chinese acceptance. The Generalissimo directed that all Chinese military vehicles be placed under the control of the Chinese SOS. It was further ordered that all Chinese Government and commercial vehicles be placed under the War Transport Board. Many years later McClure felt that this step had not been too effective, and noted that trucks meant money and power to whoever controlled or drove them.[61]

The physical aspects of the problem could not be adequately attacked until the Ledo Road was completed and until Hump tonnage was at a more satisfactory level. In anticipation of this time, now rapidly approaching, Wedemeyer requested Army Service Forces to approve shipping 2,000 6 x 6 and 5,000 Dodge trucks to China.[62]

[59] *Ibid.*
[60] Memo 286, McClure for Generalissimo, 15 Dec 44. Bk 16, ACW Corresp with Chinese.
[61] (1) History of China Theater, Ch. IV, p. 20. (2) McClure comments on drafts MS.
[62] Bykofsky MS, p. 307.

Attempts To Arm Hsueh Yueh

Because the line of communications that supported the Japanese divisions in east China ran through General Hsueh Yueh's IX War Area, and because two of the last airstrips from which Chennault could operate in east China were in General Hsueh's territory, Wedemeyer and Chennault shared a common interest in supplying Hsueh Yueh with arms. However, some months before, Stilwell's headquarters had received an order from the Generalissimo that only air force supplies were to go to east China, and had received the very strong impression that the Generalissimo did not trust Hsueh Yueh. At that time the Americans also received the impression that General Hsueh was one of a group of Nationalist war lords in east and southeast China whose loyalty to the Nationalist cause did not extend to the Generalissimo personally.[63]

During the critical months of summer 1944, when the fate of the strong Chinese city of Heng-yang was in doubt, General Chennault had repeatedly asked Stilwell to supply Hsueh Yueh with arms. Obedient to the Generalissimo's orders, Stilwell had refused. Now, in November 1944, Hsueh renewed his pleas for arms and again forwarded them through the Fourteenth Air Force. On 30 November 1944 Wedemeyer personally raised the issue with the Generalissimo. He told the Chinese leader that Hsueh had requested 3,000 rifles, 600 Bren guns, 150 mortars, and 500 grenade dischargers, with ammunition. Noting that the request had come through Fourteenth Air Force channels, Wedemeyer said he would not fill it without the Generalissimo's concurrence. In reply the Generalissimo said that Hsueh's request should be disregarded.

The Generalissimo's statement had several implications. Wedemeyer therefore asked the Generalissimo to define his policy on the issuance of American supplies to the Chinese commanders. Wedemeyer conceded that coordination between the several U.S. headquarters had not been good, for in his opinion Dorn on the Salween and Chennault in east China had become accustomed to independent action. The Generalissimo replied that he would see to it that the Chinese did not again make any approaches outside the proper channel which was through the Ordnance Department of the Ministry of War. But this reply still left unsettled the Generalissimo's attitude toward General Hsueh Yueh, and so Wedemeyer asked if Hsueh Yueh was a "loyal and effective general." The Generalissimo answered that Hsueh was "able, and had been with the Revolution a long time."[64]

---

[63] *Stilwell's Command Problems,* Ch. XI.

[64] (1) Min, Mtg 8, Wedemeyer with Generalissimo, 30 Nov 44. Bk 1, Generalissimo Minutes. (2) Rad CAK 2018, Chennault to Wedemeyer, 8 Dec 44. Item 164, Bk 1, ACW Personal File.

In the same conference the question of cutting the Japanese supply lines in east China was discussed. Stretching for hundreds of miles south of Hankow through hostile territory these seemed an obvious target for Chinese attacks. But Wedemeyer told the Generalissimo he had reports that Hsueh Yueh and General Chang Fa-kwei, who commanded the IV War Area (Kwangsi), were not obeying orders to attack, while the commander of the 24th Group Army was not only not attacking the Japanese but was reported to be looting Chinese villages. The Generalissimo answered that Hsueh Yueh had been sent orders. Chang Fa-kwei seemed to be in a different category, for Chiang remarked that orders would not be enough, a special envoy would have to be sent to him.[65]

So, Wedemeyer told Chennault on 11 December:

Subject discussed in your CAKX 2018 was taken up with the Generalissimo two days ago. I did not get any definite commitment from him. However, he stated categorically that no supplies or equipment will be given to Chinese forces without his express approval. He apparently is adamant concerning your request to provide supplies for the Ninth War Area. If you desire to pursue this request further I suggest that the Chinese commander of the Ninth War Area make his request directly to the Generalissimo. I do not feel that I can make further representations in the near future. Theater policy concerning the air-dropping of supplies was sent to you in TG 354 from Breitwiser. This policy will not be violated.[66]

Plans To Use the Chinese Communists

In the months preceding Stilwell's recall, the President and the Joint Chiefs had desired to see Stilwell, under the Generalissimo, command both Chinese Nationalist and Chinese Communist forces in the war against Japan. The War Department had contemplated giving lend-lease to a Chinese Army that might include Communist forces. Stilwell's recall had not changed these views, and the Japanese threat to the Kunming–Kweiyang–Chungking area suggested to the U.S. theater headquarters in China that Chinese Communist military help might do a great deal to stop the Japanese.

Wedemeyer had sought and obtained as his chief of staff General McClure, who arrived in Chungking on 20 November, assuming his new post on the 28th. He very soon took an active part in formulating plans and proposals to arm and use the Chinese Communists against the Japanese. In the week of his arrival he discussed the military and political problems of China with the President's personal envoy, General Hurley. With the resolution of the October 1944 command crisis, Hurley had turned his attention to the civil strife in China which so hampered the Chinese war effort. He reported every move to the President and received the President's approval and sup-

---

[65] Min cited n. 64(1).
[66] Rad CFB 28882, Wedemeyer to Chennault, 11 Dec 44. Item 172, Bk 1, ACW Personal File.

COL. DAVID D. BARRETT, *Chief of the American Observer Group at Chinese Communist Headquarters in Yenan, China.*

port of his efforts to mediate between the Nationalists and Communists. Because they thought that Communist military aid could materially assist in stopping the Japanese, Wedemeyer, McClure, and other officers of theater headquarters spent a good deal of time trying to assist Hurley in his efforts to forestall civil war and unify the Chinese.[67]

From the discussions in Wedemeyer's headquarters, three projects for using the Chinese Communists finally evolved. The earliest and simplest was to supply munitions to the Communists. Presented to the General-

[67] (1) McClure, Memo for Record. Communist File, 06104-M, 3 Nov 44–10 Dec 44, T–49–20 CBI, DRB AGO. The memorandum seems to have been written in January, certainly before 25 January 1945. (2) On Hurley's efforts, see radio, CFB 25629, Hurley to President, on 7 November 1944. Item 89, Book 1, Hurley Papers. (3) For indication of the President's support, see Item 103, Book 1, Hurley Papers, a radio in which the President authorizes Hurley to say to Chiang Kai-shek that a working arrangement between Nationalists and Communists would greatly expedite throwing the Japanese out of north China "from my point of view and also that of the Russians. You can emphasize the word 'Russians' to him." (4) For subsequent references to the Chinese Communists, see pp. 167, 249–54, 337–38, 381–85, below.

issimo by Wedemeyer on 27 November, it met with immediate rejection. The Generalissimo stated that the time was not ripe, but as soon as it was he would tell Wedemeyer.[68]

Then it became known that the head of the Office of Strategic Services, Maj. Gen. William J. Donovan, would visit China, and so McClure and Wedemeyer began to shape more comprehensive plans for presentation to General Donovan, should the Generalissimo approve them. Donovan's aid and support appeared desirable because one of the emerging plans would involve guerrilla warfare, the specialty of the OSS and an activity for which the Communists enjoyed a great reputation in the press. Moreover, Wedemeyer expected to leave for an inspection trip of his new theater and his chief of staff wanted to present the plans before Wedemeyer left.[69]

The first plan to emerge was suggested by Colonel Barrett of the American Observer Group in Yenan. This small party of American military personnel with two civilians from the State Department, John S. Service and Raymond P. Ludden, had been sent to Yenan in July 1944 to obtain intelligence and assist pilots in escape and evasion. Since then the men had been occupying themselves with order of battle, meteorological, and target data. Barrett's orders forbade the men to engage in political discussion, but in effect their party formed an American listening post behind the Communist lines, and offered an agency through which communications might be sent to the Communists.[70] McClure accepted the plan which Barrett had drafted, and in turn presented it to Wedemeyer. Wedemeyer approved, and laid the plan before the Generalissimo on 2 December 1944.[71]

The plan suggested organizing three Communist infantry regiments in Yenan, a total of about 5,000 men. The force would be armed and equipped by the U.S. Services of Supply. They would then be moved into Nationalist territory, either southwest China or the Tung-kuan–Hsian area of Shensi Province, near where the Chinese Nationalists were blockading the Communists. On their arrival they were to be commanded by an American officer with ten liaison officers attached.[72] The Generalissimo rejected the scheme, on the ground that the people in the area where the Communists were to operate would be actively hostile toward them.[73]

The other plan, prepared by McClure, called for sending U.S. airborne units of 4,000 to 5,000 well-trained technicians into Communist-held territory,

---

[68] Min, Mtg 5, Wedemeyer with Generalissimo, 27 Nov 44. Bk 1, Generalissimo Minutes.
[69] Memo cited n. 67(1).
[70] *Stilwell's Command Problems*, Ch. X.
[71] (1)Memo, Barrett for Wedemeyer, 30 Nov 44, sub: Organization of Special Units of Communist Forces. Incl to Min, Mtg 11, Wedemeyer with Generalissimo; (2) Min, Mtg 11, Wedemeyer with Generalissimo. Bk 1, Generalissimo Minutes.
[72] Memo cited n. 71(1).
[73] Memo cited n. 67(1).

providing both the Nationalists and Communists approved. Wedemeyer approved its concepts, as presented by McClure to Donovan and himself, then left for his inspection trip. McClure set about completing the draft and seeking concurrences before the plan was presented to the Generalissimo. Since Colonel Barrett was going to Yenan on a mission for Hurley, McClure told him to ask what aid and assistance the Chinese Communists might give if the plan were to be approved. The Communists were to be told the plan could not go into effect unless both Nationalists and Communists agreed. McClure then presented the plan to Hurley, adding that he, McClure, planned later to show it to General Chen Cheng, now Minister of War. At Hurley's suggestion, McClure also showed it to China's Foreign Minister, T. V. Soong. Again McClure offered cautions, saying this presentation was only so McClure could offer a mature study at a later date, and asking Soong not to tell the Generalissimo unless Soong thought it essential.[74]

So, in December 1944, McClure sought reactions and concurrences from several key figures, much as he would circulate a staff paper in his own headquarters, accompanying each presentation with oral cautions. The impact of word that an agency of the United States Government contemplated steps which if successful would ultimately result in American technicians and American supplies being committed to Communist China was some weeks in appearing.

[74] (1) Memo cited n. 67(1). (2) McClure comments on draft MS. (3) Ltr, Gen Hurley to Maj Gen R. W. Stephens, Chief of Mil History, 15 Dec 56. OCMH.

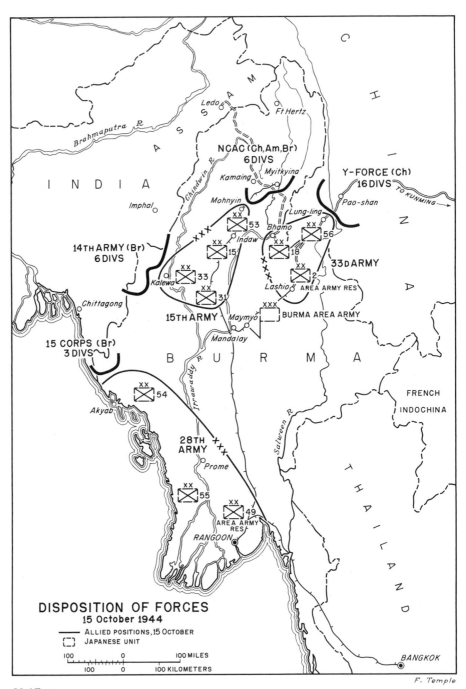

DISPOSITION OF FORCES
15 October 1944

————	ALLIED POSITIONS, 15 OCTOBER
⊏⊐	JAPANESE UNIT

100 0 100 MILES
100 0 100 KILOMETERS

F. Temple

MAP 7

CHAPTER III

Beginning the Fall Campaign in North Burma

When the monsoon rains lifted in the fall of 1944 and the ground began to dry, action in Burma started to rise to another peak of intensity. The great British victory at Imphal, on the Indo-Burmese border, in the preceding spring and summer, had fatally weakened the Japanese *15th Army,* while the Chinese and American successes in north Burma had left the Japanese *33d Army* strength only to delay. For the staffs, the questions were how far and in what direction to exploit success; for the soldiers, how to overcome the stubborn delaying action of a sorely wounded but still determined enemy.

The Situation at the Front

By September 1944 the Allies had breached the natural defenses of Burma at several points. (*Map 6—inside back cover; Map 7*) A state whose area is as large as that of Germany, Burma is essentially a group of river valleys sheltered between two major spurs of the Himalaya Mountains. On the Indo-Burmese border are the Arakan Yoma, the Chin Hills, and the Naga Hills, which curve in a great arc from the Bay of Bengal to the border of Tibet. Some of their peaks are as high as 10,000 feet, and their lower slopes are covered with tropical forest. The Sino-Burmese border runs through another complex of mountain ranges, which, unlike that on the west, is of great width. These mountains also come down to the sea, so that Burma is most readily reached by sea or air.

Burma may be regarded as the land that three great rivers flowing from north to south have carved from the mountains. The westernmost of these three is the Chindwin River. Running parallel to the mountains of the Indo-Burmese border, it offers another barrier to troop movement in either direction. The country through which it flows for most of its length is sparsely settled brush and forest. Then, at Shwegyin, it emerges from the

TANK FARM AT MYITKYINA. *Gasoline delivered by pipeline was stored in these tanks until needed.*

valley, alters its course slightly to the east, and enters the great valley of central Burma which the Irrawaddy River has cut. The Irrawaddy in central Burma inclines southwestward, then it meets the Chindwin, and the now even mightier Irrawaddy flows on for many more miles to enter the Bay of Bengal. The great port and prewar capital of Burma, Rangoon, is slightly to the east of the Irrawaddy delta. Once restored, Rangoon's port facilities would make it an excellent staging area for an amphibious attack on Malaya. In the eastern portion of Burma the Salween River flows from north to south and enters the Andamen Sea at Moulmein.

Since the principal topographic features of Burma lie along north-south lines, the problem that faced the Allies after the Japanese took Burma in April 1942 was to cut across the grain of the country from west and east until they had placed themselves in one of the major valleys, then exploit their successful crossing of the mountain barriers by a campaign down the valley into the vital airfields, oil resources, railways, highways, and seaports of central and south Burma. The greatest of the Burmese valleys is that through which the Irrawaddy flows. Myitkyina is the most important point on the northern stretches of that river.

Before the war Myitkyina was a thriving frontier town, with rail connections to Rangoon and a fair-weather road to China. Since August 1944 it had been in Allied hands, and was being rapidly converted into a great supply center.   A gasoline pipeline began deliveries to Myitkyina on 2 October. The local airstrips were being rehabilitated and expanded, and air cargo was flowing in steadily.   The Ledo Road was being extended past Myitkyina and was being joined to it by a cutoff.

South from Myitkyina, both the Burma Railways and the Irrawaddy River led to central Burma and the famous old city of Mandalay.   The railway builders had laid the tracks between two long, narrow, 3,000- to 4,000-foot hill masses which lie along a north-south line within the major valley, hence the name by which this avenue of approach was known at the time, "the Railway Corridor."   An Allied force driving down from Myitkyina would inevitably strike the flank of any Japanese force trying to stop an attack coming from the east across the grain of the country.

In the Arakan section of Burma, along the Bay of Bengal, the British 15 Corps, with the 25th and 26th Indian Divisions, and the 81st West African Division, had been forced by the monsoon rains to confine itself in August to patrolling.   It was astride the coastal range, and was in position to move down the coast.   Such an advance would open up staging areas and airfields near the most vital areas of south and central Burma—the oil fields of Yenangyaung and the seaport of Rangoon.[1]   In February 1944 the British and Indian forces in the Arakan had signally defeated the Japanese *55th Division;* opportunity to exploit this success would come when the rivers went back to their channels and the ground began to harden.

The Japanese forces in the Arakan were the *28th Army,* with the *54th* and *55th Divisions.*   This force had to defend the coast almost to Rangoon.

On the central front, opposite Imphal, where fighting heavy by any scale had taken place between the British 4 and 33 Corps and the Japanese *15th Army,* the 11th East African and 5th Indian Divisions were pursuing the survivors of the Japanese *15th* and *31st Divisions,* and the still formidable though sorely battered Japanese *33d Division.*   On 5 July Lt. Gen. William J. Slim, commanding the British Fourteenth Army, having determined to exploit the victory at Imphal, had ordered 4 and 33 Corps to destroy the Japanese *15th Army* west of the Chindwin.   This order meant keeping unremitting pressure on the Japanese through the monsoon rains.   Its execution yielded major results.   Their defeat at Imphal, plus Slim's relentless monsoon pursuit, cost the Japanese 171 guns, 2,058 vehicles, and 85,000 men.   If the Japanese were to fight again in Burma, they had to rebuild their forces and so the *33d Division* was putting up a stubborn rear guard action.   The *53d Division* was moving down from north Burma to reinforce the *15th Army.*

The terrain between Imphal in India and the Chindwin River in Burma, behind which the Japanese were now seeking shelter, is exceedingly difficult.

---

[1] Mountbatten Report, Pt. B, pars. 239–41.

463995 O–59—7

The Japanese dug themselves into the mountains, with their machine guns and mortars commanding the muddy mountain tracks. The monsoon rains poured down impartially on friend and foe. Under these circumstances, the steady advance of the two divisions was a very considerable achievement and denied the Japanese the time they so badly needed. On 30 August an Indian patrol stood on the banks of the Chindwin.[2]

In north Burma, a powerful Allied concentration faced the Japanese *33d Army.* The Northern Combat Area Command, though American, had, by common and informal consent of Chinese and Americans, come to the open exercise of the command it had hitherto exercised through the legal fiction of a headquarters with a Chinese name and Chinese authority, Chih Hui Pu.[3] Its combat elements included two Chinese armies totaling five divisions, the British 36th Division of two brigades, which had arrived at Myitkyina airstrip in mid-July, and an American brigade headquarters to which attachment of one Chinese and two American regiments was contemplated.[4] This force was deep in north Burma and firmly gripped the upper valley of the Irrawaddy River, whose lower length is Burma proper. Having relieved the "Chindits" (the airborne formation which had operated behind Japanese lines), the British 36th Division was advancing southward down the line of the Burma Railways, on a course that would, if the Japanese could not halt it, inevitably bring it to Mandalay. To the east lay China, now within striking distance.

The Japanese *33d Army* currently included the *18th, 2d,* and *56th Divisions,* plus one regiment of the *49th.* The *18th Division* was greatly reduced in strength as a result of the 1944 battles in the Hukawng and Mogaung valleys and was scheduled for reorganization and re-equipment.[5]

In the air the Allies had superiority, unchallenged and crushing. The Allied air arm for Burma, Eastern Air Command, in October 1944 had in operational condition 125 AAF fighters and 267 RAF fighters, 48 AAF heavy bombers and 38 RAF heavy bombers, 72 AAF medium bombers, 198 AAF transports, and 35 RAF transports. The transports were most important for they gave the Allied ground forces a mobility and an independence of lines of communications on the ground the Japanese could not dream of approaching.

Against this force the Japanese had their *5th Air Division.* Once masters of the Burma skies, the *5th's* pilots faced the expected Allied attack with about 12 bombers, 60 fighters, and 10 reconnaissance aircraft. With this handful

---

[2] (1) Mountbatten Report, Pt. B, pars. 251–53. (2) Japanese Study 133, p. 16. (3) Japanese Study 91 states one battalion was reduced to sixty men with three machine guns.
[3] See *Stilwell's Command Problems* and *Stilwell's Mission to China.*
[4] History of IBT, I, 38–39.
[5] (1) History of IBT, I, 7. (2) Japanese Study 91. (3) *Stilwell's Command Problems* has a brief résumé of the Chindit operation.

the *5th Air Division* was ordered to defend not only Burma but Thailand and Indochina.[6]

With the disparity in force in Burma, in great measure the result of the British and Indian victory at Imphal, Allied success was now certain. The question of defining the victory remained to be solved. Given the circumstances that Germany though defeated was still fighting desperately, that the American forces in the Pacific were capable of making a gigantic amphibious assault anywhere in the western Pacific from the Kurils to the southern tip of the Philippines regardless of what might happen in China, what plans for Southeast Asia Command would best combine the profitable and the practical?

Planning the First Directive

When plans for a fall campaign became a current topic in June 1944, the Combined Chiefs of Staff (CCS) seemed to feel that the most which could be hoped for was that SEAC should be prepared to exploit any successes gained; they did not direct the occupation of any geographical objective in Burma. In June 1944, when the Japanese were a grave threat to India, the CCS thought the main object of all operations in Burma was to send the maximum quantity of supplies over the Hump. The only indication of an offensive spirit in the CCS at that time with regard to ground operations in Burma was discussion of an airborne operation against Rangoon—but the CCS did not think the operation could be staged in time to help Pacific operations.[7]

Then came the retreat of the Japanese from their abortive attack on India, a retreat that began on 15 July. As they fell back, they left behind the unmistakable evidence of disaster in abandoned equipment and unburied dead, proof that the plan of General Slim and General Sir George Giffard to meet and break the Japanese *15th Army* on the Imphal plain had succeeded. So the question soon became that of drafting plans to exploit this success, plus those gained by Stilwell in north Burma.[8]

The SEAC planners drafted two plans, X and Y, to exploit the victories and to carry out the CCS directive of 4 June 1944. Plan X called for the NCAC forces in north Burma to move from the Mogaung–Myitkyina area to Katha and Bhamo. At the same time 4 and 33 Corps would drive in force toward the Chindwin, and an airborne operation would be undertaken in the

---

[6] (1) See *Stilwell's Command Problems*, Chapter III, for detailed information. (2) Despatch on Air Operations in Eastern Air Command (SEA) Covering the Period 15 December 1943 to 1 June 1945, prepared for Gen Stratemeyer, pp. 132, 133. OCMH. (Hereafter, EAC Despatch.) (3) Japanese Study 95.

[7] (1) CM–OUT 53610, 20 Jun 44. Case 404, OPD 381 Security. (2) CCS 166th Mtg, Item 3, 15 Jun 44.

[8] (1) Japanese Studies 91 and 133. (2) Operational Record of Eleventh Army Group and A.L.F.S.E.A., Nov 43–Aug 45, pp. 34–35. OCMH. (Hereafter, ALFSEA Record.)

Wuntho area.   The goal of Plan X was to occupy north Burma to the line Kalewa–Lashio.   Plan Y called for 4 and 33 Corps to cross the Chindwin so as to use British superiority in armor in the central Burma plain, and later to exploit as far as Mandalay.   Airborne troops would take Kalewa, and there would be a later descent at the entrance to the Mandalay plain.   This operation against central Burma would be complemented by a southward advance of the NCAC and the Y–Force.   At the suggestion of the British Chiefs and General Marshall, the Staff added Plan Z, a combined sea and air assault on Rangoon.[9]

The question then arose of how these several plans fitted into the current CCS directive to SEAC, which called on that command "to develop, maintain, broaden, and protect the air link to China, in order to provide the maximum and timely stock of petrol and stores to China in support of Pacific operations . . . to be prepared to exploit the development of overland communications to China. . . ."[10]   General Wedemeyer, who was then SEAC's deputy chief of staff and had not yet gone to China, reported to the War Department that the SEAC planners were splitting along national lines.   He believed that the British members of the planning staff interpreted the directive to the effect that there were to be no actual operations to open a line of communications to China, just preparations.   Wedemeyer reported further that the British planners were squarely behind Plan Z for an attack on Rangoon, in Wedemeyer's opinion for diplomatic reasons, while the American planners favored Plan Y for an overland offensive aimed at Mandalay and clearing north Burma.[11]

In reply to Wedemeyer, the War Department stated that the phrases in the SEAC directive had been chosen with a view to securing an early agreement on the paper.   In the War Department's opinion, the directive called on SEAC to use all its resources for an early and maximum flow of supplies to China, and to continue vigorous operations to open a land link to China.[12]

To co-ordinate and clarify the views of the British and American Chiefs of Staff on future operations in southeast Asia, Mountbatten and Wedemeyer visited London and Washington respectively in early August 1944.   Their reports to other interested officers and agencies suggest that in August there was considerable agreement among SEAC's military superiors.   On 17 August Mountbatten told Stilwell that the British Chiefs of Staff wanted Phases I and II of Plan Y, the attack on Mandalay, executed as soon as possi-

[9] (1) Mountbatten Report, Pt. B, par 221.   (2) Ltr, Wedemeyer to Col Lawrence J. Lincoln, 13 Jul 44.   Case 438, OPD 381 Security.   (3) Rpt, SAC (44) 3 (0), SAC's Visit to London, 5–21 Aug 44.   SEAC War Diary.
[10] Mountbatten Report, Pt. B, par. 185.
[11] (1) Ltr cited n. 9(2).   (2) Ltr, Wedemeyer to Marshall, 9 Jul 44.   Folder 57, OPD Exec 10.
[12] CM–OUT 71617, Marshall to Wedemeyer, 27 Jul 44.

SECOND QUEBEC CONFERENCE. *Seated, from left: General George C. Marshall, Admiral William D. Leahy, President Franklin D. Roosevelt, Prime Minister Winston S. Churchill, Field Marshal Sir Alan Brooke, Field Marshal Sir John Dill. Standing: Maj. Gen. L. C. Hollis, General Sir Hastings Ismay, Admiral Ernest J. King, Air Marshal Sir Charles Portal, General Henry H. Arnold, Admiral Sir A. B. Cunningham.*

ble, with Plan Z against Rangoon to be executed mid-March 1945 using resources from Europe.   Stilwell agreed, providing forces at hand were committed to Plan Y and not held for later use against Rangoon.[13]   A day later Wedemeyer advised Mountbatten that the Joint Chiefs of Staff (JCS) wanted Plan Y executed as soon as possible in the fall.   If the European situation permitted, an attack on Rangoon would be acceptable providing the basic objectives of Y were kept in mind.   The JCS had made it very clear they would not agree to operations against Rangoon if these militated against Phases I and II of Plan Y.[14]

---

[13] CM–IN 16319, Stilwell to Marshall, 17 Aug 44.
[14] CM–OUT 83031, Wedemeyer to Mountbatten, via Eisenhower, 18 Aug 44.

Then came the second Quebec Conference between President Roosevelt, Prime Minister Churchill, and the Combined Chiefs of Staff, which began 12 September. As discussions opened, it became apparent that the British Chiefs of Staff had changed their views since the exchanges of mid-September, when there seemed agreement on executing Phases I and II of Plan Y, or CAPITAL as it then became. Some of Churchill's comments had suggested that it was unwise to become involved in Burma operations, and were reflected in the views now offered by the British Chiefs of Staff and SEAC.[15] Remarking that it was undesirable for jungle fighting in Burma to go on indefinitely, Churchill observed it was for that reason the British Chiefs of Staff now suggested the Rangoon attack (or DRACULA), to be preceded by Phase I of CAPITAL, the taking of Kalewa and Kalemyo plus a limited advance in north Burma, as much as was needed of Phase II, which was an overland and airborne assault on the Ye-u–Shwebo area, and an advance by NCAC to the line Mongmit–Mogok–Lashio.[16] Mandalay was thus excluded as an objective, but opening a line of communications to China, though not prescribed, was within the scope of proposed operations.

In supporting these proposals, the Chief of the Imperial General Staff, General Sir Alan Brooke, said that the British desired to liquidate the Burma commitment as early as possible; it was proving a heavy one, both in casualties and in men needed to operate the long lines of communications. To liquidate this commitment, operations against Rangoon had been examined. If successful, they would end the Burma commitment, secure the air route to China (with possibly at a later date a land route), and get staging areas for further operations in Southeast Asia. Some earlier comments by Churchill forecast the nature of the further operations to which General Brooke referred. "He had always advocated an advance across the Bay of Bengal and operations to recover Singapore, the loss of which had been a grievous and shameful blow to British prestige which must be avenged. It would not be good enough for Singapore to be returned to us at the peace table. We should recover it in battle."[17]

These expressions now fell on sympathetic ears among the Americans. Once the line of communications across Burma to China had been re-established and secured, the Joint Chiefs and the President in September 1944 had no further interest in Burma operations *per se.* The British were in effect suggesting that the major Japanese concentration in central Burma be bypassed by an amphibious operation and this was a technique which the Americans, Australians, and New Zealanders had used with great effect in

[15] See *Stilwell's Mission to China,* pp. 329, 358–59, and *Stilwell's Command Problems.*
[16] The phases of CAPITAL are described in Mountbatten Report, Pt. B, par. 250.
[17] (1) CCS 174th Mtg, Item 4, Quebec, 14 Sep 44. (2) First Plenary Mtg, the Citadel, Quebec, 13 Sep 44.

the Pacific.   As Roosevelt remarked on 13 September, "American experience has been that the 'end-run' method paid a handsome dividend.   Rabaul was an example of this by-passing technique which had been employed with considerable success at small cost of life."[18]

In accepting the proposals of the British Chiefs of Staff, Generals Marshall and Arnold, the latter commanding the U.S. Army Air Forces, joined to ask that the proposed directive be amended to make clear that opening an overland line of communications to China was among the prescribed missions of SEAC.   They explained that supplies being flown to China over the Hump were accumulating at the Chinese airfields because there was no transport to move them.[19]   Trucks were urgently needed and could be put into China only by driving them over the new Ledo Road.   The amendment was accepted, and the OCTAGON directive was drawn up accordingly.   Mountbatten was ordered to seize Rangoon by an amphibious assault before the 1945 monsoon, target date 15 March, and to engage in such operations within Burma as were necessary to secure the Hump air route and open overland communications to China.   If it should be impossible to attack Rangoon before the rains began, then Mountbatten was to exploit current operations into Burma as far as possible, without impairing chances of attacking Rangoon from the sea after the monsoon's close.[20]   The importance given Rangoon reflected its strategic location and logistical importance.   Once it was in Allied hands, *Burma Area Army* would lose its only effective line of communications and be forced to evacuate Burma.

Events Cancel the Attack on Rangoon

Both before and during the Quebec Conference of 1944, at which SEAC was ordered to concentrate on taking Rangoon before the 1945 rains, the comments of various senior officers identified forces at work which might compel an alteration in the plans.   For one thing, the commanders in the field were advancing aggressively and were well into the early stages of CAPITAL, the attack toward Mandalay.   Once acquired, momentum is hard to stop.   On 1 September 1944 General Giffard was quoted, on the connection between current and future operations, to the effect that CAPITAL should be regarded as an extension of the present operations, drafted by commanders who were already in the field and carrying out the current pursuit of the beaten Japanese.[21]   A fortnight later Mountbatten told the CCS that in steadily

[18] First Plenary Mtg, the Citadel, 13 Sep 44.
[19] CCS 174th Mtg, Item 4, Quebec, 14 Sep 44.
[20] Mountbatten Report, Pt. B, par. 260.
[21] SAC (44) 5th Mtg (0), Preparation of Plans for Operation CAPITAL, 1 Sep 44.   SEAC War Diary.

exploiting the victory at Imphal SEAC's forces had carried out Phase I of CAPITAL "to an extent that would make it unreasonable to cancel Phase II." So Mountbatten told the CCS that, if he could not be given all the resources SEAC had originally stipulated as necessary to take Rangoon in March 1945 by assault from sea and air, he would be happy to investigate the possibility of conducting the same operation in March with a smaller force.[22]

Mountbatten's comments pointed to the second factor, the extent to which his superiors would reinforce SEAC to permit an attack on Rangoon together with major operations on land. In the past SEAC's operations had suffered from the higher priority given European offensives. At Quebec, on 16 September 1944, Marshall had promised to examine the possibility of sending two U.S. divisions to Burma. These would have been in addition to a very considerable British reinforcement, possibly as many as seven divisions from Europe and the Mediterranean, and would have changed the scale of operations in Southeast Asia.[23]

But as the European summer faded into fall, the German Army overcame the shock of the summer reverses in France and stiffened noticeably as British, French, and American divisions approached the German border. Supply problems sharply limited the effort the Allies could exert there. Inside the Reich, the National Socialist regime of Adolf Hitler survived an attempt at a military *Putsch*. Germany was not going to collapse in early fall 1944, and no divisions could be spared from Europe in time for Mountbatten to count on them for operations in March 1945. On 2 October 1944 the British Chiefs of Staff and the War Cabinet concluded that the assault on Rangoon could not be carried out in March 1945. The British Chiefs of Staff estimated the operation would require sending 253,000 men to India—three divisions and an armored brigade from the European Theater of Operations, two Indian divisions from the Mediterranean. They did not feel justified in withdrawing these forces when there was still hard fighting ahead for the forces of General Dwight D. Eisenhower. Instead of an attack on Rangoon, the British Chiefs suggested that Mountbatten be ordered to move aggressively into central and north Burma (CAPITAL) without prejudice to plans to carry out DRACULA after the rainy season.[24]

The Joint Chiefs did not believe that because troops could not be spared from Europe this meant Eisenhower was being given troops originally intended for Burma, and they told the President they would never have agreed

---

[22] Rad SEACOS 227, Mountbatten to CCS, 13 Sep 44.   SEAC War Diary.

[23] (1) Memo, Marshall for Dill, 22 Sep 44; Ltr, Dill to Marshall, 4 Oct 44.   Folders 57, 66, OPD Exec 10.   (2) The U.S. divisions might have been destined for China.   See *Stilwell's Command Problems*.

[24] (1) Ltr, Dill to McNarney, 5 Oct 44.   Folder 66, OPD Exec 10.   (2) CM–OUT 42323, 6 Oct 44.   Case 516, OPD 381 Security.

to any diversion from the main effort.   The transfer of divisions from Europe, in their opinion, would not be agreeable unless victory there was assured.[25] But the suggestions of the British Chiefs of Staff—that SEAC press vigorously into Burma from the west and north and prepare to attack Rangoon about November 1945—were fully satisfactory and conformed to the alternative provisions of the OCTAGON directive.   The final orders were phrased accordingly.[26]

CAPITAL, whose continuation was now the assigned task of SEAC, fell into three phases:

Phase I—the seizure of Kalewa and Kalemyo by a land advance combined with an airborne operation, while the forces of N.C.A.C. advanced via the Katha–Bhamo area towards Kunchaung, Sikaw and Namhkam.

Phase 2—an overland and airborne assault against the Ye-U-Shwebo area, while the forces of N.C.A.C., make a complementary advance to a line Mogok–Mongmit–Lashio (possibly using airborne forces to assist in the capture of the last-named place).

Phase 3—the securing of Burma down to a line Mandalay–Pakokku, while the forces of N.C.A.C. advanced to a line Maymyo–Lashio.[27]

Allied Land Forces, Southeast Asia

The final orders, to continue with CAPITAL, went to a new agency in the Southeast Asia Command structure.   This was Allied Land Forces, Southeast Asia, under Lt. Gen. Sir Oliver Leese, who had commanded the British Eighth Army in Italy.   In May 1944 Mountbatten had concluded that he needed a commander in chief for the Allied ground forces in Southeast Asia. General Giffard, commanding Eleventh Army Group, would have been the logical choice, but Stilwell was not willing to serve under Giffard.   Mountbatten put the issue to the CCS, pointing out he found it difficult to deal directly with a variety of subordinate army headquarters.   The question was raised again during the period of planning for the split of the U.S. China, Burma and India Theater of Operations into the China and India–Burma Theaters.   Stilwell then expressed his opposition.   He believed that no new channel of command was needed, that creation of an Allied land forces headquarters would emphasize American commitments in SEAC, and that the Generalissimo would resent having his troops under control of another foreign headquarters.   A few days later Stilwell modified his views to a considerable degree by stating that he was willing to accept an all-British staff in the proposed headquarters for he feared his theater could not supply qualified officers.   The British point of view, as expressed by Giffard, was that the headquarters should be an integrated one.

[25] Memo, JCS for President, 14 Oct 44.   Folder 69, OPD Exec 10.
[26] Mountbatten Report, Pt. B, par. 262.
[27] Mountbatten Report, Pt. B, par. 250.

With the ending of the monsoon and the decision to continue with operations into Burma, the creation of the new headquarters became an urgent matter; Wedemeyer reported to Marshall that the British were contemplating setting up such a headquarters without awaiting U.S. or Chinese approval.[28]   A week after Wedemeyer wrote, Mountbatten recommended to the CCS that Headquarters, Allied Land Forces, Southeast Asia (ALFSEA) should be activated to control all British land forces, NCAC, the Chinese Army in India, and Chinese forces operating within SEAC.   He conceded that the Generalissimo would have to approve where the Chinese were concerned, and that U.S. ground and service troops not under NCAC would not be under the new command.

Informal approval of the new arrangement was given by Marshall on 30 October 1944.   He explained to Mountbatten that a formal written agreement on ALFSEA's creation would require the Generalissimo's approval, but he himself saw no reason why there could not be an oral agreement for operational command by Leese.   He feared an appeal direct to the Generalissimo would complicate an already intricate situation.[29]

Mountbatten thought the Chinese aspect would offer no difficulty because he recalled that at Chungking in October 1943 and again in India in November 1943 the Generalissimo had said that all Chinese troops within SEAC's boundaries were under Mountbatten's command.   These statements were taken by Mountbatten for use as the basis for delegating authority over Chinese troops to the new headquarters.   On 6 November 1944 General Wedemeyer, who had by then become U.S. chief of staff to the Generalissimo, obtained the latter's oral agreement to the new arrangement.   On 12 November 1944 the new headquarters, essentially Headquarters, Eleventh Army Group, plus some American officers, was activated and General Leese took command.[30]

Creation of the new headquarters brought discussion of the relationship between India–Burma Theater and SEAC.   Transfer of the U.S. contingent among the SEAC Joint Planners to the Commanders-in-Chief Planners of SEAC, at a substantial saving in personnel, was quickly agreed to.   The question of the control of U.S. resources in SEAC, a question raised by Mountbatten when the theaters were split, was much more complex.   The new Allied land forces commander and the current Allied air forces commander controlled the operations of NCAC and the U.S. Air Forces units within SEAC, respectively.   Ultimate control rested with the CCS through the British Chiefs of Staff in London.   However, the right to move air or

---

[28] Ltr, Wedemeyer to Marshall, 8 Oct 44.   Item 1306, Msg Bk 23, OPD Exec 9.
[29] Ltr, Marshall to Mountbatten, no date.   Item 1359, Msg Bk 24, OPD Exec 9.
[30] (1) History of IBT, Vol. I, pp. 62–66.   (2) Mountbatten Report, Pt. B, par. 268.   (3) ALFSEA Record, p. 45.

other resources from India–Burma Theater to China subject to the needs of the fighting in Burma had always been reserved by the Joint Chiefs.   Behind the JCS's reserving this right lay the assumption that all U.S. resources in India and Burma were in the final analysis there to support China.   Since India–Burma and China were now two separate U.S. theaters of operations, Mountbatten suggested that the CCS rather than the JCS should decide when resources could be moved from one to another.   He had good reason to be anxious lest events in China result in a heavy draft on American resources from Burma.   But the JCS would not agree to his suggestion, and reserved to themselves the disposition of U.S. forces in China, Burma, and India.[31]

That the commanders in the field had continued their operations through the monsoon rains, the OCTAGON Conference, and the exchanges between the staffs meant that the situation in the field changed steadily from day to day.   Three days after ALFSEA opened for business on 12 November, the 11th East African Division entered Kalemyo in Burma, substantially completing the British part of Phase I of CAPITAL.

NCAC Prepares To Resume Operations

The operational tasks in north Burma which fell to Northern Combat Area Command under CAPITAL had of course been assigned to it well before ALFSEA began operations; NCAC had its operations under way at a correspondingly earlier date.   The general missions given NCAC were as follows:

1. Conduct offensive operations to expel or destroy the enemy east of boundary with Fourteenth Army [major British formation opposite central Burma] and north of the general line Lashio–Mongmit–Thabeikkyin by mid-February 1945.
2. Protect the air supply route and overland communication with China.
3. Secure Assam and Upper Burma north and east of the boundary with 11th Army Group.[32]

The specific tasks given to NCAC, with the desired dates for their completion, were as follows:

Phase I—(October to mid-December)—destroy and expel the enemy north of the general line to include key points: Indaw (railroad)–Kunchaung–Sikaw–Namhkam.

Phase II—(mid-December 1944 to mid-February 1945) destroy and expel the enemy north of the general line to include key points: Thabeikkyin–Mogok–Mongmit–Lashio, and be prepared to exploit in anticipation of Phases III and IV.[33]

From Myitkyina the Irrawaddy takes a course which though serpentine is generally southward until it reaches Bhamo; then it bends sharply westward

---

[31] (1) History of IBT, Vol. I, pp. 67–69.   (2) Mountbatten Report, Pt. B, par. 329.   (3) JIC 201/M, 15 Jul 44, sub: Political Effect of Present Japanese Opns in China.
[32] History of IBT, Vol. I, p. 84.
[33] Ibid.

and does not turn south again until the vicinity of Katha, which is about fifty-five air miles west of Bhamo. Its course is about equidistant between the hills that form the eastern boundary of the Railway Corridor mentioned earlier and the escarpment that in this area is the western edge of the Yunnan plateau. North of Bhamo, the Irrawaddy has cut a passage through a cluster of hills, some of which just top the 3,000-foot mark. The line NCAC sought to reach by 15 December ran from Indaw on the railway, through Katha, then south and east to the road junctions of Kunchaung and Sikaw, which are in the valley, and then plunged into the mountains to Namhkam, in the valley which the Shweli River has chiseled through them. Thirty miles northeast of Namhkam, the Burma Road enters the Shweli valley at Wanting. Completion of Phase II would involved a general southward advance of about fifty miles, some of it across the most rugged of mountain terrain.

Current plans called for brigading the 1st Chinese Separate Infantry Regiment, which had been trained at Ramgarh in long-range penetration tactics, with two American regiments, the 475th Infantry and the 124th Cavalry. The combined unit would be the equivalent of a division, but would have the designation 5332d Brigade (Provisional). The project had its origins in Stilwell's long-cherished dream of having an American division to command. In April 1944, when CBI Theater headquarters knew that a considerable body of American replacements was coming to CBI, Stilwell ordered Brig. Gen. Frank D. Merrill, then commanding the only U.S. infantry in CBI, a provisional regiment, to prepare to reorganize his command as a light division with one Chinese and two American regiments. Meanwhile, the War Department knew that Stilwell wanted another long-range penetration group, and suggested it might be possible to form a mixed Sino-American unit in India, with 30 to 40 percent Americans in key positions and the rest of the spaces filled with Chinese volunteers. Stilwell liked the idea, for he thought that Chinese and American soldiers got on well together. By 22 June the Asiatic Section of the Operations Division, War Department General Staff, was considering sending a light brigade to CBI with a view toward giving Stilwell what it could to open a land line of communications to China.[34]

To carry out the project, the 5332d Brigade (Provisional), known later as MARS Task Force, was activated 26 July 1944. Brig. Gen. Thomas S. Arms assumed command the same day.[35] The activating order provided for most of the brigade's subordinate units to be attached to it as they arrived in India or were activated—as of 26 July the brigade was still very much in the pre-

---

[34] (1) Rad CRA 1763, Sultan to Stilwell, 21 Apr 44. Item 129, Bk 6A, JWS Personal File. (2) Rad SH 64, Stilwell to Marshall, 22 Apr 44. Item 133, Bk 6A, JWS Personal File. (3) Memo for Record, 6-22/2170. Case 404-2, OPD 381 Security.
[35] Unit History, 5332d Brigade (Prov), Ch. I, p. 1. OCMH. (Hereafter, 5332d Unit History.)

paratory stage.   Thus, the 475th Infantry Regiment (Long Range Penetration Regiment, Special), Lt. Col. William L. Osborne, was not activated until 5 August 1944.   It included many survivors of the original American experiment in long-range penetration tactics—GALAHAD, or "Merrill's Marauders." [36] Its companion regiment, the 124th Cavalry (Texas National Guard), Col. Milo H. Matteson, arrived in India on 30 August 1944.   It did not reach the brigade's training area until 27 October.   Also attached were the 612th Field Artillery Battalion (Pack), Maj. John W. Read, and six quartermaster pack troops.[37]

Direct air support for NCAC was provided by the Tenth Air Force with 9 bombardment squadrons, 7 fighter squadrons, 4 combat cargo squadrons, and 3 troop carrier squadrons.   Tenth Air Force in turn was a part of Eastern Air Command, the operations of whose other components elswhere in Burma indirectly but powerfully affected the campaign in the northern part of that vast area.   The teammates of Tenth Air Force were the Strategic Air Force, which sought to destroy the Japanese transport net in Burma; 3d Tactical Air Force, which supported British operations in central and southern Burma; 293 Wing, RAF, which protected the vital industrial area centering on Calcutta; and the Photographic Reconnaissance Force.[38]

The impact of the Allied air arm on the Japanese by the time the fall 1944 campaign opened is suggested by some excerpts from captured Japanese diaries:

During the day enemy aircraft come over in formations of three and six.   As we have no aircraft we cannot do anything except take shelter.   [A superior private on the Myitkyina–Bhamo front, 24 September 1944.]

At 1825 hours enemy aircraft heavily bombed and machine-gunned positions on the opposite bank.   I wish we had even one aircraft, that would be something!   My earnest desire is that the people on the home front would speed up production and send us even one as soon as possible.   [The same soldier, 13 October.]

At times you are driven to hide food from your best friend instead of sharing it with him. . . .

We feel the noose tightening slowly, relentlessly around our necks. . . .

Enemy aircraft are over continuously in all weathers.   We can do nothing but look at them.   If we only had air power!

---

[36] The 5307th Provisional Unit (Special), code name GALAHAD, nicknamed Merrill's Marauders after General Merrill, who with Col. Charles N. Hunter took it into combat, was organized in India from volunteers obtained in the United States, the Caribbean area, and the Southwest Pacific.   It fought at Walawbum, Inkangahtawng, Nhpum Ga, and Myitkyina from March to August 1944. Disease and fatigue incurred as a result of its envelopments of the Japanese flanks and deep penetrations behind enemy lines so weakened the unit as to render it ineffective as a regiment by 1 July 1944.   Some of its survivors were then organized into a battalion and others provided stiffening for two battalions of replacements, the so-called "New GALAHAD."   So organized, they fought with distinction at Myitkyina.   The 5307th was awarded the Distinguished Unit Citation.   See *Stilwell's Command Problems.*

[37] Organizational details are from the 5332d Unit History, Chapter I.

[38] Save as noted below, material on direct air support of NCAC is drawn from History of IBT, Vol. I, pp. 95–100.

In the opening phases of the North Burma Campaign, October–November 1944, the major objective of the Tenth Air Force was to stop Japanese reinforcement of the front.   This meant pounding the railroads, primarily the bridges.   The Burma Railways then had 302 bridges of more than forty feet in length which were the principal targets.   Specializing in such attacks, the 490th Bombardment Squadron (M) won the nickname "Bridge-Busters." The 490th claimed its hundredth bridge neutralized on 8 November.   In allocating its efforts, the Tenth in December 1944, when the campaign was moving to its peak, spent 50 percent in attacks on Japanese lines of communication, 25 percent in close support of the ground forces, and 25 percent against Japanese troop concentrations and supply points.

In the close support of the infantry, air-ground liaison was far ahead of that practised in Europe.   For example, when in summer 1944 the invasion of southern France was being planned, Lt. Gen. Lucian K. Truscott sought to arrange for the presence of forward air control parties with the combat infantry.   He did not succeed, and it was months before the practice became common in Europe.[39]   Though artillery played a most valuable part in the North Burma Campaign, it could not always accompany troops penetrating behind the Japanese lines, and close air support was the only possible substitute.   By May 1944 the Air Forces in Burma had worked out the technique of forward air control.   This was exercised by a party of one or two officers plus six to eight enlisted men.   They approved targets selected by the Army, called up air strikes by radio, and if necessary guided the aircraft to the target.   On occasion, liaison aircraft would observe the strike.   In some cases, aircraft were on target thirty minutes after the request was made. This was the system controlling close air support during the fall 1944 campaign.

In addition to providing air cover and assuming all responsibility in the fields of transport and supply, the U.S. Army also provided the greater part by far of medical aid for the Chinese in north Burma.   Three field hospitals, 1 mountain medical battalion, 8 portable surgical hospitals, 2 medical collecting companies, 1 clearing company, 2 veterinary evacuation hospitals, 3 separate veterinary companies, 1 malaria survey unit, and 7 malaria control units were part of NCAC.   These evacuated to the general hospitals of the SOS in India, principally the 20th General Hospital at Ledo.   A major part of the burden of medical aid fell on the portable surgical hospitals, for "they could march with a column, perform the emergency surgery on casualties, and evacuate them by air."

Evacuation of the wounded by air was greatly appreciated by the soldier and was carried to a point that made it a distinguishing feature of the North

[39] Lt. Gen. Lucian K. Truscott, *Command Missions* (New York: E. P. Dutton and Company, 1954), p. 398.

Burma Campaign.   Writing immediately after the war, the Historical Section, India–Burma Theater, noted that "without known exception every wounded soldier, Chinese or American, evacuated out of the forward area, was transported by aircraft during part of his journey."   For the wounded, the worst part of the trip was the short journey on a stretcher to the improvised airstrip where the liaison aircraft, refitted as an ambulance, awaited them.

The Chinese, who could provide only the simplest medical care from their own resources, were responsible for transporting their own wounded within their own sectors.   NCAC assumed responsibility for further evacuation when the Chinese patient was delivered to an American medical unit, which was usually the portable surgical hospital that accompanied each Chinese division.   Then the patient was carried to a liaison plane landing strip—if he could not readily be driven to a field hospital—and from there was flown to the nearest transport strip.   Detachments of the 151st Medical Battalion met him there and supervised his journey to hospital.[40]

Burma is not a healthful place even for its inhabitants, while for the combat soldier, who is daily exposed to contaminated water, polluted soil, and disease-bearing insects, it has long been deadly.   In 1942 many medical authorities had feared disease might bring disaster to armies invading Burma and had appraised the danger in most gloomy terms.   By fall 1944, after the campaigns of the previous years, the dimensions of the problem were known and remedial measures were at hand.   Malaria and dysentery were the two great menaces.   Malaria was the greater by far.   By then commanders and medical officers had learned that routine measures of mess, water, and camp sanitation could control dysentery and that the problem was more a command than a medical problem.   Notably, the Chinese, who always ate their food hot and boiled water faithfully, suffered far less from intestinal disorders than did the Americans.[41]

Malaria was much slower in yielding to preventive measures.   In the autumn of 1943, when the fighting resumed in north Burma, malaria was attacked by the assignment of two malaria control detachments, who were to destroy the mosquitoes, and by measures of individual prevention, such as the use of repellent.   But measures of environmental control were of little use when the Allied forces began to advance rapidly, for every forward step was also a step into Japanese-held terrain that medical personnel could hardly invade.   The decision to use atebrin was not made until April 1944, then only because the monsoon rains were approaching, and it was limited to troops

---

[40] History of IBT, I, 94–95.

[41] 1st Lt. James H. Stone, U.S. Army Medical Services in Combat in India and Burma, 1942–1945, Ch. 15.   OCMH.   Unless otherwise noted, material in this section is drawn from Lieutenant Stone's manuscript.

least able to carry out measures of environmental control. NCAC slowly extended use of atebrin from combat troops to service troops south of Ledo. Late in 1944 NCAC finally decided to make its use general in north Burma. The stubborn opposition had been based on the belief that use of atebrin might lead to laxity in other control measures, but overcrowding in the hospitals made this consideration yield. A similar lag in the use of the powerful insecticide DDT may be noted; it was not available in quantity until late in 1944 and not used extensively until 1945.

Four malaria control detachments were on hand when fighting began in fall 1944. They fought the mosquito peril by "DDT residual spraying as soon as fighting had stopped; DDT spraying of occupied tents, latrines, mess halls, and other buildings; DDT perimeter spraying around the camp areas, including natural resting places within the perimeter; DDT spraying of front line installations and fortifications when combat units were static; minor larviciding and ditching around headquarters areas; and transportation and issue of anti-malaria supplies."

By early February the success of atebrin therapy and widespread use of DDT was apparent. The CBI Theater malaria rate, which was the rate of admission to hospital, had been approximately 95 per 1,000 per year in January 1943, and 75 per 1,000 per year in January 1944. The India–Burma rate in January 1945 remained at 75. But where the previous years' rates had never dropped below the 50 per 1,000 mark, the India–Burma rate was below 20 per 1,000 by the end of March 1945. In the past, May had been the month that malaria began to take the worst toll, moving rapidly up to 300 per 1,000, but in 1945 the rate stayed under 20 per 1,000. The new techniques were a success.

In mid-August 1944 the training area which had been set up about ten miles north of Myitkyina on the west bank of the Irrawaddy began receiving members of the 475th Infantry Regiment. The area was designated Camp Robert W. Landis in honor of the first member of GALAHAD to be killed in action. Unit after unit started moving into Camp Landis as the 5332d began to put on flesh and assume the likeness of a pair of regimental combat teams. Another battalion of pack artillery, the 613th under Lt. Col. James F. Donovan, the 18th Veterinary Evacuation Hospital, the 44th Portable Surgical Hospital, the 1st Chinese Separate Infantry Regiment, Col. Lin Kuan-hsiang, arrived during the fall.[42]

Units were scheduled to arrive in a way that permitted the 475th Regimental Combat Team to train in September and October, the 124th, in October and December. Training stressed the weapons and tactics used by long-range penetration units operating over wooded, hilly terrain. Physical

---

[42] 5332d Unit History, Ch. I.

BIVOUAC AREA OF THE 475TH INFANTRY *at Camp Landis. Irrawaddy River in the background.*

conditioning was emphasized. Maintenance of health during jungle operations, a factor whose difficulty and value had received local demonstration during the GALAHAD operations, was also covered.[43]

After General Arms had seen the 5332d through its organization and training phase he was so unfortunate as to be injured in a motor accident, and was succeeded on 31 October 1944 by Brig. Gen. John P. Willey. Willey had served on the NCAC staff during the North Burma Campaign, and been chief of staff of the Myitkyina Task Force from 1 June to 4 August 1944. His peacetime experience had been in armor and cavalry.[44]

The Chinese divisions also received rigorous training, which began immediately after the fall of Myitkyina on 3 August 1944. Thus, when the 22d Division departed its camp sites for Kamaing in the week of 7–14 October it had completed nine weeks of training. The 50th Division trained in

[43] Capt. Edward Fisher, History of NCAC, CBI Theater and IB Theater, II, 224. OCMH. (Hereafter, NCAC History.)
[44] 5332d Unit History, Ch. II.

the Mogaung area.   As for the 38th Division, its units began training as soon as they arrived at Myitkyina and continued until they departed for combat.[45]

As last-minute preparations were made for opening of the postmonsoon offensive, the 38th Division and two regiments of the 30th Division were training in the Myitkyina area.   The 89th Regiment, 30th Division, was ten miles south of Myitkyina on the Myitkyina–Bhamo road.   The 14th Division was around Namkwi on the Burma Railways line five miles northwest of Myitkyina.   The 50th Division had its headquarters at Mogaung, and its 150th Regiment was there.   The 149th was patrolling and training four miles southwest of Mogaung, while the 148th was in the Kamaing area, the scene of some of the bitterest fighting a few months before.   The 22d Division had its headquarters at Kamaing.[46]

Logistical Support

Given the smooth working of the Indian base described in Chapter I, the principal logistical problem as combat reopened in north Burma was that of delivering the supplies to the troops.   The method characteristic of north Burma was airdropping.[47]   By flying over the battlefield, transport aircraft could defeat all Japanese attempts at victory by encirclement and could make units at the front independent of ground lines of communications, thus greatly increasing their mobility.   Units carried three days' rations and were continually resupplied by air.   The mission of storing, packing, and loading airborne supplies was given to the Air Supply Service of Advance Section No. 3 of the SOS at Ledo.   A "British Wing" worked with Advance Section No. 3 to meet the problems of supplying the British 36th Division in the Railway Corridor.   Packing, sorting, loading, and ejecting supplies from the aircraft were performed by units called air cargo resupply squadrons, which were attached to the Air Supply Service.

Troops in the forward areas requested supplies be dropped on designated target areas, forty-eight hours in advance, when possible, but sometimes on an immediate basis to meet emergencies.   G–4 of NCAC's Forward Echelon screened the requests, then forwarded them to the Air Control Section, which in turn sent them to the Air Supply Service.   The service allocated orders among the several squadrons, according to the orders already assigned and the numbers of transport aircraft available.   To permit better liaison between the 36th Division and NCAC, a British officer, Lt. Col. George Demetriadi, served as a member of the staff.

[45] NCAC G–3 Periodic Rpts, Sep and Oct 44.   KCRC.
[46] History of IBT, I, 6.
[47] For a description of the origins, growth, and operations of air supply in CBI, see *Stilwell's Command Problems*, pp. 95ff.

Each squadron had a complete supply depot. As squadrons received orders they made up planeloads from prepacked supplies. Those rare items not habitually stocked were brought up from rear depots to the Air Supply Service. Air Supply Service controlled the mechanics by changing each request for air supply into an airdrop order which was followed through to completion or cancellation.

Because of the extremely heterogeneous nature of the Allied forces in north Burma—Chinese, British, American, Hindu, Moslem, Burmese, and so on—a corresponding variety in rations had to be delivered, posing some interesting problems in administration and in aircraft loading. The Chinese received rice, corn beef or pork link sausage, peanuts, spinach or peas, and the so-called Stilwell ration of crackers, one fruit bar, sugar, peanuts, salt, and a vitamin pill. This ration was eaten at noon when no hot lunch was served. The individual Chinese carried his own rice and at mealtime contributed his share to the cook.

The Air Supply Service combined three standardized combat rations for the MARS Task Force (5332d Brigade)—three or four days' K or C rations, D ration bars, supplemented by fruit juices, dehydrated soup, coffee, sugar, peanuts, halazone tablets, vitamins, and salt, and canned heat. This gave a much better diet than was provided by straight C or K ration. In the spring of 1944 the GALAHAD Force had found C and K rations inadequate, the resulting dietary disturbances contributed to the later fatigue and illness that so harassed GALAHAD troops. All the components of the new ration were placed in hessian cloth sacks 32 inches by 14 inches. Weighing 13 to 17 pounds, these loads fitted easily into the soldier's pack. An assembly line using mass production techniques to fill the packs kept pace with the needs of the front.

The mules, horses, and ponies that carried the heavy loads were supplied by premixed loads of cereal fodder and salt in correct proportions, twenty-five pounds to the sack. This equaled two days' rations. Bags of grain were just loosely packed in double sacks and shoved out of the aircraft. Losses were quite reasonable.

Indian-made containers, which could hold 465 pounds and cost only $3.63 as against $30 to $45 for U.S.-made equipment, were standardized in the winter of 1944–45. They proved so successful and so economical that automatic shipment of containers from the United States was canceled by the Air Service Command.[48]

But the air supply effort, though the spearhead of logistics in north Burma, was only part of the picture. Supplies had to be delivered to the forward airfields from which the transports flew, and the Ledo Road's build-

---

[48] (1) SOS in IBT, Ch. IV.   (2) Dupuy Comments.

ing and the whole complex of activities behind the fighting troops had to be supported. Fortunately, once the Chinese and Americans driving into Burma from Ledo were firmly in control of the Mogaung–Myitkyina area they were on the prewar Burmese road-river-rail network. The Ledo Road itself constantly fed tonnage into the forward area network. Parallel to and preceding the Ledo Road was the so-called combat road, in some places quickly bulldozed out of the brush, in others merging into an improved section of existing road or trail. The combat road stretched 139 miles from Shingbwiyang, in the upper Hukawng Valley, to Mogaung. An old oxcart road was rehabilitated from Mogaung to Myitkyina, which added 51 miles. Later, on the stretch from Mong Yu to Hsipaw, temporary bridges were built and the road maintained. Thanks to this ground line of communications, more tonnage was trucked forward of Ledo than was flown by aircraft. And, alongside and supplied by the Ledo Road were the forward airfields and supply depots, Shingbwiyang, Tingkawk Sakan, and Warazup, fair-weather fields at Taihpa Ga and Maingkwan, and ten strips for liaison aircraft.

As soon as the 48-mile Mogaung–Myitkyina section of the Burma Railways was in Allied hands it was put into operation by the 61st Transportation Corps Composite Company. By the end of October 1944 the 61st was running trains to Hopin, 70 miles from Myitkyina. "The detachment of two officers and 63 enlisted men operating five salvaged and repaired locomotives and several jeeps equipped with flanged wheels, carried 66,167 passengers and 14,485 long tons of supplies in August, September, and October 1944, most of this in support of the British 36th Division driving down the railway corridor." [49]

Japanese Plans and Preparations

While the Allied forces in India and Burma had been getting ready for the fall campaign—the British and Indian divisions by the steady advance of relatively fresh units and the rehabilitation of the veterans, the Chinese and Americans by training and reorganizing—and while the Allied leadership had been reaching its decision to move on Mandalay, the Japanese too had been planning and preparing. The problems the Japanese faced in September 1944 were not unlike those of Hollanders who see the sea rising higher and higher, the waves here threatening to wash right over a low spot, and the pressure there steadily gnawing a hole, while the men behind the dike wonder which holes must be plugged now, which can wait a bit, and how long before the sea washes away dike, sandbags, laborers, and all. In the Central Pacific the American flood was roaring ahead, in Burma the dike showed an ever-widening leak, in Manchuria was a supply of resources

[49] History of IBT, I, 91–93.

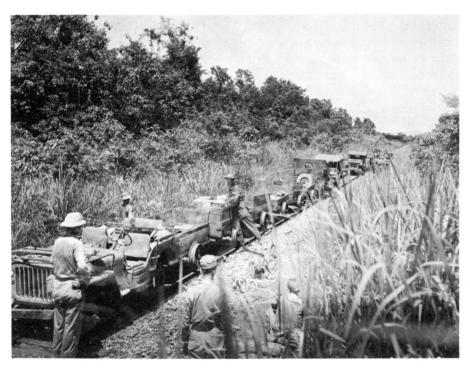

JEEP TRAIN ON A NARROW-GAUGE LINE *hauling supplies between Myitkyina and Mogaung.*

depleted by the removals of 1944, and in China was one last stockpile of arms and men.   So *Imperial General Headquarters* weighed its perils and made its decisions.

The Japanese command gave first priority to stopping the flood in the Central Pacific, and Manchuria and China yielded divisions accordingly. From Manchuria and Korea went the *1st, 8th, 10th, 12th, 19th, 23d, 24th,* and *66th Infantry Divisions,* and the *2d Armored Division* and most of the stockpiles so painstakingly accumulated.   As a replacement, five divisions were organized in Manchuria and Korea.   From China went the *62d* and *26th,* and later the *37th* and *22d,* these last two to Indochina.   These were replaced by four new divisions, organized locally.[50]

Burma, in contrast to the Central Pacific, could not expect reinforcements. The tasks of *Burma Area Army* were reduced accordingly.   Once, the mission of *Burma Area Army* had been to cut land communications from India

[50] Japanese Study 45, pp. 157–60.

to China.   Now, in September 1944, *Imperial General Headquarters* instructed *Southern Army* that its subordinate headquarters in Burma was to put a lower priority on that mission than on holding southern Burma, lest the Allies move on from southern Burma to attack Thailand and Malaya.[51]

In making detailed plans, *Southern Army* and *Burma Area Army* weighed a number of factors.   First was the state of the Japanese forces in Burma, which in the summer of 1944 were reduced to 100,000 combat troops and 60,000 in the rear area.   The Japanese system kept about 4,000 replacements a month flowing into Burma until September 1944.   These plus the *53d* and *49th Divisions* permitted rebuilding *Burma Area Army* to about 160,000 as of December 1944, which was a drop of 92,000 from the strength in March.[52] Another factor to be considered in addition to the forces available was the desirability of protecting the oil fields of Yenangyaung and the rice of lower Burma.   Then, too, the Japanese had established a puppet government in Burma, whose collapse would be a blow to Japanese prestige.   Last of all, the Japanese had fears, well founded as it developed, of the political situation in Thailand.[53]

Trying to strike a balance between their resources and their missions, the Japanese staff in Burma decided *Burma Area Army* had to hold the line Lashio–Mandalay–Yenangyaung.   Three operations were shaped to carry out the missions of holding south Burma and blocking the Allied attempts to open communications with China.   Plans to keep China blockaded received the code name *DAN.*   Plans to meet the anticipated attack of the British Fourteenth Army along the Irrawaddy in front of Mandalay were named *BAN,* and were for the decisive operation.   Defense of the coasts was called *KAN.*

The *33d Army* in north Burma was responsible for the *DAN* operation, the *15th* in central Burma for *BAN,* and the *28th* along the Arakan coast and Irrawaddy Delta, *KAN.*   The *15th Army* was allotted 3 divisions, the *28th Army* had 2, plus an independent mixed brigade, and the *33d Army,* 2 more.   Three were under *Burma Area Army* control.

Reorganizing their divisions for the decisive battles, the Japanese cut their authorized strength to 13,000, reduced artillery batteries to three guns each, disbanded the infantry headquarters of the division, reorganized reconnaissance troops as combat infantry, combed out service elements, and requisitioned oxcarts to replace the motor transport lost in the spring.   To keep supplies coming forward, trains moved only at night and during the day hid on camouflaged sidings.   The Burmese themselves moved rice between

---

[51] Japanese Study 45, p. 155.

[52] (1) Japanese Study 91, chart opposite p. 171.   (2) Japanese Officers' Comments on draft manuscript of this volume.   (3) In January 1945 *Southern Army* was told it could not rely on reinforcements from Japan.   Japanese Study 45, p. 182.

[53] Japanese Study 90.

Mandalay and Rangoon by some 20,000 oxcarts, which delivered about twenty tons a day. Small craft moved supplies on the rivers.[54]

The *33d Army,* NCAC's immediate antagonist, decided that it would try to check and delay the Allied advance as far to the north as possible, strike a sharp blow at the Chinese divisions from Yunnan, but make its final stand on the line Lashio-Bawdwin-Mong Yang. It was influenced by the belief that to reopen satisfactory ground communications the Allies would have to come as far south as Lashio, that a line opened farther north would be so rough that little could be delivered to China. Inevitably, therefore, *33d Army* and NCAC would differ in their appraisal of events in north Burma. The principal aim of *33d Army's* operations, faithfully reflecting the directives of higher headquarters, was to cover the flank of *15th Army* while the latter fought the decisive battle for Burma. If the *15th* could make its stand without interference from the American-trained Chinese divisions, then the *33d* could feel it had done its part. Certainly, a Japanese victory at Mandalay would go far to restore the situation in the north.

To fight its delaying action, screen the flank of the *15th,* and keep the Allies north of Lashio—whose possession by the Allies the Japanese thought to be essential to breaking the blockade of China—the *33d* had the *18th* and *56th Divisions,* plus the use of a regiment each of the *2d* and *49th Divisions,* at Bhamo and Lashio respectively. The link between *33d Army* and the *15th Army* was provided by the *53d Division,* which with its two regiments was under control of the *15th.*

Reopening the Fight

The plan that General Sultan adopted for NCAC to carry out Phase I of CAPITAL called for a three-pronged attack south from Myitkyina into the Japanese holdings in north Burma. (*Map 8*) On the west, the British 36th Division, followed by the Chinese 50th Division, was to move south down the Railway Corridor to secure the Katha-Indaw area. In the center, the Chinese 22d Division was ordered to move south, then east, to an area roughly halfway between the Railway Corridor to the west and the Myitkyina–Bhamo road to the east, to seize the airstrip northeast of Katha, where the 3d Indian Division had landed behind the Japanese lines in March 1944, and secure a bridgehead over the Irrawaddy at Shwegu (the Irrawaddy here flows from east to west). On the east, the Chinese 38th Division was ordered to secure the area Bhamo-Mansi. Successfully completed, these operations would place the three divisions in line across north Burma from Katha through Shwegu to Bhamo.[55]

[54] Japanese Study 133.
[55] History of IBT, I, 90–91.

The British 36th Division, Maj. Gen. Francis W. Festing, was already deep in north Burma when D Day, 15 October, arrived, for General Stilwell had used it to exploit the weaknesses in the Japanese position caused by the Allied successes at Mogaung and Myitkyina and the work of 3d Indian Division (the Chindits) in cutting the Japanese lines of communications.[56]

While the 36th was preparing for the move to north Burma it was visited by the Fourteenth Army commander, General Slim.   Addressing the commissioned and noncommissioned officers, General Slim said the 36th had been picked to serve in north Burma for two reasons: first, the high regard that Slim held for the division and General Festing, and secondly, the need for success in carrying out the task assigned to British troops in north Burma.   The setback of 1942 had in General Slim's opinion lowered British prestige.   Further, he considered that General Stilwell had little good to say about most British or Indian organizations.   Therefore Slim had chosen the 36th to play Britain's part, and had the fullest faith that his confidence would be justified.[57]

As the 72d Brigade, 36th Division, moved into the Mogaung area, it replaced the 3d Indian Division, whose weary survivors were now being evacuated.   The first Japanese position was met ten miles south of Mogaung, at Hill 60, which the exhausted Chindits had been unable to take.   There was a brisk fight, in the course of which an attempted envelopment missed its mark and had to be retrieved under cover of smoke.   Hill 60 was taken and the 72d resumed its southward advance after an enemy who now seemed bent on no more than delaying action.   Taungni, the first objective, was occupied 9 August.   Perhaps anticipating his next orders, Festing continued the advance.[58]

On the 13th new orders came, to go as far south as possible.   Aware that the last brigade of his division was now moving up to join him and that his organic division artillery was about to begin arriving, Festing gave free rein to his aggressive disposition and took Pinbaw as his next objective.   Its capture would place him twenty-six miles below Mogaung.   Air support was arranged by conference with Brig. Gen. Russell E. Randall of the Tenth Air Force, and the administrative build-up of a line of communications down the railway from Mogaung began.   Then further orders came from Stilwell, that Pinbaw was to be the limit of the 36th's advance for the time being.

Pinbaw required three days' fighting, beginning 25 August 1944, before a

---

[56] (1) Geoffrey Foster, 36th Division, The Campaign in North Burma, 1944–1945, with foreword by General Festing, pp. 7–9, 62–63. OCMH. (Hereafter, Foster.) Dr. Foster was Assistant Director of Medical Service (A.D.M.S.) for the 36th Division.   (2) NCAC Operational Highlights, period 14 Oct 44–13 Jan 45. OCMH.

[57] Foster, p. 8.

[58] (1) Extracts from War Diary of Headquarters 36th Division, 3–12 Aug 44. OCMH. (Hereafter, 36th Division Diary.)   (2) Dupuy Comments.

MAJ. GEN. FRANCIS W. FESTING AND GENERAL SULTAN *crossing the Shweli River during the latter's inspection of forward areas of the 36th Division in central Burma.*

rain-swollen stream was crossed and two outlying fortified villages cleared. On the 27th the only opposition came from rear-guard machine gunners, and that afternoon a patrol reported Pinbaw unoccupied. The village itself was no prize; the 36th's senior medical officer, Geoffrey Foster, later described it as "only a collection of wooden houses on stilts, situated in a sea of mud, slime, filth, and smells." But Pinbaw as a military objective represented a very considerable and rapid advance south under severe difficulties of terrain and weather, against a skillfully delaying enemy. Stilwell recognized the achievement and radioed Festing: "In getting your objective so promptly, congratulations to you and your men. Smart work. We are proud of you." [59] The 36th Division was now on the line of departure for the fall offensive, deep in Burma.

Ordered to wait for D Day in the Pinbaw area, Festing took the normal

[59] (1) Foster, page 14, quotes Stilwell's commendation.   (2) 36th Division Diary, 13–27 Aug 44.

precaution of patrolling, but patrolling as he defined it meant excursions in strength. Not until Festing was operating about four miles south of Namma around 24 September were Japanese encountered in a strength that this forceful reconnaissance could not master.[60]

During this period in which Festing was establishing himself well ahead of the line of departure and was leaning against the forward Japanese outposts, word came, on 12 September, that he was to be transferred back to London.[61] The NCAC staff quickly notified Stilwell, and the proposed transfer was canceled by Stilwell's personal intervention, the men of the 36th Division believed.[62] Plainly, the 36th and General Festing had won out.

From 24 September to 15 October, D Day, the 36th held its positions around Namma. A great deal of work was done on the railway in repairing bombed-out bridges and relaying track; on the eve of D Day, trains could run from the Loilaw ferry, just below Mogaung, to within six miles of the front.[63]

As the 36th prepared to attack again, NCAC believed it faced some 5,500 Japanese. These were thought to come from all three regiments of the *53d Division,* and from the *34th* and *24th Independent Mixed Brigades.*[64] After the war, officers of the *53d Division* stated that following the premonsoon fighting the division was rebuilt with 2,400 replacements. It had never had but two regiments, the *128th* and *119th,* in north Burma. These two units, with two batteries of artillery, an engineer unit, and two attached independent infantry battalions, a total of just over 4,000 Japanese, faced the 36th in the Railway Corridor. It was identifications from the two attached battalions that suggested to NCAC the presence of two independent mixed brigades.[65]

The British moved out on 15 October. At first, contact was light, but by the time they reached Mawlu on 31 October Japanese posts were stronger and closer together and their artillery and mortar fire was progressively heavier. However, at Mawlu the 36th was eighty miles south of Mogaung and very near the great bend of the Irrawaddy which was the goal for 15 December.[66] The Japanese stiffened at Mawlu, and the 1st Battalion, Royal Scots Fusiliers, met artillery, mortar, and machine gun fire that took thirteen casualties. By evening the town was occupied. Road conditions were very bad, for the ground was still wet, and vehicles had trouble moving.

[60] (1) 36th Division Diary, 7–24 Sep 44.   (2) Dupuy Comments.
[61] (1) 36th Division Diary, 12 Sep 44.   (2) Rad CHC 4313, Cannon to Hearn, Sultan, and Wessels, 13 Sep 44.   Item 2815, Bk 7, JWS Personal File.
[62] Foster, p. 9.
[63] 36th Division Diary.
[64] NCAC History, II, 180.
[65] (1) SEATIC Bull 244, pp. 21–22.   MID Library.   (2) Japanese Officers' Comments on draft MS.
[66] 36th Division Diary.

After occupying Mawlu the division paused until 9 November.   There were brushes with Japanese, snipings, patrol actions, but no heavy fighting. Festing used the lull to bring up the 72d Brigade, and so make his advance one of brigades in line, with the 72d on the east, the 29th on the west.   The 72d would make the main effort.

Moving down a dry-weather road parallel to the railway tracks, elements of the 72d Brigade on 10 November met stubborn resistance a few miles northwest of a railway station called Pinwe.   It came from a cluster of bunkers, which together with heavy artillery fire and the identification of Japanese from a number of units all pointed to one conclusion for the 36th— it had met the Japanese main line of resistance in this area centering on Pinwe.[67]

The Pinwe area was well adapted to defense.   Farther north the 36th had fought its way over rice fields, but here the bush made an impenetrable screen on either side of the jungle tracks.   Flanking movements were so difficult that they were judged to be impossible.   Frontal attacks after artillery and air preparations became the order of the day.[68]

The Japanese fought stubbornly at Pinwe.   At night their infiltration parties harassed the British rear areas and sought to destroy their artillery. On one occasion, they thrust so deftly into the British positions as to cut off two companies of infantry, which had to be withdrawn at night.   The fighting resolved itself into British attempts at prying the Japanese out of their strongpoints, while maintaining a close guard against Japanese raiding parties.   In these days the 72d Infantry Brigade, which had been trying to force its way over the stream covering the principal Japanese positions, took heavy casualties and had to be relieved by the 29th Infantry Brigade.   On 25 November the British did put a company across the stream, but found they could not reinforce or supply it.   That was the last major offensive effort; on 29 November the Japanese were found to be evacuating their positions, and the British entered Pinwe on 30 November.[69]

The Japanese lines at Pinwe were held by the *119th Regiment, 53d Division*.   Pinwe was the hardest fighting the *53d* had encountered, and the *119th* received a diploma of merit for its work there.   On 25 November the *53d Division* had received orders to fall back until it crossed to the east bank of the Irrawaddy, so that it might take part in the anticipated decisive action in central Burma, and had begun its withdrawal accordingly.[70]

A pause followed on the Pinwe action, and when the advance resumed there was no opposition.   The towns of Indaw and Katha were entered by

[67] 36th Division Diary.
[68] Foster, p. 20.
[69] 36th Division Diary.
[70] Bull cited n. 65(1).

BRITISH CASUALTIES *being treated by medics of the 60th Portable Surgical Unit (American) during the 36th Division drive on Pinwe, Burma. November 1944.*

patrols on 10 December.   Katha was a river port on the Irrawaddy, a railway terminus, and a town of some size.   Its occupation marked the successful completion of Phase I of CAPITAL by the 36th Division, four days ahead of schedule.   The only fight of consequence had been at Pinwe, and that had been the only delay the Japanese had imposed.   On 14 December the 36th Division elements in Katha were met by an American patrol of the 475th Regimental Combat Team, which meant that Sultan's drive in the center was likewise close behind the retreating Japanese.[71]

The Attack in the Center

Sultan's orders to the NCAC forces in the center called for them to advance rapidly to the old airstrip twenty miles southeast of Hopin and then swing east to seize a bridgehead over the Irrawaddy in the Shwegu area.   Only one

[71] 36th Division Diary.

PACK ARTILLERY TROOPS *of the Chinese 22d Division waiting to be ferried across the Irrawaddy River. General Sultan is in the background (right) wearing a campaign hat, November 1944.*

division, the Chinese 22d, was used, leaving the Chinese 14th Division in reserve, because the Japanese were believed to have only a light covering force between the Railway Corridor and the Myitkyina–Bhamo road. The estimate was a good one, for the Japanese did have their strongest concentrations on either flank of the Allied advance. In the center there were only two battalions, guarding a ferry across the Shweli River at Myitson. This was well to the south, and many weeks of marching, as of 15 October, lay between the Allied forces and Myitson. The Japanese *33d Army* was well aware that it had guarded the Railway Corridor and the Lashio area at the expense of the center, and narrowly watched Allied progress there.[72] From positions in the Kamaing area, far behind the outposts held by the 36th Division in the Railway Corridor, the 22d began its march on 15 October. It was to move southeast toward Mogaung, but bypassing the town to save ten miles, then toward Pinbaw, then Hopin. As the march got under way

[72] Japanese Study 91.

it appeared that the long rest after combat had left troops and animals in poor condition. The troops were traveling as light as possible, but fatigue was evident when after three days the division reached Hopin. Predawn departures were ordered to keep to a minimum the time spent marching under the full sun, and a day of rest was spent at Hopin.

At Hopin the division turned east, to take a route that would sorely test the marching powers of its troops, for the chosen trail led over the ridge that marked the eastern boundary of the Railway Corridor, down into a plain formed by a tributary of the Irrawaddy, where the old Chindit airstrip BROAD-WAY was located, and up again over a hill mass overlooking the Irrawaddy valley. On 26 October the division reached the airstrip, twenty-seven miles southeast of Hopin.

General Liao Yueh-shang, commanding the New Sixth Army, of which the 22d Division was part, flew in to BROADWAY, and gave the division detailed orders for the final move to the Irrawaddy. The division was formed into two columns. On the west, the 64th Regiment was directed to take Shwegugale, which lay on the south bank downstream from Shwegu. The 65th and 66th were to move off as one column, then to split into combat teams just north of the Irrawaddy and cross on a broad front. Kachin irregulars and patrols reported there were no Japanese ahead, and after a three-day rest the division resumed its advance.

On 3 November the division occupied the north bank of the Irrawaddy without opposition. The troops rested while commanders studied maps and waited for rubber boats and outboard motors to be airdropped. Three days later the 64th Regiment crossed the Irrawaddy and took Shwegugale against light opposition. Next day the 65th Regiment took Shwegu, and the division had its first objectives.

So far the 22d had been tested by mountain marches, with no opposition worthy the name. The orders now received at Shwegu meant that combat lay ahead, for they directed two regiments, the 65th and 66th, to occupy a point from Man Tha, on the principal road south from the Japanese strong-hold of Bhamo, to the largest Japanese concentration in the center of the north Burma combat zone, the Shweli ferry site of Myitson. The 64th was ordered to stay and garrison the Shwegu area.[73]

Man Tha was occupied without incident 14 November, and a roadblock set up to intercept any Japanese who might attempt to move south from Bhamo. There was no sign of a Japanese reaction, and the two regiments were ordered to move still farther south, straight down the Bhamo–Myitson road to a village called Si-u, which is about thirty miles south of Man Tha and separated from the Shweli valley by a narrow range of 3,000-foot hills.[74]

[73] NCAC History, II, 207–12.
[74] NCAC History, II, 213.

In its operations in the Si-u area, the 22d Division would be supported by American combat troops. The 475th Infantry, now commanded by Col. Ernest F. Easterbrook, sent the first march serial south from Camp Landis on 15 November.[75] The first serial was the 2d Battalion plus the 31st Quartermaster Pack Troop, under Lt. Col. Benjamin F. Thrailkill. The 3d Battalion left a day later, then the 612th Field Artillery Battalion, and finally the 1st Battalion, each at a day's interval. By 27 November all the serials had closed in the assembly area, on the Myitkyina–Bhamo road about twenty miles northeast of Bhamo. There the 475th reorganized as battalion combat teams; after a rest they moved down the Myitkyina–Bhamo road until they arrived at Momauk, where the road swings west to Bhamo. Bhamo was then under siege by the Chinese 38th Division; the combat teams bypassed it, then marched west. In the area south of Shwegu they began moving south again, toward Si-u and the Shweli River.[76]

In mid-November 1944 the main strength of the Japanese *18th Division,* Lt. Gen. Eitaro Naka, was moved west from around Namhkam to the area around Mongmit, a road center southeast of Myitson. Its mission was to prevent the Allies from separating the *15th* and *33d Armies.*[77] A projected move of the *2d Division* to the Mandalay area was delayed. These orders meant that GALAHAD's and the 22d's old adversaries, the *55th* and *56th Regiments* of the *18th Division,* would be barring further Allied progress south. Rebuilt to a strength of 18,000, the *18th Division* was again an effective fighting machine.[78]

Once in the Si-u area, the 22d Division sent outposts in various directions to secure the area. One of these, the 3d Battalion, 66th, went about five and one-half miles southwest of Si-u to the village of Tonkwa. In organizing the area, the Chinese put their command post at Mo-hlaing, about 2,500 yards northeast. Meanwhile, on the Japanese side of the Shweli, General Naka seems to have decided on a policy of aggressive defense. A strong Japanese task force, with elements of both the *55th* and *56th* and artillery support, was sent north across the Shweli about 6 December, aimed at Tonkwa.[79]

On that same day of 6 December the 2d and 3d Battalions of the 475th Regiment received orders to relieve the 22d Division in the region of Mo-hlaing, about a mile north of Tonkwa. General Wedemeyer's plans to strengthen the Chinese Central Government were beginning to affect the

---

[75] On activation, the 475th was commanded by Colonel Osborne, a veteran battalion commander of the GALAHAD force who was taken ill in October from the effects of the jungle campaign the spring before and had to be evacuated. His successor was Stilwell's son-in-law. Osborne commanded the 124th Cavalry Regiment in the later phases of the campaign.

[76] 475th Unit History. NCAC files, KCRC.

[77] Bull cited n. 65(1), pp. 4–5.

[78] Japanese Study 91.

[79] NCAC History, II, 213.

course of operations in Burma, for on 5 December the new Sixth Army received orders to prepare the 22d Division to be airlifted to China.[80]   The 475th would have to replace it.   If General Naka chose to stage a local attack he would find the central portion of the NCAC offensive in a difficult position.

Naka's task force made its presence felt on 8 December with an attack on Tonkwa.   The outnumbered Chinese battalion fell back to the north, and next day the Japanese were attempting to move into Mo-hlaing itself.   There with the Chinese they met the Intelligence and Reconnaissance Platoon of the 2d Battalion, 475th Infantry, which was a day's march ahead of the battalion, and once again Americans and Japanese were fighting in Burma.

Fighting Around Tonkwa

The Japanese approaching Mo-hlaing early in the morning of 9 December as though they thought it unoccupied.   They seemed to have no more than five platoons and when contact was made immediately attacked.   Moving toward the northeast on either side of the Tonkwa–Mo-hlaing road the Japanese succeeded in breaking into the Chinese perimeter.   An American counterattack restored the situation.   As the fighting went on that morning, sometimes hand to hand, Americans and Chinese shared the same foxholes and fought shoulder to shoulder in the most literal sense.[81]

About three miles to the northeast of Mo-hlaing, marching down the Si-u road, were the 2d and 3d Battalions of the 475th, less Company E of the 2d Battalion, which was acting as the advance guard.   The 1st Battalion was securing the Shwegu area.   Colonel Thrailkill of the 2d Battalion ordered the I and R Platoon to fall back on E Company.   The rest of the 2d Battalion was sent swinging round to the southwest to Tonkwa itself.   Thus, at the end of 10 December, the 475th had its two battalions in line facing west, the northernmost or 3d Battalion near Mo-hlaing, the southernmost or 2d Battalion opposite Tonkwa.   The Chinese 66th Regiment, under orders now to move to China, asked to be relieved in the Tonkwa area and the 475th agreed, moving forward accordingly.[82]   The Americans had no orders to go farther into Japanese-held territory, for the decision to move the Chinese 22d Division from Burma to China halted the center portion of the NCAC offensive.   Whether a battle would develop rested with the Japanese.

Over 11 and 12 December Japanese patrols checked American positions and sporadic Japanese artillery and mortar fire harassed the soldiers in their

---

[80] (1) 475th Unit History.   NCAC files, KCRC.   (2) NCAC History, II, 215.   (3) See Ch. IV, below.
[81] (1) NCAC History, App. 1, 5332d Brigade, Ch. V, pp. 3, 5.   (Hereafter, History of 5332d.) (2) NCAC History, II, 213.
[82] History of 5332d, Ch. V, p. 4.

FIELD CONFERENCE AT SIKAW, BURMA, *12 December 1944. From left, Col. M. Fisher, Liaison Officer, 22d Division; Maj. R. Leonard, S–3, 475th Infantry; Col. Ernest F. Easterbrook, Commanding Officer, 475th Infantry; General Willey; and Col. Joseph W. Stilwell, Jr., G–2, Northern Area Combat Command.*

foxholes.   American patrols in their turn found what seemed likely Japanese assembly areas, and American artillery shelled them.   On the 12th the Chinese withdrew.   The night was quiet, but tension was in the air for the Japanese seemed to be "all around." [83]

The Japanese activity had apparently been preparation for attack, and on the morning of the 13th men checked their weapons with care and looked to the arranging of their ammunition in convenient spots.   The American positions had the advantage of excellent fields of fire across open paddy fields. Looking toward the south and the west, the men of the 475th could see the dark green mass of leaves, trunks, and brush making the jungle that hid the Japanese assembly areas and, farther back, the Japanese gun positions.   Following a ten-minute preparation, the Japanese attacked one American flank at 0600 and the other at 0610.   The 475th's fire power met the Japanese as

[83] Quotation from diary, Lt Col John H. Lattin, 12 Dec 44.   Lattin was then executive officer of the 2d Battalion.

CHRISTMAS DAY AT TONKWA. *In the background, Marsmen attend religious services while their comrades in the foreground, manning a 75–mm. M1 A1 pack howitzer, maintain alert vigil against possible enemy attack.*

soon as they were clearly defined targets, and stopped the attacks within an hour. At one point a Japanese force of about a platoon tried to cover the open space by a concerted rush only to be cut down with thirty or forty casualties. There were no further Japanese attacks that day. The following morning, the 14th, the Japanese repeated their tactics of the 13th, and that effort too was beaten off, at the cost of several men killed. The 475th's entry into combat had the result on the men noted by observers in many previous wars, for they now spent hours digging themselves in more deeply and improving their positions.[84]

Contrary to what had been the usual Japanese tactics when on the offensive, Naka's men did not repeat their efforts, which suggests his mission had changed. What now followed was patrol activity as both sides sparred in the open space between their respective perimeters. At only one point was there continual close contact, where a body of Japanese were holding a

[84] Lattin diary, 13, 15, 16 Dec 44.

pocket close to E Company of the 2d Battalion.   Patrolling meant a series of sharp little clashes as parties from the two sides met by accident, it meant ambushes carefully laid in wooded draws near the American lines, and it meant sniping as one man stalked another.[85]   The situation of patrolling and intermittent Japanese shelling and machine gun fire continued in the area of the 2d Battalion until 15 December.

The 3d Battalion to the north near Mo-hlaing was subject only to artillery fire.   That the Japanese at one point were actually within small arms range of the 2d Battalion while apparently not capable of doing more than shelling the 3d with their infantry guns suggested that the 3d might be able to take in reverse the Japanese pocket that pressed on the 2d Battalion.

Sent into action against the Japanese the morning of 15 December, L Company (reinforced) of the 3d Battalion came down from the Mo-hlaing area to the north.   Forming an arc around the Japanese who had occupied a wooded area, adjacent to E Company's position near Tonkwa, L Company began closing in.   A paddy field lay to the west of the woods, and the Japanese sought to withdraw across it, in the process drawing fire from both the encircling and holding elements of L Company.   By midafternoon the area seemed free of Japanese.   Two Americans were killed, and nineteen Japanese.

After these small operations there followed a period of a week in which Japanese and American patrols skirmished about the 475th's perimeter defenses, and Japanese sporadically shelled the American positions.   The 475th was ordered simply to hold the area and thus cover the 22d's flight to China from a nearby airstrip, while the Japanese had not seized their opportunity to exploit their initial successes.   As Christmas 1944 drew nearer signs of Japanese grew fewer and fewer.   The command post of the 475th was moved into Tonkwa itself, patrols reported no contact, and by Christmas it was apparent that the Japanese had gone.[86]   In these actions, the 475th lost 1 officer and 14 enlisted men, and estimated that it had killed about 190 Japanese at Tonkwa and about 30 near Shwegu.[87]

After the war, Japanese senior officers said that communication intercepts had given them clear indication of the withdrawal of Chinese divisions from Burma.   Having broken the Chinese codes they felt they "knew practically everything about their opponents."   From this information they concluded that no large-scale offensive south of Lashio was planned by NCAC.   This fitted well into Japanese plans to fight a decisive battle near Mandalay.   One may therefore conclude the Japanese were content to accept the *status quo* near Tonkwa and to concentrate on what they regarded as more vital areas.[88]

---

[85] John Randolph, *Marsmen in Burma* (Houston, Tex., 1946), pp. 96–97.
[86] History of 5332d, Ch. V, pp. 7–11.
[87] Randolph, *Marsmen in Burma*, p. 99.
[88] (1) SEATIC Bull 242, pp. 76–77.   MID Library.   (2) Quotation from Col Masanobu Tsuji, former opns officer, *33d Army* Staff, in Japanese Officers' Comments.   OCMH.

CHAPTER IV

Breaking the Blockade of China

Of the three moves by NCAC, only one was aimed toward China. The drives down the Railway Corridor and toward the Shweli would keep the Japanese away from the trace of the projected line of communications, but only the easternmost drive—down the Myitkyina–Bhamo road—could clear the way for vehicles and gasoline to enter China on the ground. As the Chinese New First Army (30th and 38th Divisions) completed preparations for the 15 October 1944 offensive, a reconnaissance east from Myitkyina toward China revealed that the Japanese grip had already been pried from the northeast corner of Burma. *(See Map 8.)*

Maj. Benjamin F. Thrailkill, who as a lieutenant colonel later commanded the 2d Battalion of the 475th at Tonkwa, left Myitkyina on 27 August with a company of Chinese and a platoon of U.S. infantry, plus engineers, signal, medical, and OSS personnel, with orders to establish contact with the Chinese from Yunnan. Moving east via Fort Harrison (Sadon), Thrailkill and his force met the Yunnan Chinese on 6 September in the Kambaiti Pass (Kauliang Hkyet). Eight days later Thrailkill and his men were back at Myitkyina.

The Thrailkill expedition, as it came to be called, established that the trail to China was passable, with numerous dropping ground and camp sites. The local inhabitants were thought to be friendly toward the Americans, but not to the Chinese. No Japanese were met.[1]

NCAC Drives Toward China

The initial NCAC orders to General Sun Li-jen's New First Army called for it "to advance rapidly on Bhamo, destroy or contain enemy forces there; seize and secure the Bhamo–Mansi area, and be prepared to continue the advance."[2] The key point was Bhamo, the second largest town in north Burma and the end of navigation on the Irrawaddy. Before the war the

---

[1] History of 5332d, Ch. III.
[2] History of Combat in the India–Burma Theater, 25 Oct 44–15 Jun 45, p. 5. OCMH. (Hereafter, IBT Combat History.)

town had been a thriving river port; the great 400-foot river steamers had brought cargoes and passengers from Rangoon to Bhamo for the short overland trip to China. When in May 1944 the Chinese and Americans had struck Myitkyina that town had had only the defensive capabilities inherent in any inhabited locality. Nevertheless it had held out till August. Now, in the fall of 1944, the Chinese in north Burma faced a town that not only possessed natural defenses but had been strongly fortified in addition. Bhamo's military importance lay in that it dominated the ten-mile gap between the Irrawaddy River and the plateau that is the eastern side of the Irrawaddy valley. Through that space the Ledo Road would have to be built.

A force moving from Myitkyina to Bhamo in October 1944 would find a good prewar road connecting the two towns. The road did not parallel the Irrawaddy closely, but had been placed on higher ground to the east, in the foothills, to lift it above the monsoon floods. The wooded hills and the tributaries of the Irrawaddy that cut across the road offered obvious opportunities to a defending force. Of these tributaries the Taping is the most considerable.

Entering the Irrawaddy just above Bhamo, the Taping is a large river in its own right. Its sources extend so far into the plateau that marks the Sino-Burmese border that one of its own tributaries flows past the city of Tengchung where there had been some of the heaviest fighting of late summer 1944 between Chinese troops seeking to break into Burma from that side and the Japanese *56th Division* trying to keep a block on the Burma Road.

Japanese documents dated early September 1944 and captured a few weeks later showed that the Japanese planned to delay around Bhamo in threee stages. In the first, the Japanese outpost line would be defended from Sinbo on the Irrawaddy to Na-long on the Myitkyina–Bhamo road, about halfway down to Bhamo, and thence to the upper reaches of the Taping River. The second Japanese line was the Taping River, whose crossings were to be fortified. The third stage was Bhamo itself.

These lines were manned by the *2d Battalion, 16th Regiment,* and the *Reconnaissance Regiment* of the *2d Division.* The division was ordered to hold the outpost line until 20 September, the line of the Taping to mid-November, and Bhamo itself to late December.[3] These time limits seem not to have been known to the individual Japanese, who were exhorted:

As it was with the heroes of Myitkyina, so it must be with the Bhamo garrison. . . . Do not expect additional aid. . . . Each man will endeavor to defend his post to the

[3] (1) IBT Combat History, p. 6, and facing Japanese map. (2) Bhamo's provisions would last only until the end of December. (3) Ltr, Hq NCAC, 27 Nov 44, sub: Translation of Captured Documents. Folder, Complete Translations, Nos. 151–250, NCAC files, KCRC. (4) Ltr, Hq New First Army to CG CAI, Dec 44, sub: Captured Enemy Documents. NCAC files, KCRC.

utmost—to the death . . . If, for the success in the large sense, units in dire straits are overlooked in the interests of larger units do not expect to be relieved, but be cognizant of the sacrifice you as an entity will make to insure the success of the whole.[4]

The 38th Division led the advance of the New First Army and was charged with taking Bhamo. Possibly because D Day was 15 October, more than three weeks after the date to which the Japanese had planned to defend their outpost line, the Sinbo–Na-long line was crossed without incident. With the 113th Regiment in the lead the Chinese moved right down the road to Bhamo without a significant contact until 28 October when Japanese patrols were met two miles north of the Taping River, the next Japanese defense line. These were brushed aside, and the 113th was on the river bank, occupying Myothit.

Here was the Japanese outpost line of resistance; the Chinese patrols speedily found that the Japanese meant to defend it. Strong Japanese positions were seen on the south bank, and the commander of the 38th Division, General Li Huang, saw that he would have to force a defended river line unless he could turn the Japanese position. General Li decided to use the 112th and 114th Regiments, which had been the main body of the 38th, as an enveloping force. Since they were some seven miles to the north the 112th and 114th were out of contact with the Japanese and well placed to make a wide swing to the east. The two regiments began their march through the hills, while the 113th made a show of activity around Myothit to keep the Japanese attention focused there.

Once again envelopment proved its worth. The Japanese were too few to defend a long line, and the enveloping force was able to cross the Taping at an unguarded bridge upstream, go around the right end of the Japanese outpost line of resistance, and emerge on the Bhamo plain on 10 November. Pressing on west toward Bhamo, the enveloping force met a strong entrenched Japanese force at Momauk, which is eight miles east of Bhamo and is the point at which the Myitkyina–Bhamo road swings to the west for the last stretch into Bhamo. Here there was savage fighting between the 114th Regiment and the Japanese defenders. Heavily outnumbered, the Japanese outpost at Momauk was driven into the main defenses at Bhamo. The appearance of its survivors, some without rifles, others without shoes, depressed the Bhamo garrison.[5]

Meanwhile, the 113th Regiment at Myothit on the Taping River profited by these diversions to force a crossing. Then, instead of coming down the main road, the 113th went west along the Taping's south bank, where there

<hr>

[4] (1) IBT Combat History, p. 8.   (2) Under interrogation, one enemy prisoner stated that at first the Japanese were told they must fight to the death, but later that if they fought well they would be allowed to evacuate.   Superior Pvt Rokuro Wada, 12 Dec 44.   Folder 62J, 411–420, NCAC files, KCRC.

[5] (1) IBT Combat History, pp. 7–9.   (2) Statement of Pvt Wada cited n. 4(2).

GENERAL SULTAN AND GENERAL SUN LI-JEN, *commanding the Chinese New First Army, examine enemy equipment left behind at Momauk, Burma, by fleeing Japanese troops.*

was a fair road, and came at Bhamo from due north. The Japanese sought to delay along the road and at one point, Subbawng, three miles north of Bhamo, appeared ready to make a fight of it. Here the 113th's commander elected to rely on the unexpected. Leaving a small force to contain the garrison of Subbawng, he moved south directly across the face of the defenses, at close proximity, and only ended his march when he was south and southeast of Bhamo in the suburbs of U-ni-ya and Kuntha. As a result of these several and rather intricate maneuvers—with the 114th Regiment attacking west from Momauk, the 113th cutting between the Momauk outpost and the Bhamo garrison, and the 112th bypassing the fighting completely to move on down the Bhamo road toward Namhkam—a loose arc was drawn around the Japanese outposts in the Bhamo suburbs, with the 113th holding the south portion of the arc and the 114th the north.[6]

[6] IBT Combat History, p. 11.

Finally facing Bhamo, the Chinese saw a town that was deceptively pleasant in appearance.   Bhamo, lying between the Irrawaddy River to the west
and a ring of lagoons to the east, seemed like a city in a park.   Unlike the
close huddle of buildings and shops that is the usual settlement in Asia,
Bhamo reflected the years of peace under British rule in Burma, for its homes
and warehouses were spread out among grassy and wooded spaces.   The
Burmans, Shans, and Kachins who worked in Bhamo tended to cluster together in surburban communities.   Over all were the pagoda spires.   But
each of these features, so attractive in peace, held a menace to the Chinese.
The almost complete ring of lagoons channeled the attack.   The spaces between buildings gave fields of fire to the defense.   The pagodas were natural
observation posts.   And the thick brick and concrete walls that had been
meant to give coolness now gave protection against Chinese shells and bullets.   The Japanese were known from aerial photography to have been for-
tifying Bhamo; how well, the infantry would soon find out.[7]

Attack on Bhamo

The first Chinese attack on Bhamo itself was given the mission of driving
right into the city.   Made on the south by the Chinese 113th Regiment, the
attack received heavy air support from the Tenth Air Force.   It succeeded in
moving up to the main Japanese defenses in its sector, but no farther.
American liaison officers with the 113th reported that the regimental commander was not accepting their advice to co-ordinate the different elements
of the Allied force under his command or supporting him into an artillery-
infantry-air team, and that he was halting the several portions of his attack
as soon as the Japanese made their presence known.[8]

However, the 113th's commander might well have argued that he and his
men faced the most formidable Japanese position yet encountered in Burma.
Aerial photography, prisoner of war interrogation, and patrolling revealed
that the Japanese had been working on Bhamo since the spring of 1944.
They had divided the town into three self-contained fortress areas and a headquarters area.   Each fortress area was placed on higher ground that commanded good fields of fire.   Japanese automatic weapons well emplaced in
strong bunkers covered fields of sharpened bamboo stakes which in turn were
stiffened with barbed wire.   Antitank ditches closed the gaps between the
lagoons that covered so much of the Japanese front.   Within the Japanese
positions deep dugouts protected aid stations, headquarters, and communica-

_____
[7] Capt. Erle L. Stewart, Asst G–2 NCAC, The Japanese Defense of Bhamo, 3 Mar 45.   OCMH.
(Hereafter, The Japanese Defense of Bhamo.)   This study has an excellent aerial photograph as
its Appendix VII.
[8] NCAC History, II, 201–03.

tions centers.   The hastily improvised defenses of Myitkyina were nothing like this elaborate and scientific fortification.   Manned by some 1,200 Japanese under Col. Kozo Hara and provisioned to hold out until mid-January 1945, Bhamo was not something to be overrun by infantry assault.[9]

Meanwhile, north of Bhamo, where the Chinese had not moved closer to the city than the containing detachment the 113th had left opposite the Japanese outpost at Subbawng, the 114th was making more progress.   That regiment bypassed the Subbawng position on 21 November and moved two miles west along the south bank of the Taping River into Shwekyina.   Outflanked, the Japanese quickly abandoned Subbawng and the rest of the 114th came up to mop up the Shwekyina area, freeing advance elements of the 114th to move directly south through the outlying villages on Bhamo.

On 28 November the 114th was pressing on the main northern defenses of Bhamo.   In this period of 21–28 November the division commander, General Li, did not alter the mission he had given the 113th of entering Bhamo, but by his attention to the 114th he seemed to give tacit recognition to the altered state of affairs.[10]

The Chinese lines around Bhamo were strengthened by putting the 3d Battalion of the 112th into place on the southern side between the Irrawaddy River and the road to Namhkam.   This permitted a heavier concentration of the 113th east of Bhamo, and that unit was given another chance at a major attack.   Such an effort would be supported by twelve 75-mm., eight 105-mm., and four 155-mm. howitzers and a company of 4.2-inch mortars.[11]   Supported by air and medium artillery, the 113th on the east again showed itself willing to move up to the Japanese defenses but no further.   Moreover, it did not appear able to take advantage of the artillery concentrations laid down for it. At this point, an American division commander would have relieved the 113th's commander, but the Chinese response was to shift air and artillery support to the 114th.

The 114th's aggressive commander had been most successful in the early days of December.   With less than half the air support given the 113th and with no help from the 155-mm. howitzers, he had broken into the northern defenses and held his gains.   The decision to give the 114th first call on artillery support posed a problem in human relations as well as tactics.   This was the first time the 38th Division had ever engaged in the attack of a fortified town.   All its experience had been in jungle war.   Faced with this new situation, the 113th Regiment's commander seemed to have been at a loss to know what to do.   The 114th, on the contrary, had gone ahead with conspicuous success on its own, and now was being asked to attempt close co-

[9] (1) The Japanese Defense of Bhamo.   (2) Japanese Officers' Comments on draft MS.
[10] NCAC History, II, 201–03.
[11] IBT Combat History, p. 13.

ordination with artillery and air support.   Its commander hesitated for a day, then agreed to try an attack along the lines suggested by the Americans.[12]

The tactics developed by the 114th Regiment by 9 December took full advantage of the capabilities of air and artillery support.   Since the blast of aerial bombardment had stripped the Japanese northern defenses of camouflage and tree cover it was possible for aerial observers to adjust on individual bunkers.   So it became practice to attempt the occupation of one small area at a time.   First, there would be an artillery preparation.   Two 155-mm. howitzers firing from positions at right angles to the direction of attack would attempt to neutralize bunkers in an area roughly 100 by 300 yards. Thanks to the small margin of error in deflection, the Chinese infantry could approach very close to await the lifting of fire.   The 105's would lay down smoke and high explosive on the flanks and rear of the selected enemy positions.   Aerial observers would adjust the 155's on individual positions. When it was believed that all Japanese positions had been silenced the Chinese infantry would assault across the last thirty-five yards with bayonet and grenade.[13]

Meanwhile, the Japanese *33d Army* sent a strong task force under a Colonel Yamazaki to attack toward Bhamo in the hopes of creating a diversion that would cover the breakout of the Bhamo garrison.   Comprising about 3,000 men with nine guns, the *Yamazaki Detachment* moved north from Namhkam the evening of 5 December to move on Bhamo via Namyu.[14] Operating south of Bhamo was the Chinese 30th Division, which had been ordered to move on down the general line of the Bhamo road to take Namhkam.   Twenty-two miles south of Bhamo the leading regiment, the 90th, encountered rough country, with hills up to 6,000 feet, and six miles farther on the first Japanese patrols and outposts were encountered.   The 2d Battalion, on the far right, pulled up along a ridge about 1 December.   The dominant height in the area, Hill 5338, was the object for the next ten days of operations that to American liaison officers appeared prolonged beyond all reason.   When it was finally occupied, the Japanese immediately began attacking in strength, and the battalion soon showed itself as stubborn in defense as it had been lethargic in attack.[15]   These Japanese attacks, regarded as a reaction to the loss of Hill 5338, were actually the *Yamazaki Detachment* making its arrival known.

To the left of the 2d Battalion, across the road, was the 1st Battalion, with the mission of keeping contact between the 90th Regiment and the rest of the division and of protecting a battery of the division artillery.   In at-

[12] NCAC History, II, 203–04.
[13] The Japanese Defense of Bhamo.
[14] Japanese Study 148, pp. 40–41.
[15] NCAC History, II, 253–57.

FRONT-LINE POSITION, *30th Chinese Division sector. Two American liaison officers discuss the tactical situation.*

tempting to execute this mission the battalion spread itself over a two-mile front. On the night of 9 December the battalion received a heavy bombardment followed by a Japanese attack which penetrated its lines and isolated its 1st and 2d Companies. This was bad enough, but worse followed the next morning. Colonel Yamazaki massed three battalions in column to the east of the road, and, attacking on a narrow front, broke clean through by leapfrogging one battalion over another as soon as the attack lost momentum. The third Japanese battalion overran the 2d Artillery Battery, 30th Division, and captured four cannon and 100 animals. The battery commander died at his post.[16]

The Chinese were not dismayed by the setback but fought with a spirit novel to the Japanese. The 88th Regiment swung its forces toward the Japanese penetration, which was on a narrow front, and since the terrain was

[16] (1) NCAC History, II, 258, 259. (2) Japanese Study 148, App. D, The Yamazaki Detachment in the Battle at Namyu.

hilly in the extreme the Japanese could see Chinese reinforcements converging on the battle site. So vigorously did the Chinese counterattack that one lone Chinese soldier fought his way almost into the trench that held Colonel Yamazaki and the *33d Army* liaison officer, Colonel Tsuji. Writing in his diary, Tsuji remarked: "This was the first experience in my long military life that a Chinese soldier charged Japanese forces all alone." [17]

The Chinese, comprising as they did three regiments of a good division, could not be indefinitely withstood by the four Japanese battalions. Destroying the four pack howitzers they had captured, the Japanese sought only to hold their positions until the Bhamo garrison could escape.[18]

Meanwhile, within Bhamo, the Japanese garrison was making preparations to break out. Its mission of delay was well-nigh accomplished, and a further reason for its departure was provided by the increasing successes of the 114th Regiment in the northern part of Bhamo. By 13 December this unit had penetrated the northern defenses and was cutting its way into the central part of Bhamo.[19]

At this point, Chinese techniques of war intervened to change what might have been the inevitable end of the story, a heroic suicidal dash by the Bhamo garrison on the machine guns of the besiegers, the so-called banzai charge that had been the final episode for so many Japanese garrisons before. American liaison officers with the Chinese formed the impression that a co-ordinated attack by the Chinese had been planned and ordered for 15 December.[20]

On the night of the 14th the Japanese in the garrison tried to fire off all their ammunition. Then they moved out into the river bed of the Irrawaddy and charged the Chinese lines along the river at daybreak. Taking advantage of the early morning mists, they moved through the Chinese lines to safety. As soon as the garrison was clear, the Japanese word for "success" was broadcast to the waiting *Yamazaki Detachment,* which promptly began to disengage. The Japanese claim that 950 of the garrison's 1,200 men made their way safely to Namhkam. American records support the claim of a successful withdrawal. After the war, the Chinese chronicler, Dr. Ho Yung-chi, former vice-commander of the 38th, stated that the Bhamo garrison was allowed by General Sun Li-jen to escape, only to be annihilated later. However, the agreement between the Japanese and American accounts, plus the fact that the American liaison officers with the 38th Division were told

---

[17] Japanese Study 148.

[18] Japanese Study 148, p. 42.

[19] (1) Japanese Study 148. (2) Japanese PW Statements. Folder 62J, 411–420, Japanese Documents, NCAC files, KCRC. (3) NCAC History, II, 204.

[20] The American combat narratives, prepared in 1945 from sources at the disposal of NCAC, such as liaison officers' reports, Daily Operational and Intelligence Summaries, and the like, refer to the proposed attack of 15 December. There is no hint that the American liaison officers knew Sun had ordered that the Japanese were to be allowed to escape.

nothing either of Sun's order to let the Japanese garrison through his lines
or of any later annihilation of 950 Japanese, suggests that there are some
flaws in the Chinese account.[21]

If to Western minds the reasoning which permitted the Japanese garrison
of Bhamo to live to fight another day was difficult to follow, a Western
observer had to admit that the performance of the Chinese 38th Division at
Bhamo compared most favorably with that of the combined Chinese and
American forces at Myitkyina six months before. That within thirty days
the Chinese 114th Regiment should have hacked a way through defenses
the Japanese had been six months preparing and have accomplished the feat
with artillery and air support that was slight in comparison with that at the
disposal of Allied forces elsewhere reflected the greatest credit on the unit
and its commander.

Last Days of the Burma Blockade

After the fall of Bhamo, the Chinese Army in India and the Chinese
Yunnan divisions, or Y–Force, were within fifty air miles of each other.
This narrow strip of rugged, highly defensible terrain was the last Japanese
block across the road to China. (*Map 9*)

The Chinese Army in India had before it a march of twenty miles south-
southeast over fairly level country; then it met the escarpment that was the
western edge of the great plateau through which the Shweli and Salween
Rivers had cut their valleys, the great plateau on which, far to the east, was
China's Yunnan Province, Kunming, and the Hump terminals. The road
the Chinese took was an extension of the Myitkyina–Bhamo road, one-way
and fair-weather but leading directly to the old Burma Road. All the road
needed was metaling and widening and it would be ready for heavy traffic
as the easternmost end of the Ledo Road. The road met the hills about
twenty miles south of Bhamo. Crossing a series of ridges it entered the
Shweli valley. It then swung northeast for about thirty miles and linked
with the old Burma Road at Mong Yu. East of the Shweli valley, over
fifteen miles of 5,000-foot hills, was the Burma Road.

Therefore, after the fall of Bhamo, the task facing the Allies in north
Burma was to clear the *33d Army* with its approximately 19,500 Japanese
from the remaining fifty-mile stretch that lay between the two Chinese
armies.

---

[21] (1) Japanese Study 91 states the Bhamo garrison made good its escape and rejoined the *2d Division.* (2) Japanese prisoners of war taken later in December 1944 state that 400 to 600 Japanese evacuated Bhamo. Folder 62J, 411–420, Japanese Documents, NCAC files, KCRC. (3) NCAC History, II, 205, says that an attempt was made to intercept the Japanese but failed because reserves were too far away. (4) Dr. Ho Yung-chi, *The Big Circle* (New York: The Exposition Press, 1948,) p. 130.

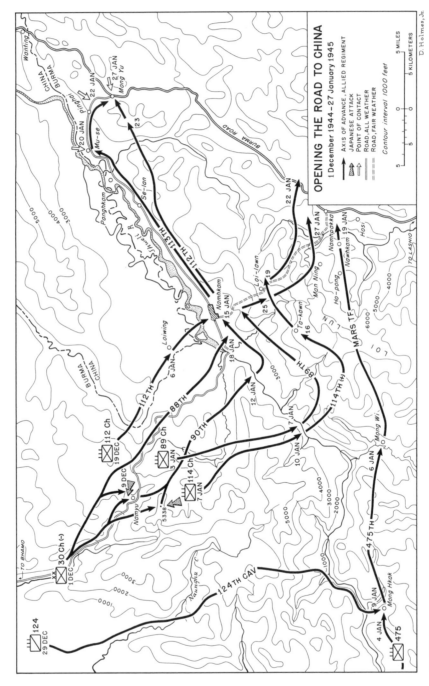

OPENING THE ROAD TO CHINA
1 December 1944–27 January 1945

AXIS OF ADVANCE, ALLIED REGIMENT
JAPANESE ATTACK
POINT OF CONTACT
ROAD, ALL WEATHER
ROAD, FAIR WEATHER

Contour Interval 1000 feet

5   0   5 MILES
5   0   5 KILOMETERS

D. Holmes, Jr.

MAP 9

The positions the Japanese held in the Shweli valley from Namhkam to Wanting could have been most formidable. Namhkam, for example, had originally been fortified with the expectation that the whole of the *18th Division* would hold it. However, the *33d Army's* mission was only to delay the Chinese while the decisive battle was fought out around Mandalay; there was no thought of fighting to a finish and the *33d* organized itself for combat accordingly. The Japanese positions in the vicinity of the valley covered the Burma Road, the main avenue of approach to Mandalay from the northeast. The bulk of the Japanese forces was deployed in the Wanting–Mong Yu area facing the Y–Force. The strongly fortified Wanting was held by the *56th Division,* and ten miles to the rear along the Burma Road at Mong Yu was the *168th Infantry Regiment* of the *49th Division,* Colonel Yoshida. Thirty miles to the southwest of Wanting the *Yamazaki Detachment,* 3,000 strong, manned the Namhkam defenses astride the route of advance of the Chinese New First Army, thus protecting the left and the rear of the main body of Japanese troops in the Wanting–Mong Yu area. The *4th Infantry Regiment, 2d Division,* Colonel Ichikari, located at Namhpakka on the Burma Road near its intersection with the road leading to Namhkam, was in a good position to be used as a tactical reserve along either of the roads. *Thirty-third Army* had expected that the Ichikari and Yoshida regiments would be transferred to the Mandalay area and the Japanese intended to keep them in reserve, but the Chinese pressure forced their commitment.[22]

As of 17 December NCAC headquarters believed, and correctly, that in the Tonkwa–Mongmit area, the center of the Japanese position in north Burma, they faced a strong force of the *18th Division.* At Namhkam, NCAC estimated there were 2,500 Japanese, and from Namhpakka to the north edge of the Shweli valley, 2,500 more. In the north end of the valley, around Wanting, NCAC placed the *56th* itself. A week later NCAC's G–2, Col. Joseph W. Stilwell, Jr., estimated that only delaying action and minor counterattacks were to be expected from the Japanese.[23]

When the Chinese 22d Division was recalled to China, in mid-December, General Sultan changed his plans and regrouped his forces. His original thought had been to send the 22d Division wide to the south and then east to place it across the old Burma Road in the Namhpakka area. This would cut off almost the whole of the *33d Army* to the north and make inevitable its withdrawal, which in turn would clear the way for the Ledo Road to be linked with the Burma Road. In so planning, he was aware of the possibility that some Chinese divisions might be recalled to China and arranged his dispositions accordingly. He hoped that his forces might swing east like a giant gate whose southernmost edge would hit Lashio, but if he lost some

[22] Japanese Study 148, pp. 43–44.
[23] NCAC G–2 Rpts, 17, 24 Dec 44. NCAC G–2 files, KCRC.

of his Chinese troops then he planned to compensate by shortening his gate and making a shallower swing to the east.   Across the Allied line from west to east Sultan's new orders directed the following moves: (*See Map 8.*)

(1) The British 36th Division would move east of the Irrawaddy, then southeast via Mongmit to cut the old Burma Road in the Kyaukme–Hsipaw area, well south of Lashio.

(2) The 5332d Brigade (MARS Task Force) would make a most difficult march across hill country to the Mong Wi area, then cut the Burma Road near Hosi.   Essentially, this was the mission once contemplated for the 22d Division.

(3) The Chinese 50th Division, which had been following the British 36th Division down the Railway Corridor, would move just to the east of that unit, cross the Shweli River near Molo, and then move southeast to take Lashio.   It thus moved into the area formerly occupied by elements of MARS Task Force.

(4) The Chinese New First Army would occupy the upper Shweli valley from Namhkam to Wanting and reopen the road to China.[24]

The earliest action in the drive south from Bhamo to link up with the Y–Force and clear the road fell to the Chinese 30th Division.   While the 38th had been besieging Bhamo, the 30th had been sent past it; the 30th was the division that had fought the *Yamazaki Detachment* at Namyu when the latter sought to relieve Bhamo.   General Sun Li-jen, army commander, now ordered the 90th Regiment, 30th Division, to move straight down the road toward Namhkam.   The 88th and 89th Regiments were sent on a shallow envelopment south of the road, to come up on Namhkam from that direction.   The 38th Division was used for wide envelopments to either side of the 30th Division, and one of its regiments was kept in army reserve.[25]

After the heavy fighting of mid-December, the 30th Division did not find the Japanese to its front intent on anything more than light delaying action. The stage was set for a swift advance into the Shweli valley, but the commander of the 90th Regiment was not so inclined and, as he had the center of the Chinese line, the flanks delayed accordingly.   His repeated failures to advance, and his practice of abandoning supplies and then requesting more by airdrop, were regarded by the American liaison officers as having wasted two weeks after the action at Namyu; his relief was arranged in early January.   The new regimental commander, Colonel Wang, was energetic and a sound tactician; the regiment's performance improved at once.[26]

The 90th Regiment now moved with more speed, and soon reached the

---

[24] History of IBT, I, 137–39.
[25] History of IBT, I, 182.
[26] (1) History of NCAC, II, 260–61.   (2) The Japanese remarked on the slow progress of the Chinese advance.   Japanese Study 148, p. 45.

hill dominating the southwestern entrance to Shweli valley. The term valley as applied here refers to a stretch of flat ground about 25 miles long and from 4 to 6 miles wide carved from the mountains by the Shweli River and its tributaries between Mu-se and Namhkam. The floor of the valley, 2,400 feet above sea level, is dotted with villages. The existing road, whose trace the engineers planned to follow, closely hugged the hills forming the southeastern edge of the valley. Namhkam was built along the road near the southwestern end of the valley and its immediate approaches were dominated by a hill mass abutting the Bhamo road between the river and its small tributary to the north.

Facing this terrain, the Chinese chose to circle around the southwestern end of the valley with the 90th Regiment, while the 112th Regiment was ordered to move directly across the valley on Namhkam. Units of the regiment began crossing the Shweli on 5 January 1945; the whole regiment was across in fifty hours. The regiment now came swinging around the southeast corner of the valley and up the eastern side of Namhkam. Meanwhile, the 88th Regiment had entered the valley along the road and cut across the little plain directly toward Namhkam.

Namhkam itself was occupied on 16 January by the 2d Battalion of the 90th. Only a few shots marked the change in ownership, and two Japanese were killed. Inspecting the settlement, the Chinese realized that the Japanese had not planned to stand there. So there was no dramatic battle. The significance lay in that the Japanese had been pushed away from the lower end of the Shweli valley. Once the valley was in Allied hands, the road to China was open, and on 15 January the Japanese *33d Army,* which attached little significance now to blockading China, was slowly pulling back off the trace of the road to China.[27]

Since the 38th Division had been engaged at Bhamo while the 30th Division had bypassed the fighting there and gone on toward the Shweli valley, its regiments were behind the 30th and, in effect, had to follow it in column before they could swing wide to envelop the Shweli valley. The 112th Regiment had been pulled out of the lines at Bhamo just before the city fell and sent toward the Shweli valley along trails running through the hills north of the Bhamo road. There was little contact with the Japanese, and as the 112th moved along it stopped on Chinese soil, so close is the Bhamo area to China. This made the 38th the first Chinese unit to fight its way back to Chinese soil. Moving steadily on, the regiment was in the Loiwing area on 6 January 1945. In 1941 Loiwing had been the site of the Central Aircraft Manufacturing Company plant. In 1942 Chennault and the American Volunteer Group had operated from the Loiwing field for several

---

[27] History of NCAC, II, 261–62.

BURMESE IDOL IN NAMHKAM. *American and Chinese soldiers are from the Northern Combat Area Command.*

months. Now, it was back in Allied hands. Patrolling from the Loiwing area across the Shweli to Namhkam, the 112th concluded that the road to Namhkam was open. It requested permission to take the town, but was held back until the 30th Division occupied it.[28]

The 114th Regiment, which had so distinguished itself at Bhamo, was given the mission of swinging wide around the southern end of the Shweli valley. Because of the casualties the 114th had taken at Bhamo it had to be reinforced with the 1st Battalion of the 113th. The mission it received was to be a severe test of its marching powers, for on reaching the south end of the Shweli valley it was to ford the Shweli, move south and east through the hills on the right flank of the 89th Regiment as the latter moved on Namhkam, then continue its march to cut the Namhkam–Namhpakka trail about midway. At the mid-point, the village of Loi-lawn, it would be about

[28] History of NCAC, II, 272–74.

TWO SOLDIERS. *An American-trained and -equipped soldier of the Chinese Army in India (left), compares lots with a Chinese Expeditionary Force soldier at Mu-se, Burma.*

seven miles from the old Burma Road, which was the line of communications to the Japanese *56th Division* in the Wanting area. Crossing the Shweli on 10 January, it reached Ta-kawn on the 16th. Making this the regimental base with a garrison and air supply facilities, Col. Peng Ko-li sent two battalions off to cut the Namhkam–Namhpakka trail. The Japanese resisted stubbornly, and not until the 19th were the Chinese across the trail.[29]

With the southern end of the Shweli valley firmly in Chinese hands by 17 January, General Sun issued his next orders, which called for the 112th and 113th Regiments to move up the Shweli valley toward Wanting and secure the trace of the Ledo Road. At this point the conceptions of the battle held by NCAC and *33d Army* were very much at odds. NCAC saw its men as fighting their way up the valley in a northeasterly direction. The

[29] History of NCAC, II, 275–76.

Japanese saw themselves as falling slowly back from the Shweli under pressure from the northwest. Actually, the only pressure from the northwest was that of the 30th Division and the MARS Task Force, which after rounding the Namhkam corner were moving southward toward the Burma Road. In the northern two thirds of the Shweli valley, the 38th Division's flank guards, as they drove northeast, were brushing across the Japanese rear guards, which were falling back to the southeast and attempting to cover the Burma Road, their line of communications and avenue of retreat.

Such being the case, the 38th not surprisingly met little resistance as it drove up the Shweli valley. The *56th Division* was holding strongly only at Wanting, where the road up the valley met the Burma Road, and not until the 38th Division approached Wanting did Japanese resistance stiffen.

First contact with the Japanese came at Panghkam, a village near the northern exit of the valley. The 113th stayed in the valley, and the 112th was sent wide into the hills to the right of the road near Se-lan. Japanese resistance was of the rear-guard variety; the 113th was only slowed, not stopped. As it approached Mu-se, the exit of the valley, its leading elements on 20 January joined with Chinese troops of the Yunnan divisions.[30] These men had entered the Shweli valley by enveloping its northern end, much as Sun Li-jen's troops had enveloped the southern, then driving directly across to the southern side. The trace of the road was not yet open, but the presence of the Yunnan troops meant formal opening was only a matter of days.

The End of the Salween Campaign

While the Chinese Army in India had been moving on and then encircling Bhamo, the battered divisions of General Wei Li-huang's Chinese Expeditionary Force had been trying to recover from the blows inflicted on them by the September Japanese counteroffensive, which the Chinese had manfully stemmed.[31] At the end of the battle, both sides were exhausted, but the Chinese could claim the advantage. They had kept the Japanese from reoccupying the terrain about Teng-chung and Ping-ka, which controlled passes into Burma north and south of the Burma Road, and they had held on to Sung Shan, from which Japanese artillery had once controlled the ascent of the Burma Road from the Salween gorge. On the Burma Road itself, the Chinese, with the survivors of seven divisions, were in a semicircle to the east of Lung-ling.

As October began, American liaison officers with the Chinese saw traffic movements and demolitions within the Japanese lines that convinced them,

---

[30] *Ibid.*
[31] For a description of the September fighting, see *Stilwell's Command Problems,* Chapter XI.

and correctly, that the Japanese were thinning their lines, that only rear-guard action was contemplated.[32]

The Chinese of XI Group Army completed their preparations for the next attack, and on 29 October it began.   Thirty-seven P–40's from the Four-teenth Air Force flew close support for the Chinese 200th Division, a veteran of the 1942 campaign, which led the assault.   South and west of Lung-ling, elements of the Chinese 200th swung around to attack positions along the Burma Road behind Lung-ling.   Meanwhile, two divisions of the 71st Army put heavy pressure on the Japanese garrison, with artillery support up to 1,700 rounds and 30–40 air sorties per day.   Late on 3 November the last Japanese left Lung-ling and at 2300 the Honorable 1st Division moved through the gutted center of the town.[33]   (*Map 10*)

A pause followed which thoroughly disturbed General Dorn, the chief of the Y–Force Operations Staff advising General Wei.   Dorn saw no reason why the Chinese should not follow closely on the Japanese rear guards, feared that the Chinese were delaying, and asked Wedemeyer to intervene with the Generalissimo.   Wedemeyer agreed, and pointed out to the Gen-eralissimo that it was important to finish the campaign and free the Y–Force for service in China.   On 9 November the Generalissimo agreed to give the necessary orders.

In addition to advising on strategy and tactics and furnishing air support, the American forces gave medical aid.   From the opening of the campaign in May 1944 to November they treated 9,428 Chinese, of whom only 492 died.   Many wounded never reached an American hospital because of the rough terrain, but even so this was the best medical aid Chinese forces in China had yet enjoyed.

Receiving the Generalissimo's orders to advance, General Wei sent his XI Group Army (53d, 2d, 71st, 6th Armies) against Mang-shih, the *56th Division's* former headquarters.   One army moved through the hills on the north side of the Burma Road, and two on the south, while the 71st came down the road itself.   Having strict orders to avoid any decisive battle, the *56th Division* contended itself with demolitions, burning the rice harvest, and delaying the Chinese with rear-guard actions.   Casualties were light among the Chinese as they advanced through Mang-shih on 20 November.   At this point the Chinese were about seventy miles away from Namhkam in the Shweli valley.   Mang-shih was a valuable prize because of its airstrip. Speedily repaired, it permitted the C–46's of the 27th Troop Carrier Squadron to land supplies, a much more economical and satisfactory means than air-

---

[32] (1) Y–FOS Journal, KCRC.   (2) Japanese Studies 93 and 148.   This section, unless other-wise noted, is based on these sources.

[33] Comments of Col. John H. Stodter on draft MS of this volume.

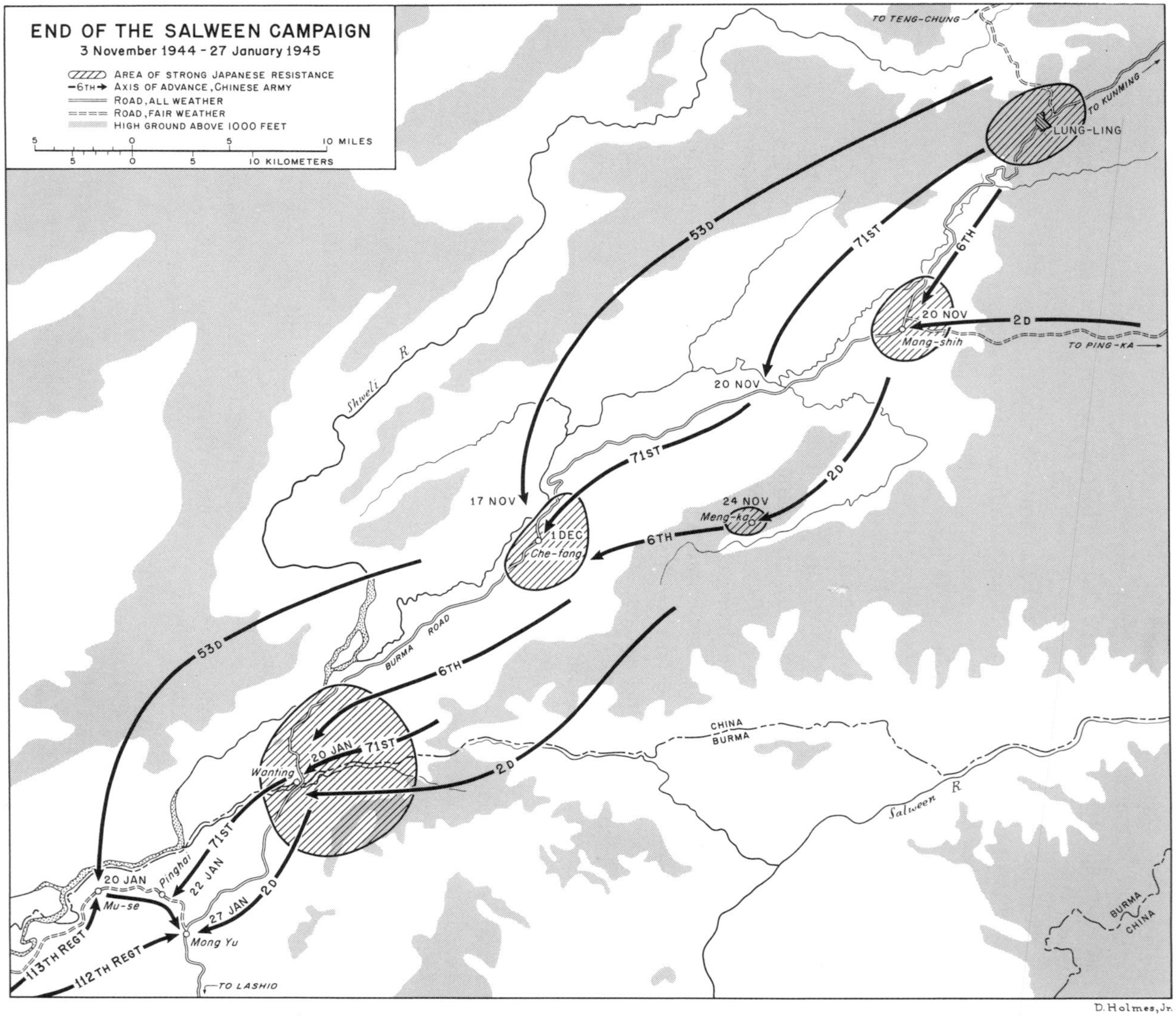
END OF THE SALWEEN CAMPAIGN
3 November 1944 - 27 January 1945
AREA OF STRONG JAPANESE RESISTANCE
6TH AXIS OF ADVANCE, CHINESE ARMY
ROAD, ALL WEATHER
ROAD, FAIR WEATHER
HIGH GROUND ABOVE 1000 FEET
5 0 5 10 MILES
5 0 5 10 KILOMETERS
TO TENG-CHUNG
TO KUNMING
LUNG-LING
53D
71ST
6TH
2D
20 NOV
Mang-shih
TO PING-KA
20 NOV
Shweli R
71ST
2D
24 NOV
Meng-ka
6TH
17 NOV
1 DEC
Che-fang
BURMA ROAD
53D
6TH
CHINA
BURMA
20 JAN
71ST
Wanting
2D
Salween R
71ST
22 JAN
2D
27 JAN
20 JAN
Pinghai
Mu-se
Mong Yu
113TH REGT
112TH REGT
TO LASHIO
BURMA
CHINA
D. Holmes, Jr.

MAP 10

dropping.[34]   Meanwhile, the Fourteenth Air Force continued to harass the retreating Japanese, bombing all bridges and likely Japanese billets.   The Japanese were careful to stay clear of the Burma Road in daylight, but contacts with their rear guards gave the P–40's opportunity to demonstrate close air support.

By this time Wei had a solution to his tactical problems.   One army moved along each of the ridges that paralleled the road, and the rest of his forces came straight down the road.   If the Japanese, as at the divide between Mang-shih and the next town twenty-four miles away, Che-fang, attempted a delaying action with a small force, the wings of Wei's force simply outflanked them and forced them back.   If the Japanese, as seemed likely to be the case at Wanting, attempted a stronger stand, then Wei was advancing in a formation well adapted to rapid deployment and encirclement.   Che-fang fell on 1 December, and Wanting was the next target.

Lying as it does at the northeastern exit of the Shweli valley, on the Burma Road, Wanting had to be taken.   Moreover, pressure on Wanting would make it difficult for the Japanese to transfer units from that front to meet the NCAC troops at the southwestern end of the Shweli valley.

Not for another thirty days did the Chinese resume their offensive down the Burma Road.   Asked by Y-Force Operations Staff to send out strong patrols at least, the Chinese were willing, but ordered their patrols to stay out of Wanting.   The Chinese unwillingness to advance down the Burma Road and end the blockade of China as quickly as possible, at a time when Wedemeyer was making every effort to bring aid to China, moved the latter to make very strong representations to the Generalissimo.   After describing the situation around Wanting, Wedemeyer wrote:

1. It is a policy of the China Theater not to give aid to those who will not advance; therefore, no air support has been given to these divisions nor to the others in that section who, apparently having similar instructions, cannot advance.   The Chief of Staff [General Ho] has been promised renewed efforts when he puts into effect plans which are now being developed to take Wanting.   His earlier plans to send two regiments as patrols into Wanting did not materialize.

2. I feel certain that if you will issue orders to these C.E.F. [Chinese Expeditionary Force] forces to take Wanting, they have the ability to do so in a short time.   I certainly will provide all the air support possible which should greatly facilitate the capture of the objective.[35]

Then, on 15 December, Bhamo was evacuated by the Japanese.   General Wei may have wanted to delay his attack until he could be sure that the NCAC forces would not be delayed by another siege like that of Myitkyina.

---

[34] See *Stilwell's Command Problems,* Chapter III, for a discussion of the several techniques of air supply.

[35] Memo 275, Wedemeyer for Generalissimo, 10 Dec 44.   Bk 16, ACW Corresp with Chinese.

Wei's divisions were now far understrength, since replacements had not been supplied, and lacked 170,000 men of their prescribed strength.[36]

As part of his swing around China Theater, Wedemeyer visited Wei on 20 December. The American commander urged Wei to resume the offensive, to link his forces with Sultan's because the east China situation demanded everyone's aid. Apparently, Wei's circumstances were changing, because in late December the Y–Force began its last battle.

The first Chinese attack was made by the 2d Army on the Japanese right flank, in the area of Wanting. Initially, it went very well. The Chinese 9th Division on 3 January broke through to the village streets, finally reaching the Japanese artillery positions. The Japanese rallied, and there was bitter hand-to-hand fighting—"pistols, clubs, and bayonets"— according to the Japanese account. That night the Japanese counterattacked successfully and drove out the Chinese.

Wei then shifted his attack to the Japanese left flank, which lay along the Shweli River. The Chinese succeeded in establishing a bridgehead but could not hold it against Japanese counterattacks by two regiments, and the attempt failed. A pause of a week or so followed.

The Japanese defense of Wanting had been successful, but while the *56th Division* had been fighting in that area, Sultan's NCAC forces in the Namhkam area, including the MARS Task Force, had begun moving eastward toward the Burma Road. If they succeeded in blocking the Burma Road, the *56th Division's* position obviously would be compromised. So the problem the Japanese faced was to know how long they could afford to fight at Wanting before the exit slammed shut. As noted above, the MARS Task Force had been dispatched by Sultan to block the Burma Road, and by 17 January it was clashing with Japanese outposts adjacent to it. Weighing all these factors, the *56th Division* in mid-January estimated it could hold its present positions about one week more. The *33d Army* could not afford to cut things too fine, and so the *56th* began to shorten its perimeter as it prepared to withdraw south down the Burma Road while time remained.

Since attempts at enveloping the Japanese position had been successfully countered by the alert defenders, the American liaison section with XI Group Army, Col. John H. Stodter commanding, suggested that Wei try a surprise attack on the center, which seemed to be lightly held. American liaison officers took an active part in the planning. After the war, as he looked back with satisfaction on the careful co-ordination of air, artillery, and infantry weapons that distinguished this attack from many of its unsuccessful predecessors along the Salween, Stodter thought it the "best coordinated" he

---

[36] Memo 304, McClure for Generalissimo, 20 Dec 44. Bk 16, ACW Corresp with Chinese. This memorandum describes Wedemeyer as being disturbed over the replacement problem in the Y–Force.

had seen to that time in the Y–Force. From his observation post, Stodter watched the Chinese infantry attack on 19 January and climb up the dominant local peak, the Hwei Lung Shan. Chinese artillery, mortar, and machine gun fire pounded the Japanese trenches until the last moment, then the Chinese infantry attacked with grenade and bayonet. The attack succeeded, Japanese counterattacks failed, and the Japanese hold on Wanting was no longer firm.[37]

On 20 January elements of the Chinese 9th Division found Wanting empty. Later in that day patrols from Wei's army met other patrols from Sultan's Chinese divisions. The long Salween campaign was drawing to a victorious close; the road to China was almost open.

The final work in opening the Burma Road would have to be done by the Chinese Army in India. On 22 January the Generalissimo ordered the Chinese Expeditionary Force to concentrate north of the Sino-Burmese border. He informed his commanders that remaining Japanese resistance would be cleared away by the Chinese Army in India. Two days later General Wei ended his offensive, and ordered his units to stay in place until relieved by one of Sultan's. The Salween campaign was thus formally ended 24 January 1945.

On the vast panorama of the world conflict the Salween campaign did not loom very large to the Western world. But the Chinese had succeeded in reoccupying 24,000 square miles of Chinese territory. It was the first time in the history of Sino-Japanese relations that the Chinese forces had driven Japanese troops from an area the Japanese wanted to hold. To this effort China had contributed initially perhaps 72,000 troops and in the fall of 1944 some 8,000 to 10,000 replacements, plus the elite 200th Division. The United States had given 244 75-mm. pack howitzers, 189 37-mm. antitank guns, and infantry weapons, plus sufficient ammunition. American instructors and liaison officers had sought to assist the Chinese in their conduct of operations. The Fourteenth Air Force had been ordered to draw heavily on its small resources to support the operation. The Japanese had initially faced Wei's men with 11,000 soldiers and thirty-six cannon. For their fall offensive they had reinforced the much-reduced original garrison with 9,000 more soldiers from the *2d* and *49th Divisions*.

The military significance of Wei's victory lay in the trucks and artillery which now would move into China, and in the three elite divisions released for service there. For the future, the Salween campaign demonstrated that, given artillery and heavy weapons plus technical advice, Chinese troops, if enjoying numerical superiority of five to one or better, could defeat the forces

---

[37] Stodter comments on draft MS. Elsewhere in his comments, Stodter remarks that Chinese noncommissioned officers and junior officers, though inexperienced, appeared brave and intelligent, while the Chinese private won the affectionate regard of those Americans who served with him.

of the Great Powers.   Observing the campaign, the American liaison officers had concluded that technical errors by the Chinese reduced the combat efficiency of the Chinese forces.   Failure to bypass isolated Japanese units; inability to co-ordinate infantry and artillery; faulty maintenance of equipment and poor ammunition discipline—all tended to offset the valor and hardihood of the Chinese soldier.   None of the practices was beyond correction.   As the Chinese improved, they would require less in the way of numbers.[38]

Opening the Ledo Road

In the period between the split of the CBI Theater in October 1944 and the fall of Bhamo on 15 December, the Ledo Road engineers under General Pick brought the survey of the Ledo Road from a point just below and east of Kamaing, 211 miles from Ledo, to a juncture with the Myitkyina–Bhamo road.   The Ledo Road was to bypass Myitkyina, for there was no point to running heavy traffic through an inhabited place, and Myitkyina's supply needs could be served by an access road.   Metaling and grading were complete almost to Mogaung.   The Mogaung River had been bridged near Kamaing, and a temporary bridge placed across the Irrawaddy.   Tonnage carried on the road for use within Burma was steadily rising.   In early October it had carried 275 tons a day; by the latter part of the month the rate was twice that.[39]   Immediately after Bhamo's capture, the advance headquarters of the road engineers was moved to that town.   A combat supply road was made from Mogaung, below Myitkyina, to a point just ten miles west of Namhkam.

Progress during December was steady, swift, and uneventful because once the roadbuilders reached the Myitkyina area of north Burma only routine engineering remained.   In mid-January the Ledo Road was linked with the Myitkyina–Bhamo road, at a point 271 miles from Ledo.   The Myitkyina–Bhamo road was being metaled, and, significant of the state of the link to China, the first truck convoy was poised at Ledo ready to drive to Kunming. The road to China was complete, as far as the engineers were concerned. Beginning the traffic flow now depended on driving away the Japanese.   A four-inch pipeline paralleled the road as far as Bhamo, where the intent was to send the line cross country to China, rather than along the next stretch of road.   The mission of clearing the Japanese rear guards from the last stretch of the road trace was given to the 112th and 113th Regiments of the Chinese 38th Division, with the 113th moving up the valley along the existing road

[38] Liaison officer reports in Y–FOS files, Kansas City Records Center, contain many comments on Chinese tactics and techniques, 1943–45.
[39] History of IBT, I, 172–73.

PONTON BRIDGE OVER THE IRRAWADDY RIVER *was an important link in the Ledo Road.*

from Panghkam and the 112th going through the hills. By 23 January the 112th had reached a point in the hills south of the valley road from which it could, through a gap in the hills, see the Shweli valley road behind the Japanese lines but at a range too great to bring fire to bear. The regiment halted that afternoon and formed its defenses for the night. The precaution was wise, for that afternoon and evening several Japanese detachments withdrawing from the valley area found the 112th across their projected routes and at once tried to fight their way through. There was brisk fighting, and sixty-seven dead Japanese were later buried around the regiment's positions.

Meanwhile, the first convoy had closed on the Namhkam area and was waiting for the all-clear signal. The road stretch from Namhkam to the northeast was being efficiently interdicted by fire from a Japanese 150-mm. howitzer. The convoy was heavily laden with representatives of the press; there would be a great to-do if a 150-mm. shell burst among them on a section of road that the Army had designated as clear, and so the convoy was held up several days at Namhkam while NCAC pressed the Chinese to open the road and also tried to silence the 150-mm. howitzer by counterbattery.

An artillery observation craft was sent aloft and after some time managed to locate the Japanese howitzer. Several rounds were fired; the Japanese finally displaced the howitzer to a safer spot.[40]

To expedite the clearing of the road, the NCAC chief of staff, Brig. Gen. Robert M. Cannon, conferred with the Chinese commander, General Sun Li-jen, on 24 January and received General Sun's promise that the road would be open on 27 January. Unknown to the two Allied officers, the Japanese began withdrawing the *56th Division* from the Wanting area on 23 January, beginning with their casualties and ammunition.[41] Reflecting the decisions of the conference, the 113th Regiment moved forward on the 25th, and by the night of the 26th there were only five miles of Japanese-held territory between the two Chinese armies.

On the night of the 26th plans were made for an attack by armor and infantry, supported by artillery, to clear the last five miles. Careful co-ordination was needed lest the attack carry on into the Y–Force, beyond, and conferences between U.S. liaison officers from Y–Force and NCAC sought to arrange it. The attack moved off the morning of the 27th, with the tanks overrunning the little village of Pinghai, the last known enemy position. It fell without opposition. Meanwhile, an air observer reported that he saw troops in blue uniforms, undoubtedly Y–Force soldiers, in the area where the Shweli valley road joined with the Burma Road. A message was sent out canceling all artillery fire. Unfortunately, soldiers of the 38th opened small arms fire on the Y–Force troops.

At this point, Brig. Gen. George W. Sliney, who had been an artillery officer in the First Burma Campaign, intervened to halt what might have become an ugly incident. Fearlessly exposing himself to the Chinese bullets, he walked across the line of fire and forced it to stop. Sliney then walked over to the Y–Force lines. So ended the blockade of China.

Soon after, some tanks with the 38th mistakenly fired on Y–Force men. Their artillery retaliated. Only prompt action by General Sun Li-jen and the liaison officers with the 112th straightened out the affair. With this misunderstanding ended, the road to China was open, and the first convoy was ready to roll. The Ledo Road, built at an estimated cost of $148,000,000, was open.[42]

The confusion that attended the meeting between Y–Force and the

---

[40] NCAC History, III, 282, hints the piece was destroyed, but Lt. Col. Trevor N. Dupuy, who was in the area, states it was merely forced to move.

[41] Japanese Study 148, p. 48.

[42] (1) NCAC History, III, 283–85. (2) Dupuy witnessed Sliney's act. Dupuy comments on draft MS. (3) Stodter comments on draft MS. (4) Memo, Engr Hist Div, Office, Chief of Engrs, 25 Mar 53. OCMH.

CHINESE COOLIES LEVELING A ROADBED *for the Teng-chung cutoff route to Kunming.*

Chinese Army in India was only a reflection of the greater confusion that surrounded the actual declaration that the road to China was open and the blockade broken. The several headquarters involved in the operation were aware of the public relations aspect of the feat; there were sixty-five press and public relations people in the first convoy as one indication of it—more reporters than there were guards.

The inaugural convoy had departed from Ledo on 12 January. Its trucks and towed artillery, with Negro and Chinese drivers, the latter added for ceremonial reasons, reached Myitkyina on the 15th, and then had to wait there until the 23d because the Japanese still interfered with traffic past Namhkam. On the night of the 22d, Lt. Gen. Daniel I. Sultan, India–Burma Theater commander, made some rough calculations of space and time, and announced that the road was open. Probably he expected the Japanese to be gone by the time the convoy reached the combat area. Next morning the caravan got under way again. It reached Namhkam without incident, and then confusion began.

The newsmen and public relations officers were surprised to learn on the 24th that the British Broadcasting Corporation had just announced the arrival of the first truck convoy at Kunming, China, via Teng-chung, on 20 January. India–Burma and China Theater authorities had long known that a rough trail, capable of improvement, linked Myitkyina and Kunming via Teng-chung. There had been considerable discussion of the respective merits of the Bhamo and Teng-chung routes, with General Pick firm for the Bhamo trace. The Chinese liked the idea of a Teng-chung route, and had advocated the Teng-chung cutoff as an alternative to and a supplement of the Bhamo route. Their laborers to the number of 20,000 were put to work on the stretch beyond Teng-chung, beginning 29 September 1944 and were supported by the small force of American engineers under Colonel Seedlock who had been assisting in reconstructing the Chinese portion of the Burma Road In less than sixty days, 145 miles were cleared.[43]

On 20 January 1945, two trucks and an 11-ton wrecker commanded by Lt. Hugh A. Pock of Stillwater, Oklahoma, arrived at Kunming after a sixteen-day trip from Myitkyina. At one point, at a precipitous pass, the back wheels of the lead truck had slid out over empty space; the vehicle had to be winched back. At another point Lieutenant Pock had to halt his little convoy while one of Seedlock's bulldozers cleared a path. But this was minor compared to the fact that a truck convoy had reached China.[44] No more than sixty-five vehicles crossed into China via Teng-chung, for the route was a rough one, and not paralleled by a pipeline as was the route via

---

[43] (1) Ltr, Col Seedlock to Romanus, 21 Dec 50. OCMH. (2) Rpt, Board of Officers re Pipelines and Burma Road, Including Teng-chung Cutoff, 31 Oct 45. CT 41, Dr 1, KCRC.
[44] History of IBT, I, 188.

Bhamo.   The impact of the news was immediate.   As a result of some of the announcements that followed, General Merrill radioed Sultan:

> A Reuter's report has been published and broadcast to the effect that convoys from India have been reported by Chinese sources to have crossed overland from India to China via Teng-chung.   The Supreme Allied Commander is quoted as radioing Churchill and Roosevelt: "In accordance with orders you gave me at Quebec, the road to China is opened."
>
> Wheeler's PRO [Public Relations Officer] has sent to Washington a blurb saying that the "plan drawn up by Lt. Gen. Raymond A. Wheeler two years ago is now about to pay off."
>
> The Chinese censors have scooped your correspondents, but events in Europe and the Pacific are dwarfing the story.   I recommend you take no action except to get your convoy across the border fast.[45]

On the morning of the 28th, the official inaugural convoy from India–Burma Theater resumed the often-interrupted journey.   There was a two-hour ceremony at Mu-se, and then, a few miles beyond, a road junction with a macadam road.   As the trucks swung out onto it realization flashed down the line that they were at last on the Burma Road and in China.   Two days later, as the convoy crossed the Salween, an air raid alarm brought a flurry of excitement.   Then came the long drive through Yunnan Province to Kunming, through dry, hilly, brown land, a contrast to the green and blue of the Burmese hills.   The night of 3 February the convoy bivouacked at the lake Tien Chih, and next morning Chinese drivers took over for the ceremonial entry.

On 4 February the line of 6 x 6 trucks and jeeps, some of the prime movers towing 105-mm. and 75-mm. howitzers, entered Kunming.   General Pick led the parade, standing erect in his jeep.   Firecrackers crackled and children screamed; American missionary nuns waved greetings, and Chinese bands added their din.   That night Governor Lung Yun of Yunnan gave a banquet which was graced by the presence of an American operatic star, Lily Pons, and her husband, a widely known conductor, Andre Kostelanetz. The occasion had its ironic side, unknown to the Americans as they rejoiced in the completion of the engineering feat; for, if General Okamura's memory is to be trusted, Lung Yun corresponded with him throughout the war.[46]

Shortly after the road was opened, the Generalissimo suggested that it be renamed the Stilwell Road.   The idea received general approval, and so the man who was primarily a tactician and troop trainer, whose mission and greatest interest was the reshaping of the Chinese Army into an efficient force, had his name applied to one of the great engineering feats of history, and was indelibly associated with it in the public mind.   The soldiers called it either the Ledo Road or "Pick's Pike."[47]

[45] History of IBT, I, 189.
[46] (1) History of IBT, I, 191–92.   (2) Japanese Officers' Comments, Okamura, p. 6.   OCMH.
[47] Mountbatten Report, Pt. B, par. 393.

CHAPTER V

The Crest of the Flood in China

In December 1944 Wedemeyer faced a grave test of his ability as a commander and staff officer. While he was still shaping his new command, the Japanese *11th Army* sent two of its divisions to the border of Kweichow Province. (*See Map 1—inside back cover.*) If they drew closer to Kunming there would be an obvious menace to the principal U.S. base in China. Wedemeyer would then have to carry out two major tasks simultaneously: recommend and obtain Chinese approval of actions that could stop the Japanese; and continue with the setting up of his command and the Chinese participation in ALPHA.

Wedemeyer Asks Help From SEAC

The original orders of the Japanese command in China had directed the *11th Army* to halt at the border of Kweichow Province. Taking the bit in its teeth, *11th Army* raced across the boundary, with the later approval of higher authority. However, it thought of pursuit, not Kunming.[1] Its *13th Division* took the town of Tushan, finding there considerable quantities of arms, and defeated some fresh Chinese troops, whose presence on the scene was among the first results of ALPHA. Local Chinese command problems had been greatly complicated by a tragic error of the Fourteenth Air Force, which bombed Chang Fa-kwei's headquarters on 27 November, destroying most of his transport and signal equipment.

The road up which the Japanese were moving forked not far above Tushan, one leg of the Y leading to Kunming on the west, the other, to Chungking. This was the strategic Kweiyang area. Americans were sent there to advise and assist the Chinese on technical and operational problems: Col. Frederic W. Boye, who assisted General Tang En-po throughout the rest of the war; Colonel Bowman, who in addition to aiding Chang Fa-kwei sent out OSS demolition teams led by Cols. Dan Mallon and Alexander H.

---

[1] (1) Japanese Study 130, pp. 26, 30. (2) Japanese Officers' Comments on draft MS.

Cummings and Lt. Col. H. V. Ennor.   That colonels should lead demolition teams on hazardous missions suggests the improvisations resorted to under the Japanese pressure.   Bridges had to be blown and roads trenched to slow the Japanese, and officers of colonel's rank could successfully negotiate the details with the responsible Chinese officers.[2]

Not even the most optimistic Chinese could for the moment interpret this Japanese move as a thrust confined to the American air bases in China, and no one on the Allied side could feel really sure where the *11th Army* would halt, though the summer uniforms worn by the Japanese suggested to American observers that the Japanese might be outrunning their supply lines.   It could not have occurred to anyone that the Japanese command itself was equally uncertain.   Theater headquarters concluded that Chungking and Kunming were under direct, immediate threat, and high Chinese personages began to interview Wedemeyer about flying out to India.[3]

This Japanese thrust into Kweichow meant that Wedemeyer had to give immediate attention to bolstering the defenses of Kunming and Chungking. One of his radios of this period to Sultan suggests the nature of his thinking about his problems.   Wedemeyer observed that where the ordinary military commander had but one great unknown, the enemy, he himself had two, the enemy and the combat effectiveness of the Chinese forces.   He added that he was "doing everything possible to create ground forces which are fed, trained, equipped, and led properly.   This will require several months, and during that period these two divisions [from Burma] must be practically my chief reliance in holding the Kunming area."[4]

On 30 November Wedemeyer told the Joint Chiefs and Admiral Mountbatten that the Generalissimo had decided the Chinese 22d and 38th Divisions must be transferred from Burma to China and that he concurred in the Generalissimo's conclusion.   Wedemeyer stated that if Kunming was not held, operations in Burma would become meaningless and the Chinese Government might reasonably be expected to collapse.   He added that his directive required that he "maintain and support the Chinese Government,"[5] and conduct operations to contain and divert the Japanese and support Pacific operations.   He added further that he knew Admiral Mountbatten believed

---

[2] (1) Comments on draft MS by Col Cummings, Brig Gen Frederic W. Boye, and Brig Gen Harwood C. Bowman.   (2) Colonel Mallon was a veterinarian who had gone to Command and General Staff School.   He was given the G–2 role when Z–FOS personnel took the field after the Japanese advance halted their training programs.

[3] (1) Japanese Study 130, p. 30.   (2) Memo, Marshall for President, 20 Dec 44.   Item 20, WDCSA 091 China (20 Dec 44).   (3) Rad CFB 28167, Wedemeyer to Marshall for JCS, 4 Dec 44.   Item 6, Wedemeyer Data Book.   (4) Bowman comments refer to the uniforms and to the Tushan arms store.   (5) Min, Mtg 6, Wedemeyer with Generalissimo, 28 Nov 44, Bk 1, Generalissimo Minutes, has Wedemeyer's apology for the bombing.

[4] Rad SIG 1442, Wedemeyer to Sultan, info Chennault, McClure, Cheves, Dorn, Tunner, 21 Dec 44.   Item 196, Bks 1 and 2, ACW Personal File.

[5] Wedemeyer's directive does not contain this phrase.

463995 O–59—11

withdrawing the two divisions would imperil current Allied operations in Burma. Wedemeyer also contemplated that the Y–Force would return some of its units to Kunming immediately, and that the rest of the force would not proceed much farther into Burma.[6]

In addition to requesting the 22d and 38th Divisions, Wedemeyer also wanted India–Burma Theater and SEAC to send two combat cargo groups of transport aircraft to China. Since the whole Allied combat operation in Burma was based on air supply, here was a proposal that affected anything SEAC might hope to do in Burma. These requests, made as they were by an American general officer, were thought by India–Burma Theater to have implications embarrassing to the American leadership. The United States had long been the ardent advocate of a campaign in Burma to aid China, to which the British Commonwealth would of necessity contribute the majority of the combat troops—even as the United States did in the Pacific. In December 1944 the British Commonwealth was moving toward the climax of the Burma campaign, with its divisions deep in the jungle, and now Wedemeyer was urging, and the Generalissimo demanding, that two Chinese divisions and about one half of SEAC's resources in transports be sent from Burma to China.[7]

Mountbatten was so strongly opposed to Wedemeyer's requests that he appealed to the British Chiefs of Staff. We do not know on what view of the situation in China he acted, but it was presumably that of SEAC's Director of Intelligence who assured him that there was little likelihood of a collapse of the Generalissimo's armies even if the Japanese took Kunming or Chungking. Behind this view was the British intelligence system in China. So he protested most vigorously to the British Chiefs of Staff the proposal to withdraw the two combat cargo groups and only slightly less so the recommendation that the 22d and 38th Divisions return to China.[8] Depriving SEAC of the two combat cargo groups would, he thought, force the Fourteenth Army to halt, and might even require it to return across the Chindwin River, for its supply situation would be jeopardized. Returning the 22d and 38th Divisions to China would be "disastrous," for it would imperil the campaign in north Burma and delay the opening of the road to China. Morever, because time was required to concentrate the two divisions, fly them to China, and redeploy them within China, Mountbatten feared they would be lost to both Burma and China at a critical period. Though

---

[6] (1) Rad CFB 27686, Wedemeyer to Marshall for JCS, info Mountbatten, 30 Nov 44. OCMH. (2) History of IBT, I, 121.

[7] *Ibid.,* pp. 123–24.

[8] (1) Mountbatten Report, Pt. B, par. 330.   (2) For a description of the British intelligence system in China, see History of China Theater, Chapter III. (3) Item 20, Wedemeyer Data Book. (4) In SEAC headquarters, the Japanese drive was sometimes called, sardonically, "the Wedemeyer Offensive." Ltr, Gen Creasy to Gen Smith, 16 Jun 54.

he did not want to see the transports moved from service in Burma, Mountbatten was willing to release forty-eight B–24's of the U.S. 7th Heavy Bombardment Group for transport service in China.[9] The steady progress of the Burma campaign was reducing the number of targets suitable for strategic bombardment and there was precedent in the theater for using B–24's in a transport role.

Wedemeyer's recommendation, the Generalissimo's demand, and Mountbatten's reluctance raised a major problem of inter-Allied and intertheater relations which had to be solved to permit bringing to China the two battle-tested and reliable divisions on which Wedemeyer's plans placed such emphasis.

Reaching a Decision

In apportioning resources between India, Southeast Asia, and China, bids for a change in the existing allocation made by a local theater commander might fall into either of two categories. Procedures were at hand to deal with each.

(1) If Wedemeyer desired the transfer of resources not under the operational control of SEAC, his requests were to go to Sultan who would relay them to the War Department. If Sultan concurred, the transfer followed. If Sultan objected, then the Joint Chiefs were called on to decide.

(2) If Wedemeyer wanted resources that were under SEAC's operational control, as in the present case, then Sultan was to relay his requests to Mountbatten. If Mountbatten approved, transfer was automatic. But if, as in this case, there was dissent, then Sultan was to present the case to the Joint Chiefs from his point of view, and Mountbatten, to the British Chiefs of Staff from his. The two staffs would then meet as the Combined Chiefs to render their decision.

Mountbatten had recommended against acceptance of Wedemeyer's request for the resources, and so, too, did Sultan, though the latter somewhat qualified his objections. Sultan believed that moving the 22d and 38th Divisions would "nullify" efforts to open the Burma Road, but he added that if Wedemeyer believed that Kunming was definitely threatened, then he would agree that the divisions should return to China. As of 30 November Wedemeyer did believe that Kunming was in danger, and said the divisions would be needed within a month to forestall disaster. Since Wedemeyer had met Sultan's point, there was now a clear-cut division between the British and the Americans in Asia and so the matter was one for decision by the Combined Chiefs of Staff.

The Joint Chiefs took the position that they could not question the

[9] History of IBT, I, 126.

Generalissimo's right to use his own Chinese forces on China's behalf, but having regard to the state of operations in Burma, where the 22d and 38th Divisions were in actual contact with the enemy, they recommended that these latter two go only if the other three divisions of the Chinese Army in India, which were not in combat, could not be used. The Joint Chiefs suggested the principle that the Generalissimo's requests should be met with the least possible damage to operations in Burma. As for the transfer of the American combat cargo groups from Burma to China, the Joint Chiefs believed China Theater should be able to call up any transport aircraft, the Air Transport Command included, that would be needed to move two divisions to China and support them once they were there. But the JCS added the significant modification that such demands should be limited to aircraft that were not engaged in supplying Allied forces in combat.

Initially, both Prime Minister Churchill and the British Chiefs of Staff agreed with Mountbatten that it would not be desirable to move the 22d and 38th from Burma to China. This support would have postponed the transfer of the divisions for several weeks and perhaps indefinitely while the CCS considered the question. Then Admiral Mountbatten reversed himself and on 3 December 1944 agreed that two Chinese divisions could be released. Reflection and survey had shown that the Japanese in Burma were so badly weakened that the transfer could safely be made.[10]

The question of transferring transport aircraft from Burma to China was a more vital one to SEAC because its ability to operate in Burma was directly related to air supply. Mountbatten took exception to the unilateral character of the JCS's pronouncement that China Theater might call on any U.S. transport aircraft in India–Burma Theater that were needed to move and support the two Chinese divisions. Such a step appeared to compromise Allied unity in Burma. He reminded the Joint Chiefs that the campaign in Burma had been undertaken on the basis of resources pledged to SEAC by the United States to help carry out a directive in whose drafting the United States had shared.

However, the Combined Chiefs of Staff took a broader view, and regarded the emergency nature of the need as the standard of judgment. In the spring of 1944 they had acquiesced in Mountbatten's diverting transports from the Hump to meet the situation created by the Japanese attack on India.

Now that the American Chiefs of Staff believed there was an emergency in China, the Combined Chiefs were willing to divert resources from SEAC on an emergency basis. Therefore the Combined Chiefs agreed that some transport aircraft could go to China on loan, rather than on permanent assignment. They were to be returned to Burma by 1 March 1945. On the larger

---

[10] *Ibid.,* pp. 127–30.

issue, of transferring U.S. resources from India and Burma to China, the Combined Chiefs agreed that the American Chiefs of Staff could transfer any U. S. resources without awaiting CCS action, if the American Chiefs believed an emergency existed in China. At the time the British Chiefs were quite explicit in concurring only on an emergency basis and until they could review the whole matter.[11]

Moving Reinforcements to China

With agreement on moving two divisions, plus transport aircraft for intratheater troop movements, to China, the question became one of choosing the units to go, after which the logistical problem of flying men, mules, and artillery to China would have to be solved. When in late November it first became likely that NCAC would have to send two of its Chinese divisions back to China, the NCAC and IBT commander, General Sultan, had asked Wedemeyer and the Generalissimo if it would be possible to substitute the 14th and 50th Divisions, neither of which was in contact with the Japanese, for the 22d and 38th, which were engaged, the latter heavily so at Bhamo. The China Theater authorities considered that the veteran 22d and 38th were elite units, and did not want to forego the services of both. In the light of this, Sultan suggested a compromise, the 14th Division and either the 22d or the 38th. When China Theater accepted, the selection of the 22d became automatic, since it was not so deeply involved in operations as was the 38th.

With regard to selection of transport aircraft, after discussion between India–Burma and China Theaters reduced the number to be lent to China from six squadrons to three, General Wedemeyer stated that two of the three would be used to move some of the Y–Force to the Kunming area and the third, to support the Fourteenth Air Force. To replace these transports, Mountbatten curtailed paratroop training activities.[12]

The actual movement of the divisions to China in time for them to be of use in defending Kunming presented some difficult problems. It was necessary to find the aircraft to fly them over the Hump, and to make arrangements to redeploy them once they had arrived in China. Moving the divisions over the Hump might result in a heavy cost to Hump tonnage flown to China. And, such was the lack of transport facilities within China, moving the troops off the airfields once they arrived was a complicated problem involving the most careful scheduling of truck and aircraft movements within China.

In the beginning China Theater held most strongly to the view that Hump deliveries should not suffer because of these troop movements, for Hump tonnage was just as vital as were the troops in stopping the Japanese. SEAC, on the other hand, maintained that the Hump operation should be

[11] *Ibid.*
[12] History of IBT, I, 130–34.

drawn on first because SEAC's remaining aircraft resources were all engaged in supporting the offensive into Burma. As so often in Allied operations attempts were made to compromise and many organizations were drawn on for transport aircraft. For example, NCAC cut its airdrop requirements to thirty C–47 sorties a day. The Fourteenth Air Force from its meager resources was able to carry 5 percent of the total. Eastern Air Command gave two squadrons, which were engaged in the lift throughout its operation. These expedients unfortunately were not enough to eliminate calls on the ATC, which ultimately carried 40 percent of the load, at the cost of a slight reduction in Hump tonnage.[13]

There were some difficulties in keeping up an orderly flow of men and matériel across the Hump, and on occasion sparks flew as the India–Burma and China Theaters sought to co-ordinate their operations. Because the 14th Division was in reserve in the Myitkyina and Warazup areas, its concentration and emplaning presented a minimum of difficulty. On 5 December the first of the 14th's men and matériel began the flight back to China. The initial flow of reinforcements seemed to be progressing smoothly, the 22d Division was preparing to return, and then came administrative troubles. On one occasion, troops flown over the Hump from Burma to Chanyi field in China had to be flown back to Burma because China Theater was not ready to receive them. When the time came for the 22d Division to move, on 22 December 1944, India–Burma Theater had units ready to go on twenty-four hours' notice, and had sent the leading elements on a correspondingly tight time schedule only to receive a radio from China Theater headquarters that the move should be postponed. Since operations in Burma had been affected in order to meet what China Theater had represented as a grave emergency, Sultan reacted strongly to these delays and postponements, placing the matter before the Army's Chief of Staff, General Marshall, as well as his colleague, Wedemeyer.[14]

Some of Sultan's concern possibly may be traced to the fact that just a week earlier he had asked Wedemeyer if the move of the 22d could be delayed for a while until NCAC could regroup the 50th Division and begin moving the 38th away from the Bhamo area. Wedemeyer had not felt able to agree, for as of 16 December he thought that the vital Kweiyang area, gateway to both Chungking and Kunming, was still menaced, and that only the Fourteenth Air Force and the rough terrain were shielding Kunming.[15]

---

[13] *Ibid.* pp. 136–7.

[14] Rad CHC 5743, Sultan to Wedemeyer, info Marshall, 25 Dec 44. Item 232, Bks 1 and 2, ACW Personal File.

[15] (1) Rad CHC 5532, Sultan to Wedemeyer, 14 Dec 44; Rad, CFB 29155, McClure to Chennault for Wedemeyer, 14 Dec 44; Rad CSF 4920, Wedemeyer to McClure, 16 Dec 44; Rad CFB 29422, Wedemeyer to Sultan, 18 Dec 44. Items 180, 181, 186, 188, Bks 1 and 2, ACW Personal File. (2) History of IBT, I, 135.

CHINESE 22D DIVISION TROOPS *waiting with their weapons to board C–47's of the Tenth Air Force for the return flight over the Hump to China, 22 December 1944.*

Wedemeyer, in a strongly worded telegram, took Sultan to task for placing the matter before their common superior, General Marshall. Wedemeyer did not comment on the difficulties involved in moving Chinese troops within China, which tied up trucks that otherwise would have been available to move troops from the airfields, but put his reply on the grounds that such matters should be adjusted locally between theaters. Sultan hastened to agree, and the matter was closed amicably.[16]

So with Wedemeyer insisting that the 22d Division had to be moved to China, even though the actual flights were a problem in intertheater coordination, the division began its move on 22 December, from an emergency airstrip at Nansin completed just one day before. By 5 January 1945 the movement was complete.

[16] (1) The problems Wedemeyer found in trying to make the troop movements called for by ALPHA are discussed below. (2) Rad CFB 29872, Wedemeyer to Sultan, 26 Dec 44; Rad CHC 5812, Sultan to Wedemeyer, 29 Dec 44. Items 234, 222, Bks 1 and 2, ACW Personal File.

Flying the 14th and 22d Divisions back to China was an impressive achievement. This was a powerful force, well able to handle the same number of Japanese divisions, and better equipped than all but a few of those in China. The two comprised: [17]

25,105 Chinese soldiers
   249 American liaison personnel
 1,596 horses and mules
    42 ¼-ton trucks
    48 75-mm. howitzers
    48 4.2-inch mortars
    48 37-mm. guns, antitank

With the flow of well-trained, well-equipped, and well-led Chinese troops into China which got under way in early December 1944, and with the Chinese 38th Division occupying Bhamo on the 15th of that month, the road to China would soon be open to bring in trucks and artillery. Because of the limitations which in August 1944 the War Department had set for the road's development,[18] the road would not deliver supplies at the impressive rate the Hump was now approaching, but the psychological impact of opening a ground line of communications would be present once the road was opened. Some at least of the elite troops who had opened the road could go on to China for the defense of Kunming. Ultimately, the rest of the five Chinese divisions in Burma would follow. If the Japanese overran the Kunming airfields, the Hump operation would be ended. But at the same time the Japanese in Burma would be hard put in December 1944 to find troops with which again to cut the Burma Road once it had been reopened.

The balance was beginning to tilt in Wedemeyer's favor, though the outcome was uncertain. Wedemeyer, struggling with the complex responsibilities of China, still had to face the possibility that the Japanese at the last moment might break through Kunming's defenses and seize the Hump terminals. All the results of such a stroke could not be predicted, but they would certainly interrupt his process of reinforcement and rebuilding before it was fairly under way. So in early December, as Bhamo was about to be yielded by the Japanese, China Theater applied itself to reinforce the Chinese units that were between the Japanese and Kunming.

Attempts To Reinforce the Kweiyang Area

The most immediately important part of ALPHA was the redeployment of reliable Chinese troops to stiffen the defenses of Kunming and Chungking

---

[17] History of IBT, I, 134–35.
[18] *Stilwell's Command Problems,* p. 389.

against the two Japanese divisions which were in early December moving steadily onward toward the vital Kweiyang area. [19]

The American command believed that the defense of the Kunming area was absolutely essential, that if the Hump terminals there were lost it would probably mean the end of the war in China. Three Chinese armies were scheduled by the ALPHA plan to move to the Kunming area, the 57th from Sian, the 53d from the Salween front, and the 5th Army, which had done well in 1942 in the First Burma Campaign, from Yunnan.[20] General Wedemeyer believed that the Generalissimo had approved ALPHA and that the Chinese were therefore committed to carry out their part of the plan.[21]

The first hitch in the troop movements called for by ALPHA came with the Chinese 53d Army on the Salween front, which refused to move. When the issue was raised with the Generalissimo by General Wedemeyer, General Chien Ta-chun of the National Military Council said that the fault lay with the commander of the 53d. It later appeared that the Chinese authorities had issued orders on short notice canceling the movement but had not notified the Americans, who had kept their trucks and aircraft standing by to no avail.[22]

As to the 5th Army, which was to have completed this concentration, the Generalissimo announced that he had decided not to move it out of Yunnan, that it would defend Kunming the way the 10th Army had defended Heng-yang. This was an allusion to the long defense of the walled city of Heng-yang by the 10th, which had shut itself up within the city walls in July 1944 and defended the city until 8 August when it was overwhelmed by the Japanese. Wedemeyer's headquarters did not consider a heroic defense of Kunming as useful as stopping the Japanese some miles away.[23]

In the light of the difficulties caused by the Chinese decision to cancel the movements of the 53d and 5th Armies, General Wedemeyer felt obliged to protest to the Generalissimo on 9 December. Consistent with his appreciation of the Generalissimo's position, his approach was tactful, for he asked that all those present, save the Generalissimo, General Chen Cheng, General McClure, and the interpreter leave the room before he offered his views to China's leader:

Our memo No. 272 re operation, we think, is absolutely vital if we are to properly defend Chungking and Kunming. We have a Chinese copy attached to it. Here it is. One month ago we got together. One thing I told you then was, we must not lose the Kunming area which is our terminal of supply. It is also my understanding that you

---

[19] Memo cited n. 3(2).

[20] For Wedemeyer's views on holding Kunming, see Rad CFB 26558, Wedemeyer to Marshall for JCS, 17 Nov 44. Wedemeyer Data Book.

[21] Min, Mtg 3, Wedemeyer with Generalissimo, 21 Nov 44. Bk 1, Generalissimo Minutes.

[22] (1) Min, Mtg 14, Wedemeyer with Generalissimo, 6 Dec 44. Bk 1, Generalissimo Minutes. (2) History of China Theater, Ch. VI, p. 20.

[23] Min, Mtg 15, Wedemeyer with Generalissimo, 8 Dec 44. Bk 1, Generalissimo Minutes.

agreed. The second thing we talked about was the defense of Chungking and the ALPHA Plan was explained to you in full. The reason why I asked for special privacy to talk to you is that I want to talk to you directly and frankly. I hope you will accept it in the spirit given. Many decisions have been made, and I was told the Gimo made them. The result was the ALPHA Plan was disrupted, precluding orderly disposition of forces and supplies. Not knowing about these decisions, it is well nigh impossible as chief of staff to the Gimo to coordinate our efforts. I would like to have permission to draft directives to commanders in the field . . . have the Gimo and his Minister of War read and approve them . . . and then send them out . . . so that we can stop interfere {sic} with the execution of these directives from Chungking. This is serious. Americans like Gens. Chennault, Cheves and Dorn are working hard, trying to help; but constant changes of order rendered such help impossible. They appeal through me to get Gimo to approve a firm plan and stick to it. Changing of troop movement is easy for your staff—e. g., changing the 57A [57th Army] from Chanyi to Peishiyi, but a lot work is involved. As regards this change, I am told it is impossible to comply with the changed order, because thousands of gallons of gas will have to be moved from Chanyi to Peishiyi. The 57A must go to Chanyi. I have been here only a month; I feel we are having coordination and I hope to be able to help. When I have reports from the field—the airmen and the SOS men showing that they do not know what to do, that they do not have any firm orders and if there are, they change daily, I feel it is impossible for me as you {sic} chief of staff to serve well. I feel badly and concerned about this. Therefore I ask for privacy to talk to you. Time is short, and unless firm decision is made so that we don't have so many changes, I don't know how to cope with the situation. I do want to serve China.

Chen: It is true that the SOS orders often conflict with Operation orders.

Wedemeyer: I don't want to interfere. Now the Gimo may want to comment on the memo. These details should be known to the others too. Do you want the others to come in?

Gimo: Alright lets get the others to come in now. [The others re-entered.] I think all the troubles are results of bad liaison.

Chen: In the CEF [Chinese Expeditionary Force; the Chinese armies on the Salween front] there are one American officer and one Chinese officer who are made responsible to make a decision. If a decision could not be made then the issue would be submitted to the Gimo. At any rate, bad liaison does bring about misunderstanding.

Wedemeyer: Right now it is important to have good liaison. We must do it immediately. Will appreciate if you do so.

Chen: In the interim the remedy would be to have the heads of different ministries to work directly with the Americans, if they cannot settle a problem, submit it to General Wedemeyer who will make a decision and then go to the Gimo for approval.[24]

. . . .

In the discussion which followed, the Generalissimo remarked that he had diverted the troops from Chanyi because he feared that with the troops returning from Burma there might be congestion at Chanyi. Wedemeyer assured him that he and his American SOS would take care of any congestion that might develop. The Generalissimo suggested the immediate creation of a "combined staff," presumably an integrated Sino-American group,

---

[24] Min, Mtg 16, Wedemeyer with Generalissimo, 9 Dec 44. AG 337, Combined Staff Meetings with the Generalissimo, 1945–1946. Cabinet 2533, Dr 3, CT files, KCRC.

CHINESE-AMERICAN STAFF CONFERENCE *in China Theater Headquarters, Chungking. Around the table (left to right): General Chang Ping-chun, Director of Department, Chinese Ministry of Military Operations; General Chu Shih-Ta-chun, personal Chief of Staff to the Generalissimo; General Wedemeyer; Brig. Gen. Mervin E. Gross, Acting Chief of Staff, United States Forces, China Theater; General Liu Fei, Vice Minister of the Chinese Ministry of Military Operations; Col. L. G. Clarke, Assistant Chief of Staff, G–1, United States Forces, China Theater; and General Hsu En-sui, Director of the Chinese Services of Supply. (Photograph taken in 1945.)*

but Wedemeyer demurred because he currently lacked personnel. So the Generalissimo moved to solve the problems of co-ordination by suggesting that Chen Cheng, General Liu Fei of the Chinese Board of Military Operations, General Yu Ta-Wei of the Chinese Ministry of War, and General Chien Ta-chun, director of the Generalissimo's headquarters, join in the staff conferences with Wedemeyer and his assistants. Then, said the Generalissimo, "Preliminary decision should be made in these meetings and then submit to me for approval, and not vice versa." Wedemeyer agreed. [25]

[25] *Ibid.*

Then word came to theater headquarters from General Dorn that the 57th Army in Hsian, under General Liu, was refusing to move. The American SOS in China had trucks standing by all day long waiting for General Liu, as a result disrupting its supply schedules for that area. The American liaison officer reported to theater headquarters that Liu was in possession of proper orders but refused to heed them because he wanted to move his forces to the west. Such incidents as those of the 57th and 53d Armies could disrupt the whole of the ALPHA plan, while the resultant delay was a serious matter. Since Wedemeyer as of mid-December was in the field inspecting his theater, his chief of staff, General McClure, raised the issue with the Generalissimo on 16 December.

The Generalissimo's reaction was that the commander of the 57th Army was not to blame if he had not received his movement orders. Responsibility fell on General Ho, in Chiang Kai-shek's opinion. His final decision was that Ho should investigate while General Liu would be ordered back to Chungking to explain. Later that day it appeared that General Liu was charging that the U.S. liaison officer had tried to give him orders, to which the American reaction was that the liaison officer had simply been trying to get the movement under way according to plan.[26]

A few days later General Ho gave his version of what had happened to the 57th Army. Orders to move the 57th Army had been received through the American liaison officer but General Liu had received so many different orders about the 57th Army's movements that he had refused to comply with this order. Then General Ho passed to the heart of the matter, the Chinese doctrine on command. He explained that a field commander would take orders only from his superior officer, not from a liaison or staff officer. Therefore, by implication, although these orders had been issued by the Generalissimo or the National Military Council they would not be binding on General Liu because they had not been transmitted directly.[27]

These delays in troop movements meant that not all of the reinforcements called for by ALPHA were in place by mid-December. Part of the 57th Army was finally flown toward the Kweiyang area. The 94th Army was en route by truck and foot from its stations around Chihchiang to reinforce the 17,000-man 13th Army which was already at Kweiyang. The New Sixth Army from Burma was on the way to move into reserve behind Kweiyang; most of one division was back in China by mid-December. Falling back toward Kweiyang from the south and southeast were the remnants of the 67th and 64th Armies. These scratch forces, the Fourteenth Air Force, and moun-

---

[26] (1) Rad CFB 29139, McClure to Dorn, 14 Dec 44; Rad CFB 29244, McClure to Dorn, 16 Dec 44. Items 175, 177, Bk 1, ACW Personal File. (2) Min, Mtgs 20 and 22, Wedemeyer with Generalissimo, 16 Dec 44. Bk 1, Generalissimo Minutes.
[27] History of China Theater, Ch. VIII, pp. 10–12.

tainous terrain stood between the Japanese and a great triumph, if the enemy was of a mind to attempt the seizure of Kunming and Chungking.[28]

Wedemeyer Reshapes His Organization

Having initiated troop dispositions to enable China Theater to ride out what seemed an approaching storm, Wedemeyer applied himself to setting up an organization to carry out his mission of advising and assisting the Chinese Government. His first weeks of command had been spent in studying his situation, and he had necessarily exercised command through the machinery he had inherited. Now, by mid-December, his ideas had taken form and he was ready to create an administrative machine in harmony with them.

When Wedemeyer arrived in China to take command, he found that the headquarters staff he inherited in Chungking was a small one. In March 1944 the old CBI headquarters had been divided between Chungking and New Delhi. The greater part of the staff went to New Delhi, while the members who remained in China as the Forward Echelon had duties limited to liaison with Chinese agencies, co-ordinating and supervising within China the execution of theater directives, and aiding theater headquarters in policy preparation and planning for operations in China.[29] This mission resulted in a staff so small that the G-1 section, for example, had but one member. Plainly, such a staff could serve as the nucleus of a theater headquarters, but badly needed expansion.

When in December Wedemeyer reorganized his headquarters he took great care to provide continuing attention to advising and assisting the Chinese and to his own logistical problems. On 13 December 1944 Wedemeyer divided his headquarters into a forward and a rear echelon. At Chungking, the wartime capital of China, was the Forward Echelon with the assistant chiefs of staff for intelligence, operations, plans, supply, and, in January, civil affairs (G-5). The Assistant Chief of Staff, Plans, had two subsections in his office, the U.S. Joint Planning Staff and the Theater Planning Section. In addition to the general staff sections came those of the special staff, including offices for psychological warfare, air, air-ground aid, plus the adjutant general, signal officer, judge advocate general, and the engineer.

The new Rear Echelon, at Kunming, was headed by General Cheves, SOS commander, with the title of theater Deputy Chief of Staff. Cheves was also made G-1 and assistant to the China Theater G-4. Also present was the Hump Allocation Officer, with a staff channel to G-4 at Chungking. Special staff sections included the assistant adjutant general, engineer, and signal

---

[28] *Ibid.,* pp. 14–15.
[29] See *Stilwell's Command Problems,* Ch. VII.

officer, plus the ordnance officer, surgeon, provost marshal, inspector general, fiscal officer, and finance officer. Rear Echelon was therefore organized and staffed to work closely with the SOS on problems of logistics and administration, with matters arranged so that both types of problems would cross Cheves' desk. Moreover, if Japanese pressure should force Wedemeyer to evacuate Chungking, there would be administrative machinery in Kunming to which he could join the Forward Echelon at short notice. An evacuation plan was drawn up in November and December, and was ready if the Japanese moved into west China.

General Cheves had a key role in the new organization, that of coordinating logistics and administration. One of his duties was to preside over the mechanism of Hump tonnage allocation. In explaining the new arrangements to Cheves, Wedemeyer pointed out to him that he had to know both the Chinese and American deployments, since Cheves would be called on to equip the U.S.-sponsored Chinese divisions. In this connection the fact was brought out that 70 percent of the needed equipment was in China, 10 percent in India, and the rest on the way. The Chinese Combat Command, to be discussed below, was the headquarters through which Wedemeyer planned to supervise and control the operation of the ALPHA plan.

On 20 December, meeting at Kunming with senior officers of the India-Burma and China Theaters, Wedemeyer explained the thinking behind his arrangements. He intended that the greater part of China Theater's effort would be supervision over operations and supply of the ALPHA divisions. This supervision he broke down into three phases: (1) combat, in which the Americans would come very close to having operational control; (2) training, which they would completely supervise; (3) supply, where Americans would be present at every level. He remarked that it was imperative that the Chinese ground forces perform more effectively, that only the Fourteenth Air Force was presently between this conference and the Japanese.[30]

Wedemeyer's initial directives to his principal subordinates were issued very early in December, after consultation with Chennault (air), Cheves (SOS), and Dorn (Chinese ground operations). The theater commander's radio books reveal that his approach to these commanders was very similar to his approach to his staff; information was widely disseminated, opinions were sought, and decisions announced with enough background data to make the principal commanders in the field aware of what the theater commander was seeking.

---

[30] (1) Organization charts, Item 2, Wedemeyer Data Book. (2) Conf, Wedemeyer and Cheves, 17 Dec 44, Kunming, China. OCMH. (3) Min, IBT and CT Conf, 20 Dec 44, Kunming, China. OCMH. (4) The evacuation plan is described in Radiogram CFB 28509, and is also in the China Theater files, KCRC. (5) Min, Conf, McClure and subordinate comdrs, USFCT, 3 Jan 45. OCMH.

The directive to Chennault, like that of 1942, made defense of the airline to China (the Hump) Chennault's first task.   Then came, in order, air support for the troops protecting the ground line of communications to China; air cover for the SOS and air installations; air support for troops defending Kunming, including interdiction of Japanese communications; support of U.S. operations in the Pacific; air cover for the B–29's; reconnaissance; attacks on Japanese communications and supply installations; and prompt dissemination of intelligence to adjacent and higher headquarters.   On the logistical side, Chennault finally received command of the Air Service Command, and was made responsible for supply of all technical items for the Air Forces.[31]

The SOS had vast responsibilities, for, in addition to its normal duty of logistical support to U.S. military activities, it was given "the responsibility of insuring an uninterrupted and adequate flow of supplies, equipment, matériel, and personnel to . . . certain stipulated Chinese Forces in the Chinese Theater of Operations."   This included lend-lease.   Cheves was charged with requisitioning lend-lease from India–Burma Theater for initial equipment (in accord with the 36-division program) and for replacements.   SOS was to receive, store, maintain, distribute, and issue these stores.[32]

That the SOS would support certain Chinese forces was a great step forward for it meant that these troops would be assured a steady flow of food and ammunition.   Many Chinese military problems, in retrospect, seem to have arisen from logistical difficulties, the sheer uncertainty as to whether food and ammunition would reach troops in battle or on a long march.   Now, American logistical techniques were to be applied to supporting a select group of Chinese divisions.

On 17 November 1944 the American officers of the old Y–Force and Z–Force became the Chinese Training and Combat Command, the China Theater equivalent of a theater ground force, which received an operational directive on 2 December.   This organization was superseded in January 1945 by the Chinese Combat Command.   The December directive was, however, a milestone in Wedemeyer's evolving a solution to the problem of creating an effective Chinese Army.   It showed that Wedemeyer now gave a dual role to the American officers going out into the field; they were to advise the Chinese officers to whose headquarters they were accredited and also to keep in close liaison with subordinate and superior U.S. headquarters so that the American forces might have a steady flow of information.   Unit training was

---

[31](1) Chennault's comments on the draft manuscript of this volume underscore his feeling of satisfaction at the ending of a situation in which he did not control his direct logistical support. (2) Opnl Dir 1 to CG Fourteenth USAF, Hq USFCT, 1 Dec 44. Item 3, Wedemeyer Data Book. (3) Previous directives to Chennault are discussed in *Stilwell's Mission to China*, p. 187.
[32] Opnl Dir 2, Hq USFCT, 1 Dec 44.   Item 3, Wedemeyer Data Book.

to be in the areas assigned to the several armies under the ALPHA Plan. Two
service schools would present artillery and general staff training. Three
training cycles were projected for the troops. Into the first of two months
was to be crammed all the basic training possible. Phases two and three
would depend on the tactical situation.[33]

Therefore, in December, Wedemeyer set up machinery that permitted
him to keep in close touch with the Generalissimo and his government at
Chungking, provided a U.S. headquarters for administrative work in the rear
area, gave Chennault his taks in an order of priority that would permit the
airman to be increasingly aggressive as the situation improved, gave the SOS
the task of supporting selected Chinese troops, and provided for closer supervision of the training and operations of the Chinese ground forces designated
by Chiang to carry out Wedemeyer's plans.

Moving Toward Better Co-ordination

Because China Theater was an Allied theater, further complicated by the
presence of independent agencies, many of them in the field of intelligence,
machinery alone would not solve problems unless it was harmoniously
adjusted. So Wedemeyer made further efforts to better co-ordinate the different Allied agencies in China and his headquarters; the several U.S. commands and the Generalissimo; Wedemeyer and the Chinese troops in the
field. Since the question of Hump tonnage entered into most Allied activities in China, control of it gave Wedemeyer a powerful lever, which he soon
began applying to the Allied intelligence agencies.

In the winter of 1944–45, Wedemeyer's personal data book listed a variety of these: the Office of Strategic Services; Navy Group, China (which also
functioned in another capacity as part of a Sino-American agency for guerrilla warfare under the Generalissimo's chief of secret police); the 5329th Air
Ground Force Resources Technical Staff, which functioned as the Fourteenth
Air Force's intelligence net; the Air-Ground Aid Section; and the British intelligence agencies in China. Some of the problems created for Wedemeyer,
whether as the Generalissimo's U.S. chief of staff or as U.S. theater commander, by this group of semi-independent or completely independent organizations, can be suggested by the status of Navy Group, China. Its director,
Commodore Milton E. Miles, USN, was also deputy director of the Sino-
American Special Technical Cooperative Organization (SACO) whose director was General Tai Li, chief of the Generalissimo's secret police. Navy
Group, China, as such, supplied meteorological and ship movement data to
the U.S. Pacific Fleet. As part of SACO it trained and equipped guerrilla
fighters and assisted guerrilla operations. Beginning in July 1944 it received

[33] Opnl Dir 3, Hq USFCT, 2 Dec 44. Item 3, Wedemeyer Data Book.

a fair amount of Hump tonnage, about 175 tons a month, most of it small arms ammunition, semiautomatic arms, and high explosives.   Created in 1943 by special agreement between China and the United States on the cabinet level and commanded by the Commander in Chief, U.S. Fleet, Navy Group, China, was independent of Wedemeyer, but a potential source of embarrassment to him.[34]

British intelligence activities in China were a cause for concern.   Theater headquarters believed that the British had several thousand agents in China, whose primary mission was gathering intelligence on the Chinese, rather than on the enemy.   Preparation for the postwar period and protection of the British stakes in China, such as Hong Kong, appeared to the Americans to be high on the list of British interests.   From this intelligence activity the Americans received excellent target and shipping data, but little more.[35]

Wedemeyer believed this British activity concerned him both as U.S. theater commander and as a chief of staff to the Generalissimo.   He feared there was a clash of national policy between the United States and the British Commonwealth.   Thoroughly aware that the United States was trying to make China a Great Power, he felt that British activity was inimical to that purpose, and so warned the Generalissimo on 26 December 1944. Two days later he took action, asking the Generalissimo for permission to send a questionnaire to the several Allied agencies in China.   Precipitating this move was a British request for a fairly large allocation of Hump tonnage.   Wedemeyer was willing to give it if the Generalissimo so directed, but felt that as the Generalissimo's U.S. chief of staff he should know what was being attempted by the other Allied powers in China Theater.[36]

Giving weight to this warning, Wedemeyer sent the Chinese two memorandums which claimed that the uncontrolled activities of the various Allied military and political agencies in China held inherent dangers to the joint efforts of China and the United States, that the military activities of the other Allied powers in China might interfere with the military and political capabilities of the Chinese forces.   Thoroughly alert to the diplomatic implications of these steps, Wedemeyer kept in close touch with Ambassador Hurley.   On 2 January 1945 Hurley was advised by Wedemeyer that the intelligence situation was confused and potentially dangerous, and warned that integration and improvement were needed.

Shortly after, the situation and the measures taken were summed up by General McClure:

Because the Commanding General does not presently know about all groups operating in the Theater and having no control over them, the Generalissimo and the American

---

[34] Incls E, H, Item 17, Wedemeyer Data Book.
[35] Item 20, Wedemeyer Data Book.
[36] Min. Mtg 23, Wedemeyer with Generalissimo, 26 Dec 44; Mtg 24, 28 Dec 44.   Bk 1, Generalissimo Minutes.

B-29's HEAD FOR RANGOON *to bomb Japanese installations in support of British operations in Burma.*

Embassy are cooperating with the CG by actually tabulating the activities of all United Nations' efforts in China.   The information will include the number of organizations, personnel, missions, locations, and authority for being in the China Theater.   It is hoped that all American organizations such as OSS, SACO, etc. will be placed under the American second-in-command [in China Theater?].   It is recognized that there will always be some free agents moving about in the Theater, but it is desirable that there be control at least to the extent of a check in whereby the CG will know who these people are, what they are doing, and under what instructions.[37]

After the war, as he looked back on the intelligence problem, the theater's chief of staff, General McClure, doubted that a great deal had been accomplished toward unification of intelligence agencies.   He concluded that there had been a greater flow of low-grade information between agencies, but he had also seen evidence that separate agencies were purchasing the same information from the same sources.[38]

[37] Quotation from History of China Theater, Ch. III, p. 2, quoting Notes on Theater Conf, 3 Jan 45, in Wedemeyer Personal Ltr File 2.
[38] McClure comments on draft MS.

Another semi-independent agency in China, and one that bore heavily on theater resources, was the XX Bomber Command with its B–29's. In June 1944 the JCS had believed that B–29 operations from China would do more to help the Allied cause there than would turning over the B–29 stockpile to Chennault. So the B–29's flew their missions, under great logistical difficulties, and dropped 3,623 tons of bombs in Japan, Formosa, and on a few targets in China.

If this helped China, theater headquarters was not aware of it. Weighing results against costs, as early as summer 1944 General Arnold, commander of the Army Air Forces and a member of the JCS, had considered reducing the effort. From time to time, others within the Air Forces had criticized the costly B–29 effort from China.

In late October 1944, on the eve of Wedemeyer's arrival in China, General Hurley, the President's special representative in China, suggested to Roosevelt that the B–29's be withdrawn. Hurley argued that intensive air operations would hold southwestern China, that the Fourteenth Air Force was sorely handicapped because the B–29 Hump allocations were consuming its proper share of Hump tonnage. Believing that B–29 operations could not be justified in view of the emergency in China, he suggested moving them to Pacific bases. He closed by observing: "If we can hold the situation in China until National and Communist troops are united and Chinese Armies regrouped, then Chinese troops rather than Americans will be in a position to drive the Japs out of the country." The JCS asked Wedemeyer for his opinion, adding that they had planned for some time to move the B–29's to the Pacific when bases were available. But for the time being Wedemeyer was willing to have them stay.

By 4 December he concluded that the B–29's should go. Their presence in China put "prohibitive" limitations on his efforts. They consumed 14 percent of Hump tonnage in December 1944, and he felt that much greater results would be obtained, for example, by devoting that tonnage to equipping the Chinese forces and supporting the Fourteenth Air Force. On 12 January 1945 Wedemeyer repeated his recommendation.[39]

On 16 January 1945 China Theater received the JCS decision that the B–29's would at once move from bases in China to their home stations in India. There they would conduct limited operations before moving to the Mariana Islands in the Pacific. Having anticipated such orders, members of the XX Bomber Command staff had their plans ready; by 27 January the

---

[39] (1) Rad CFB 28167, Wedemeyer to Marshall, 4 Dec 44. Item 6, Wedemeyer Data Book. (2) History of IBT, II, 146. (3) Wesley Frank Craven and James Lea Cate, eds., *The Army Air Forces in World War II: V, The Pacific: MATTERHORN to Nagasaki, June 1944 to August 1945* (Chicago: The University of Chicago Press, 1953), pp. 150–51. (4) CM–OUT 55263, JCS to Wedemeyer, 31 Oct 44.

bulk of the command was back in India.   From then until the last India-
based mission on 30 March, the B–29's attacked Japanese-held ports and
Japanese shipping lanes around the Bay of Bengal, from Rangoon to Singapore.   As training their attacks were invaluable, but save for their bombing
of the great dry docks at Singapore, they contributed little to the war;
Japanese shipping by spring 1945 was an expended asset.[40]

On 17 December 1944 the Hump Tonnage Allocation and Control Office
was established in Rear Echelon, China Theater headquarters.   Its purpose
was ". . . to effect a proper balance of logistical support between the various
agencies within this Theater and to facilitate allocations to meet radically
changed tactical situations or other unpredictable or unforeseen contingencies."[41]   Every month, the new office, soon called HUMPALCO, received
from the Air Transport Command an estimate of its capacity for each of the
next four months, and from every agency in China that needed Hump tonnage an estimate of its needs for the next four months.   Estimates for the
immediate future were regarded as firm, and for the following three months
as planning data.

Then HUMPALCO's members, who included representatives of the China
Theater air, service, and ground force commands, and India–Burma Theater,
prepared a recommended allocation, which in turn went to the Chief of Staff,
U.S. Forces, China Theater.   On Wedemeyer's approving the recommendations as reworked or accepted by his own staff, the allocations became firm.

In the days ahead HUMPALCO was able to work out detailed data on
Hump support, what tonnage would be needed to equip and support the
ALPHA forces, what was the ceiling on U.S. personnel strength in China, and
so on.   In addition, since every soldier who entered China from abroad was
a burden on Hump tonnage, small individually but great in the aggregate,
Wedemeyer's headquarters through HUMPALCO sought to control the
influx of personnel.[42]

Still pursuing the theme of co-ordination, anxious to be sure that as
Chiang's U.S. chief of staff he would in the future know what orders were
going from Chungking to the Chinese armies in the ALPHA plan, wanting
to give General Ho, the ALPHA divisions' commander, proper discretion in
the conduct of operations, and hoping to arrange these matters during his
forthcoming inspection of China Theater, Wedemeyer in the second week of
December sought to persuade the Chinese to modify their system of command.   When on 6 December the Generalissimo commented on some orders
he had sent to Generals Hsueh Yueh and Chang Fa-kwei, Wedemeyer re-

[40] (1) Item 9, Wedemeyer Data Book.   (2) *The Army Air Forces, V,* 158–67.
[41] Cir 8, Hq USFCT, 17 Dec 44.
[42] Ltr, Col Louis W. Haskell, HUMPALCO officer, to Wedemeyer, 11 Oct 45, sub: Hist Rpt
of the China Hump Tonnage Allocation and Control Off.   OCMH.

GENERAL WEDEMEYER VISITS WESTERN COMMAND HEADQUARTERS, *Kweiyang, China, December 1944. From left, Col. John K. Sells, Commanding Officer, Western Combat Command; General Dorn; General Huang; General Szhung; General Wedemeyer; General Wei Li-huang; Lt. Gen. Yu Ta-wei, Chinese Vice Minister of War.*

marked that the commander in the field, who was now General Ho, should make his own troop dispositions. To this theme Wedemeyer returned again and again in the days ahead, stressing that Ho should have a broad directive within which to operate. Wedemeyer pointed out that the Generalissimo was making, in Wedemeyer's phrase, "too many decisions," and that this was disrupting the ALPHA plan. There should be a firm plan, adhered to by all.[43]

Having prepared the groundwork, Wedemeyer next on 11 December asked if he could draft directives of the sort he had in mind. The Generalissimo was, it appeared, happy to see such, so next day they were submitted to him. With them went the polite request that they be approved by 14 December, the day Wedemeyer planned to leave for the field. The Generalissimo on

---

[43] See Ch. III, above.

the 13th promised that the directives as submitted by Wedemeyer would be on hand at the airfield, approved, when Wedemeyer departed on the 14th.[44]

The order of 11 December 1944 the Chinese sent to General Ho placed him in command of the ALPHA forces. His duties would be to protect Kunming and Kweiyang, train reserves, safeguard communications, and stop enemy raids. He was to keep the enemy off balance so the concentration around Kweiyang could be completed. All air forces in the area would be under Chennault's command. The American SOS would assist Ho in solving his supply problem. Other war areas were to co-operate by attacking enemy lines of communications passing through them.[45] Taking the directive with him, Wedemeyer left for the area around Kweiyang.

The Japanese Menace at Its Height

Overcoming difficulties of terrain and more especially of supply, the Japanese *3d* and *13th Divisions* pressed on into Kweichow Province in three columns. The *13th Division* was moving up the main road on Tushan while the *3d Division* moved along mountain trails to reach Pa-chai (Tan-chai), about seventy-five miles southeast of Kweiyang. A third column, thought by the Chinese to be much smaller, began attacking Li-po, well to the rear of these two advancing columns, on 3 December.

For the defenders, the situation was enormously complicated by the lack of reliable information. General Tang En-po, who was in local command, had been hastily rushed to that area, and not all the members of his staff were with him. Communications had broken in the retreat, and in many cases General Tang did not know just where his units were.[46] Moreover, the condition of the defenders' morale disturbed Wedemeyer's staff; his chief of staff, McClure, told the Generalissimo that the troops south of Kweiyang were rife with desertion because their food was bad and that something had to be done to improve the rations.[47] Wedemeyer had hoped that Generals Chang Fa-kwei and Hsueh Yueh would be able to put pressure on the tenuous Japanese lines of communications, but on 8 December he was obliged to report to the Generalissimo that they were not obeying orders to do so. Even worse, the XXIV Group Army had gotten out of hand and was looting Chinese villages.[48]

To this picture, alarming to the American command in China, the Generalissimo added a reassuring touch. He impressed upon Wedemeyer that

---

[44] Min, Mtgs, Wedemeyer with Generalissimo: 14, 6 Dec 44; 15, 8 Dec 44; 16, 9 Dec 44; 17, 11 Dec 44; 19 13 Dec 44. Bk 1, Generalissimo Minutes.
[45] Ltr O, Generalissimo to Ho, 11 Dec 44. AG 300.4 (USFCT), KCRC.
[46] (1) Japanese Study 130, p. 30. (2) History of China Theater, Ch. VIII, pp. 13, 15.
[47] Min, Mtg 15, Wedemeyer with Generalissimo, 8 Dec 44. Bk 1, Generalissimo Minutes.
[48] *Ibid.*

the troops who were to defend Kunming and Chungking would do well, for they were Nationalist troops, whereas those who had sought to defend the east China airfields were provincial troops, and he considered that this explained the latter's poor performance in combat.[49]

At this moment, which appeared so pregnant with disaster, the Japanese halted. The *11th Army* had extended its pursuit beyond the prescribed limits and stopped only when its supplies were exhausted. It reported as much to the *6th Area Army,* which with a nice appreciation of the *11th's* sensitivities designated the present position of the *11th Army* as the limit of the pursuit. Soon after, the *11th Army* was ordered to pull the *3d Division* back to the area south of Liuchow while the *13th Division* was ordered to garrison the Kwangsi-Kweichow railway.[50]

When the Japanese withdrawal was discussed between Wedemeyer and the Generalissimo on 12 December, the latter correctly analyzed the Japanese movement, remarking that the enemy "had insufficient strength and was running out of time, anticipating Allied landings on the Asiatic mainland at any moment. The advance to Kweiyang was not part of the enemy's plan." [51]

Wedemeyer's Views on China's Problems

Wedemeyer was now forming more sharply defined views of China's problems, with which he as the Generalissimo's U.S. chief of staff daily had to deal. He presented them with candor and impartiality to his Chinese and American superiors. To General Marshall he sent on 16 December a long letter which Marshall forwarded to President Roosevelt:

(a) We must retain the Kunming area as our terminal of supply.

(b) Chungking should receive second priority, for its loss unquestionably would have disastrous political, economic, as well as psychological effects.

(c) The Chinese have no conception of organization, logistics, or modern warfare.

(d) The Generalissimo is striving to conduct the war from Chungking. The management of affairs of state in itself would require a Disraeli, Churchill, and Machiavelli all combined in one. The Gissimo will not decentralize power to subordinates.

In early conferences with the Generalissimo, I pointed out that we should make disposition of forces and allocation of equipment as early as possible to insure the defense of the Kunming area. I presented a plan for this purpose and he approved that plan. This was about four weeks ago. Now I find that he is vacillating—in fact, he has ordered movements of divisions from the Kunming area without my knowledge. There are increasing indications that he no longer accepts the premise that Kunming should receive first priority. Apparently his advisers in the interim have emphasized the necessity for holding Chungking which, as stated above, we agree is necessary, but only after we have made appropriate preparations for the defense of Kunming.

---

[49] Min, Mtg 12, Wedemeyer with Generalissimo, 4 Dec 44. Bk 1, Generalissimo Minutes.
[50] Japanese Study 130, p. 31.
[51] Min, Mtg 18, Wedemeyer with Generalissimo, 12 Dec 44. Bk 1, Generalissimo Minutes.

Recently in discussing the defense of Chungking with the Generalissimo, I mentioned that we should make plans now for evacuation should the enemy advance continue on the capitol and require our withdrawal. The Generalissimo categorically stated that he intended to remain in the capitol and die here, if necessary. He has stated this on two other occasions, General, once in Nanking and again in Hankow, but was prevailed upon by his advisors to get out at the last minute. My purpose in making plans is to preclude chaos and confusion under the circumstances and to insure that we could set up a seat of government in some other appropriate location, preferably Kunming. There are so many political implications in everything we do here that this may not materialize. For example, the Governor of Yunnan Province and the Generalissimo are very unfriendly. Further, the Generalissimo wants to remain near Szechuan Province . . . . If he goes to the Kunming area, the Governor of Yunnan may kidnap him or at least place him under protective custody. Also, he would be cut off from provinces to the north, Szechuan, for example.

In connection with the Americans, I have plans for their evacuation—in fact, I am gradually moving officers and men to the Kunming area. I will remain here with the Generalissimo as long as possible. . . .

[Wedemeyer here remarked that if he could obtain Chinese co-operation, stop vacillations, and inspire some will to fight on the part of the Chinese, all might yet be well. Then he resumed:]

My approach to the Generalissimo has been friendly, direct, and firm. I believe that he likes and respects me now. It is the influence and chicanery of his advisers, who have selfish, mercurial motives and who persuade him when I am not present to take action which conflicts with agreed plans. . . .

We have recommended dispositions which, if the Chinese will fight with determination and elan, should insure the security of the capitol. Also, we are moving an ample supply of munitions centrally located for the troops. We could make a continued Japanese advance costly, in fact prohibitive, in time and effort. It is difficult to imagine the pressure that is being brought to bear from various facets and high officials to concentrate for the defense of Chungking in lieu of Kunming. In this connection it is amusing and also tragic to note that many high-ranking Chinese officials are asking me to facilitate their evacuation to America by air. [Two such requests by senior Chinese generals are] indicative of the psychological approach of Chinese who should know better. Self-sacrifice and patriotism are unknown quantities among the educated and privileged classes.

We have taken steps to improve the diet of Chinese soldiers. The Chinese soldiers are starving by the hundreds. . . .

In connection with troop movements, the Chinese march an outfit from A to B and make no provision for bivouacs, food, and so forth along the route. This is being taken care of. If only the Chinese will cooperate! American officers have been designated to supervise such movements and we are well on the way to exercising constructive influence with regard to this very important factor. The Generalissimo often asks me to move by air 50,000 men from A to B, and after carefully studying such movement we make appropriate arrangements. Suddenly he will order a change and there are all kinds of ramifications involved which render it impossible or at least impracticable to comply with his wishes. Neither he nor his advisers really understand supply and movement problems. But they ask for the most astounding troop movements to implement their strategy, which is really piecemeal, uncoordinated employment of forces.

The Chinese SOS is terrifyingly inefficient. . . .

I have already indicated to the Generalissimo that here in Chungking we must issue broad policies and directives to responsible commanders in the field and that we definitely must not tell them how to carry them out. If we find that these commanders are not complying, then relieve them. I emphasized that it is wrong to direct operations from Chungking. Although he has agreed to the soundness of this approach, he violates his agreement almost daily, and this adds to our difficulties. I told you that he did not give me the best Chinese general for the command of the ALPHA Plan, yet I impressed upon him that it was the most important military operation with which any Chinese had ever been charged. I receive continual reports of the inefficiency of General Ho. . . . For political reasons the Generalissimo does not desire to remove him from a position of responsibility in the war effort.[52]

Wedemeyer also reported to the Generalissimo on the state of the Chinese armed forces and the reasons for it. On 26 December he met with the Generalissimo, U.S. Ambassador Hurley, and T. V. Soong. The occasion on which Wedemeyer spoke thus to the Generalissimo was in many ways an auspicious one. The Generalissimo, working closely with Ambassador Hurley, had effected a considerable reorganization of his government, in which Chinese who had impressed some influential Americans as being both liberal and efficient had been brought to positions of responsibility. Moreover, Hurley thought he had made considerable progress in his attempt to unify the Communist and Nationalist forces under the over-all leadership of the Generalissimo. In these weeks, T. V. Soong on 4 December became Premier of China, as well as Foreign Minister, and there was considerable optimism as to the immediate future.[53]

It was against this background, and to these high personages—the Generalissimo, Soong, and Hurley—that Wedemeyer offered his observations and remedies. His comments were significant in their implicit rejection of the Chinese claim that lack of arms was responsible for Chinese setbacks at Japanese hands. Rather, Wedemeyer stated in so many words, the Chinese had neglected their armed forces, and this was why Japan had been able to move her forces at will over China.

Wedemeyer introduced the topic by commenting on the problems raised by the return of the 14th and 22d Divisions to China. The two divisions had become accustomed to being properly fed and to receiving their pay in full and on time. If these two divisions, on which Wedemeyer had earlier said he placed primary reliance for the defense of Kunming, were to be placed on what Wedemeyer thought the usual Chinese standards, the resulting morale problem might cause serious concern were the Japanese to resume their drive. After contrasting the men of the 22d and 14th Divisions with

---

[52] The remainder of his letter General Wedemeyer devoted to military matters, such as permission to use the B–29's against Hankow. Memo cited n. 3(2).
[53] Rpt, Hurley to State Dept, 23 Dec 44. Hurley Papers.

those barefooted, poorly clothed, and ill-fed Chinese troops he had seen in east China, Wedemeyer told the Generalissimo, Soong, and Hurley:

> . . . We must do something although it would cost the government a great deal of money. He [Wedemeyer] has told the Generalissimo several times that the Army must be well fed, clothed, and paid in order to fight and be kept in the Army [*sic*]. Divisions which are loyal to the Generalissimo and soldiers who are willing to fight should receive priority in such a program. While we have the east wall secure against the Japanese attacks, we have to train. We have several hundred divisions now. That is too many. If we can train and equip 36–50 divisions well, we can drive the Japanese out.
>
> Generalissimo said he quite agreed and had talked to General Chen Cheng about this.
>
> General Wedemeyer said he too had talked to General Chen Cheng who agreed. About the size of a division, we feel that 10,000 should be the strength of a division. This is a good size to be adopted, at least for the remainder of the war. We don't like the tremendous number of porters in a division, for example—it was found upon inquiry that an Army of 30,000 had but 2,000 rifles to go around.

Then the issue of pay for the Chinese Army in India arose. Their pay in India had been regular, and by constant effort NCAC had seen to it that the men were able both to receive and to keep their pay. The Generalissimo's comment was that the returning soldiers should have their pay cut to the usual level. This drew a strong reaction from Wedemeyer, who ". . . replied that he didn't mean special treatment but that he thought the Chinese Government had neglected the Army. That is why the Japanese have had a free hand. He proposed to raise the standard of all other armies. Since Generalissimo has reorganized the Government, this is a psychological moment to do this and raise morale."

Taking a constructive approach to the problem, Wedemeyer said that he might be able to give each Chinese soldier $1.00 in U.S. currency a month. Acceptance of this proposal by the Generalissimo would mean that the United States might ultimately become the paymaster of the Nationalist forces. The Generalissimo at once offered a major qualification, for he insisted that the money should not be given directly to the soldier (for him to exchange on the local money market as a sort of hedge against inflation), but that the United States should give the dollars directly to the Central Government, which would then given the soldier $100 a month in Chinese Nationalist currency. This would in effect set the rate of exchange at 100 to 1. Since the black market rate was about five times that, and rising daily, the whole purpose of Wedemeyer's suggestion, which was to give the soldier some pay in stable currency, would be lost, and instead the Central Government would receive a direct monthly subsidy in U.S. dollars.

Wedemeyer replied that ". . . he didn't wish to butt in, but the Generalissimo said he would like for me to be frank. The Army is neglected and the rich do not want to sacrifice. He fully agreed with the Generalissimo that there should be no special privilege. The standard I have in Burma, should be the standard they have in the entire Chinese Army."

The last major issue raised at the conference was a brief comment by Wedemeyer, advising the Generalissimo and Soong that Wedemeyer's staff was working on Plan BETA, for an offensive against Kweilin, Liuchow, and Canton.[54]

Cherry Blossom and Sea Wind

Meanwhile, in the south of China, the Japanese *23d Army* was establishing contact with the *French Indochina Garrison Army*. The *23d Independent Mixed Brigade* took Nanning on 24 November after brushing aside the provincial levies who were in the way. Behind at a leisurely pace followed the *22d Division*. It was then transferred from the *23d Army* to the *11th Army,* and the principal strength of the *23d Army* began to return to home stations in the Canton–Hong Kong area. Taking over the establishment of contact to the south, *11th Army* opened the road on 10 December. It then began preparations to transfer the *37th* and *22d Divisions* to Indochina to bolster that area against the feared American amphibious assault.

Establishment of contact with the *French Indochina Garrison Army* did not mean the establishment of a workable line of communications from Korea to Indochina as current Japanese propaganda claimed. Facing the realities of transport in China, *6th Area Army* concluded that "The improvement in the strategic situation by the occupation of the route between Yungning and French Indochina served as practically nothing but a temporary route for passage of small groups," by means of which the Japanese sent the *22d* and *37th Divisions* to Indochina. The transfer made, the link "lost its practical significance."[55]

The week's span between 3 December 1944, when the Japanese halted their incursion into Kweichow Province, and 10 December, when they linked their forces in South China with those in Indochina, is the high-water mark of Japanese conquest on the mainland of Asia in the first half of the twentieth century. The Japanese had accomplished great martial deeds. They had carried their emblem of the Rising Sun from the border of Siberia through the great empire and culture of China, the nations and European colonies of Southeast Asia, and on to the soil of India. In so doing they had inflicted grievous wounds on that Chinese Nationalist regime which had appeared so promising in 1937, torn great provinces from the French and British imperial domains, driven the United States from the Philippines, and by shattering the

---

[54] (1) Min, Mtg 23, Wedemeyer with Generalissimo, 26 Dec 44. Bk 1, Generalissimo Minutes. (2) See also Meeting 21 of 15 December, at which the Generalissimo said he wanted to bring the whole Chinese Army to the standard of the Chinese Army in India. (3) Exchange rate from Chart B, Annex E, History of the Procurement Branch, G–5 Section of the General Staff, Hq, U.S. Forces, China Theater. OCMH. It was 1,000 to 1 in June 1945, 3,500 in August, 1,200 in September.

[55] Japanese Study 130, pp. 40, 64.

existing order given opportunity and encouragement to revolutionary forces, some of them genuinely nationalist but others deeply committed to an imperialism as militant, if more subtle, than the Japanese.

The Japanese conquest had been a tremendous feat. The empires of Genghis Kahn, Tamerlane, and Attila had been succeeded by one as vast as any of theirs, ruling over populations as great, but now to prove as ephemeral as the cherry blossom. Because the Japanese conquest was in the Oriental tradition it was to Western eyes of the twentieth century stained by deeds of cruelty. The sack of Nanking in 1938 paralleled the Mongol slaughter at Ctesiphon, centuries before. The massacre of prisoners was the fate of those who had, in Oriental eyes, by their surrender forfeited claim to consideration. Now, in December 1944, the moment of greatest expanse, the Japanese conquests were in their gravest peril.

In the Pacific, the American forces had everywhere burst through the island barrier that was to have defended Japan from attack on and over the seas. Those islands were bits of land on which the great figures of Oriental history had never gazed but their possession in the end meant more to Japan's destiny than did that of the great cities of China. On 24 November 1944, 111 B–29 bombers attacked Tokyo from bases in the Marianas, the first of many similar raids. About a month later, the Japanese line on Leyte Island in the Philippines was broken and the Americans' hold on that island was secure. The *SHO* Operation, the Japanese attempt at a decisive counterattack, was a failure, while the Americans had bases from which they could attack Japan itself. In Burma, British forces in strength crossed the Chindwin River in early December. This was the major thrust into central Burma, and its goal was Mandalay. The time had come for the Japanese to shape a new strategy and both *Imperial General Headquarters* and Okamura's headquarters undertook the necessary studies. Drafting new plans would take time. Meanwhile *China Expeditionary Army* began to prepare operations of very direct interest to the Fourteenth Air Force.

The Fourteenth Air Force Versus the Japanese

In the Suichuan area of east China, about 130 miles east-southeast of Heng-yang, the Fourteenth Air Force had an airfield from which it had staged operations toward the east in 1943. In line south of Suichuan were two other fields, Kanchow (Kan-hsien) and Namyung (Nan-hsiung). After the loss of his major fields in east China, Chennault moved a task force to these fields, which lay well to the east of the Japanese corridor through east China and so were supplied by transports flying across the Japanese lines.[56]

---

[56] Chennault, *Way of a Fighter*, p. 326.

To the west of the Japanese corridor was Chihchiang, about 185 miles from Heng-yang, and this too became a base.

In their planning for *ICHIGO,* the Japanese had appreciated Suichuan's importance and assigned it as an operational goal, to be taken after Kweilin and Liuchow. Another mission to be completed about then was the clearing of the southern end of the Hankow–Canton railway—it will be remembered that the Japanese drive on the east China air bases had swung west in a great arc past this segment of rail line. This planning had been completed between January and March 1944, and much had happened since then. The American advance westward across the Pacific made it appear that landings on the China coast were an imminent probability. The solution to the problem set by these three factors, of which clearing the rail line seemed the most important to the Japanese, was issued as an order in early December.[57]

The plan called for the *40th* and *27th Divisions* to move south from the Heng-yang area, target date mid-January 1945. The *40th Division* was to proceed down the railroad. Because the rail line was to be captured intact, the Japanese began training special raiding parties to race ahead and seize the bridges and tunnels before the Chinese could destroy them. The *27th Division* was ordered to swing wide from Heng-yang to the Suichuan area, and overrun the airfields. The *23d Army* at Canton was to send two columns north which would meet the *40th* and *27th Divisions* coming south. On the successful completion of the operation, the *40th* and *27th* would proceed to Canton to join the garrison there.[58]

Chennault appreciated Japanese capabilities and had no illusions that the enemy would leave him alone in Suichuan. The Chinese troops around Suichuan were those of General Hsueh Yueh, who had sacrificed his Tenth Army to hold Heng-yang, and Chennault did his best to obtain arms for Hsueh, as has been noted above. Hsueh was not in the good graces of the Generalissimo, and these requests were all turned down, the Generalissimo saying that Hsueh's pleas should be "disregarded."[59]

In the meantime, there was work to be done, and Chennault bent himself to it. After the war he looked back on the achievements of the Fourteenth Air Force in December 1944 and called then "phenomenal." Several factors contributed to the Fourteenth's ability to surmount the loss of its old fields. Its supply situation was much easier. In the last quarter of 1944, the Fourteenth received a monthly average of 9,274 tons of gasoline and lubricants as against a monthly average of 5,987 tons the quarter before. That much of

---

[57] (1) *Imperial General Headquarters* (Army) Order Regarding Execution of Operation No. 1, 24 Jan 44, App. 1; Plan for Operation No. 1, 10 Mar 44, App. 3. Japanese Study 129. (2) Japanese Study 130, p. 43. (3) Japanese Study 129, pp. 65–66.

[58] Japanese Study 130, pp. 43–44.

[59] Min, Mtg 16, Wedemeyer with Generalissimo, 9 Dec 44. Bk 1, Generalissimo Minutes.

FOURTEENTH AIR FORCE B–24 *heads for home after bombing Japanese supply dumps at Hengyang, China.*

this was flown to Suichuan instead of Kweilin did not eliminate the effect of the increase. The Fourteenth had more aircraft, and better. Chennault himself in retrospect gave first importance to having a theater commander whom he believed to be sympathetic to him, and second to his no longer having to give close support to the Chinese, which meant he was free to attack prizes greater than well-dispersed and cleverly camouflaged Japanese infantry.[60]

The Fourteenth Air Force was organized into two composite wings of the Army Air Forces, one Chinese-American Composite Wing, a fighter wing, and one group of heavy bombers. The 69th Composite Wing in west China had four fighter squadrons and three medium bomber squadrons; in east China the 68th Composite Wing had three fighter squadrons with bombers attached when necessary. Covering the Yangtze River, the Chinese-American Composite Wing, which offered the hope of expansion into a future Chinese Air Force, comprised eight fighter squadrons and four squadrons of

---

[60] (1) Chennault, *Way of a Fighter,* pp. 329–31. (2) Fourteenth AF Annual Summary, 1944. OCMH.

mediums.   The 312th Fighter Wing had five squadrons for the defense of Cheng-tu.   In terms of aircraft assigned, the average monthly strength in the last quarters of 1944 was 501 fighters, 106 medium bombers, and 46 heavy bombers.   These were supported by 30 transport aircraft and 31 photo reconnaissance aircraft.[61]

The opposing Japanese *5th Air Army* was a much smaller and weaker force, whose principal combat elements as of mid-November had 56 fighters and 38 medium bombers and a grand total of 152 aircraft of all types.   The Japanese in China were fully aware of the cumulative effect of their long series of defeats in the air.   They sadly lacked experienced pilots, while there was such a shortage of aircraft that even two old biplane fighters were pressed into service.   Capture of the Fourteenth's fields had not eased the problems of the Japanese, for their radar was inadequate, the bases were open to surprise attacks, and the poorly functioning Japanese lines of communications made it hard to obtain spare parts and fuel.   However, the Japanese decided they would occupy Heng-yang and attempt operations from there.[62]

The Japanese attempt to base squadrons at a forward airfield that lacked radar warning, in the presence of an aggressive opponent, was a venture as costly as had been similar Allied efforts in 1942.   On Armistice Day of 1944 the Fourteenth Air Force sent fighters against Heng-yang; the Japanese successfully intercepted.   The Americans had a slight edge in the fighting which followed, and then both sides separated to refuel.   While the Japanese service crews worked over their fighters, Chennaults' real effort of the day appeared—the Chinese-American Composite Wing, coming in at low level.   The Japanese were strafed and bombed heavily.   The Fourteenth viewed its attack as a complete success; the Japanese admit that they had to withdraw the air regiments they had attempted to base at Heng-yang.   Thereafter, the Japanese operated only army co-operation aircraft out of Heng-yang, camouflaging them with care, and taking full advantage of low visibility and bad weather.[63]

Since the Fourteenth's supply situation permitted it to average only eight fighter and four medium bomber sorties per aircraft a month, there was a lapse of a few weeks, and then the Fourteenth marked the anniversary of the Japanese attack on Pearl Harbor in 1941 with operations against Hong Kong and Nanking.   Fifteen fighters were sent against Hong Kong, and a similar force against Nanking.   When the fighters returned from Hong Kong they reported sinking a 10,000-ton liner and a destroyer and damaging four trans-

[61] (1) Organization Chart, Fourteenth AF, 1 Jan 45.   Item 8, Wedemeyer Data Book.   (2) Fourteenth AF Annual Summary, 1944, p. 8.   OCMH.   (3) Chennault comments on draft MS.
[62] Japanese Study 82, pp. 118–19.
[63] (1) Japanese Study 82, pp. 117–19.   (2) Chennault, *Way of a Fighter,* p. 327.

ports but postwar examination of the Japanese records does not support the claim.[64]

Ten days later the Cheng-tu-based B–29's were directed against Hankow, Okamura's headquarters and the supply base for Japanese activities in central and south China. When in June 1944 Stilwell had sought permission from the Joint Chiefs to use the B–29's against Hankow it had been refused on the ground that the B–29's could help more in China by attacking Japan's industry than they could by bombing Hankow. Now the Joint Chiefs were willing to let them be used against major targets in China.[65]

Hankow seemed a most profitable target. It was a center of industry for the Japanese, who had long stressed local procurement, e. g., "coal, alcohol, weapons, and clothing." The prosaic fighter sweeps over the Japanese rail system in north and central China and the attacks on Japanese river shipping in central China, which when lucky could produce a spectacular blaze as ship and cargo exploded, had caused a massive congestion of Japanese transport facilities in the Hankow area. Over 100,000 tons of supplies were stalled at various way points. The Japanese had pinned high hopes on rebuilding the Peiping–Hankow railway, and had it almost ready for traffic by late November. Then Chennault's airmen damaged some of the key bridges and ended for the time hopes of using that rail line to replace the Yangtze River as a line of communications. So all this complex of stockpiles, factories, and warehouses in the Hankow area was sprawled out below the American bombsights.[66]

The effort made by the Fourteenth Air Force and XX Bomber Command against Hankow was in proportion to its importance. Seventy-seven B–29's and 200 of the Fourteenth's fighters and bombers were sent against Hankow in the course of 18 December 1944. When the day's action was over there was a thick pall of smoke over the three Wuhan cities loosely known as Hankow. There were follow-up raids over Hankow for the rest of the month, though not on the scale of that effort. It was a dramatic operation, which ten years later the Japanese rated as "highly effective." They did not attempt retaliation.[67] Their attempts to give air cover to Hankow and to their new airfields had sharply reduced their aircraft strength. What was left was deployed to the coast to counter the feared American landing.

The next phase in the Fourteenth's operations was a major effort against the rail lines that the Japanese were using. In early January 1945 the Jap-

[64] (1) Chennault, *Way of a Fighter,* p. 328.   (2) Opnl Summary, Fourteenth AF.   Item 8, Wedemeyer Data Book.   (3) Mil Hist Sec, Special Staff, GHQ FECOM, The Imperial Japanese Navy in World War II, 1952 (Japanese Study 116).   OCMH.
[65] See *Stilwell's Command Problems,* p. 369.
[66] Japanese Study 130, pp. 40–41.
[67] (1) Japanese Comments on draft MS.   (2) Chennault, *Way of a Fighter,* pp. 329–30.

anese succeeded in opening the Peiping-Hankow railway to through traffic. South of Hankow, on the line to Changsha, there were still gaps in the line where key bridges were down, but by unloading at some breaks and ferrying trains across others the Japanese found it possible to conduct a certain amount of traffic. Though the rail line was open, its performance was a disappointment because the Fourteenth Air Force destroyed so many locomotives. The cumulative effect was serious. The Japanese had planned to deliver 45,000 tons to Hankow by rail in January. They were only able to deliver 12,000, and had to supplement this figure by bringing 8,000 tons up the Yangtze.

In February the picture brightened. Twenty-five thousand tons were carried down from Peiping, and 8,000 again came up the Yangtze. But the rolling stock situation was serious. Chennault's new P-51's, with their great range, were all over north China, hitherto the citadel of Japanese power in China, and losses of locomotives were "very heavy." The Japanese had planned to move rolling stock from north China into central and south China. Now, they found that they could move only about 10 percent of the amount they had wanted to bring down, while the Fourteenth Air Force made the Yangtze almost useless. Given the cumulative effect of the Fourteenth's raids, the headquarters responsible for operations in central and south China, *6th Area Army,* could see the day was fast approaching when the Japanese would be unable to use their railroads south of the Yangtze.

The supply situation with regard to food, ammunition, and clothing was satisfactory. One of the fruits of *ICHIGO* had been the capture of more than 10,000 tons of munitions from the Chinese. Added to local procurement and what trickled down the line of communications from Hankow, this gave the Japanese enough to eat, wear, and shoot. There was, however, a significant shortage of motor gasoline and motor alcohol. Casting up their accounts, balancing their consumption against their resources plus their expected receipts, the staff of *6th Area Army* expected that 1 June 1945 would see the end of their gasoline stocks, and not until November did they expect to have alcohol in sufficient quantities.[68]

Therefore the grave shortage of motor fuel and the anticipated collapse of rail transport south of the Yangtze, the latter directly attributable to Fourteenth Air Force operations, caused the Japanese staff most directly concerned, that of *6th Area Army,* in late January 1945 to believe that the day was coming when the Japanese would have to loosen their grip on China south of the Yangtze. These conclusions were not shared by *China Expeditionary Army,* which under Okamura's guidance was meditating a spectacular drive

---

[68] (1) Japanese Study 130, pp. 35, 61–63. (2) Japanese Comments on draft MS.

on Chungking,[69] nor were they known to the American theater headquarters, which considered that the Japanese possessed "complete freedom of action."[70] Such conclusions by the Americans possibly reflected the vigorous operations that were being carried out by the troops of *6th Area Army* even as the Japanese staff was making its studies. As the estimate that the Japanese had complete operational freedom was being dispatched to Washington, the Japanese were on their way to occupy the Suichuan fields from which Chennault had in effect set a time limit to their further stay in south China.

The Suichuan Operation

Though there was a brief lull in operations following the Japanese withdrawal from before Kweiyang, beginning 5 December 1944, Wedemeyer was not complacent. His current appraisals correctly estimated that the Japanese were thinking of strengthening themselves against an American landing, but as he read the reports on the strength the Japanese had available he was at a loss to account for the pause in what had seemed a threat to Kunming. There was an explanation currently circulating, and on 10 January 1945 Wedemeyer called it to the Generalissimo's attention:

> The temporary slow-up of the Japanese, General Wedemeyer said, does not mean that the danger period is over. There are persistent rumors circulating that through the puppet Nanking Government [which the Japanese had set up under Wang Ching-wei to attract dissident war lords to their side] an understanding has been arrived at between the Japanese and the Generalissimo, and this understanding accounts for the Japanese slow-up. The strong Japanese force concentrated does not explain the slow-up. It is inconceivable that the Generalissimo would do such a thing without consulting his Chief of Staff. No doubt, these are malicious prevarications whose origin may be traced to the enemy.
>
> To this the Generalissimo was absolutely non-committal. There was no indication, emotional or otherwise, that he either denied or admitted it. His spontaneous reaction was a dry cackle.[71]

As noted above, the Japanese were later to deny such reports, but their circulation on so high a level suggests some of the tension underlying the grave courtesy of Wedemeyer's meetings with Chiang.

Even as Wedemeyer was hinting to the Generalissimo that sinister conclusions were being drawn from the very recent course of events in east China where the local commanders had been left to face the Japanese as best they could without arms or reinforcements from the Nationalist Government, reports were arriving in theater headquarters that the Japanese were building up their strength around Heng-yang. Intelligence reports spoke ominously of Japanese troop movements into the Heng-yang area and gave details about

---

[69] Japanese Study 129, p. 70.
[70] Rad CFB 31783, Wedemeyer to Marshall for JCS, 22 Jan 45. Wedemeyer Data Book.
[71] Min, Mtg 27, Wedemeyer with Generalissimo, 10 Jan 45. Bk 1, Generalissimo Minutes.

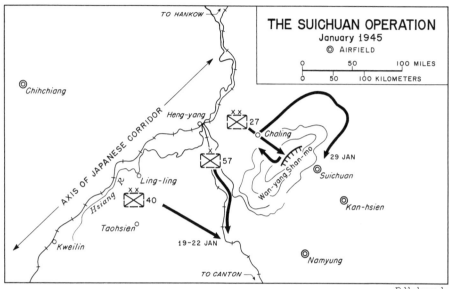

MAP 11

D. Holmes, Jr.

troop trains moving south from Peiping to Hankow, probably the *47th Division* as it moved into south China from Japan.   From these reports theater headquarters concluded that the odds favored a Japanese drive to open the Canton–Heng-yang stretch of the Canton–Hankow railway and to take the Suichuan fields.[72]   *(Map 11)*

In deploying for the attack to open the railroad and take the airfields, the Japanese spread out over a wide front, two divisions and one brigade over 180 miles.   At the extreme right, between Ling-ling and Tao-hsien, the *40th Division* sent specially trained raiding squads forward about 10 January. Their course was at about a 45-degree angle to the railroad, and as they made their way cross country they sought to avoid giving the alarm.   Between 19 and 22 January they reached the railroad and succeeded in occupying the key bridges and tunnels before the Chinese could destroy them.   In the center of the line, one brigade, the *57th,* made its way down the railway without incident.   Only on the left of the long, 180-mile line, where the Japanese *27th Division* was moving on the airfields directly, did the Japanese encounter resistance.   They had not expected this; their comments suggest they had not been impressed by the caliber of Chinese opposition during the east China campaign: "Judging from the enemy strength, existing situation and former tactics, it was more apparent that he would resist our attacks as a for-

[72] (1) History of China Theater, Ch. VIII, pp. 28–29.   (2) Japanese Study 129, p. 57.

mal gesture while his main body retired into the mountainous area to conserve its strength. It was estimated it would be difficult to make contact."[73]

The Japanese driving on the Suichuan fields moved in two columns. One, of probably no more than a regiment in strength, moved southeast from Chaling toward the airfields. The rest, "the main body of the *27th Division* with the attached *Iwamoto Detachment*," took the principal roads which swung first north, then east to the airfields, thus avoiding a hill mass, the Wan-yang Shan-mo. Because in mid-January the weather in east China becomes unsuitable for air operations, the Fourteenth Air Force was unable to give support to General Hsueh Yueh's troops.

The resistance offered by that commander's troops was somewhat spotty. In the neighborhood of Chaling, northwest of Suichuan, it was completely successful. The Japanese force there failed to penetrate the Chinese lines and had to be moved back to the rest of the *27th Division*. The main Japanese force seems not to have encountered serious resistance, for it covered 120 miles in ten days to occupy Suichuan on 29 January.[74]

With the Japanese actually on the move, Chennault again pressed Wedemeyer to obtain arms for Hsueh Yueh. A subsequent letter of Chennault's would indicate that General Hsueh had sought to bypass the Generalissimo, and had been rebuffed by Wedemeyer. In compliance with the policy guidance given him by Wedemeyer, Chennault warned Hsueh that the latter could hope to receive arms only from the Generalissimo. In a later radio, Chennault added: "In my opinion, Hsueh Yueh has now definitely affirmed his allegiance to Chungking, having learned for good and all from this episode that he cannot expect aid as an independent leader." In retrospect, it appears that perhaps it was General Hsueh's attempt to be an independent leader that lay behind the loss of the east China airfields and the reverses of the summer of 1944. The Generalissimo was not willing to send arms and reinforcements to so ambitious a subordinate, especially since a resounding victory over the Japanese by Hsueh Yueh might well result in the latter's gaining stature that would make him a rival of the Generalissimo. In any case, the Generalissimo had embargoed all arms and reinforcements for Hsueh. Now that Hsueh had made his submission, reconciliation and arms speedily followed, but far too late to affect the issue. Not until 22 February, many days after Suichuan's loss, did Hsueh tell Chennault that the Chinese Military Affairs Department in Chungking had issued him 1,200,000 rounds of rifle ammunition, 3,000 mortar shells, 270,000 hand grenades, all of which were in Chihchiang ready for delivery. Chungking also issued him

---

[73] Japanese Study 130, pp. 44–46.
[74] (1) Japanese Study 130, pp. 45–47.   (2) Chennault, *Way of a Fighter*, pp. 333–34.

150 heavy machine guns, 300 light machine guns, and 30 mortars, which were not yet in Chihchiang.[75]

Japanese occupation of Suichuan was an empty victory. The Fourteenth evacuated its ground personnel and aircraft to other fields. Since its operations had been on a hand-to-mouth basis there were no great stockpiles to be destroyed. All the Japanese inherited were empty runways, while Chennault's aircraft were active as before. However, the Japanese had opened the Canton–Hankow railway, and greatly reinforced the Canton area against the prospects of an American landing in that area.

Japanese estimates of the situation, as of late January 1945, differed according to the headquarters forming them. *Imperial General Headquarters,* noting that the Americans had established themselves in force in the Philippines near the Canton–Hong Kong area and being in the process of reshaping its strategy to cope with the danger of invasion that now faced Japan itself, found that the completion of *ICHIGO* had placed strong Japanese forces in a position to counter an American attempt to move from the Philippines to the Canton–Hong Kong–Formosa area. Okamura's headquarters, *China Expeditionary Army,* thought that Tokyo overestimated the danger of an American landing, and wanted to attack Chungking. *Sixth Area Army,* which was concerned with the day-to-day conduct of operations, viewed the future with apprehension, and the recent past without satisfaction:

The immediate objective of the Hunan–Kwangsi Operation, the destruction of the United States air force bases, had been accomplished and several of the marked air bases completely destroyed. However, we checked the enemy's action only temporarily and were unable to strike a fatal blow. Our speed and limited scale of operation, based chiefly on ground operations, could hardly cope with the enemy's speed in changing and equipping airfields. The only practical fruit of this operation was the expansion of a large zone extending from North China to French Indo-China for lookouts and observation of enemy air activities.[76]

---

[75] Rad CAK 5697, Chennault to Wedemeyer, 15 Feb 45; Rad CAK 6017, Chennault to Gross, 21 Feb 45; Rad, Chennault to West, 21 Feb 45; Rad CAK 6126, Glenn to Chennault, 22 Feb 45. Items 411, 432, 438, 439, Bks 1 and 2, ACW Personal File.

[76] (1) Quotation from Japanese Study 130, p. 31. (2) Japanese Study 129, p. 66. (3) Japanese Study 45, p. 173.

PART TWO

PLANS AND PREPARATIONS FOR OPENING A PORT IN CHINA

CHAPTER VI

The MARS Force and the Burma Road

While the Chinese divisions in north Burma had been pushing the Japanese out of the upper reaches of the Shweli valley and so off the trace of the almost completed ground line of communications to China, the moment had been approaching when the small American force in Burma was to receive its greatest test. It was given the mission of striking across the lower end of the Shweli valley to the old Burma Road and hastening the advance of the Chinese forces against the Japanese still on the upper trace of that road. The significance of this mission was that as long as substantially intact and battleworthy Japanese forces remained in north central Burma neither the operation of the new Ledo Road nor the flank and rear of the British forces now driving deep into Burma could be secured. Nor could the three American-trained Chinese divisions in Burma and the MARS Force be released to reinforce Wedemeyer. It was believed that the MARS Task Force, acting as a goad on the flank of the Japanese line of communications, could make a significant contribution to victory, while its performance would show whether the lessons of the GALAHAD experiment in long-range penetration warfare had been learned.

Marsmen Prepare for Battle

Though pushing the Japanese off the trace of the Burma Road tended to overshadow events elsewhere, it was only part of a larger operation, CAPITAL. Phase II of CAPITAL called for taking the general line Thabeikkyin–Mogok–Mongmit–Lashio by mid-February 1945; operations looking directly toward the completion of that mission had been under way simultaneously with those to clear the road. Sultan's current plan called for the forces under his command to swing east like a closing gate. To the north, this maneuver had pushed the Japanese off the trace of the road to China, but the rest of the swing was still to be made. MARS Task Force, the Chinese 30th Division, and the Chinese 114th Regiment had still to move east and cut the Burma Road below the Namhkam–Wanting area, the Chinese 50th Division had to take Lashio, and the British 36th Division had to cross the Burma

Road south of Lashio. This swing would sweep the Japanese from the area north of CAPITAL's Phase II line.[1] Meanwhile, the 38th Division (−) of the Chinese New First Army would be operating to the north in the Namhkam–Wanting area. The fighting in the northern part of the NCAC front, where NCAC's divisions had driven northeast to link with the Y–Force and break the blockade of China, has been described.[2]

The work of the rest of NCAC's forces, which did not reach its climax until February 1945, after the Ledo Road had gone into operation, developed south of the Shweli valley area, in and a little to the southeast of the triangle Namhkam–Mong Yu–Namhpakka. The Chinese forces from Burma and China, CAI and Y–Force, had met in the vicinity of the apex, at Mong Yu. The west side of the triangle was the Shweli valley, with Namhkam at its western corner. Forming the eastern side of the triangle was the Burma Road, on which were Mong Yu and Namhpakka. (Map 12)

NCAC believed that if MARS Task Force would thrust across the base of the triangle to the Burma Road, thus placing it closer to the locally well-known town of Lashio than were the Chinese, the latter might well be roused to emulate it through considerations of face. MARS would, it was hoped, spur the Chinese to greater activity in their operations.[3]

In deciding where to reach the Burma Road, Sultan rejected a suggestion, advanced by Easterbrook, the commander of the 475th Infantry, and adopted by General Willey, that MARS cut the Burma Road at a suspension bridge about twelve miles south of Namhpakka. A good trail led to the spot, the hills west of the road were within machine gun range of its traffic, and the Japanese could not easily bypass a roadblock there. But Sultan ruled otherwise. He did not think the Chinese would support a venture so deep into Japanese territory, and noted that the area did not offer a good site for a landing strip. He preferred the Ho-si area, farther north on somewhat flatter ground. But Ho-si had disadvantages, for there the Burma Road is beyond machine gun range from the ridge paralleling the road on the west.[4] There were also secondary roads in the hills to the east, by which the Japanese could escape.

The first step toward blocking the Burma Road would be the forward concentration of the whole MARS Task Force, which meant bringing up the 124th Cavalry to join the 475th. Since the 124th did not arrive at Myitkyina until late October 1944, it was not until December that its commanding officer, Col. Thomas J. Heavey, and NCAC thought it ready for the long march to combat. On 16 December the 124th moved south in an administrative march,

---

[1] See pp. 89–90, above.
[2] See Ch. IV, above.
[3] (1) NCAC History, II, 237.   (2) Willey comments on draft MS.
[4] (1) NCAC History, II, pp. 237–38.   (2) Willey comments on draft MS.

MULE SKINNERS AND PACK ANIMALS *of the MARS Task Force plod through the hills toward the Burma Road, January 1945.*

to proceed to the Bhamo area and there receive further orders.   Five days later MARS headquarters followed, and reopened at Momauk.[5]

Supply arrangements revealed how completely the campaign had come to depend on air supply.   The 124th was to report drop field locations forty-eight hours in advance; as they left camp the men would carry three days' rations and minimum combat loads of ammunition.   Animal pack transport, to face the hills ahead, was heavily relied on, though a few trucks had been improvised from the derelicts that dotted the Myitkyina landscape.[6]

As they left Myitkyina, the men of the 124th revealed in little ways that they had been a cavalry regiment, still felt like a cavalry regiment, and were walking to war though no fault of theirs.   Many of the troopers wore their old high-top cavalry boots, cut down an inch or two.   Here and there in the columns were small two-wheeled carts, improvised by the men, and pulled

[5] History of the 5332d, Chs. VI, IV.
[6] *Ibid.*

by ponies and little Burmese horses that the horse-wise 124th had enlisted for the duration. When called into federal service the 124th had been a Texas National Guard regiment. Transfers had diluted it, but 27 percent of the troopers were Texans.[7]

Marching along, the 124th passed through a settled area of Burma, part teak forest, part bamboo jungle with village clearings, and part rice paddy. The Burmese, from several tribes and peoples, would appear during breaks and bivouacs to barter or sell their chickens, eggs, rice, and vegetables. They rarely begged, unlike the Indians with their eternal cry of "baksheesh, sahib," nor were they endlessly persistent like the Chinese troops, but traded quietly and courteously. Sometimes the troopers descended on unwatched garden plots. Foraging and cooking, finding water, the occasional novelty of a pagoda, the problems of getting a good night's sleep and improvising a good meal, varied the days of slogging through dust and heat until the 124th reached Momauk, about six miles east of Bhamo. The hills were at hand, the Japanese were in them somewhere, the shakedown march was over.[8]

While the 124th was marching toward Momauk, the 475th and its supporting elements (the 612th Field Artillery Battalion, 31st, 33d, and 35th Pack Troops, 44th Portable Surgical Hospital) had been clearing the Japanese from the vicinity of Tonkwa. By Christmas Day it was apparent the Japanese had left the area,[9] and as soon as elements of the Chinese 50th Division should take over in the Tonkwa area the 475th would be ready to join the 124th. When it did, the 5332d would operate as a brigade for the first time. Originally, MARS was to have been an American-style division, composed of the two U.S. infantry regiments and the Chinese 1st Separate Regiment. The concept was fading, for the same order that directed the 124th and 475th to assemble kept the Chinese regiment in NCAC general reserve.[10] The 5332d would assemble in the Mong Wi area, within striking distance of the Burma Road. But between the two regiments and Mong Wi lay the Shweli River, and some of the roughest mountain country in north Burma.

Over the Hills and Through the Woods

Because Tonkwa is only some forty-five miles from Mong Wi, the 475th faced a shorter march than did the 124th, and was also closer to the mountains, two ranges of which, on either side of the Shweli, stood between it and Mong Wi. As 1944 closed, elements of the Chinese 50th Division were already across the Shweli on their way east, so the 475th would not have to

---

[7] Randolph, *Marsmen in Burma*, pp. 17, 56.
[8] *Ibid.*, pp. 73–92.
[9] See Ch. III, above.
[10] (1) FO 22, Hq NCAC, 26 Dec 44.   (2) Willey comments on draft MS.

worry about an opposed crossing but could follow the Chinese over the vine and bamboo bridge the 50th had built.   On New Year's Eve the American infantry left bivouac.   With them were 220 replacements that had been flown to the Tonkwa area and so began a rough march without the hardening their comrades had received during the journey south from Myitkyina.[11]

So close is Tonkwa to the mountains that the 475th found the trail rising steeply on the first day's march east.   Like a crazily twisted drill it bored its way farther east and ever higher.   In some places it was fifteen to twenty feet across; in others, just wide enough for a man and a mule.   As they rounded the turns, the men would peer ahead and look out across the valleys to where lay row on row of hills, like the waves of a frozen sea.   Trees were everywhere.   In flat places carved by erosion, the Burmese had cut and farmed terraces, and little villages clung to the mountains like limpets to a rock.

Because existing maps were unreliable, so that map reconnaissance could not locate water and bivouac areas, and because the sheer fatigue of climbing the steeper slopes was formidable, march schedules went out the window, or rather, down the mountain side, with quite a few steel helmets and an occasional mule.   Halts were a matter of common sense leadership at platoon or company level.

The march was tactical but no Japanese were encountered, though rumor of their nearness kept the men alert.   The Chinese had passed that way before, while a screen of Kachin Rangers was preceding the American column.   Speaking the local dialects and carrying radios and automatic weapons, the Kachins were an excellent screen which masked the MARS Task Force while reporting anything that might be suspicious.

The 124th also found the mountains worse than it had expected. Though there had been four organized attempts to lighten the baggage load, and much was left behind at Momauk, still, when two days' march from that village the men began their climb, they found that the steep incline forced them to jettison cargo in earnest.   The little two-wheeled carts made with such effort and ingenuity were no help; the trail was too much for them. The Burmese must have thought the lightening process a bonanza of cooking utensils, boots, underwear, spare fatigues, paper, and so forth.

For the 475th in the lead, crossing the 400-foot wide Shweli was not too hard.   The bridge built by the Chinese some weeks before still stood, a triumph of Oriental ingenuity, with bundles of bamboo for pontons and vines for cable.   The Shweli was beginning to tear it apart, but work parties from the 475th kept it operable.   Once on the far side, the 475th found its march more difficult than before.   The mountains were steeper and higher.

[11] Rad, TOO 0640, 31 Dec 44.   475th Radio File, NCAC Files, KCRC.

BAMBOO BRIDGE OVER THE SHWELI RIVER

Being higher, they were often hidden by cloud, so that air supply was impossible and the men went hungry.   Just as they were approaching Mong Wi, and the 124th was about to cross the Shweli, rain began.   Trails became extremely slippery and hazardous, and even the mules sometimes slid into ravines.   That day, 6 January, the 2d Battalion of the 475th evacuated twelve men as march casualties.

The rain fell on the 124th as it began descending to the Shweli.   The trail was over a fine red clay; when soaked, the footing became quite slippery. Men and mules skidded right on down to the river edge, in a mad muddy slide that mixed the comic and the hazardous.   Colonel Heavey would have preferred to cross elsewhere, but after the 124th had lost 4 January in looking for crossing points and waiting for an airdrop, and a series of radios had been exchanged between Heavey and NCAC, the 124th was told to cross where it could, providing it reached Mong Wi on schedule.   That time limit committed it to the muddy slide and the Chinese bridge.

Thanks to the rains, the Shweli was now in flood and pulling the bridge

apart.   Considerable rebuilding was necessary, while the bridge's flimsy, un-
stable nature made it a real hazard.   Mules were taken over one at a time;
not till one was safely off was another allowed on.   Sometimes the artillery
pack mules were unloaded and the cannoneers manhandled howitzer components.   When night came, crossing stopped.   Meanwhile, the rains fell.
Bad visibility precluded airdropping, so it was a wet, cold, and hungry unit
that finally stumbled into bivouac across the Shweli.   Because of the rain
and the search for a crossing site, it was not until 10 January that the 124th
was over the river and ready to march for Mong Wi.[12]   Heavey was not to
have the privilege of taking the 124th into combat.   The strain of the march
was too much; he was relieved and evacuated from a liaison plane strip cut
out near the Shweli.[13]

Concentration of MARS Task Force was screened by two patrol bases of
battalion strength, established by the 475th on 6 January.   Behind them the
475th waited for a supply drop at Mong Wi, as the 124th pressed eastward.
The 475th's wait was a wet and hungry one, then the weather cleared and
the transports brought food.   Their stomachs full at last, the combat infantry
troops were ready to move, and received their orders 8 January.   From the
soldiers' point of view the ground between Mong Wi and the Burma Road
was no improvement over that between Tonkwa and Mong Wi.   The central portion of the Loi Lum Range that separates Mong Wi and the Burma
Road is between 5,000 and 7,000 feet high, with trails so difficult that some
of the mules could not hold to them, and fell over the side.   Some stretches
were so steep that men could climb only for a minute or two, then had to
rest.

General Willey began to deploy his two regiments over 10 and 11
January.   Easterbrook was made responsible for the opening of operations
against the road.   Willey told him that with help from the 124th he was to
disrupt traffic on the Burma Road and to prepare a detailed plan of operations and submit it for approval.   The 124th would occupy the Mong Wi
area and free the 475th to advance.   Then Willey reflected, and decided that
more than the 475th would be needed along the Burma Road, for on 13
January both regiments were alerted for operations against the road.   Willey
also tried, but unsuccessfully, to obtain the services of the Chinese 1st Separate Regiment.   NCAC refused, but Willey's request made clear that he
wanted to drive on the Burma Road with the equivalent of a U.S. division.[14]

    [12] (1) Daily Jnl, 124th Cavalry.   NCAC Files, KCRC.   (2) Diary of Lt Col John H. Lattin,
Exec Officer, 2d Bn, 475th Inf.   OCMH.   (Hereafter, Lattin Diary.) (3) Randolph, *Marsmen in
Burma,* pp. 108–27.
    [13] Randolph, *Marsmen in Burma,* p. 125.
    [14] Rad, NCAC to 5332d, 0617 10 Jan 45; Rad, Willey to Easterbrook, 7 Jan 45; Rad, Willey
to Heavey, 10 Jan 45; Warning Order, 13 Jan 45; Rad, Willey to NCAC, 11 Jan 45.   5332d G–3
Jnl, KCRC.

While the 475th had been moving forward, the 124th had been resting and resupplying at Mong Wi. The break ended 15 January, and it set out for the Burma Road in the wake of the 475th. Again the march was a hungry one. The 124th's destination was Kawngsong, to the north and somewhat forward of the points the 475th was to seize. This meant that the 124th had to swing around the 475th and up ahead of it. To do this in rain, night, and woods was not easy; as the men moved into line two squadrons lost their way and bumped into the rear elements of the 475th. The tangle was straightened out, and as the scouts of the 475th were eying a quiet group of bamboo huts, the 124th was moving around the 475th's left flank.[15]

Harassing Japanese Traffic

Since General Willey understood that the MARS role was to encourage the Chinese to greater celerity in doing their part to secure the land route to China and had been ordered to hold down casualties, he did not try to place the 475th squarely astride the Burma Road, but gave it a mission that was qualified and hedged. He directed Easterbrook to strike against the Wanting–Hsenwi section of the Burma Road, to disrupt supply arrangements, and to place a roadblock, but not to become so deeply involved that he could not extricate his force. Willey also warned him to consider that he might be attacked from almost any side.[16]

The Japanese, for their part, had the *56th Division* plus the *168th Regiment* of the *49th Division* well north of the Hosi area, and the *4th Regiment* (Ichikari), *2d Division,* and the *Yamazaki Detachment* (about a regiment) just south and northwest of Namhpakka respectively. Namhpakka was a sensitive point, for it held a big Japanese ammunition dump. The *4th Regiment,* of about 1,000 men, was the unit that MARS now faced. But the other Japanese to the north and west were expected by MARS to react strongly, though for obvious reasons their strength, which was 11,500, was unknown. Since their mission was to help in the decisive struggle now taking form around Mandalay, the Japanese had no alternative but to make their way past MARS as best geography and the fortunes of battle permitted.[17]

The ground over which MARS and the Japanese clashed changed in character east of a north-south line about two miles east of Ho-pong. (*Map 13*) West of that imaginary line, the streams, flowing west, carved the earth so that the ridge lines ran east and west; MARS had gone east along the ridge

---

[15] (1) NCAC History, III, 302. (2) Daily Jnl, 2/475th Bn. KCRC.

[16] (1) Rad, Willey to Easterbrook, 10 Jan 45. 5332d G-3 Jnl. (2) Willey comments on draft MS: "Orders to me from the start not to lose U.S. men unnecessarily." (3) The Chinese did not know of these restrictions on MARS Force and expected it to block the road. Dupuy Comments.

[17] Japanese Study 148.

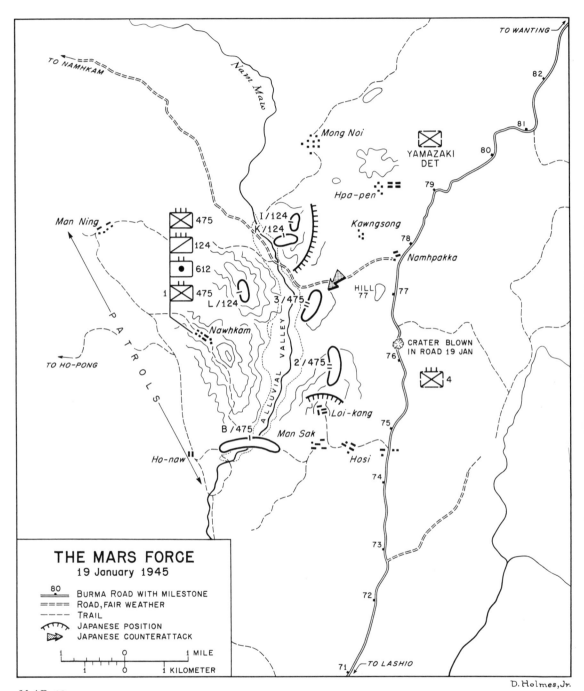

TO WANTING

TO NAMHKAM

Nam Mau

Mong Noi

YAMAZAKI DET

Hpa-pen

Kawngsong

Man Ning

475

124

612

1 475

I/124

K/124

L/124

3/475

HILL 77

77

Namhpakka

78

79

80

81

82

CRATER BLOWN
IN ROAD 19 JAN

76

4

Nawhkam

2/475

PATROLS

TO HO-PONG

ALLUVIAL VALLEY

Loi-kang

75

B/475

Man Sak

Hosi

74

Ho-naw

73

72

71

TO LASHIO

THE MARS FORCE
19 January 1945

80 — BURMA ROAD WITH MILESTONE
==== ROAD, FAIR WEATHER
---- TRAIL
JAPANESE POSITION
JAPANESE COUNTERATTACK

1   0   1 MILE
1   0   1 KILOMETER

D. Holmes, Jr.

MAP 13

463995 O–59—14

lines. Now, east of Ho-pong, the Americans found that the drainage pattern and the terrain had changed, for here the ridges, streams, and valleys ran generally north and south. One reason was a fair-sized stream about five miles to the south whose tributaries were cutting the ground along north-south lines.

About two and one half miles east of the ridge on which squats Ho-pong village, the next ridge line, reflecting the changed topography, bends to the south and east in an arc. On one of its peaks is a village of the Palaung tribe, Nawhkam, consisting of some forty bamboo huts or bashas on either side of the ridge-top trail. One mile east of Nawhkam is a little alluvial valley, perhaps three miles long and a half mile wide. One can imagine that the Palaungs tilled their rice fields there in better days, and perched their village on the ridge line for coolness and defense. Along the eastern edge of this narrow valley a string of three hills rises from 250 to 900 feet above the valley floor which is 3,600 feet above sea level. The southernmost and the highest of the three (in reality the northern end of a larger ridge) became known to the Americans as the Loi-kang ridge, after the Kachin village on its crest. The bean-shaped 3,850-foot hill in the center is the lowest, while the sprawling mass of the third hill near the northern end of the valley is approximately 4,250 feet high. From one to one and a half miles to the east of the hills is the Burma Road, the ultimate objective of the MARS Task Force. On the road, and behind the 4,250-foot hill, is Namhpakka. The size of the area can be estimated from Nawhkam's being three miles from the Burma Road. The action would be fought in an arena about four miles by four miles.

The terrain features are covered with woods and undergrowth. Visibility along the ground is often restricted and fields of fire are not too good. The Burma Road, however, is clearly visible from the dominant features.

The immediate objective of the 475th, the first step toward the Burma Road, was the high ground (estimated at the time to be 4,750 feet in altitude) in the area of Nawhkam village. The trail from Ho-pong led east, down a ravine, up the steep hillside, then onto the ridge where Nawhkam stood. Once this ridge was taken, the little alluvial valley that offered a protected site for supply installations would be dominated; the next step would be to cross the valley and get on top of Loi-kang ridge.

To hold off possible Japanese reinforcements, Company I of the 3d Battalion and two companies of Kachin Rangers were sent five miles north with orders to block the road from the Shweli valley to Namhpakka on the Burma Road.

The 1st Battalion moved out 17 January, behind the Intelligence and Reconnaissance Platoon, and ahead of both, in that loneliest of positions, lead scout, were two veterans of the GALAHAD Force, S. Sgts. Ernest Reid

MARSMEN CUT CROSS-COUNTRY *over mountainous terrain to reach their objective,* *15 January 1945.*

and Chester C. Wilson. The march went on, a quick tumble down the slope
to the ravine, then the slow climb up, and the advance south and east on the
ridge top. The hours went by, to about 1000. Approaching Nawhkam, the
scouts moved off to the north flank, then cut south into the scraggly line of
bashas. Down the trail which formed the main—and only—street they went.
At the south end a Japanese soldier at the door of a basha saw them, and
fired at Sergeant Reid. Reid's luck held, for the shot missed. Japanese
scrambled out of the bashas at the end of the village, ran south, and the
fight was on. The Japanese, later estimated at two squads, quickly took
position on a knoll seventy-five yards south. The Intelligence and Reconnaissance Platoon deployed and under cover of its fire Reid and Wilson
pulled back into safety. The battalion commander, Lt. Col. Caifson Johnson,
a former Big Ten wrestling champion and football player from Minnesota,
committed Company B, and in eighty minutes the now smoking village was
free of the Japanese outposts, at a cost of one American wounded.

Clearing the ridge continued in the afternoon. Another Japanese outpost
was discovered at the southern end of the ridge, contained, and disposed of
on 18 January. While the action was under way, an airdrop, most welcome to
the hungry troops, was received at 1430.

Late in the afternoon, the move toward the Burma Road began to yield
its first dividends. The 612th Field Artillery, beginning its occupation of
position around 1630, immediately registered on the Burma Road, range
about 4,000 yards, with good observation. Japanese daylight traffic along
the Burma Road to the *56th Division* could now be interdicted.

At this point the 1st Battalion had secured the ridge top, and the 2d Battalion was in position about two miles southwest of the south end of the
ridge line, separated from the 1st Battalion by another ridge on which was
the Japanese-occupied village of Ho-naw. Until the Japanese were driven
from Ho-Naw, the 1st Battalion was to hold on the ridge. The 3d Battalion
was in the process of moving northeast through the 1st Battalion's position,
on its way to assembly areas from which to seize ground directly overlooking
the Burma Road.[18] So far the operation had gone like clockwork against
the lightest of opposition from outposts.

The morning of 18 January efforts began to take positions dominating
the Burma Road. The objectives of the attack were the three hills along
the eastern edge of the little alluvial valley. The plan called for the 2d Battalion, 475th, to establish a position on the north end of Loi-kang ridge, the
3d Battalion to take the 3,850-foot hill, and the 3d Squadron, the hill which
overlooks Namhpakka.

The 3d Battalion took its objective with ease, moving up the hillside

[18] Ltr, Easterbrook to Col J. W. Stilwell, Jr., 28 Jan 45; Easterbrook Notebook, 17 Jan 45.
Easterbrook Papers.

against minor opposition, estimated at perhaps two squads.   For the Japanese as yet had not reacted to the MARS advance by bringing troops from
elsewhere.   The 2d Battalion, which had to use a circuitous route from its
positions to the south, did not attack until afternoon.   Crossing the valley,
it climbed up the north end of Loi-kang ridge, and began moving south.
Around 1600 it met the first real opposition, as "all hell broke loose" from
Japanese fire strong enough to stop the battalion's advance.   The fire came
from elements of the local garrison, the *1st* and *2d Battalions, 4th Regiment,
2d Division.*[19]

The 3d Squadron in advancing to its jump-off position moved behind the
2d Battalion until such time as the latter turned east to its objective; then
the cavalrymen continued on north and east toward theirs.   This procedure
was time consuming; the 124th would not be in place to attack until 19 January.   The troops had but the lightest contact with the Japanese on the
18th, resulting in one trooper slightly wounded.[20]

Meanwhile the 2d Battalion found itself in a fight.   The Japanese had
fortified the ridge north of Loi-Kang village, and held stubbornly along the
crest.   The battalion had a hard time establishing itself on the ridge, what
with darkness falling and wounded having to be brought down.   Japanese
counterattacks briefly cut off a platoon, but by evening the 2d Battalion had
a perimeter on the side of the hill and was firmly in place, though the crest
and the southern end, on which was Loi-kang village, still were in Japanese
hands.   The 1st Battalion took its objective, Ho-naw village, with two men
wounded.   Johnson's men found twenty-four Japanese packs, suggesting a
hasty flight.[21]

The 612th Field Artillery took advantage of its commanding position and
excellent observation to attack what the 475th's commander recorded as
"beautiful targets."   The Tenth Air Force, which, co-ordinated by an air support liaison group, was to be much in evidence in the days ahead, bombed
Namhpakka.   The transports came in for airdrops in the valley, and the drop
field began operation under hazards that were to last for the rest of the action, for the Japanese on their end of Loi-kang ridge had perfect observation
down the little valley.   They promptly called for artillery and mortar fire.
The Japanese had two 150-mm. howitzers in the area; their presence was
soon felt.[22]

---

[19] (1) Easterbrook Notebook, 18 Jan 45.   (2) Daily Jnl, 2/475th Bn.   (3) Japanese Study
148, p. 46.   (4) Statement, Superior Private Yoshio Sato.   Folder 62J, 441–450, NCAC Files,
KCRC.   Sato claimed that the *3d Battalion* was in Java.   (5) Johnson comments on draft MS.
(6) Quote from Lattin Diary.
[20] Daily Jnl, 124th Cav.
[21] (1) NCAC History, III, 301.   (2) Easterbrook Situation Map.   (3) Quote from Easterbrook Notebook, 19 Jan 45.   (4) Johnson comments on draft MS.   (5) Lattin Diary.
[22] (1) Easterbrook Notebook, 18 Jan 45.   (2) Willey comments on draft MS.

MARSMEN ON LOI-KANG RIDGE. *The Japanese were driven from the crest of the ridge by the 2d Battalion, 475th Infantry, 19 January 1945.*

While these operations were under way, Willey sought to bring up reinforcements of men and artillery. On 18 January he tried to persuade NCAC to use the Chinese 1st Separate Infantry Regiment. Sultan disapproved the request. Attempts to obtain the presence of Chinese 105- and 155-mm. artillery, to counter the effective Japanese 150-mm. howitzers, also failed. After the war Willey was at a loss to know why the Chinese 1st Separate Infantry Regiment, originally intended to operate as part of a division, was kept in NCAC reserve. He surmised that the Chinese objected to its being under American command, and that for essentially diplomatic reasons General Sultan had yielded.[23]

General Willey also recalled later that another command problem concerned and hindered him. He believed that his airdrop field had to be

---

[23] (1) Willey comments on draft MS. (2) Rad, Willey to NCAC, 18 Jan 45; Rad, NCAC to Willey, 19 Jan 45. 5332d G–3 Jnl.

JAPANESE TRUCK AND TANKETTE *trapped by crater blown in the Burma Road by MARS demolition men.*

covered at all costs, and so he could not maneuver as freely as he would have liked. A quarterback whose team had the ball within its 10-yard line would sympathize with the military problem; both Willey and the quarterback would be limited in their choice of maneuvers even though both were on the attack.[24]

That night, the 18th, the Japanese received reinforcements for their position in the Namhpakka area. The *Yamazaki Detachment*, under orders from *33d Army*, was moved back from the vicinity of Namhkam to link the *4th Regiment* with the main concentration to the north.[25]

On 19 January, MARS Task Force made an attempt to block the Burma Road by demolition. From the 3d Battalion, a patrol was sent out under T. Sgt. Alfred T. Martin. Sergeant Martin had the distinction of being the

[24] Willey comments on draft MS.
[25] Japanese Study 148, p. 46.

first American to set foot on the Burma Road in this area.   He and his patrol successfully blew a crater in the road, then withdrew.   The 612th Field Artillery, meanwhile, fired on a number of profitable Japanese targets, and believed they succeeded in knocking out four Japanese tankettes.   Two were caught on the road, and two more to the north of the 3d Battalion.

This same day the 2d Battalion reached the crest of Loi-kang ridge. When the battalion had organized its position, the executive, Maj. John H. Lattin, noted in his diary that the first attack at 0900 had "bogged down" with Japanese dug in on both the sides and crest of the ridge.   Around 1300 hours the decision was made to charge straight ahead for there was no room to maneuver.   At 1400 Thrailkill's men went right on up the ridge and had the satisfaction of seeing the Japanese run.   The Americans lost seven killed and seventeen wounded but had driven the Japanese from the crest of a very defensible position.[26]

To the north, the 3d Squadron of the cavalry moved on to its hill top objective, also on 19 January, in late afternoon under Japanese mortar and artillery fire.   Two brushes with Japanese patrols, one of which was hit by an artillery concentration for twelve counted dead, gave the 124th its first contact with the Japanese soldier.   That night the troopers dug in where they were to wait for morning and a chance to organize a systematic defense.[27]

The 124th's artillery support was being given by the 613th Field Artillery, which brought its twelve 75-mm. pack howitzers into action on 19 January. The 613th's commander, Colonel Donovan, was able to fight his battalion as a unit, with batteries under the control of fire direction center, and battalion concentrations ready on call.   After the war Donovan stated that, in contrast, the batteries of the 612th Field Artillery were usually detached to the control of the 475th's battalion commanders.   Using aerial observation, the 613th put a Japanese 150-mm. howitzer out of action at the extreme range of its little howitzers.[28]

To these activities the Japanese began to react more strongly than they had earlier.   Two attacks at daybreak on the 3d Battalion suggest that the *Yamazaki Detachment* was making its presence felt.[29]

Sergeant Martin's blowing a crater in the Burma Road, the artillery's placing fire on what had been the artery of supply and evacuation of the *56th Division,* and the fact that three battalions were less than 2,000 yards from the road suggested to the local commanders that the time had come to move

---

[26] Lattin Diary, 19 Jan 45.

[27] (1) Daily Jnl, 124th Cav.   (2) Randolph, *Marsmen in Burma,* pp. 149–50.

[28] (1) Ltr, Col Donovan to Gen Smith, 6 Nov 53.   OCMH.   (2) Willey comments on the draft manuscript of this volume also mentions the successful counterbattery by the 613th.

[29] (1) NCAC History, III, 302.   (2) Easterbrook Notebook, 19 Jan 45.   (3) Daily Jnl, 124th Cav.

across the Burma Road and clamp it shut.   The first phase, that of getting established along the road, was over.

The Block Disapproved

For a day or two heavy action seemed imminent as troops of the 2d Battalion tried to move south on 19 January from their part of Loi-kang ridge and consolidate their positions.   Between the 2d Battalion and Loi-kang village was a group of Japanese, well dug in, and with plenty of machine guns and 82-mm. mortars.   The local terrain favored the defense, for the ridge at this point was a razorback.   Trying to advance off the trail, which ran along the crest directly into the Japanese machine guns, the men of the 2d Battalion found themselves on slopes so steep they had to cling to the brush with their hands or creep on all fours.   Frontal assault seemed the only solution, and the 3d Platoon, Company F, T. Sgt. Patrick W. Murphy, delivered one that took the Japanese positions to the direct front.   At the day's end, the battalion had a better position but the Japanese at their end of the ridge were still able to place observed fire on American supply and command installations in the little valley.   Something would have to be done about the Japanese end of Loi-kang ridge.[30]

Dawn of 20 January revealed to the 3d Squadron troopers that their first positions were on the reverse crest of their objective.   Being on the reverse, they lacked the observation and fields of fire over the Burma Road that were their aim.   There were Japanese to the direct front and it was necessary to attack.   The hill was carried against opposition that yielded fifty counted Japanese dead; then, as the squadron was reorganizing, the Japanese struck back twice supported by strong artillery fire.   The squadron at 1100 withdrew slightly to obtain a smaller perimeter.   Fortunately, by noon the 1st Squadron was within supporting distance.   Troops A and B were attached to the 3d Squadron while Troop C and headquarters went on to their objective, a hill about two miles northwest of Namhpakka.   The 3d Squadron attacked again on the morning of the 21st.   By afternoon it could report the situation secure and ask for a mail drop.   The squadron had lost only four killed, seven wounded.   This success of the 124th meant that by morning of the 21st four battalions were lined up along the Burma Road.   Of the four, only the 2d had encountered stiff resistance, but some at least of the problems it faced could be ascribed to the difficulty of bringing heavy pressure to bear under the peculiar terrain conditions.[31]

Japanese resistance to date was not imposing, and Colonel Easterbrook

---

[30] (1) Easterbrook Notebook, 20 Jan 45.   (2) Randolph, *Marsmen in Burma*, pp. 148–49.
[31] (1) Daily Jnl, 124th Cav.   (2) Randolph, *Marsmen in Burma*.

decided to request permission to take further offensive action.   Although
Japanese counterattacks, like those on the 20th against the 124th, and two
more launched against the 3d Battalion had been repulsed, Japanese artillery
fire at night was a distinct hazard, and was causing heavy casualties among
the mules.

On 21 January Easterbrook asked General Willey for permission to move
the 3d Battalion to a ridge just east of the Burma Road, "if and when we
get some supplies."   In justification for the move it could be argued that
while MARS was harassing Japanese traffic along the Burma Road it was not
stopping it.   Thus, the 2d Battalion that same day had planted mines and
booby traps along the road.   The next night two Japanese trucks blew up
on the road, but the night after that Japanese armor was using the road at a
cost of only one tankette disabled by a mine.   As for the 124th, its unofficial
unit historian noted that "nearly every night" Japanese trucks could be heard
going by.   Plainly, the mines and ambushes of the MARS Task Force were
not cutting off traffic on the Burma Road, to say nothing of the bypass trails
to the east.   Moreover, on 21 January, leading elements of the Chinese 114th
Regiment contacted U.S. patrols as they entered the area to the north, so the
Allied position was growing stronger.   On 22 January patrols actually
reached the ridge on the far side of the road; the battalion might have been
able to follow.[32]

But on that same day of 22 January, word came back from 5332d Brigade
headquarters at Myitkyina that the plan to move east was disapproved "at
this time."   "Plan is good," radioed Willey, "but I have no report on Allied
activities to the north."   After the war, Willey recalled having considered
that the success of the proposed operation depended upon its co-ordination
with the Chinese and upon the supply situation.   Willey's radio shows that
he was concerned about co-ordination.   So, for the present, MARS Task Force
would confine itself to patrols, demolitions, and artillery fire.[33]

Patrols and ambushes offered ample scope for courage and enterprise
among small unit commanders.   Between 21 and 28 January the patrols made
their sweeps and laid their ambushes with varying results.   Ration deliveries
were irregular because Japanese fire interfered with the transports as they
came over for their supply drops.   From 14 to 26 January the 2d Battalion,
475th, was on reduced rations, though ammunition came in steadily.[34]

During this week of patrolling by day and Japanese raids and artillery fire
by night, several incidents of note occurred.   The 124th Cavalry located a

---

[32] (1) Easterbrook Notebook.   (2) Randolph, *Marsmen in Burma,* p. 158.   (3) Opns Jnl,
2/475th Inf, 21–23 Jan 45.   (4) The proposal is Item 12, 21 Jan 45, 5332d G–3 Jnl.
[33] (1) Easterbrook Notebook.   (2) Quotation is from Rad, Willey to Easterbrook, 21 Jan 45.
5332d G–3 Jnl.   (3) Willey comments on draft MS.
[34] Lattin Diary.

MORTAR SQUAD, 124TH CAVALRY, *cleans and oils an 81-mm. M1 mortar during a lull in operations, 22 January 1945.*

Japanese ammunition dump near the 3d Battalion's positions.   The 3d sent out a patrol and blew up the stockpile, with 3,000 rounds of 70-, 75-, and 105-mm., 400 rounds of grenade discharger, and 12 cans of small arms ammunition, and 18 drums of gasoline.   Two tankettes were destroyed the night of 23–24 January.   The Japanese tallied on the 25th by ambushing a 2d Battalion patrol, killing three Americans and wounding four.[35]

Meanwhile, this pressure by MARS Task Force and that of the Chinese forces in the north began to register on the Japanese.   The soldiers of the *4th Regiment, 2d Division,* could see the aerial activity that kept MARS supplied.   Not recognizing what they saw, they were so impressed by a big supply drop on the 24th that they sent a report to the *56th Division* of a large

---

[35] (1) Easterbrook Notebook.   (2) Daily Jnls, 124th Cav, 475th Inf.

airborne force being landed along the Burma Road. Accepting this report, the *56th's* commander passed it on to the *33d Army* and *Burma Area Army*. He added that he proposed to destroy his ammunition and retreat south. His superiors on 24 January agreed to let him retreat, but only after he had evacuated casualties and ammunition. Forty vehicles with gasoline accompanied by a Major Kibino of the *33d Army* staff were sent north to support the *56th* in its withdrawal.[36]

The Japanese truck convoy made its run north the night of 24 January. The trucks were heard, and the Americans placed heavy fire on the road. Kibino had been making the trip in a tankette. Hit by a 4.2-inch mortar shell, it burst into flames clearly visible from the American lines. Kibino clambered out, jumped on a truck, and succeeded in getting his convoy through to the *56th Division*. Next day the derelict tankette was credited to the 2d Battalion, 475th Infantry.[37]

With fuel and additional trucks at their disposal the Japanese began the difficult and dangerous task of running past the MARS positions. The Japanese of necessity had to move by night, and they seem to have adopted, for this reason, the tactic of keeping the Americans under pressure by heavy shelling during the night, by counterbattery with 150-mm. artillery, and by night raids. These diversionary operations were personally directed by the *33d Army* chief of staff.[38]

Meanwhile, the Chinese 114th Regiment, which had arrived in the general area 21 January, was slowly moving toward the road, north of MARS's lines and much closer to the *56th Division*. The commander Col. Peng Ko-li had conferred with Colonels Osborne and Easterbrook and, after the meeting, gave the impression that their plans had not been clearly defined to him.[39] Peng's comments to higher Chinese authority may have been fairly vigorous, for the commander of the New First Army, General Sun Li-jen, through his American liaison officer, told Headquarters, NCAC, that MARS Task Force had not cut the Burma Road near Hosi. Instead it had five battalions lined up on the hills and the Americans had refused to let the 114th Regiment through their lines to attack Namhpakka, so that the 3d Battalion, 114th Regiment, had turned northeast and cut the Burma Road at the eighty-mile road mark from Lashio on 22 January.[40]

According to the American records, based on liaison officer reports, the Chinese occupied two blocking positions on 27 January, suggesting that they

[36] Japanese Study 148, pp. 47–48.

[37] (1) *Ibid.,* p. 48. (2) Easterbrook Notebook, 24 January 1945, speaks of the "fireworks" on the road.

[38] (1) Japanese Study 148, p. 49. (2) Easterbrook Notebook, 29 January 1945, mentions 150-mm. counterbattery. (3) Lattin Diary.

[39] NCAC History, III, 277.

[40] Rad 310, 22 Jan 45. 38th Div Rad File, NCAC Files, KCRC.

had used the interim in moving up. The 3d Battalion took high ground just east of Milestone 82, five miles north of MARS's lines, while the 1st Battalion put a company less a platoon on the east side of the road at Milestone 81. A Chinese battery took position about two miles west, in the hills.

Between the 23d and the 27th, the latter being the date the road to China was opened, the Japanese had evacuated "more than a thousand casualties and several hundred tons of ammunition." Their account lacks detail, but references to the situation's becoming critical around 30 January probably tell what followed when the Chinese actually crossed the road.

The 3d Battalion was shelled and attacked for five days running, until the men were falling asleep in their foxholes. As for the lone Chinese company blocking the Burma Road, the Japanese reconnoitered its position the night of 28 January and also checked the defenses of the Chinese battery supporting the 114th. Next night the Japanese attacked. The battery position was overrun and three howitzers neutralized by demolition charges. The solitary Chinese company trying to stand between the *56th Division* and safety was almost destroyed. As these disasters were being suffered the Japanese were continuing their blows at the 3d Battalion, Chinese 114th Regiment, which stoutly held its hilltop positions.

The successes of the Japanese on the night of 29 January were sufficient for their purpose. Colonel Peng had advanced a minor piece on the game board and lost it. He accepted the situation and did not again try to stop the *56th Division's* retreat by a roadblock. The events of 27–29 January, when the Japanese succeeded in getting past the Chinese while the American forces were not astride the Burma Road or supporting the Chinese, brought some later recrimination. The vice-commander of the 38th Division, Dr. Ho, writing after the war, echoed General Sun's complaint that MARS had failed to cut the Burma Road, thus permitting the Japanese to concentrate on his men.[41]

In their battalion perimeter defenses along the west side of the Burma Road, the Americans during this period received some of the impact of the Japanese effort, mostly persistent shelling, the greater weight of which may have fallen on the 2d Battalion, 475th. The Japanese did not neglect counterbattery, and by 29 January the 612th Field Artillery had three of its 75-mm. howitzers silenced by 150-mm. shells. On the 26th four men of the 2d Battalion were almost buried alive by a Japanese shell, while two U.S. machine guns were destroyed. Casualty figures for the 475th show that by 29 January there had been 32 men killed and 199 wounded. The 612th Field Artillery had twice as many casualties as did the 1st Battalion, which was then in reserve, and the 2d Battalion had as many as the other two bat-

[41] (1) NCAC History, III, 277–79.   (2) Ho Yung-chi, *The Big Circle,* p. 139.   (3) Japanese Study 148.   (4) Dupuy Comments.

talions and the artillery combined. For their part, the men of Mars Task Force continued with daylight patrolling, booby-trapping, mining, and shelling the road, plus some minor offensive action.[42]

An attempt by Company L, 3d Battalion, to clear the Japanese from Hill 77, just west of Milestone 77 on the Burma Road, whence its name, was a failure. After a heavy mortar barrage on 28 January, Company L went forward. The Japanese were unshaken, and swept the company headquarters with machine gun fire. The company commander and forward platoon leader with four enlisted men were killed. 1st Lt. Aaron E. Hawes, Jr., took command and brought the company back to the battalion perimeter.[43]

To the north of the valley, the 124th Cavalry had found that Japanese fire from a small hill just a few hundred yards from its lines was a serious hazard. The final decision was to drive off the Japanese with Troop A, reinforced by a platoon of C, on 29 January. Troop B and the 613th Field Artillery would give supporting fire. Since the attack was mounted in broad daylight, witnessed by many men from their hillside vantage spots, and executed with speed and precision, witnesses were inevitably reminded of a service school demonstration to show the advantages of fire and movement in the attack.

The Japanese held a ring of little bunkers around the crest of the hill. Each attacking platoon had a rocket launcher team attached to smash firing slits and blind the defenders. Moving as fast as the rough terrain permitted, the troopers used a small draw for their avenue of approach, then spread out for the climb up the hill. They fired as they moved. When the range permitted, grenades were hurled into the Japanese bunkers and dugouts. The combination of speed, fire, and movement worked well, and in two hours the fight was over, at a cost of eleven wounded. Thirty-four dead Japanese were found.[44]

The Japanese retaliated with heavy artillery fire all day and on into the night. As the darkness fell, there was apprehension that the Japanese would attack in strength that night. They did, twice, and in one desperate rush broke into Troop B's perimeter, overrunning a platoon command post. There was a brief, murderous clash in the darkness, and then the Japanese were gone, leaving four dead. Elsewhere, sounds in the darkness indicated that other Japanese were looking for the airdrop field. Later discoveries of U.S. rations in enemy positions suggest that the Japanese succeeded in getting some supplies.[45]

---

[42] (1) Daily Jnl, 2/475th Inf. (2) Easterbrook Notebook, 26–29 Jan 45.
[43] (1) Easterbrook Notebook, 28 Jan 45. (2) Hawes won the Silver Star. GO 81, par. V, Hq USF IBT, 26 Apr 45.
[44] (1) Randolph, *Marsmen in Burma*, p. 168, describes the fight. (2) Rpt, 1st Lt Arthur A. Rubli, Adj 3d Squadron, to CO 124th Cav, 12 Feb 45, sub: Casualties. Daily Jnl, 124th Cav.
[45] Randolph, *Marsmen in Burma*, pp. 169–70.

An 81-mm. Mortar Crew *shelling the Burma Road.*

In these minor episodes gradually disappeared any thought that MARS's presence on the battlefield might lead the Chinese to greater speed of movement. The principal impact on Sino-American relations in the local scene seems to have been the misunderstanding as to whether MARS was to place itself squarely across the Burma Road. Elsewhere in Burma the failure of the Chinese and American forces under NCAC to hold the *56th Division* in north Burma severely limited their contribution to SEAC's operations farther south, while their inability to destroy the *56th* meant that not until the Japanese withdrawal from north Burma made further progress could MARS and the Chinese be released for service in China.

CHAPTER VII

Victory in Burma Frees Troops for China

The situation in Northern Combat Area Command about 30 January was that the 112th and 113th Regiments, Chinese 38th Division, which had made the final link with China, were now at the junction of the Ledo and Burma Roads around Mong Yu with orders to fight down the Burma Road to Lashio. The Japanese *56th Division,* using both the Burma Road and bypass trails in the hills to the east, was successfully making its way past the Chinese 114th and MARS Task Force, which NCAC had placed in the path of the *56th* with very restricting orders. At this time, the 5332d's headquarters was at Man Wing, in the southwest end of the Shweli valley.

The Chinese 30th Division, which had fought in the Namhkam area of the Shweli valley, had been ordered to move to the Hosi–Namhpakka area north of the MARS Force.[1] The leading regiment of the 30th Division, the 89th, left the Namhkam area 25 January and met Japanese resistance almost at once. The Japanese held their hill and ridge-top positions for almost two days, then broke contact on 26 January. Next day the Chinese were in the area around Man Ning village, three miles west of the 124th's positions. Given the roughness of the terrain and the heavy woods which so restricted visibility, the Japanese facing the 30th Division probably did not find it difficult to move east through the gap between the 124th's lines and those of the Chinese 114th Regiment. From the vicinity of Man Ning, the Chinese moved around to the north of the 124th's position and finally established themselves on a prominent hill about one and one half miles north of Hpapen village, which in turn was a mile northeast of the cavalry position.[2]

MARS's Last Fight

In moving past the entrenched Chinese and Americans, the Japanese were executing one of the most delicate operations in war, a movement along the

---

[1] See p. 127, above.
[2] History of IBT, I, 47–48.

front of an enemy's lines. Very probably the Japanese watched their opponents with care and sought to guard against a thrust that would catch them in flank. The events of early February suggest that the point at which some at least of the Japanese were leaving the Burma Road to bypass MARS Task Force along the trails to the east was somewhere near Hpa-pen. Just north of Hpa-pen, the Chinese 114th Regiment had sought to cross the Burma Road, and the Japanese had fought back vigorously. The high ground around Hpa-pen stood between the 124th and the Burma Road to the northeast; American interest in the Hpa-pen area might draw a very strong reaction from the Japanese.

Such was the conformation of the ground between the 124th and the Burma Road that observation and lines of fire in the quadrant from north to east were masked by the high ground on which Hpa-pen stood. This area was about a mile and a quarter northeast of the 124th's foxholes. Occupation of the square mile of high ground around Hpa-pen, which was a part of the large hill mass lying west of the road, and of a smaller hill about a mile due east of the cavalry's lines would make it easier for the 124th to obstruct Japanese traffic along the Burma Road.

Seizure of the Hpa-pen area was originally conceived as a Sino-American effort. By this time the Chinese 88th Regiment, 30th Division, was in the area, and so it was contemplated that the 88th and the 2d Squadron would attack together, on 31 January. The Chinese on 30 January said they wanted to postpone the attack until 2 February, and the delay was agreed on. On the 31st the Chinese stated that they would prefer to wait until the 3d.[3] Apparently this decision was not taken as final, for Colonel Osborne, the 124th's commander, spent the night of the 1st at the 88th Regiment command post, trying to arrange a co-ordinated attack.

To gain surprise and facilitate co-operation with the Chinese, the 2d Squadron was moved to an assembly area at Mong Noi, a mile and a half west of Hpa-pen, and by a most circuitous route. Since the Japanese had excellent observation, a ruse was attempted. On 1 February parties of men were sent rather openly into the forward perimeter, with orders to fall back under cover by ones and twos. The Japanese probably could see the perimeter being reinforced, but the 124th hoped that no Japanese would recognize the steady movement of individuals to the rear.

On 2 February the 2d Squadron was on the line of departure, about one mile west of the Japanese positions. There was a preparation from 0600 to 0620 by every weapon that could reach the Japanese positions, then the 2d Battalion moved out, with Troops E and F abreast and D in support. In fifty minutes Troop F had moved out of the little wooded draw that offered

[3] History of 5332d, Ch. VI, p. 8.

a natural avenue of approach and was coming up on the high ground.[4] Troop E, to its left, encountered more difficult terrain and reached the top at 0800.

As Troop F moved up the rough trail in an open column, the commander, 1st Lt. Jack L. Knight, was well to the front, and when two Japanese suddenly appeared at the crest, Knight killed them both. So began a display of stern valor and martial skill. Crossing the hill to the reverse slope, Knight found a cluster of Japanese emplacements. Calling up his men, he attacked one after another of the emplacements with grenades. When the Japanese, who seem to have been surprised, steadied and began inflicting heavy casualties on Troop F, Knight kept his attack organized and under control. Though half-blinded by grenade fragments, bleeding heavily, and having seen his brother, Curtis, shot while running to his aid, Knight still fought, still commanded his men, and died as his stubborn will was dragging his shattered body toward one more Japanese emplacement.[5]

The pillbox whose crew had killed Lieutenant Knight had been under fire from a rocket launcher manned by Pfc. Anthony Whitaker. Whitaker put three rounds on the emplacement, all of which failed to explode. Throwing aside his launcher, Whitaker took rifle and grenades and rushed on the pillbox. His effort succeeded, and may have been the turning point.[6]

Initially, Troop E, in the middle of the high ground and left of Troop F, did not have so difficult a time as F. Advancing with a will, E found itself rather forward of F's positions, and at one time was out of contact. Japanese counterattacks were met several times. Firing was heavy during the morning of the 2d, and as the hours passed the ammunition supply caused serious concern.[7]

With the action so heavy on F's front, and with E meeting strong counterattacks as soon as it was on its objective, Osborne elected to send in his reserve, Troop G, in midmorning. G was to take position on the north, on E's left. Where F had met Japanese intrenchments just beyond its objective, Capt. William A. Wood of G found Japanese fortifications barring his path. With a machine gun, and then with grenades, Wood kept his attack moving. When the way was opened, Wood reorganized his force. Finding his forward observer dead, he took over the radio. Wood arranged

---

[4] (1) Randolph, *Marsmen in Burma*, p. 190, is the only account to mention the attempt to achieve surprise. (2) History of IBT, I, 53.

[5] (1) Troop F was originally the National Guard troop of Mineral Wells, Texas. Knight, who entered service from Weatherford, Texas, received the Congressional Medal of Honor. His brother recovered from his wound. (2) NCAC History, III, 322–23. (3) Randolph, *Marsmen in Burma*, pp. 191–93.

[6] Whitaker received the Distinguished Service Cross posthumously. (1) GO 81, par. I, Hq USF IBT, 26 Apr 45. (2) History of 5332d, Ch. VI, p. 9. (3) History of IBT, I, 54.

[7] (1) Randolph, *Marsmen in Burma*, pp. 194–95. (2) History of 5332d, Ch. VI, p. 10.

to have a shell burst put where he could see it, then proceeded to adjust fire on the remaining Japanese positions, describing the relation of the burst to his targets as best he could.   These concentrations were most effective, and the troop took its objective with little further opposition.[8]

Smoke from burning brush and from the phosphorous drifted across the lines.   Japanese, possibly running from the fire, came against E's and F's positions in what looked very like a counterattack in the bad visibility. With the problem of getting supplies up through the difficult terrain, the general confusion of battle, and the poor light, there were moments when the situation seemed in the balance.   But emergency expedients, like sending supplies forward by returning evacuation teams, helped, and by early afternoon the situation appeared to be, and was, under control.   The day's fighting cost the 2d Squadron twenty-two dead.[9]

The Chinese contribution to this hard-fought action was a minor one. The Chinese regiments were not pledged to attack on 2 February, and did not.   The 30th Division may have agreed to contribute a company, and that afternoon a Chinese company took its place in the perimeter for a day. About one mile to the south of this action, the 3d Squadron had less difficulty.   Troop L with a platoon of K attached carried its objective in about an hour's time, with a cost of one dead and fifteen wounded.   Pvt. Solomon O. Cureton and Pfc. Bertie W. Beacon, Jr., played a conspicuous part in the action by their singlehanded attacks on enemy bunkers.[10]

Clearing Loi-kang Ridge

Next day, 3 February, found the 475th in its last regimental fight.   Holding its positions on Loi-kang ridge had strained the 2d Battalion.   As noted before, its casualties had been the heaviest, while lack of sleep and nervous tension were wearing on the men.   Since arriving on the ridge, the battalion had not been directed to remove the Japanese from the south end.   Around 31 January Easterbrook concluded that the time had come to take aggressive action to improve the 2d's position.   At a conference with the 2d's commander, Colonel Thrailkill, on 1 February, Easterbrook learned that the 2d did not want to be relieved, and supported the plan of the 475th's headquarters for an operation against the south end of Loi-kang ridge.   Willey accepted Thrailkill's plea to finish the job, and countermanded the relief order.

---

[8] (1) NCAC History, III, 318.   (2) Randolph, *Marsmen in Burma,* p. 193.   (3) GO 81, par. VII, Hq USF IBT, 26 Apr 45, awarded Wood the Bronze Star.
[9] Randolph, *Marsmen in Burma,* p. 194.
[10] (1) Randolph, *Marsmen in Burma.*   (2) History of 5332d, Ch. VI, pp. 9–10.   (3) Affidavits in Daily Jnl, 124th Cav.

It was Thrailkill's last day of command. That night, a Japanese shell hit an observation post, killing him and three enlisted men. S. Sgt. Milton Kornfeld had his leg so badly mangled that the battalion surgeon, Capt. Joseph P. Worley, on the scene quickly, had to amputate at once, and without anesthetics.[11]

The plan of attack assumed that the Japanese in the garrison on Loi-kang's southern knoll would long have had their attention fixed on the 2d Battalion to the north, and so might well be open to attack from another direction. The 1st Battalion, on the other side of the little valley that held the supply installations, and blocking the trails to west and south, was in excellent position to come at the Japanese from an unexpected angle. The decision therefore was for the 2d to make a holding attack from the north while the 1st Battalion swung around the high ground south of the valley and attacked Loi-kang from the south.

At midnight, 2 February, Companies B and C were on the line of departure, just west of little Nam Maw River, which had carved out the valley. Their route would be a trail that went round the south end of the valley—to a village, Man Sak, which was half a mile south of and below Loi-kang—then went north and on up the ridge to Loi-kang. At 0400 the two companies led out, with Colonel Johnson, the battalion commander, in the lead. The men moved as quietly as possible. At 0545 the 612th Field Artillery, 4.2-inch and 81-mm. mortars, and heavy machine guns began a fifteen-minute preparation on Loi-kang. P–47 fighters of the Tenth Air Force aided. When the fire was lifted, the 2d Battalion, now under Major Lattin, attacked the Japanese with two platoons, their objective a small knoll. They met intense fire from two Japanese machine gun emplacements, and were stopped within forty yards of the enemy. Pfc. Clifton L. Henderson, a BAR man, volunteered to clear away this barrier. Silencing one gun with a grenade, he crawled around to the rear door and, under heavy fire from the supporting machine gun, shot the crew as they tried to run out. He then occupied the emplacement and put such heavy fire on the other gun as to silence it too. His platoon "took the objective without further loss of life."[12]

Meanwhile the 1st Battalion troops were advancing steadily in column of companies, C in the lead, bypassing Man Sak to avoid alerting any Japanese who might be there. At 0530 they were past Man Sak and on a small peak just south of Loi-kang. Very soon after, apparently before the preparation, they surprised a party of Japanese, who retreated to a small ravine and were there killed. The advance continued for about 1,000 yards more, to the

---

[11] (1) Easterbrook Notebook, 31 Jan–2 Feb 45. (2) Randolph, *Marsmen in Burma,* p. 174. (3) Willey comments on draft MS.

[12] (1) Henderson's heroism was recognized by the award of the Distinguished Service Cross. GO 72, par. IV, Hq USF IBT, 9 Apr 45. (2) Easterbrook Notebook, 3 Feb 45.

southern outskirts of the burned-out huts that had been Loi-kang village. Here they were surprised by a well-hidden Japanese strongpoint and were pinned down. At this point T. Sgt. David M. Akui and S. Sgt. Sylvester G. Garrison joined in a two-man assault on the Japanese, using submachine guns. This action drew away the Japanese fire, and Company C could pull back to reorganize.

Beyond the village, and about 500 yards from Lattin's men, Company C found the keystone of the Japanese position. This was a fortified knoll, organized for all-around defense and well covered by brush and trees. The only approach from the south was over a narrow ridge. The time was now about 1600, and it seemed late in the day for an attempt at this last barrier. So Company C pulled back, and the 1st Battalion proceeded to organize itself for the night.

A preparation would be needed for the morning's attack; this raised the anxious question of just how far apart the two battalions were. The map's contour lines had been found to be unreliable, and aerial photographs were misleading because of the thick cover. By sending up a flare, the 2d Battalion marked its forward positions in the dark. This revealed enough room for artillery fire, and a fifteen-minute concentration was placed on the Japanese to keep them quiet as the 1st Battalion settled down for the night.

Next morning there was another preparation and at 0800 Company B made the final assault. During the night most of the Japanese had withdrawn and there was little resistance, but enough to make it 1000 before the two battalions established contact. The cost of the operation to the 1st Battalion was two killed and fifteen wounded, only four seriously. Because the Japanese had been well dug in and had fought stubbornly, the 475th and General Willey believed that the success and low casualty rate for the operation reflected great credit on the battalion commander, Colonel Johnson.[13]

From Combat to Administration

After 4 February contacts between the Japanese and the MARS Task Force were patrol actions and artillery exchanges. One of them, on 4 February when a platoon of the 124th was ambushed, was a bitter encounter, but most were brushes with stragglers and the tag ends of the Japanese rear guards, growing fewer as the days passed.

In the action of the 4th, a platoon of Troop I, accompanied but not led by the troop commander, 1st Lt. Hobart T. Kavel, had been sent to establish ground contact between the 1st and 3d Squadrons. The patrol moved

[13] (1) Easterbrook Situation Map. (2) Easterbrook Notebook, 2–4 Feb 45. (3) History of 5332d, Ch. V, p. 20. (4) Randolph, *Marsmen in Burma*, pp. 198–200. (5) Akui was a Hawaiian. (6) Colonel Johnson was awarded the Silver Star.

into a patch of low ground which, unknown to the 124th, lay in the field of fire of some well-hidden Japanese emplacements. Heavy fire from four machine guns tooks the troopers by surprise. Lieutenant Kavel was wounded almost at once. The patrol leader, 2d Lt. Burr L. Hughes, was ordered by him to attack. As Hughes did so, a rifle bullet in the leg toppled him to the ground. Meanwhile, men were falling all about. At this critical point, Hughes told Pfc. George A. Owen to take command, while Hughes by shouting the messages kept a link open between Owen and the radio man to the rear. Every shout brought a burst of Japanese fire. These hasty, desperate arrangements worked. Owen controlled the platoon, while the radio summoned Troop K. One squad leader, Cpl. Pierce W. Moore, despite heavy wounds, led his squad in knocking out two emplacements, greatly helping the patrol's later withdrawal. The arrival of two squads from Troop K enabled the survivors to be withdrawn. The action cost six dead, twenty-seven wounded. Among the dead was Kavel.[14]

After this painful episode, contacts with the Japanese grew steadily fewer, though deadly enough. The 124th Cavalry on 6 February reported fourteen Japanese killed by booby traps and in patrol clashes. Next day the men drove off some Japanese with mortar fire. On 9 February the 124th reported no further contact with the Japanese. Then the long arm of the S-3 and his training schedule reached out and on 10 February the troopers began to build a firing range.[15]

The 475th was harassed by Japanese 150-mm. fire until aerial observation on 8 February revealed some suspicious-looking tracks in the area east of the Burma Road. An air strike was hastily whistled up. When the bombers had finished their mission, secondary explosions were seen and no more 150-mm. shells were received. The Japanese medium artillery had been most effective, for the first time in the fall 1944 campaign, and inflicted considerable punishment on the 475th's command and artillery installations. There followed a few days of cleaning up the neighborhood, and then on 10 February the 475th went into more comfortable positions behind a screen of outposts.[16] The Japanese were now well down the Burma Road to the south, and the Chinese had reached the MARS area in strength.

When the troops began to clean up, get some sleep, and write some letters and the commanders began to get caught up on administrative details, it was

---

[14] For their display of leadership under harrowing conditions, Owen and Moore won the Distinguished Service Cross. (1) GO 72, pars. I and IV, Hq USF IBT, 9 Apr 45. (2) GO 99, par. I, Hq USF IBT, 22 May 45. (3) Well known among veterans of the North Burma Campaign, the aggressive and colorful Kavel won his first decorations with the GALAHAD Force (Merrill's Marauders). Randolph, *Marsmen in Burma,* p. 150. (4) Affidavits in Daily Jnl, 124th Cav.
[15] Daily Jnl, 124th Cav.
[16] (1) Easterbrook Notebook. (2) Willey comments on draft MS.

SILVER RUPEES FOR BATTLE DAMAGE. *Capt. Terence Carroll, Civil Affairs Officer, NCAC forces, pays Burmese headmen for livestock killed in recent action between Americans and Japanese.*

possible to note the casualty figures. These totaled 115 killed in action and 938 wounded. One man was missing.[17]

Medical procedures were greatly affected by the tropical hill country in which the campaign was fought. In evacuating wounded, much use was made of Burmese litter bearers hired through the civil affairs officer of the brigade. Carrying wounded uphill and down over rough trails was a tremendous job. If the combat troops had had to do it the drain on personnel strength would have been marked. The three portable surgical hospitals, 42d, 44th, and 49th, dispatched the litter squads. Men were carried from

[17] (1) History of 5332d, Med Sec, Chart E. (2) "Lt. Irving Kofer was wounded and apparently carried away by the Japs. When the platoon took the site they found Kofer's binoculars with lenses smashed and his maps with charred edges, as though he tried to burn them. . . . I do not believe his body was ever found, and I think he was the 124th's only 'missing in action.'" Comments on draft manuscript by Edward R. Bishop, formerly a lieutenant in the 124th Cavalry who commanded a regimental intelligence and reconnaissance platoon of the MARS Task Force.

hospital to landing strip where the L-5's of the 5th Liaison Squadron picked them up and flew them back.   Intestinal disease was attacked by chlorinating and filtering water, boiling it twenty minutes, then rechlorinating.   The Burmese were not allowed in kitchen areas.   To avoid scrub typhus the medical officers tried to keep troops out of abandoned native huts, but with indifferent success.   One problem was the so-called "march fracture," a break-ing of the arch from carrying heavy packs over steep trails.   The cumula-tive effect of these different problems was serious.   From 15 November to 15 February the 475th evacuated 929 men.   Of these, about 750 were evacuated from causes not arising in battle, a serious drain on the regiment's strength.[18]

In anticipation of the troops' arrival along the Burma Road, a big supply drop was laid on well in advance, with rations packed and ready.   The ar-rangement worked well for the 475th's supplies but when the 124th came into line the circling transports encountered ground fire which made them reluctant to drop in the area.   The shortfall in deliveries in turn made the supply situation critical for a few days.   It seems to have been solved by the progress of the battle.   The Japanese were gradually pushed off terrain features from which they could menace the transports.[19]

Relations with the Burmese were the province of a British officer, Capt. Terrance Carroll.   The Mars Task Force could have been greatly handi-capped by Burmese hostility; conversely, as litter bearers, guides, informants, laborers, and food peddlers the Burmese could have been most useful.   The policy was adopted of paying one silver rupee a day in the forward area for labor, and also of recompensing the Burmese for nonbattle damage to homes and gardens.   Thus, after Tonkwa, the local inhabitants were recompensed for damage by the 475th in silver rupees of prewar coinage, currency of im-pressive weight and fineness.   Sharply contrasting with Japanese invasion paper money, the silver rupees were a potent argument for co-operation; the bamboo telegraph did the rest.   The Burmese of the Kachin, Shan, and Palaung tribes worked cheerfully and well, were steady under shellfire, and gave an excellent impression of the peoples of Burma.   Captain Carroll's services were regarded as "very valuable."[20]

The British 36th Division Wins Its Hardest Fight

While the Chinese 38th and 30th Divisions plus Mars Task Force were pushing the Japanese away from the land route to China, the British Four-teenth Army from the west plus two of NCAC's other divisions, the British

[18] (1) History of 5332d, Med Sec.   (2) Easterbrook Notebook.   (3) NCAC History, III, 312.
[19] History of 5332d, G-4 and QM Secs.
[20] History of 5332d, Civil Affairs and G-4 Secs.

36th and the Chinese 50th from the north, were steadily, and in places even rapidly, advancing toward central Burma. (*See Map 12.*)

Of the two NCAC divisions, only the British 36th under General Festing met heavy opposition, from the veteran Japanese *18th Division* as the latter sought to guard the Japanese northern flank. After taking Katha and Indaw in December, the 36th Division had been relieved of primary responsibility for the Railway Corridor, as part of the General eastward shift of the NCAC forces. Accordingly, General Festing's force was split into two columns. The 29th Brigade continued down the Irrawaddy to a point from which it might swerve to the east and attack the next divisional objective, Mongmit, from the west. The remaining two brigades, 26th Indian Infantry and British 72d, were to cross the Shweli at Myitson and appear at Mongmit from the north. The Chinese 50th Division was sent south and east to the Si-u-Tonkwa area, replacing the Chinese 22d Division and MARS Task Force. From this area, the 50th's three regiments, moving in as many columns, came in line along the Shweli River from Molo to Mong Hkak about mid-January 1945. Save for the destruction of a Japanese rifle company south of Tonkwa the 50th had had only light contact with the retreating Japanese, but since by moving southeast from its present position it could cut the Burma Road southwest of Lashio it was in a position to attempt the interception of the retreating Japanese *56th Division.* For the immediate present, the hard work fell to the British 36th Division.[21]

On 16 December the 36th Division made contact with the advance elements of the 19th Indian Division, which had marched overland from India across Burma. This meant a solid link had been established between NCAC and the British forces; the two fronts were now joined. When the brigades reached the Shweli River, a patrol sent across the night of 31 January found Japanese bunkers unoccupied. Next day, an attempt to cross in force met strong Japanese small arms fire, later stiffened with mortar and 75-mm. shells, after the first wave of about 130 men was across. A sandbar in the Shweli, on which assault boats grounded and were then shot up by the Japanese, made reinforcement most difficult. By morning of 2 February it was necessary to withdraw the survivors.

Unwilling to repeat their previous tactics, the British chose to deceive the enemy. A small island near the crossing point had been a Japanese strongpoint and most troublesome during the previous attack, so ostensible preparations were made to cross via the island. A rough trail was cut in the jungle and supply dumps accumulated. Meanwhile, the division made ready to send a brigade across the Shweli downstream and attack from the west. On 8 February the 26th Brigade made its crossing. Its leading ele-

---

[21] IBT Combat History, p. 71.

ments were seen in the assembly area, which the Japanese shelled, but they did not react quickly enough to keep the brigade from taking Myitson on 10 February.

Over the next few days the 26th Brigade improved its positions, against opposition that grew daily heavier. Perhaps the *18th Division* was committing its troops piecemeal as they moved up north from the Mongmit area, for the result of the Japanese efforts was a steadily increasing scale of fire on the bridgehead and stronger resistance to attempts at expanding it. Small arms and artillery fire made supply and evacuation most hazardous, while Japanese attacks alternated with the 26th Brigade's efforts. Japanese attempts at infiltration on 13 February were successful. Enemy soldiers first cut the wires and supply route to brigade headquarters within the perimeter, then were driven off. Next day they were back again and were not cleared away till late afternoon. For many hours brigade headquarters was cut off from the troops manning the perimeter, during a time when Japanese attacks were rising in intensity. Finally, the headquarters had to withdraw, covered by two rifle companies.

The major Japanese effort was made on 17 February, a furious thrust preceded by an estimated 2,000 rounds of shellfire and marked by Japanese use of flame throwers. The heaviest weight fell on two Indian battalions, 2d Battalion, 8th Punjab, and 1st Battalion, 19th Hyderabad. The Indians stood their ground with fortitude and valor and when day fell every position was intact. This was the supreme effort of the Japanese at Myitson; next day over 350 Japanese dead were counted. Illustrative of the difficulty faced in supplying the bridgehead, food, water, and ammunition came in by airdrop.

Not until four days later could the 36th Division bring supplies across the Shweli by daylight, suggesting the stubbornness with which the Japanese had clung to their positions around the 26th's perimeter, and the slowness with which their grip was pried loose. Meanwhile, unknown to the bridgehead's grim defenders, the Japanese command in Burma found it had to respond to the initiative now securely in British hands. The Japanese feared that the much-battered divisions of the Japanese *15th Army* needed help to meet the British forces now closing in on Mandalay, and so on 25 February *33d Army* was ordered to send the *18th Division* (less one regimental combat team) to Mandalay to reinforce *15th Army*. The *18th* at once began to disengage and fell back on Mongmit. After the war the Japanese claimed to have estimated that the 36th Division would attack toward Maymyo or Hsipaw, and so not be a potential factor in the Mandalay area.[22]

While the British 36th Division had been fighting at Myitson the Chinese

---

[22] (1) 36th Div War Diary. (2) Foster, Ch. IV. (3) Japanese Study 148, p. 51.

50th Division to its east had been moving unopposed on a southeast course as part of Sultan's eastward wheel. In its path were the great nonferrous Bawdwin mines and the town of Namtu. While the mines were of substantial economic value, of more immediate concern was a fair road that led directly south from Namtu to Hsipaw, on the Burma Road below Lashio. The Japanese did not attempt a serious stand above the Myitnge River, but at a point nine miles below the town they fought with determination. In late February the 149th Regiment opened a bridgehead, but Japanese from the *113th Regiment* made nine separate counterattacks before conceding its establishment. Perhaps decisive in ending Japanese resistance around Namtu was the arrival in the area of the First Chinese Separate Regiment. This powerful force, organized and equipped to the U.S. Army scale, was now attached to the 50th. By early March the 50th Division was ready to drive south to Hsipaw.[23]

From Myitson, the 36th Division went on to Mongmit, and thence on toward Mogok, famous for its ruby mines. It met little opposition as it continued south and east, until it was within five miles of Mogok. The 36th was now in the area the *56th Division* was holding to screen the Japanese flank, and fighting flared again. The fight was brief, and as March drew to a close the 36th Division stood on the Burma Road at Kyaukme. On 1 April General Festing and the 36th returned to Fourteenth Army command.[24]

The Burma Campaign Moves Toward a Climax

While the 36th Division and the rest of NCAC had been wheeling ponderously eastward to clear the Burma Road, the British Fourteenth Army under General Slim was attempting a series of complex and difficult maneuvers with the aim of destroying the major part of the Japanese Army in Burma. For this attempt, Slim would have five divisions, an East African brigade, and a tank brigade, grouped as 4 and 33 Corps. Between this force and Mandalay were not the Japanese alone but a major mountain chain, the Chindwin River, and then the sheer distance of 400 miles from the railhead in India to the projected battleground in Burma. The transport aircraft would be of the greatest aid in bridging that long gap—but the number of available transports was always a matter for concern. The Chindwin River flowed down to the vicinity of Mandalay, and was navigable—but ever since 1942 the river craft had been a prime target for the RAF and AAF and were now very scarce. Plainly, brilliance would be required in logistics as well as in tactics and strategy. To ease his task, Slim had complete and unchallenged air superiority.

At the end of the long march into Burma there waited the Japanese *15th*

[23] History of IBT, II, 323–24.
[24] History of IBT, II, 320.

Army, under Lt. Gen. Shihachi Katamura, and a new Japanese commander for Burma, General Hoyotaro Kimura. The Japanese had available in the Mandalay area four understrength divisions, the *15th, 31st, 33d,* and *53d,* a regiment of nationalist Indians of the *Indian National Army,* and the prospect of reinforcement by the *2d* and *49th Divisions,* under control of *Burma Area Army,* and the *18th Division* of *33d Army.*

Kimura's orders, dating back to October, called for a battle along the Irrawaddy River. Operations out of a bridgehead over the Irrawaddy west of Mandalay would be used to harry and impede the British and Indian forces as they approached the great river; then, as they were astride it, vigorous counterattacks would be launched against them. One division, the *15th,* would be north of Mandalay, and three to the south. As of the date these orders were issued the Japanese had still not completed their withdrawal into central Burma. The withdrawal was made successfully, in that not until December was Fourteenth Army aware that the Japanese planned to make their stand along the Irrawaddy rather than, as had been assumed, on the outer rim of the central Burmese plain. In December the Japanese somewhat redefined their plans and put the *53d Division* in mobile reserve in the vital Meiktila communications and airfield center south of Mandalay.

When Slim's staff had clear evidence that it would not be possible to trap and destroy the Japanese in the central plain west of the Irrawaddy, that commander at once altered his plans accordingly. He now determined to take advantage of the road net to move the 4 Corps around from the left to the right flank of 33 Corps, with the vital exception of the 19th Indian Division, left in place with the hope that the Japanese would think 4 Corps still in its sector. The 19th Indian Division was given the further task of crossing the Irrawaddy above Mandalay to draw Japanese reserves northward—an intention which fit well into Kimura's announced policies. Another crossing of the Irrawaddy was to be made by 33 Corps near Mandalay as a further distraction. Then 33 Corps and 4 Corps would make their major efforts almost simultaneously, that of 4 Corps being the master stroke. Near Pakokku, 4 Corps was to establish a bridgehead, then from it launch a strong armored task force on the road and rail centers south of Mandalay. (*Map 14*) For the first time in the Burma fighting, the Japanese were to be confronted with the concentrated weight of the modern armor-air-artillery team. Previously, fighting had been in close jungle country, where armor, though on occasion dramatically effective, as at Walawbum in the Hukawng Valley in March 1944, was handicapped.[25] The area around Meiktila, dry, barren, rolling, with a cover of cactus and scraggly palms, was far better suited to armor, and Slim proposed to offer Kimura and Katamura new problems to solve.

---

[25] See *Stilwell's Command Problems,* Ch. IV.

New air bases, closer to central and south Burma than those in Assam, were regarded as essential to support Slim's projected offensive, and 15 Corps was directed to take the Akyab airfields.   Four divisions were provided. Much battered the preceding spring, the Japanese in the Arakan now had but the *54th Division* plus the equivalent of a regimental combat team.   The new offensive in the Arakan crossed the line of departure on 12 December.   The Japanese had previously decided that their regimental combat team in the Akyab area should withdraw to central Burma if circumstances warranted it. Because the British advance was both powerful and swift, the Japanese on 26 December decided that the situation in central Burma required the immediate withdrawal of their force in the Akyab area and the town fell without a fight on 4 January.   SEAC was beginning to pluck the fruits of its 1944 victories.

Meanwhile, the 82d West African Division had been moving southward east of the coastal ridge.   Fifteen Corps decided on a shore-to-shore amphibious assault southeast and inland from Akyab to cut off the Japanese facing the Africans.   The chosen site was Myebon, thirty-five miles to east-southeast.   The initial landing on 12 January went smoothly, but heavy fighting developed soon after, in the mangrove swamps and tidal inlets, as the 25th Indian Division moved up the little Myebon peninsula toward the Japanese flanks and rear.   Myebon once secure, the next targets were Ramree Island, as an airfield site, and Kangaw, about ten miles northeast of Myebon, and so a grave threat to the Japanese *54th Division* as it faced the Africans coming down from the north.

The first landings on Ramree Island were made 21 January by an Indian brigade, and in the ensuing fighting the Japanese garrison on 9 February was finally forced to "a withdrawal which went badly."   In the Arakan fighting the Japanese were forced to maneuver across a network of tidal inlets that often went many miles inland.   Time and again motor gunboats of the Royal Navy caught Japanese rafts and native fishing craft in the streams.   There would be a burst of machine gun and 20- and 40-mm. fire, and a Japanese platoon or section would be shattered.

Kangaw, upstream from Myebon, was assualted 22 January.   The Japanese had the better part of two regiments north of Kangaw, and one regiment down the coast at Taungup, with strong garrisons at coastal points.   The Japanese therefore reacted energetically to this landing behind them.   In his report, Mountbatten compares the resultant fighting to that of Kohima in 1944, thus rating it as heavy as any in Burma.   Beginning 17 February, the Japanese withdrew to the east and south along the coastal ridge, and into inland hill masses.

The Arakan coast slants southeast, the coastal inlets go relatively far inland, and so geography made it easy to keep herding the Japanese into the mountains to the east, toward the African troops coming down from the north. Therefore, 15 Corps decided to send a force ashore at Ru-ywa. From Ru-ywa the troops were to move on air supply to the An area, where they were to meet the 82d West African Division moving down from the north. It was hoped that the *54th Division* could be caught between them. The landing at Ru-ywa was made on 17 February. The West Africans came down punctually from the north and hopes were high; then higher authority directed suspension of the operation.

To date, 15 Corps had been allotted 130 tons a day of air supply. This was now reduced to 30 tons a day, because all available resources had to be devoted to the central Burma offensive. Reluctantly, 15 Corps suspended major operations, and began to withdraw its units to where their support would be less difficult. Fighting continued, but with occupation of Akyab and Ramree the goals of the campaign had been reached.[26]

Slim Wins the Decisive Battle

While 15 Corps had been taking the Arakan fields from which the transports could move deep into central Burma from Mandalay, 4 and 33 Corps had been drawing closer to that city. Almost together, on 7 and 8 January, the 19th Indian and British 2d Divisions arrived at Shwebo on the Burma Railways line, fifty miles north of Mandalay and twenty miles from the Irrawaddy. Covering its south flank with one brigade, the 19th swung east and crossed the Irrawaddy with two brigades on 14 January. The Japanese thought this was the moment for which they had been waiting and sent the *15th* and *53d Divisions* to attack the 19th. They were sure this was 4 Corps, and still thought so after the war. The disparity in force was not what might be imagined, for the Japanese divisions had but 4,500 men each, and the *53d* had been weakened by detachments which were, however, ordered to rejoin. From 20 January to 20 February the battle around the 19th Indian Division's bridgehead went on, costing the *15th Division* about 30 percent casualties, embroiling Kimura's reserves north of Mandalay, and depleting his very small store of medium artillery. The fight was hot and heavy, with the Indian troops withstanding every Japanese effort.

While the Indian troops were distracting the Japanese for precious weeks, 4 Corps was completing its shift and preparing to swing out around the right end of Slim's team. The engineers and mechanics, no less than the pilots and aircrews, made the advance possible, for in places along the trails through central Burma the dust was three feet deep, a tremendous burden on maintenance and road-building personnel. But 33 Corps and 4 Corps pressed on with vigor, despite the often desperate resistance of Japanese outposts, and

[26] (1) ALFSEA Record, Ch. VII. (2) Mountbatten Report, Pt. B, pars. 343–77. (3) Japanese Study 132, pp. 18–34. (4) Japanese Officers' comments on draft MS.

by 12 February, the 20th Indian Division, 33 Corps, was ready to cross the Irrawaddy at its great bend west of Mandalay. The 20th was in position to offer an obvious threat to Mandalay and Slim hoped it would further distract the Japanese while the 4 Corps was readying itself for the eastward thrust to cut below the main Japanese concentration at Mandalay. On the night of 12 February the division made its initial crossing, on the boundary between the Japanese *31st* and *33d Divisions*.

That same night 4 Corps crossed over. Further deception was involved here, for an East African brigade had moved south along the Irrawaddy's west bank as if to menace the great oil fields at Yenangyaung. The ruse worked, for 33d Indian Infantry Brigade, 7th Indian Division, crossed the Irrawaddy south of Pakokku against some perfunctory machine gun fire. The Japanese, using a regiment of the *49th Division* under *28th Army* command, later reacted vigorously against the East Africans, even driving them back up the river, but the 33d Indian Infantry Brigade, soon joined by the 89th, was not seriously attacked. The 33 Corps was applying such heavy pressure that the Japanese troops originally destined for Pakokku could not be moved there.[27]

The Japanese failure to appreciate the menace created by the 33d's bridgehead permitted two mechanized brigades (63d, 48th) of the 17th Indian Division and the 255th Indian Tank Brigade to be concentrated in it, after the aircraft necessary to maintain these units had been obtained.[28] On 21 February the 17th Indian Division and the armor burst out of the bridgehead and rushed on Meiktila, moving on a wide front to minimize terrain problems.

An airfield about twenty-five miles from Meiktila was captured early 26 February and the third brigade of the 17th, organized on an air-transportable basis, prepared to emplane and begin the flight from the rear, several hundred miles away. Its fly-in was complete 2 March. As these reinforcements were hurrying forward, the task force was deploying around Meiktila. So far it had been more than a match for the tag ends and service troops that had been in its way, though they had resisted with the accustomed sacrificial valor of the Japanese. Meanwhile, *15th Army* failed to appreciate the threat and was several days reacting.

Meiktila was garrisoned by a collection of service troops later estimated at 3,500, well able to find cover and concealment in the town. Moreover, the approaches to the town from the west were channeled between small lakes. Despite these obstacles, the Indian infantry and armor had the town secure by 4 March, after but three days' fighting. A comparison between the siege of Myitkyina and the battle of Meiktila displays the advantages of veteran troops under skilled commanders, with adequate artillery, armor, and

---

[27] (1) Japanese Study 132, p. 16. (2) Japanese Officers' comments on draft MS.
[28] The complicated question of transport aircraft resources will be discussed in Chapter X, below.

air support, as against the heterogeneous force from three nations and several divisions, with little artillery and no armor, that finally took Myitkyina.[29]

After taking Meiktila, the victors fanned out over the communications network of which that town was the hub. In so doing, one armored task force met the first evidence of Japanese disorganization. The *168th Regiment, 49th Division,* which had fought in the Shweli and Salween area under *33d Army,* was marching along in administrative fashion. Taken by surprise, the *168th* was cut to pieces on the road before it could deploy. Even after this episode, the Japanese were slow to react, and for some days treated the loss of Meiktila as relatively minor.

While the 17th Indian Division and 255th Tank Brigade were drawing up around Meiktila, the troops Slim had put across the Irrawaddy north of Mandalay began to reap the rewards of their increasing advantages in strength, organization, training, and equipment over the battered Japanese who faced them. On 20 February the 19th Indian Division broke out of its bridgehead and began moving south. Bypassing strongpoints that could not be quickly reduced, it exploited its breakthrough and arrived on the outskirts of Mandalay with two brigades on 9 March. The third brigade moved east to take Maymyo, the prewar summer capital of Burma in the hills, of more importance as a key point on the line of communications to the Japanese *56th Division.*

Kimura now faced two crises, at Meiktila and Mandalay. He had already detached the *18th Division* from *33d Army* and sent it toward Mandalay. He now found Mandalay threatened, Meiktila gone, and the British across the Irrawaddy on a wide front. He decided Mandalay was the crucial point and did not turn his full attention to Meiktila until mid-March. Actually, the decisive battle was that fought out around Meiktila in late March. To wage it, Kimura summoned *Headquarters, 33d Army,* from the Northern Combat Area Command front, and attached to it the *18th Division* (less one regiment), the *49th Division* (less one regiment) from the delta area of south Burma, the remnants of the *53 Division,* and a regiment of the *33d.* The *15th Army* was left with the *15th, 33d,* and *31st Divisions,* and the *4th Regiment* of the *2d* from the NCAC front. The other two regiments of the *2d Division* were en route to Indochina because of orders from the highest Japanese headquarters in southeast Asia, *Joint Expeditionary Forces, Southern Regions,* so the decisive battle was fought without them.[30]

In the region of Mandalay, Slim had the 19th and 20th Indian Divisions and the British 2d, which proved enough, but for the situation around Meiktila he felt that he needed more troops. These were provided by a

---

[29] (1) For a description of the siege of Myitkyina, see *Stilwell's Command Problems,* Ch. VI. (2) Japanese Officers' comments on draft MS.
[30] (1) SEATIC Bull 247, pp. 46–47. (2) Japanese Officers' comments on draft MS.

brigade of the 5th Indian Division, landed on Meiktila airfield under Japanese shell fire.   The other two brigades moved from Assam to the battle area by truck, arriving there in mid-March.

The fight around Meiktila was bitter.   The Japanese did their very best to cut the line of communications from Meiktila west to the bridgehead, and succeeded, cutting off the services of supply elements of the 17th Indian Division, which had to stay under cover of the 7th Indian Division in the bridgehead area.   At Meiktila the veteran *18th Division* reached the main airstrip in a night attack and dug in at its fringe.   The Japanese were pushed back, but attacked again and succeeded in overrunning the whole field.   Airdropping was now necessary to supply the 17th and the armor.   But the Indian and British troops never faltered, and counterattacked ceaselessly.   To the north, three of Slim's divisions were tearing apart the Mandalay garrison, and to the west, 7th Indian Division was assaulting to open communications to Meiktila.

The battle for Meiktila was decided the night of 28 March when the Japanese conceded defeat in the decisive struggle for central Burma.   Visiting the *33d Army* headquarters, the chief of staff of *Burma Area Army,* General Tanaka, who had been Stilwell's opponent in north Burma, on his own authority ordered the *33d Army* to pass to a holding role so that the *15th Army* might withdraw from the Mandalay area.   Next day the 17th Indian Division was able to report the airstrip cleared, before the changed orders issued midnight 29 March could reach the Japanese at the front, and on 30 March the 161st Indian Infantry Brigade from the west broke the Japanese block on the line of communication to Meiktila.

The victory in central Burma was Slim's, though there was still hard fighting ahead along the Irrawaddy.   Henceforth, though Japanese regiments and some divisions could keep a fair amount of cohesion, the Japanese command in Burma slowly began to disintegrate on the retreat south and west.   Army headquarters troops found themselves fighting as infantry.   Confusion and disorganization began to spread through the Japanese rear areas as Slim's armored columns, moving ever faster, knifed through them.   Thereafter, whether or not SEAC would take Rangoon depended primarily on the logistical support that could be allotted.[31]

Reinforcements for China Theater

The logistical support available for Slim's campaigns and the extent to which the Chinese Army in India and MARS Task Force would contribute

---

[31] (1) 36th Div Diary.   (2) Mountbatten Report, Pt. B., Secs. 5, 6.   (3) ALFSEA Record, Chs. VIII, IX.   (4) Japanese Study 148, Ch. V.   (5) Japanese Study 134, pp. 99–107.   (6) Brigadier M. R. Roberts, *Golden Arrow* (Aldershot, England: Gale and Polden, 1952), Chs. XIX, XX.

ALLIED LEADERS PLAN OPERATIONS *in China and Burma early in 1945. General Wedemeyer stands behind (from left to right) General Sultan, Admiral Mountbatten, and Maj. Gen. William J. Donovan.*

further to victory in Burma were problems difficult to assess. The United States had long insisted on a Burma campaign to support China. Now when that campaign was at its height and British forces were fully involved at the end of a tenuous line of communications of which air transport was an integral part, events in China made the Chinese Government, Wedemeyer, and the Joint Chiefs anxious to move Chinese and American resources from Burma to China as quickly as possible. Though procedures had been established to deal with requests for such transfers,[32] these procedures did not provide guarantees against an outcome possibly injurious to SEAC's current campaign in Burma. So the British Chiefs of Staff sought assurances and on 31 January asked that no further transfer of resources from India–Burma–China that was unacceptable to SEAC be made without CCS approval.[33]

[32] See above, p. 145.
[33] CCS 747/7, 31 Jan 45, sub: Allocation of Resources Between IB and CT.

To this the Joint Chiefs gave an assent so highly qualified as to disturb Mountbatten, for they agreed only that the CCS should "discuss" transfer, whereas the British had wanted the CCS to control.   The JCS based their stand on the ground that: "The primary military object of the United States in the China and India–Burma Theaters is the continuance of aid to China on a scale that will permit the fullest utilization of the area and resources of China for operations against the Japanese.   United States resources are deployed in India–Burma to provide direct or indirect support for China." Mountbatten was concerned that his resources in transport aircraft might be lost to him.[34]

Mountbatten's fears were apparently shared by the British Chiefs of Staff, for they suggested to the CCS that there should be no withdrawal of U.S. resources from Burma to support China without prior discussion by the CCS, lest approved operations in Burma be thereby endangered.   The merits of this contention were recognized by the Combined Chiefs, who found themselves reluctant to deprive Mountbatten of forces upon which he had counted without first examining the issues.   They therefore agreed that if the British Chiefs of Staff objected to any transfer of U.S. forces from SEAC the matter would be referred to the CCS.[35]

Meanwhile, in China, Wedemeyer was reaching conclusions that would bring forth just the contingency Mountbatten feared.   Looking beyond the present China situation toward a day when the Allies could seize the initiative in China, he told the Generalissimo on 5 January that the center of strategic gravity should shift east into China rather than south to Rangoon. The Generalissimo agreed.   Wedemeyer announced that studies would be made.   A week later he was prepared to recommend that the entire Chinese Army in India should return to China.   He was not suggesting hasty action and pointed out that the United States had urged Britain to take action in Burma, that moral obligations to the British were involved.   Wedemeyer in January–February 1945 hoped to begin concentration for the offensive toward Canton–Hong Kong on 1 May.   This meant the Chinese would have to leave Burma in time to arrive in east China by 1 May.   He also looked forward to intensified air activity; the Tenth Air Force was the nearest source of reinforcements.[36]

Meeting with Mountbatten and Sultan at Myitkyina around 16 February, Wedemeyer told Mountbatten of his desire to bring all the Chinese troops

[34] (1) CCS 452/37, 1 Feb 45, sub: Opns in SEAC.   This paper was approved by the CCS and reported to the President and Prime Minister.   (2) Mountbatten Report, Pt. B, par. 397.
[35] Min, Mtg of CCS, 1 Feb 45.   *Foreign Relations of the United States: Diplomatic Papers.* Dept State Pub 6199, *The Conferences at Malta and Yalta, 1945* (Washington, 1955).
[36] (1) Min, Mtg 27, Wedemeyer With Generalissimo, 5 Jan 45; Mtg 28, 13 Jan 45.   Bk 1, Generalissimo Minutes.   (2) Rad CFB 32476, Wedemeyer to MacArthur and Nimitz, info Marshall, 5 Feb 45.   Bks 1 and 2, ACW Personal File.

back to China.   Mountbatten, anxious to complete the Burma campaign and with the fight for Mandalay still under way, not unnaturally opposed the suggestion.   Sultan, however, was reported to have agreed that after Lashio was taken it would be possible to move the Chinese Army in India back to the homeland and to rely upon two or three Y–Force divisions to protect the Burma Road and pipeline.[37]

For his part, Mountbatten may have decided that the Combined Chiefs would keep the Chinese divisions in Burma long enough to permit a successful conclusion of the campaign, for he directed his planners and commanders in chief to consider the aggressive exploitation of Slim's successes around Mandalay.   Assuming they would be able to use the Chinese Army in India, the SEAC staffs began to weigh the possibility of taking Rangoon by 1 June.   If they decided this was possible, they had to determine whether it would be better to take it by overland attack from the north after capture of Mandalay, or by amphibious assault, thus reviving Operation DRACULA.

Mountbatten further directed that an attack be made on the Isthmus of Kra of the Malay Peninsula by June and as soon as possible after Rangoon was taken and its port back in operation.   On 23 February Mountbatten and his senior commanders and staff took what appeared the determining decisions—to seize Rangoon by overland assault, and use the amphibious resources thus freed for an attack on the Isthmus of Kra, by 1 June if possible.[38]

That same day, 23 February, brought the message that Mountbatten must have anticipated with concern, a radio from Sultan warning that China Theater was about to ask that all U.S. and Chinese forces in north Burma—MARS Task Force and three Chinese divisions—be sent to China.   Shortly after, Wedemeyer stated that he needed MARS Task Force immediately, and requested one regiment by 10 March and the other by 1 April.[39]

Lashio and the Reinforcement Problem

This request focused new attention on the drive for Lashio, because it had been agreed that Lashio's capture, which would place a wide belt of liberated territory south of the ground line of communications across north Burma, would mark the end of Phase II of CAPITAL.   After the Japanese broke contact with MARS Task Force it had been pulled back into reserve and Sultan ordered the Chinese New First Army to move southwest down the Burma Road and take Lashio.   The Chinese 50th Division was directed to move

---

[37] Min, Mtg 30, Wedemeyer with Generalissimo, 19 Jan 45.   Bk 1, Generalissimo Minutes.
[38] Mountbatten Report, Pt. B, pars. 398–408.
[39] Mountbatten Report, Pt. B, par. 446.

south from Namtu, take Hsipaw, and establish itself across the Burma Road. The hope was that the 50th would be the anvil for the hammer of the New First Army. (*See Map 12.*)

Between the Chinese positions in the Hosi–Namhpakka area and Lashio the two principal towns are Kutkai and Hsenwi. Kutkai fell without a fight, the Chinese finding there prepared positions abandoned by the Japanese. Four miles north of Hsenwi came that rarity in Burma, a fight between armored units. These were Chinese tanks of the First Provisional Tank Group, now back in the fight since the campaign was moving out of the jungles, and a Japanese armored column. The heavier Chinese armor won the day, and Hsenwi was taken 19 February.

Around Lashio itself the Kachin Rangers of OSS Detachment 101 had been most active, harassing the Japanese and directing the Tenth Air Force on to profitable targets. With their growing strength and increasing Japanese weakness they were becoming strong enough to try open warfare. On 26 February four Kachin companies held a hilltop overlooking the road between Hsenwi and Lashio against an estimated 500 Japanese. Not till the following day did the Rangers withdraw, feeling that they had inflicted heavy casualties at light cost.

By this time, the *56th Division,* now in independent command of this sector, was concerned only with delaying action and placed no strong obstacles before the Chinese 38th Division. Old Lashio, the prewar settlement, and the suburb of New Lashio, which had been born of Burma Road traffic before 1942, were occupied by the Chinese over 6 and 7 March. The question of the next mission for the Chinese Army in India now became acute.[40]

Mountbatten feared that if more Chinese troops were withdrawn from Burma it might not be possible to take Rangoon before the monsoon rains began. Capture of Rangoon's harbor facilities was essential if Slim's troops were to be supported in Burma. Otherwise the monsoon, whose rains would turn the roads east of Imphal into quagmires, would find Slim's six divisions and two tank brigades dependent on an airlift at almost the maximum range of the transports. This was an unpleasant prospect, so Mountbatten went to Chungking on 8 March for two days of conference with the Generalissimo.[41]

When the conference of 9 March concluded, the Generalissimo, according to the American minutes, said that he would recapitulate. In so doing, he remarked that the details of withdrawal would be settled later and that no final decisions would be made before General Wedemeyer was able to take part in them. Then he stated that unless there was a simultaneous amphibious attack on Rangoon, operations would stop at Lashio and Mandalay and

[40] History of IBT, II, 316–18.
[41] Mountbatten Report, Pt. B, Par. 448.

the Allies would assume the defensive. The Chinese would stop at Lashio, but details of their operations between Lashio and Mandalay would be settled later between the staffs. And he took note of Mountbatten's statement that the Chinese would not be asked to go south of Mandalay.[42]

That the Generalissimo should include in his recapitulation points to which SEAC was unalterably opposed, such as stopping operations at Mandalay, suggests that the conference did not clarify matters. The exchange of radios which soon followed showed that in fact there had been no more than an exchange of views.

It soon became apparent that Mountbatten did not want to use the Chinese south of Mandalay, but he did not believe that their actual withdrawal would be on any date set by the conferences but rather would be determined by the course of the battle. The Chinese, on the other hand, did not want their troops to take on further obligations once they had entered the Lashio–Hsipaw area.

The misunderstanding became quite apparent in mid-March when General Sultan, under whose command the Chinese were, received conflicting orders. In mid-March it was apparent that the 38th and 30th Divisions coming down the Burma Road were about to link with the Chinese 50th Division moving southeast, that Hsipaw would soon be taken. Therefore, SEAC ordered Sultan to move his forces southwestward toward Mandalay, while the Generalissimo directed that the Chinese divisions stay in the Lashio area.

As a compromise and to avoid having the Chinese wait idly around Lashio, Sultan suggested that a smaller task force be directed to proceed south. But the Generalissimo and his American advisers stood firm, lest the shift of troops to China be delayed. This in turn caused the British to believe that if the Chinese were not going to advance they should be withdrawn forthwith and end the burden on the line of communications. Behind this attitude lay the fact that as of 20 March the fight for Mandalay was obviously a British victory. However, the trend toward a speedy departure of the Chinese did not lead to rigidity on either side; later in March it was agreed the Chinese would advance westward from Hsipaw along the Lashio–Mandalay rail line to take the town of Kyaukme. Kyaukme taken, SEAC requested a further advance, but here the Generalissimo had, it developed, made his final concession.

While these high-level discussions had been taking place, the New First Army from Lashio and the 50th Division from Namtu had been steadily advancing. By 13 March the 50th was moving on Hsipaw. Curiously, the Japanese yielded Hsipaw without a fight, then counterattacked bitterly on 17, 18, 19, and 20 March. The Chinese held, then, sending one regiment south

---

[42] Min, American Mtg Held in Generalissimo's Presidential Residence in the Country, 1015, 9 Mar 45. OCMH.

MEN OF THE 988TH SIGNAL BATTALION, *attached to the Chinese 50th Division, send a message on 22 March from the occupied town of Hsipaw.*

and dispatching another one northward up the Burma Road to assist the Chinese 38th Division driving south, from a point sixty miles away. The 38th on occasion met fierce resistance coming down the road, but the Japanese had no intention of being caught between the 38th and tne 50th when they could so easily sideslip away to the south. On 24 March, seven miles east of Hsipaw, the two divisions met, and the whole of the Burma Road from Hsipaw to Kunming was in Chinese hands.[43]

Sultan believed that this was the final move, and so he recommended that the Chinese be moved back to the Myitkyina area, save only those troops needed to guard the Lashio–Hsipaw area. At Myitkyina they would be easier to supply until the time came to move them to China. The Chinese were moved back accordingly and plans made to have them in China by 1 July, the move beginning on 1 June.[44]

The MARS Task Force was first to move to China. In the discussions on the employment of the Chinese in Burma, Sultan had observed that MARS made far heavier demands on air supply than would an equivalent number of Chinese troops. For that reason he doubted whether he could afford to use them to pursue the Japanese. Therefore, on 11 March, Mountbatten ordered that one MARS regiment be released at once for China service, and the rest of the force on 1 April. The move began 14 March and was completed 14 May.[45]

Therefore, as a result of the victories in Burma, Wedemeyer's position in China was soon to be bolstered by powerful reinforcements. Two good divisions had been moved to China; three more were to come. The MARS Task Force would provide a very welcome source of experienced U.S. personnel.

[43] History of IBT, II, 324–25.
[44] History of IBT, II, 327–32.
[45] (1) Mountbatten Report, Pt. B, par. 452.   (2) NCAC History, III, 324.

CHAPTER VIII

Finding a Way To Advise and Assist

Since the Japanese forces that threatened Kunming in December 1944 had not been part of a Japanese design to take that city, the American arrangements to defend it had not been subjected to the test of battle. Such a test in December would have fallen on Chinese troops which lack of time had prevented Wedemeyer from improving and about whose quality, save for the 14th and 22d Divisions, he had the most serious doubts. But the storm passed by. So there was to be a chance to reorganize and train thirty-six Chinese divisions, and give them some measure of logistical support.

Making Liaison Effective

Among the directives that Wedemeyer issued to his major U.S. commands in mid-December was an interim directive to the officers who were to work with the Chinese ALPHA forces.[1] It ordered them to advise the Chinese and also keep theater headquarters promptly informed of the local situation. The problem lay in making this intention operative in the face of Chinese practices and attitudes that had created difficulties in the past.

Believing he had to have some assurance that the Chinese commander would accept advice once it had been offered, and being anxious to avoid what he described as "polite agreement and Chinese niceties followed by vacillation or no agreement," Wedemeyer told the War Department on 1 January 1945 he had arranged a liaison system with the Chinese to which the Generalissimo had agreed.[2] Wedemeyer planned ultimately to have a U.S. officer advising every Chinese ALPHA force commander from the regiment right up through army and group army headquarters to General Ho Ying-chin himself. If a Chinese commander were to refuse to accept the suggestions offered by the American working with him, the matter would be referred

---

[1] See Ch. V, above.
[2] Quotation from radiogram CFB 30283, 1 January 1945. This radio was probably addressed primarily to Lt. Gen. John E. Hull of the Operations Division, War Department, with whom Wedemeyer often corresponded.

TABLE 2—COMPARISON OF JAPANESE AND CHINESE DIVISION FIREPOWER

	Alpha Division table of equipment	Old Chinese table of equipment	Japanese table of equipment [a]
Rifles	6, 103	2, 400	9, 000
Light machine gun	334	212	382
Heavy machine gun	72	70	112
60-mm. mortar	162	97	([b])
82-mm. mortar	36	22	([b])
37-mm. AT gun	24	14	22
Infantry cannon	none	none	30
Grenade discharger	([c])	([c])	350

[a] The Japanese freely modified their tables of organization and equipment to meet local situations but it can be assumed that the Japanese three-regiment or triangular infantry division would probably not depart significantly from the above.

[b] Trench mortars were not organic to the Japanese infantry division unless used to replace the 70-mm. battalion gun, in which case 36 81-mm. mortars would substitute for 18 battalion guns.

[c] Chinese divisions were known to have some grenade dischargers, either captured or locally made. The number would vary, depending on the preference of the division commander and the past successes of his unit in obtaining this weapon.

Source: Data on the Chinese forces from Staff Study 11, Theater Planning Sec, 24 Mar 45. USFCT Files, DRB AGO. Data on the Japanese forces from TM–E 30–480, *Handbook on Japanese Military Forces*. OCMH.

in twenty-four hours to their respective superiors, Chinese and American. Ultimately, if the matter could not be resolved, it would end up before the Generalissimo and Wedemeyer. In effect, as Wedemeyer clearly recognized and intended, he and his staff would exercise operational control in the Generalissimo's name. "Any Chinese commander who continually fails to follow the well considered advice of his U.S. advisor will be replaced or have U.S. assistance withdrawn from his unit." [3]

Wedemeyer sketched his hopes and beliefs about the thirty-six divisions. He wanted them to be equipped and maintained as were the divisions in the Chinese Army in India, with better pay and better food than they currently had. "I have emphasized that if we could create 36 well-trained, well-fed, and well-led divisions we could recover the vital airfields recently lost in Central [*sic*] China. At the present time China's resources, money, food, and equipment (all of which are limited) are being further dissipated by an attempt to maintain the semblance of 300 to 400 divisions. I pointed out to the Generalissimo that we require quality not quantity. He appears to be in complete accord."

The concept underlying the structure of the U.S.-sponsored Chinese division was that, with its 10,000 men and battalion of artillery, it would be more than a match for a Japanese regiment. The Chinese army, with 30,000 men, three battalions of 75-mm. pack howitzers, and one battalion of 105-mm.

[3] Opnl Dir 5, Hq USFCT to CG CCC, 15 Feb 45, par. 3B. KCRC.

howitzers, was more nearly comparable to the division as understood in Western armies. Table 2 is illustrative only.

Wedemeyer commented on the quality of Chinese officers as they had appeared to him: "incapable, inept, untrained, petty . . . altogether inefficient." By, as he wrote, "superimposing" his liaison system on the ALPHA divisions Wedemeyer thought he had the only way to obtain effective employment of the Chinese in the war.[4]

The new organization, foreshadowed and explained by Wedemeyer's 1 January 1945 radio to the War Department, was activated a week later. The two-months old Chinese Training and Combat Command was now split in two, with the cleavage along the line that separates training and operations.

In its stead were set up a Chinese Combat Command (CCC) and a Chinese Training Center. The center, at Kunming, consisted of Headquarters, Chinese Training Center, and, under its command, a General Staff School, Infantry Training Center, Field Artillery Training Center, Automotive School for Drivers and Mechanics, and a Chinese Ordnance Training Center. Its mission was to supervise and conduct schools, and to prepare and distribute training literature, programs, and training aids. The Americans were most anxious to have as many Chinese senior officers as possible receive staff training because they believed that in many cases the senior Chinese were not as well qualified as were the junior officers. Unit training and troop schools were to be conducted in the field by the new Chinese Combat Command.

The proposed Chinese Combat Command was described by General McClure at a commanders' conference 3 January. Briefly, it comprised the U.S. liaison personnel with the 36 divisions, plus headquarters personnel. During the time of preparation for battle, its program included training, equipping, and giving supplemental pay and rations to 36 divisions of 10,000 men each, with service troops—some 500,000 men. Later the number might be expanded to 50 divisions. In addition, there would be 30 so-called commando units of 150 to 200 Chinese officered and trained by Americans.

When combat began, the Americans would ensure effective leadership. "The Chinese chain of combat command will come down from supreme headquarters through General Ho Ying-chin to divisions in the field where the Chinese senior officers will be in command with the Americans exercising a field command only through the Chinese with whom they are associated." McClure pointed out that the only means the Americans had to make their control effective was "the denial of weapons and essential equipment to those groups who do not cooperate with us."

---

[4] (1) Rad cited n. 2. (2) Brig. Gen. Paul W. Caraway, in reviewing the draft manuscript in October 1956, commented that General Wedemeyer "did not see or have contact with many junior [Chinese] officers." Caraway comments on draft MS. OCMH.

CHINESE SENIOR OFFICERS *attend a chemical warfare demonstration at Kunming.*

The Americans working directly with the thirty-six divisions would be organized into two major groupings, those assigned to the CCC and the service troops under General Cheves of the SOS. The liaison sections of the Chinese Combat Command were to be attached to each of the major Chinese area commands that would be set up under General Ho. The several senior U.S. officers in turn would command a pyramid of U.S. liaison personnel down to division level. For the time being, since personnel strengths were so low, U.S. liaison officers and men would not have fixed attachments at the regimental level. The Americans were to be picked from different arms and services so that qualified technicians organized as Ordnance, Quartermaster, Surgical, and Signal Sections would be present to help the Chinese.

The SOS, under General Cheves, would control all supply and transport facilities for the thirty-six divisions and CCC. When McClure spoke, this system was in the planning phase, but on 9 February it became a reality as Cheves took charge of the Chinese Services of Supply for the thirty-six divisions. The basic plan contemplated that the American technical service officers would forward requisitions either through command channels or direct to SOS, as might later be agreed. SOS would be responsible for procurement and delivery. At this time McClure understood that Cheves planned to deliver to the Chinese division dump. There the American G–4 of the division liaison team would become responsible for delivering supplies to the individual Chinese soldier.

Linking these activities would be a series of radio nets joining the radio teams that were integral parts of the liaison sections. At the top of the pyramid would be a high-level net joining General McClure, Commanding General, CCC, at Kunming or in the field, General Ho at Kunming, and Chungking. Kunming in turn would operate in a net that would include liaison sections with all group armies. Group armies would be netted with subordinate army liaison sections, which in turn would be netted with division liaison sections. Within divisions, a mobile radio team was to operate behind the lines.

To anticipate, it may be noted that when the liaison teams, or "U.S. combat sections" as they were officially called, took the field, each, regardless of the level at which it operated, had a Table of Organization strength of about 25 officers and 50 enlisted men. Thus, some 4,000 Americans were to assist the headquarters of 4 Chinese group armies, 12 armies, and 36 divisions (though personnel shortages kept the final total to 3,147). In addition, to each combat section there was to be attached an air-ground liaison section of 2 officers and 4 enlisted men, which would also operate a separate and parallel radio net to control the allotted air support.[5]

Chinese Combat Command headquarters on being activated further specified the reports it wanted from the field. In years past, the Chinese had been reluctant to let American Army liaison teams go out into the field. Detailed, accurate knowledge of the Chinese Army was correspondingly lacking, while the Americans hesitated to accept Chinese War Ministry statistics and communiques at face value. The U.S. liaison teams were now directed to keep a stream of statistical data, strength reports, personnel data, training reports, and situation reports flowing up the chain of command to Chinese Combat Command and theater headquarters. As the months went by, these reports would create the most complete sort of picture of the ALPHA forces and would give data on which sound policy recommendations could be based.[6]

[5] (1) Conf Notes, Off CG CT&CC CT, 3 Jan 45. AG 337 Misc Folder, Meetings 1944 to 30 Aug 45, CT Files, Box BA 51513, KCRC. (2) Ltr O, Wedemeyer to all officers CCC, 18 Feb 45, sub: Ltr of Instruction to All U.S. Officers Serving With the CCC. OCMH. (3) Ltr, Wedemeyer to CO Chinese Training Center, 26 Jan 45, sub: Organization and Mission of Chinese Training Center. OCMH. (4) Strength figures on CCC from Ltr, Col Raymond W. McNamee, ACofS G–3, Hq USFCT, to CofS Hq USFCT, 14 Aug 45, sub: Plan for Liaison Personnel with Occupying Forces. OCMH.
[6] Memos, Gen McClure, CG CCC, 17 Feb 45, 9 Jul 45, for all Sector Comdrs, sub: Rpts. AG (CCC) 319.1, KCRC.

On 25 January Wedemeyer told the Generalissimo he was sending General McClure, his own chief of staff and deputy U.S. chief of staff to Chiang Kai-shek, to Kunming to take over the Chinese Combat Command, as he was not satisfied with its progress to that date. Wedemeyer thought that some of the men who had been Stilwell's aides showed the strain of their years in Asia and, in this case, McClure succeeded the veteran Dorn. Wedemeyer was now also contemplating a change in the air force organization by bringing in the Tenth Air Force to join the Fourteenth, the Fourteenth to be a strategic air force, the Tenth to have a tactical role, and Lt. Gen. George E. Stratemeyer from India–Burma Theater to command both.[7]

Shortly after McClure took command, the Chinese forces assigned to ALPHA were divided among six area commands, in a sort of great circle around the vital Kunming area.[8] This was a radical departure from the old system of dividing all China among a few vast war areas under semi-independent commanders. On 29 January General Ho presented his proposals for organizing his troops on the new basis. Accepting Wedemeyer's views, Ho suggested the creation of an offensive force of 36 divisions and a defensive force of 9 divisions. *(Chart 4)* The first would be organized under the November 1944 tables which would give each of the divisions about two-thirds of the fire power of a Class A Japanese division. The defensive force would follow the old Y–Force Table of Organization. In previous conferences the Americans had been quite clear in stating that they could equip only thirty-six divisions; Ho's plan finally accepted this. Ho's plan went to the Generalissimo's headquarters where it was approved, and went into operation in February with only minor changes in troop assignments and deployments.[9] With the Generalissimo's approval, the Chinese Combat Command's officers in the field were authorized to proceed with the thirty-six-division plan.

The Chinese Training Center, Col. John Middleton commanding, encountered problems in beginning its work, for Chinese students were slow in appearing. On 6 March McClure told the Chinese officers of Ho's headquarters, with whom CCC's staff now met regularly, that the Chinese Training Center's Command and General Staff and Infantry Schools were ready to go but had no Chinese students. In reply, General Hsiao I-hsu, who had been General Wei Li-huang's chief of staff on the Salween front, stated that the

---

[7] (1) Min, Mtg 33, Wedemeyer with Generalissimo, 25 Jan 45. Bk 1, Generalissimo Minutes. (2) Ltr, Wedemeyer to Hull, 29 Jan 45. Case 37, OPD 381 (TS), Sec II.

[8] See pp. 264–69, below, for detailed description.

[9] (1) Min, Combined Staff Mtgs Between Chinese and American Hq, 15 Jan–3 Feb 45. AG (CCC) 337.1, KCRC. (2) Rad CFB 32878, Wedemeyer to McClure, 11 Feb 45, Item 393, ACW Personal File, says formal approval will be sent.

CHART 4—CHINESE ALPHA FORCES: 36-DIVISION FORCE

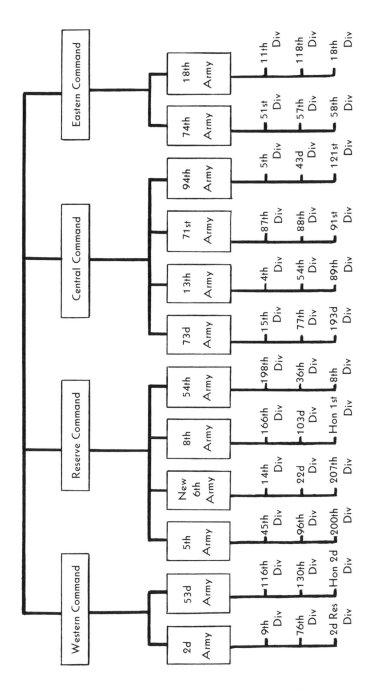

*After the return of the New First Army (30th, 38th, and 50th Divisions) in June 1945, China Theater used the term 39-Division or Chinese Army Program (CAP) in plans and preparations for the BETA Operation.

Chinese had been so busy reorganizing that they could not yet send students, but hoped to have them there by mid-April.[10]

Working Out the Thirty-six-Division Plan

The details of Ho's plan had taken some days to work out, for they involved the question of priorities in distributing equipment among the divisions under Ho's command. Who was to get what supplies in what order? When the thirty-six-division scheme began to get under way, McClure stated on 31 January that the United States had in China four complete division sets with enough infantry weapons for ten more divisions to start training. For the future, complete equipment for the thirty-six divisions was to be flown over the Hump by 1 September 1945. Arms shipments had to be meshed with General Chennault's needs; the Fourteenth Air Force had its daily requirements that had to be met.

To take care of the fact that all equipment would not be on hand at once, Wedemeyer had ordered that twenty ALPHA divisions, plus five returning from Burma, would be completely equipped first. That done, the next flow of equipment would be allocated among the remaining eleven ALPHA divisions. Fitting his plans to this, Ho began setting his own priorities. In them he seems to have accepted two principles: first, to equip six divisions on the natural avenues of approach to Kunming and Chungking, like the Kweiyang and Chihchiang areas; second, to equip two divisions of each army first. The remaining division could borrow and train with this equipment, but Ho decided it should not be spread out within the army.

Ho's plan called for first priority in equipping the 13th Army (two divisions); the 94th (one division); the 8th Army (two divisions); the 18th Army (one division). In the next group, the 94th, and 18th Armies would each get another division set, and the 5th, 54th, and 74th Armies would get two division sets. McClure's comments in the staff meetings that shaped these plans made it plain that infantry weapons would receive first priority, in shipment and issue.[11]

The emphasis McClure placed on infantry weapons implied that he was willing to defer organization of artillery battalions for some time. Indeed, he so stated on 12 February, and added that the artillery problem could be postponed for two months. The artillery component of the ALPHA forces was to comprise 12 battalions of 105-mm. howitzers divided among the 12 armies, 1 battalion of 75-mm. pack howitzers for each division, and 3 bat-

[10] Min, Combined Staff Mtg Between Chinese and American Hq, 6 Mar 45. AG (CCC) 337.1, KCRC.
[11] Min, Combined Staff Mtgs Between Chinese and American Hq, 31 Jan–26 Feb 45. AG (CCC) 337.1, KCRC.

CHINESE ARTILLERYMEN *demonstrating how to pack a 75-mm. M1A1 pack howitzer for transport.*

talions of 155-mm. howitzers and 192 4.2-inch mortars for Supreme Head-quarters reserve. The modesty of the level of artillery support was more apparent than real, for the 4.2-inch mortars would be a powerful reinforcement.[12] The Americans did not know it, but the above would have about equaled what the Japanese had.

The Japanese artillery in China had never been strong. Only the elite divisions had cannon. Essentially, the Japanese had depended upon their hardy infantry to garrison north China and watch the Nationalist forces. In 1944 their reinforcement program had brought 8 more battalions of artillery to China. Their postwar accounts, which list 3 Class A divisions, 5 Class B divisions, 11 independent mixed brigades, plus army artillery, would indicate that *China Expeditionary Army* had the equivalent of 50 battalions of

---

[12] Min, Combined Staff Mtgs Between Chinese and American Hq, Mtg 17, 19 Feb 45. AG (CCC) 337.1, KCRC.

field artillery.   If, then, the new Chinese ALPHA battalions were added to the Chinese' own stores of several hundred artillery pieces, the weight of metal would, on completion of the ALPHA program, be about equal.[13]

Substantial progress had already been made in creating Chinese artillery battalions armed with U.S. 75-mm. pack howitzers.   Since most roads in the southeast Chinese provinces were little more than narrow paths between the rice paddies, sure-footed mules carrying pack howitzers gave the best combination of fire power and mobility; this weapon was preferred for division artillery.   On 28 February General Hsiao reported to the Chinese and American staffs working on the ALPHA divisions that 25 pack artillery battalions were ready for assignment to the 36 divisions.   Equipment for 32 battalions had been received, and 4 more sets were on the way.   General Hsiao accounted for the difference between 32 and 25 by remarking that the 31st and 4th Armies had lost all their howitzers in the 1944 East China campaign, that the 46th Army had lost all but 4 pieces, and that 1 more battalion had been lost in action.[14]

The ALPHA divisions would soon have the benefit of logistical support from a revitalized Chinese supply system.   The December 1944 directive to Cheves's American SOS had given him those responsibilities.   Preliminary negotiations on Cheves's part took some weeks.   The final solution was that Cheves was to be given the rank of a lieutenant general in the Chinese Army, and the post of commanding general of the Chinese Services of Supply assigned to Ho's ALPHA forces.   As such, he was to supervise all ammunition, food, clothing, bedding, and pay of these troops.   Though Wedemeyer consistently refused to exercise formal command over Chinese troops, for he understood President Roosevelt's policy was opposed to it, and though Wedemeyer had refused to let General Chennault accept an appointment from the Generalissimo to command the Chinese Air Force, he was willing to let Cheves head the ALPHA SOS forces, on the ground that, as it was a staff appointment, Cheves would be issuing his orders "by command of General Ho Ying-chin." [15]

[13] (1) An estimate of China's artillery resources is given in *Stilwell's Mission to China*, pp 234–35.   (2) Ltr, Col Murphy, Chief Mil Hist Sec FECOM, to Gen Ward, 18 Nov 52, and Incl, Chart 1.   OCMH.   (3) The Japanese Order of Battle Bulletins, published for this period by the Military Intelligence Division, War Department, show no awareness of the 15 or so Class C divisions without artillery.   (4) Japanese Officers' comments on draft MS.   The Japanese claim to have had little ammunition.

[14] (1) Min, Combined Staff Mtg 21, 28 Feb 45.   AG (CCC) 337.1, KCRC.   (2) General Dorn reported to McClure on 11 December 1944 that of 72 75-mm. howitzers sent to the Kweilin–Heng-yang area, 62 were lost with most of the ammunition sent.   Some of the pieces lost at Kweilin were still in their shipping cases.   Memo, Dorn for McClure, 11 Dec 44.   AG (CCC) 381, Folder A, KCRC.

[15] Min, Combined Staff Mtg, 31 Jan 45, 1 Feb 45.   AG (CCC) 337.1, KCRC.   (2) Rad CFB 28804, Generalissimo to Chennault, 9 Dec 44.   Item 163, Bk 1, ACW Personal File.   (3) Min, Mtg 18, Wedemeyer with Generalissimo, 12 Dec 44.   Bk 1, Generalissimo Minutes.   (4) Rad CFB 28962, Wedemeyer to Chennault, 12 Dec 44.   Item 169, Bk 1, ACW Personal File.

Cheves and the Chinese proceeded to organize a Headquarters, Services of Supply, Southwest District, attached to Supreme Headquarters, Chinese Ground Forces (General Ho), Kunming. Under the Chinese SOS were seven area commands, each of which, in a complete departure from past Chinese practice, was put under command of the Chinese general commanding the combat forces in that area. Previously, the Chinese SOS had been independent. Under these area commands were set up branch SOS commands, one for each Chinese army. The Chinese depot system was to be reorganized to match the new area system. General depots were to be organized under Cheves's command. The Chinese area commanders were to command the intermediate depots, and the army commanders, the branch headquarters serving that particular army.

The truckheads in the army area were to be the end of the SOS responsibility. There the using agencies were to take delivery, under supervision of the Chinese Combat Command. As in the American service, the impetus of supply was to be from rear to front, to end the existing Chinese practices of cash allotments and foraging.[16]

While the new SOS organization and the basic plan for thirty-six divisions were taking shape, Wedemeyer and his subordinates also applied themselves to solving some of the basic problems of the ALPHA divisions. It was not necessary to wait on formal approval of every detail of the ALPHA plan to begin work on, for example, the ration question, and ALPHA would never work unless the questions were at least partly answered.

Food for the ALPHA Soldiers

By December 1944 Wedemeyer had, according to his chief of staff, General McClure, concluded that food was the most important Chinese military problem, and on 6 December had offered the Generalissimo a comprehensive plan to improve the soldier's dietary.[17] That the Chinese soldier needed a better diet had long been apparent to students of Chinese military affairs. The ALPHA plan would not work unless the soldiers had the strength to march and fight.

In September 1944 General Joseph W. Stilwell had arranged for the War Department to send Col. Paul P. Logan, Deputy Director of the Subsistence Division, Office of the Quartermaster General, to China to study the problem of feeding the Chinese soldier.[18] Logan's studies formed the basis for one of Wedemeyer's most considerable achievements.

[16] SOS USFCT History, OCMH.
[17] See Ch. II, above.
[18] Memo, Logan for Wedemeyer, 20 Jan 45, sub: Rpt on Nutritional Status and Requirements of Chinese Troops . . . , par. 1. OCMH. (Hereafter, Logan Report.) Logan received his orders on 15 September 1944.

The basic Chinese ration system, when Logan arrived to begin his work and when Wedemeyer made his representations to the Generalissimo, was for the Chinese Army to issue rice and salt to its soldiers, plus a monetary allowance to supplement this ration. Garrison troops were issued CN$ 190 and troops in the field CN$ 240 a month.[19] This monetary supplement would buy about one pound of pork. Not only was the supplement inadequate but in the opinion of the Americans "in too many cases the soldier never got the food it might buy, or if he was lucky a small part of it. The money had to pass through too many hands for much to reach the soldier or to be spent for his food."[20]

In describing the impact of this system on the Chinese Army, American officers working with the Chinese SOS reported:

One of the first things that strikes the eye of an American in China is the physical condition of the troops dragging along the streets and highways. Their clothes are old, patched, and tattered, but far worse is their physical condition. Obviously they are suffering from every sort of disease and are just able to walk. Occasional stretchers carry those too weak to make even an attempt to walk. It is not unusual to see the occupants of the litters dumped by the road either dead or soon to die. . . . The worst groups are the replacements. . . .

A later paragraph pictured a Replacement Depot near Kunming as the American officers and enlisted men of Ration Purchasing Commission No. 3 found it in June 1945:

A start toward feeding the replacements was made at the Replacement Depot at Hilanpo near Kunming. On investigation conditions proved horrible beyond imagination. The Depot had an overhead of 4,400. There were supposed to be 4,400 replacements, actually there were 2,000. One hundred per cent were suffering from malnutrition, T.B., and other diseases, but no medical care was being given. With an overhead of 4,400 the seriously sick replacements had to cook for themselves in kitchens which were immediately adjacent to latrines. About one blanket was provided for each three men. The dead were lying next to the barely living and left there at times for several days. Many replacements were unable even to eat the rice and should have had special therapeutic diet.

This was a problem for the medics but since no one was doing anything about it R.P.C. No. 3 went to work. . . . Singlehanded the Americans made an impressive improvement in the situation. However, how lasting this improvement will be may be judged from the fact that after the Americans left the vitamin pills provided for the patients which were in good condition [*sic*] were declared "poisonous" and condemned.[21]

As Colonel Logan neared the completion of his surveys as to the needs of the soldiers and the availability of food for them, Wedemeyer's representations began to bring a response from the Chinese. The vice-commander of

---

[19] Chinese National currency used the decimal system and a dollar unit of value.

[20] Rpt, Food Dept, Hq SOS, Supreme Hq, Chinese Army, Supplemental Food Section History, 9 Oct 45, par. 3b. OCMH. The report was prepared by U.S. personnel under Col. Charles F. Kearney, who was Chief QM, SOS, and Chief QM Ln Officer with the Chinese Armies. Colonel Kearney, like Cheves, had a major general's rank in the Chinese Army.

[21] Quoted from paragraph E2(j) of Rpt cited n. 20.

the Chinese SOS ordered that all soldiers receive an added issue of thirty-five ounces of meat and thirty-five ounces of beans per month.   Unfortunately, this did not bring results.   In the opinion of General Cheves, the orders, though issued in Chungking, had not been passed down to units in the field.[22]

Then Colonel Logan submitted his report, on 20 January 1945, and Wedemeyer had the benefit of a systematic study of the food problem.   Logan did not believe the answer to the soldier's inadequate diet lay in any shortage of food within the area under control of the Central Government for he wrote: "It is estimated that foodstuffs indigenous to 'Free China' can be obtained in sufficient quantity within the area of practical transportation from points of issue to provide an adequate and balanced dietary for Chinese Armed Forces in the southwestern area."   As for the state of the Chinese soldier, Logan based his conclusions on the examination of a sample of 1,200 men from five divisions, three corps, and replacement units, which he examined at different points from Kunming to Kweiyang.   Fifty-seven percent of these troops showed evidence of one or more nutritional deficiencies.   He believed that "All deficiences however were sufficient to affect significantly the health and efficiency of the troops though capable of relatively rapid correction under proper conditions."[23]

In conclusion Logan recommended that an adequate ration be provided at once; that multivitamin capsules be provided each man every day for at least sixty days; that all rations be issued in kind rather than by monetary allowances; that a central procurement agency consisting of Chinese and American representatives be set up within the Services of Supply to plan, purchase, transport, store, and distribute the ration to divisions; that a Food Service Program, assisted by American liaison officers, be set up in each divi-sion by appointing organization mess officers, battalion and regimental super-visors, plus a division mess inspector (this last to be responsible for proper distribution of the food); and finally that a specially trained nutrition officer of the U.S. Army be assigned to each Chinese army to report on the nutri-tional status of the troops.

The report prescribed what later became known in China Theater as the Logan Ration.   Modified at a joint Sino-American conference, 18 February, it set for the Chinese soldier a ration (in American ounces) of: rice, 27.3 ounces; beans, 2.2 ounces; peanuts, 1.1 ounces; vegetable oil, 1 ounce; salt, .35 ounce; meat, 1.1 ounces; vegetables, 11 ounces; fuel, 29.43 ounces.[24]

Completion of the Logan Report found the Chinese willing to receive suggestions that their soldiers should be adequately fed.   On 1 February, a

---

[22] Memo 321, Wedemeyer for Generalissimo, undated.   Bk 16, ACW Corresp with Chinese.
[23] Quote from App. A to Logan Report, p. 5.
[24] (1) Logan Report, Pt IV.   (2) Ltr, Brig Gen Mervin E. Gross, Actg CofS, to Gen Chen Cheng, Minister of War, 28 Feb 45.   Rpt cited n. 20.

few days after Logan submitted his study, the Generalissimo approved a greatly improved Chinese ration, but since only CN$ 600 a month was set as the limit to be spent per ration it was not possible for the Chinese actually to feed their troops the improved ration; it was estimated that in the Kunming area CN$ 2,000 would be the monthly cost of the Logan Ration.[25]

Wedemeyer on 31 January presented the gist of the Logan Report to the Generalissimo together with a draft of a directive to Cheves which would require him to give needed logistical support to the task of properly feeding the ALPHA troops.[26] Since the food problem was regarded by Wedemeyer as one of the most important he faced, he followed up his recommendations to the Generalissimo on 17 February, pointing out that as he (Wedemeyer) was about to visit the United States in mid-February for conferences (to present his plan to take a major port on the China coast) he would be able to obtain U.S. aid, vitamins for example, if the Generalissimo desired. Wedemeyer added that there was plenty of food in China, that the problem was one of distribution. To this the Minister of War, General Chen Cheng, agreed, saying that transport was the main problem. Here the Generalissimo observed that if he had had 5,000 more trucks he could have saved most of the east China airfields.[27]

Over the weeks ahead the Chinese indicated approval of many of Logan's ideas. The modified Logan Ration was adopted 28 February.[28] By 6 March a great deal of progress had been made in planning the new program. Detailed surveys of the food-producing areas had been made by U.S. officers. Vitamin tablets were scheduled for shipment from the United States. The War Department had been asked to send out qualified personnel for food procurement. The scope of the program was clearly understood: 1,650,000 pounds of food, 275,000 pounds of fuel, and 275,000 pounds of forage per day for the ALPHA divisions. By mid-March, the planning was done and the task was now one of carrying out the project.[29]

Carrying Out the Food Program

The American share of the work involved in supplying adequate food to the ALPHA divisions was begun under the China Aid Section of the American SOS in China. The section had been organized in December 1944. When on 9 February 1945 a Chinese SOS was organized, the China Aid Section was

[25] Rpt cited n. 20.

[26] Memo 398, Wedemeyer for Generalissimo, 31 Jan 45.   Bk 16, ACW Corresp with Chinese.

[27] For another explanation by the Generalissimo of the east China campaign, see *Stilwell's Command Problems,* Chapter XII.

[28] Rpt cited n. 20.

[29] Memo 463, Gen Gross, Actg CofS, for Generalissimo, 6 Mar 45.   Bk 16, ACW Corresp with Chinese.

absorbed into the American component working with the Chinese SOS. Where the initial work of the Americans had been to secure an adequate ration for the two Chinese divisions flown back from Burma to China, they now in late February began the work of obtaining food for all the thirty-six U.S.-sponsored divisions in the ALPHA plan.[30] The need for such work was obvious among the units that were to be in position to stop the Japanese if they chose to drive on Kunming. The American staff of the Food Department, Chinese SOS, later reported to General Wedemeyer that in March 1945 they found the Chinese 13th Army unable to make even a short hike "without men falling out wholesale and many dying from utter starvation."

The first step was to send U.S. officers and men fanning out over the Chinese countryside to see what food was procurable locally. The Americans formed the impression that Chinese statistics on food were nonexistent or unreliable. Local magistrates might be underestimating to avoid excessive confiscation or taxation, but even so, "no one really knew." It appeared that vegetable production was geared to the needs of the local countryside, and that as far as statistics might show there was no surplus for the Army. It was therefore necessary to secure an immediate increase in the vegetable supply, and since the need was pressing there could be no time to wait till the next harvest. The Chinese and Americans agreed that the way to obtain more food was to set a fair price, end confiscation, and stop organized foraging by the Chinese Army.

Issue of perishable meat items was a real problem because refrigeration, transport, and storage facilities were not present in the Chinese countryside. The solution finally adopted was to issue livestock, which could be carried or driven to the troops. This might not give each man his prescribed ration of meat every day but it was thought that over a month's time the issues would balance out.

The Chinese Army had supply depots, which the Americans hoped could be brought to play a part in the food plan. Village magistrates, the traditional source of local authority, could be of great help in persuading farmers to sell their produce and their aid was sought.

The foundation of the whole ration scheme was the work of the Americans in the six ration purchasing commissions which were sent into the field, beginning on 11 April 1945. Ultimately, by exercising authority far beyond that prescribed for them, they were able to supplement the diet of 185,000 Chinese soldiers.

The ration purchasing commissions were placed at strategic spots to function as parts of the ALPHA plan. The first commission was placed in the vital Kweiyang area and began operations 11 April 1945. It fed the Chinese

[30] The report cited in note 20 is the source for this and the following section of the chapter.

13th Army, the animals of the 71st Army, and units passing through Kweiyang, such as the Chinese 22d Division.   The average number of men being fed at any time was 35,000.   The work of this commission was singled out by Col. Charles F. Kearney, director of the food program, who reported that, whereas in March the 13th Army could not make even a short march without casualties from hunger, by August 1945 the 13th was "a physically magnificent army, in excellent march order."

At Chanyi, which was on the eastern line of communications between Kunming and Kweiyang, Ration Purchasing Commission No. 2 fed the troops from Burma, the New 1st and New 6th Armies, as they flew in from Burma and began moving to east China.

Ration Purchasing Commission No. 4 at Chihchiang was in an area from which the Fourteenth Air Force began operating after the loss of the Suichuan airfields, and so was a likely target for a Japanese attack.   Established 1 May, it began feeding the New 6th Army (28,000 men) from Burma after the men were moved to the Chihchiang area to counter a Japanese threat.

On 1 June Ration Purchasing Commission No. 3 began its work in the Kunming area.

To support the projected drive to the coast (Operation BETA), Ration Purchasing Commission No. 5 was activated 15 June 1945 at Poseh, about 100 miles south of Kweiyang on the road to Nanning and Port Bayard, the latter a small seaport very near the island of Hainan.   The commission later moved forward to Nanning.   It fed about 30,000 men.   Several higher-numbered commissions were planned and one was activated but played little part in the progress of events.

Problems and Accomplishments of the Food Program

In trying to appraise the results of the food program, its director, Colonel Kearney, gave first place to the development of an adequate ration and its adoption by the Chinese Army, and second place to the actual feeding of the 185,000 men affected by the program at its peak operation.   His report touched on other points which suggest the Chinese were being offered lessons and procedures whose influence might be felt long after the Americans went home.   The Chinese were shown that armies on the march could be given an adequate, balanced diet.   From among the Chinese who had worked with the Americans on the program grew the nucleus of an organization that might cope with the problems of procurement, storage, and transport.   The pages of Kearney's report suggest that the operation was in many ways a demonstration to the Chinese of what the Americans thought to be effective procedures.   Kearney did not consider that a permanent and lasting reform had been accomplished within the Chinese Army.   It may be noted that the Americans were withdrawn on 10 August 1945, with the end of the war, although, in Kearney's opinion, "Chinese personnel were not really considered adequate, competent, and suitably trained."

In reflecting on the problems met in carrying out Wedemeyer's projects for giving adequate food to the troops of the ALPHA plan, Kearney gave considerable space to the Chinese Army food depots, whose inadequacies seem to have given the ration purchasing commissions one of their major problems:

Securing the cooperation of depots was a great difficulty. They have either refused to perform what was set out as their function or performed inadequately. They refused because of inadequate personnel, rigid depot regulations which cannot meet the needs of this type of operation, inadequate instruction in the requirements of their part in the supplemental food program, inadequate transportation, non-cooperation or opposition on the part of troops being fed, the physical inadequacy of their equipment and totally insufficient and incomplete records for a successful operation. R.P.C. personnel were forced in many cases to by-pass depots and go beyond their original responsibility and issue food directly to the troops if they were to be fed. This was caused by the fact that there was no American personnel with the depots, and the time required for orders from higher authority to be received would have required months. If the R.P.C.'s had not extended beyond their normal function the troops would have not been fed.

But though the depots were a problem the picture was not uniformly dark, for as the depots together with the local magistrates and the Chinese armies being fed became familiar with the operations of the commissions relations with all of them slowly improved. As for the several army headquarters, they took some time in adjusting themselves to the new system. They appeared to the ration purchasing commissions to be "determined to get as much as possible, aften threatening physical violence and at times practicing it. They attempted in some cases to discredit the system in hopes the system would fail and they again would be issued money to use as they saw fit."

Thanks to this venture in Sino-American co-operation, by the time summer arrived 185,000 Chinese troops had been put in condition for more vigorous offensive action than China had seen since 1939.

The Student Volunteers

The Chinese conscription system, as noted earlier,[31] did not send a steady flow of useful replacements into the Chinese Army. And, sharing the traditional Chinese esteem for the scholar, the Central Government had exempted students from Army service. As a result, the Chinese Army had been handicapped in trying to obtain qualified noncommissioned and junior officers.

Late in 1944 the Chinese Government decided to change its policy, and to bring students into its armed forces. This immediately raised the issue of how and where they could best be used. The Americans recommended that

[31] See Ch. II, above.

they be distributed among the thirty-six U.S.-sponsored divisions as a means of improving them. The Generalissimo raised the student issue on 29 November, telling Wedemeyer that 60,000 students would be ready for service by 30 January 1945, and the remaining 40,000 by 31 March. Wedemeyer heartily indorsed the project of bringing the students into the Army. The Chinese, however, soon revealed that they intended to organize the 100,000 students into ten elite divisions. Wedemeyer objected, for he thought that the students would be better used as replacements for the ALPHA divisions, that assigning them would raise the morale of the units upon which so much depended.[32]

In January Wedemeyer again alluded to the student question and related it to the largest issues of Chinese social policy:

The object of war is to guarantee a just peace in which the people of the world can share its privileges. In China itself one object must be to reduce the differences between the "haves" and the "have nots" to guarantee a happier and more contented people. With this background in mind plans must be drawn for the use of 100,000 students. To form them into a "corps d'elite" with favored treatment would defeat the aims for which the war is being waged, but to use them on the same basis as all the other troops would be a big step toward forming a united, strong China.[33]

Shortly after, Wedemeyer discussed another aspect of the student question, the Chinese practice of sending young men to the United States. In the past Wedemeyer had always maintained, he reminded the Generalissimo, that it was unwise to send young, capable, and English-speaking officers out of China in time of crisis. If such were available in numbers Wedemeyer had requested they be attached to the Sino-American Chinese Combat Command where they could be used very profitably. Wedemeyer had understood that the Generalissimo agreed with him and had undertaken to make such officers available.

It now appeared, Wedemeyer told the Chinese, that 1,024 able-bodied young men had just been sent to India, to go from there to the United States for naval training. In addition, the Chinese had requested that 154 Chinese be sent to the United States to study armored warfare. Because he thought that the next six months of 1945 would be the most critical in the history of China, Wedemeyer believed these young men could make a far greater contribution in China Theater.[34]

These representations from Wedemeyer brought favorable comment from the Generalissimo. When on 17 February 1945 Wedemeyer remarked that

---

[32] (1) History of China Theater, Ch. VII, p. 21. (2) Memo 304, McClure for Generalissimo, 20 Dec 44. Bk 16, ACW Corresp with Chinese. (3) Min, Mtg 25, Wedemeyer with Generalissimo, 31 Dec 44. Bk 1, Generalissimo Minutes. (4) Memo 555, Wedemeyer for Generalissimo, 5 May 45. Bk 9, ACW Corresp with Chinese. This latter memorandum reviews the whole question as of 5 May 1945.
[33] History of China Theater, Ch VII, p. 21.
[34] Memo 418, Wedemeyer for Generalissimo, 9 Feb 45. Bk 16, ACW Corresp with Chinese.

it would be a mistake to give special privileges to the students, the General-issimo replied that they would be given the same treatment as the members of the U.S.-sponsored ALPHA divisions. Wedemeyer added that as soon as the student volunteers were trained they should be sent out in groups of three or four thousand to fill the ranks of the various units, and "The Generalissimo said he endorsed this idea." [35]

For the time being the solution reached was a nominal compromise between the Chinese and American views, one that gave the Chinese their wishes in concrete form in exchange for a promised future compliance with General Wedemeyer's views. A Student Volunteer Army of ten divisions, each of 10,000 students, was organized, under the current tables of organization and equipment of the Chinese Army, subject to the understanding, on the part of the Americans, that these divisions would not be permanent. It was further understood by the Americans that these units would train for two or three months (a period of time regarded by the American service as appropriate for basic training but far less than that needed to produce the infantry-artillery team that is a division), and then the students would be distributed among the ALPHA troops. When the training period came to an end in May 1945 Wedemeyer began to urge the Generalissimo to initiate the next phase. [36]

No Arms for the Chinese Communists

During November and December 1944, when the Japanese were thought by the Americans to be offering a serious threat to Kunming, Wedemeyer and his staff had spent much time trying to find ways in which the Chinese Communist forces could be effectively used against the Japanese. Two proposals to that end were presented to the Generalissimo, who rejected them. General McClure had been preparing a third, which Wedemeyer approved before he left Chungking in December to inspect his theater. Meanwhile General Hurley had been attempting to effect a reconciliation of the Nationalists and Communists that would be consistent with the American policy of supporting the Generalissimo and his government. [37] Hurley's task was one of major historic importance; that he might be the better equipped

---

[35] Min, Mtg 40, Wedemeyer with Generalissimo, 17 Feb 45. Bk 1, Generalissimo Minutes.
[36] (1) History of China Theater, Ch. VII, p. 22. (2) Memo cited n. 32(4). (3) McClure believed in 1954 that the student units remained intact, and were kept in training. McClure comments on draft MS.
[37] (1) General Hurley, in his comments on the draft manuscript of this volume, describes the difficulties he encountered. Ltr, Hurley to Maj Gen R. W. Stephens, Chief of Mil History, 15 Dec 56. OCMH. (2) See Ch. II, above. (3) McClure comments on draft MS.

THE HONORABLE PATRICK J. HURLEY, *new U.S. Ambassador to China, stands at attention outside National Government House in Chungking as he arrives to present his credentials to the President of the National Government of the Republic of China, Generalissimo Chiang Kai-shek.*

for the effort, President Roosevelt on 30 November 1944 had nominated him for the post of Ambassador to China.[38]

A detailed examination of Hurley's effort to prevent civil war in China is beyond the scope of this volume, but the chronology of the major episodes in this period may be significant. On 10 November the Chairman of the Chinese Communist Party, Mao Tse-tung, signed a five-point statement drafted by Hurley, which the latter thought a suitable basis for the unification of China. The Nationalists rejected it, and offered a three-point draft which omitted mention of a coalition government. Hurley took both drafts to be statements of the initial bargaining positions of the parties. On 8 December the Communists rejected the government offer, and added that its terms in their phrase precluded any possibility of their representatives returning to Chungking. Hurley's initial reaction, of 12 December, was that the

[38] United States Department of State, *United States Relations With China* (Washington 1949), p. 59.

Nationalists should reopen the negotiations. At least outwardly unperturbed, he continued his work and felt that he was persuading the Nationalists to soften their stand.[39]

While Hurley, Wedemeyer, and McClure had been engaged in the proposals and negotiations mentioned above, the Office of Strategic Services in China was contemplating far-reaching negotiations with the Chinese Communists. Wedemeyer's later reports suggest he did not know of this OSS project until January, and Hurley's papers do not refer to it.[40]

In the meantime, whether aware or not of what was about to be undertaken by the OSS, McClure took the occasion of a trip to Yenan by Colonel Barrett, accompanied by Lt. Col. Willis H. Bird of the OSS, to have Barrett present the Communists with McClure's own plan for co-operation between them and Nationalist China. McClure recommended having U.S. airborne units totaling 4,000 to 5,000 well-trained technicians operate in Communist-held territories on missions of demolition and sabotage of Japanese installations. McClure later stated that Barrett and Bird had orders to make it plain to the Chinese Communists that the McClure plan was being offered for their reactions only and was not being formally presented by the U.S. Government; such presentation, prior to the Generalissimo's consent, would have been a flagrant breach of diplomatic etiquette and tantamount to recognition of the Communists. McClure's later report does not give the Communist reaction to his plan.[41]

Independently, Colonel Bird entered upon his own negotiations with the Communists on behalf of the OSS, and reached a tentative agreement with them, on the same day that Barrett presented the McClure plan and a message from Hurley to the Communists. Not until 24 January did Wedemeyer, the theater commander, learn what Colonel Bird had proposed to the Chinese Communists, and then he was given only a portion of Bird's report to his OSS superiors in Washington:

All agreements made on DIXIE Mission tentative and based on our government's approval of project. Theater Command already agreed on principle of support to fullest extent of Communists and feel it is an OSS type project. If the government approves the following is tentative agreement:

a. To place our S.O. [Special Operations] men with their units for purposes of destroying Jap communications, air fields, and blockhouses, and to generally raise hell and run.

---

[39] (1) *United States Relations With China*, pp. 74–76. (2) Rad, CFB 26390, Hurley to Roosevelt, 16 Nov. 44. Item 97, Hurley Bk 1. (3) Ltr, Chou En-lai to Hurley, 8 Dec 44. Item 122, Hurley Bk 1. (4) Rad, Hurley to Roosevelt, 12 Dec 44. Item 126, Hurley Bk 1. (5) Hurley to State Dept, 23 Oct 44. Hurley Papers.

[40] The OSS project is described in a letter, Lt Col Willis H. Bird, Deputy Chief, OSS in China, to McClure, 24 January 1945, subject: Yenan Trip. Folder, Eyes Alone Wires re Communists, Communist File, Items 1–5, 3 Nov–10 Dec 44, Register No. 06104–M, USFCT Files, DRB AGO. The detail and scope of the plans are such as to suggest they were drafted before Bird arrived in Yenan on or about 15 December 1944.

[41] (1) Memo for Record, Gen McClure; Handwritten Incl to Ltr, McClure to Barrett, 18 Jan 45. Communist File cited n. 40. (2) See Ch. II, above.

b. To fully equip units assisting and protecting our men in sabotage work.

c. Points of attack to be selected in general by Wedemeyer. Details to be worked out in co-operation with the Communists in that territory.

d. To provide complete equipment for up to twenty-five thousand guerrillas except food and clothing.

e. Set up school to instruct in use of American arms, demolitions, communications, etc.

f. Set up intelligence radio network in co-operation with 18th Route Army.

g. To supply at least 100,000 Woolworth one shot pistols for Peoples Militia.

h. To receive complete co-operation of their army of six hundred fifty thousand and People's Militia of two and one half million when strategic use required by Wedemeyer.[42]

This incomplete version of the Bird message to the OSS in Washington is not without its puzzling aspects which may, however, be explained in the missing portions. For in an afternoon Bird succeeded in reaching tentative agreement on matters of the highest importance to both parties. It may be that the Bird message describes only the last stage in a long and complicated series of negotiations, brought to fruition on or about 15 December, and never reported to General Wedemeyer.

So far as Hurley knew, Barrett was in Yenan to deliver a message from Hurley to the Chinese Communists. On 16 December, Chou En-lai, whose post with the Yenan regime corresponded to that of foreign minister, wrote his answer to that message. It again implied that the negotiations between Nationalists and Communists were at an end.[43] Later messages from the Chinese Communists in December had the same theme, and Hurley was at a loss to know why the Communists were so intransigent.

By 15 January 1945 Hurley was satisfied that he had the answer and hastened to put the matter before President Roosevelt and General McClure. Hurley told McClure on 15 January (Chungking time) that the previous weekend he had visited the Generalissimo's residence and had there learned from Navy Group, China—which with the Generalissimo's secret police under General Tai Li formed the Sino-American Cooperative Organization—that the Communists had heard of a plan to use U.S. paratroopers in the Communist areas to lead Communist guerrillas. To the President he added that this plan was predicated on direct negotiations between the Communists and the U.S. Government. In Hurley's opinion, this amounted to recognition of the Communists and gave them their objectives—destruction of the Nationalist regime and lend-lease arms from the United States.[44]

At this same time, a spate of reports from observers in the field told of clashes between Nationalist and Communist forces, while the American Ob-

---

[42] Ltr cited n. 40.

[43] Ltr, Chou to Hurley, 16 Dec 44. Item 126, Hurley Bk 1.

[44] (1) Memo cited n. 41. (2) Rad War 21084, Marshall to Wedemeyer, 15 Jan 44. Item 265, Bks 1 and 2, ACW Personal File.

server Group in Yenan was of the opinion that the Communist leadership seemed willing to contemplate immediate civil war.[45]

The authorities in Washington reacted strongly to Hurley's report. Marshall ordered Wedemeyer to investigate and report at once.[46] This he did. In his report to General Marshall, 27 January, he stated that he had informed all officers of his command that "we must support the Chinese National Government" and that no negotiations were to be carried out with Chinese not approved or recognized by the Generalissimo. Wedemeyer believed that Barrett and Bird were aware of these orders. He added that he had not been aware of Bird's accompanying Barrett to Yenan and, by quoting Bird's message to Washington as it has been quoted above, implied that he had not known of Bird's discussions. Wedemeyer closed his report by telling Marshall, "Needless to say I am extremely sorry that my people became involved in such a delicate situation. I do not believe that this instance is the main cause of the breakdown of negotiations but I am fully aware that unauthorized loose discussions by my officers employed in good faith by General Hurley could have strongly contributed to the latter's difficulties in bringing about a solution to the problem." [47]

Negotiations between Nationalists and Communists resumed on 24 January 1945, so the breach was not permanent, but the incident made its impression on Wedemeyer. He had been aware that General Chennault had been closely associated with General Hsueh Yueh and that the latter was not in the Generalissimo's good graces. Now, officers on his own staff were becoming involved in Chinese politics to such an extent that Ambassador Hurley thought they had created a major obstacle to his diplomatic efforts. Wedemeyer's solution was to issue an order removing both the Army and himself from any possibility of further involvement: "Officers in China Theater will not assist, negotiate, or collaborate in any way with Chinese political parties, activities, or persons not specifically authorized by Commanding General, U.S. Forces, China Theater. This includes discussing hypothetical aid or employment of U.S. resources to assist any effort of an unapproved political party, activity, or persons. This also forbids rendering local assistance. . . ." [48]

According to General McClure's recollections, this development ended

[45] (1) Rad CAK 3705, Chennault to Wedemeyer, 10 Jan 45. Chennault had liaison officers with the Communists, e.g., Maj. Fred W. Eggers. See Memo Maj E. T. Cowen for G-2, USFCT, 11 Jan 45; Rad 322, Wedemeyer for Dickey to Evans sgd Cromley, 9 Jan 45. Communist File cited n. 40.

[46] Rad cited n. 44(2).

[47] Rad CFB 32080, Wedemeyer to Marshall, 27 Jan 45. Communist File cited n. 40.

[48] (1) Memo for CG 14th USAF *et al.*, 30 Jan 45, sub: Support of U.S. policy. Item 1, Chinese Agreements, Items 1 to 11, Register No. 06105–1, USFCT Files, DRB AGO. (2) *United States Relations With China*, p. 78. (3) Ltr cited n. 37(1).

the period of close operational contact between the embassy and theater head-quarters. Thereafter, the relationship between Hurley and Wedemeyer was one of close liaison rather than mutual use of the theater's resources in staff officers. However, Hurley attended nine of tne twenty-two meetings between Wedemeyer and Chiang that were held until the end of the war, and so was conversant with the main trends in theater policy and planning.[49]

Six months later, Wedemeyer explained his stand to Lt. Gen. John E. Hull, the Assistant Chief of Staff, OPD. Telling Hull that Hurley and the Generalissimo had just asked him to negotiate with the Communists, that they had been flattering in their comments about what he might do, Wedemeyer added, "After my experience last December with Hurley concerning McClure and Barrett in which he blamed the Army for breakdown in his negotiations, I am very wary." So he told the Generalissimo and Hurley that he did not intend to visit Yenan, for he did not wish to jeopardize their success, which Hurley thought imminent. As for the political activities of other U.S. agencies and personnel in China, he told Hull: "If the American public ever learned that we poured supplies to a questionable organization such as Tai Li operates, without any accounting, it would be most unfortunate indeed. . . . I rather question the Navy's concern about the Chinese attitude. Miles [commanding Navy Group, China] had been Santa Claus out here for a long time and just between you and me Chennault has given supplies to a certain war lord friend without accounting for them. All I am doing, and I am sure you would do the same, is trying to conduct this show in a straightforward manner."[50]

Conducting a Straightforward Show

Wedemeyer's remark to Hull, that he was trying to conduct his theater's operations in a proper and businesslike manner, was a description of his policy. He was fully aware of the impact of American lend-lease and American expenditures on the Chinese economy and Chinese politics, and resolved that no corruption or waste or unauthorized intervention would result from any action within his sphere. Several antecedents may be distinguished.

The Chinese inflation gathered momentum throughout 1945. The whole-sale price index rose in geometric ratio, while the exchange rate between Chinese and U.S. currency held at roughly 500 to 1 from January to April, then bounded to another plateau at 750 to 1 from April to June, before it rocketed to the stratosphere of 3,000 to 1 in a vain attempt to catch the wholesale price index, which was by then in outer space. Meanwhile, the numerical strength of the U.S. forces in China was steadily growing, from

[49] (1) McClure comments on draft MS.   (2) Bk 1, Generalissimo Minutes.
[50] Ltr, Wedemeyer to Hull, 5 Jul 45. Case 49, OPD 319.1, TS Sec I.

32,956 in January to 58,975 in June, with all the implied demand for construction. As the troops increased, so did U.S. expenditures in China, from about one billion National currency dollars in November 1944 to six billion National currency dollars in April 1945, and twenty billion National currency dollars in May. All the while, U.S. lend-lease to China, which would be a counterbalancing charge on China against these expenditures and also against Chinese contributions in kind, *e. g.,* food and shelter in Chinese hostels, was being distributed.[51]

Therefore, China Theater headquarters had to keep accurate records against settlement day, plan its purchases carefully so that the U.S. taxpayer would receive his dollar's worth, and conduct its affairs with meticulous care so that Chinese traders would not receive advance notice of heavy purchases and profiteer accordingly. Moreover, China Theater was also interested in developing sources of Chinese production.

Several developments in December and January 1944–45 preceded the decision to create the post of Assistant Chief of Staff, G–5 (Civil Affairs), to assist the theater commander in dealing with these and other problems of relations with civil authority. In fall 1944 the Chinese created their own War Production Board, whose basic charter ("organic law" in Chinese terminology) gave it the most sweeping powers over the procurement and distribution of matériel for the war in China. China was after all a sovereign power, free to renounce her previous engagements; this law seemed to China Theater headquarters to come very close to asserting Chinese control over every aspect of lend-lease. Theater headquarters was also aware that a considerable quantity of supplies from the United States had been procured by Chinese and American agencies under various programs to aid China, many of which had little relation to the thirty-six-division program. Control of lend-lease was Wedemeyer's ace card, and he could not afford to have it trumped by American supplies brought into China without his consent.

On 25 December Wedemeyer protested that as Commanding General, U.S. Forces, China Theater, he was vested with control over lend-lease which it was not in his power to relinquish. Nor could he relinquish control over transport facilities to China, and therefore over the allocation of Hump tonnage. Then he proceeded a step further, by recommending that all supplies entering China be placed under his control, that Chinese agencies be asked to submit their requisitions to him so that as the Generalissimo's chief of staff he could determine to what degree they furthered the war effort. The Chinese did not immediately respond.[52]

Then, in January, T. V. Soong asked Wedemeyer publicly to refute an

---

[51] (1) Data from History of the Procurement Branch, G–5 Section of the General Staff, Hq USFCT. OCMH. (2) See Table 3.
[52] History of China Theater, Ch. III, pp. 1–10.

CHINESE MECHANICS REASSEMBLING LEND-LEASE JEEP *under the direction of an American liaison man.*

article in an American magazine which charged mishandling, misdirection, and misappropriation of foreign supplies entering China. Wedemeyer told the Generalissimo that he would be happy to do it, but added that since he did not have access to the facts he honestly could not do so. Therefore he recommended that incoming supplies of whatever origin should be stored in warehouses under U.S. military control and Chinese representation. The Generalissimo agreed, then again asked that Wedemeyer tell the press that all lend-lease had been properly handled. The press release was to be on Wedemeyer's own authority, Soong quickly explained, and was not to quote the Generalissimo. When the Generalissimo pressed Wedemeyer again to issue such a statement, the latter replied that he would consider it, and several days later told Chiang that War Department policy would not permit his issuing such a refutation. For his part, the Generalissimo agreed to consider a unified control system.[53]

---

[53] Min, Mtg 29, Wedemeyer with Generalissimo, 13 Jan 45; Mtg 30, 29 Jan 45. Bk 1, Generalissimo Minutes.

CHINESE HOSTEL AT AN AMERICAN AIR BASE, *where men of the 308th Bomb Group lived and worked.*

In mid-January two of the American agencies in China—the War Production Mission, headed by Donald M. Nelson, which was working to improve Chinese war production, and the Foreign Economic Administration—fell in behind the Wedemeyer policy of central control. The FEA's concurrence was important, for it was then engaged in a major project to bring 15,000 trucks to China. By agreeing that the SOS would receive and issue all spare parts and maintenance equipment brought in under its program it gave Wedemeyer a way of directing this vitally needed transportation to support of the war effort.[54]

To bring these complicated and potentially embarrasing activities under effective control of the theater commander, the post of Assistant Chief of Staff, G–5, was created 30 January 1945, and Col. George H. Olmstead was appointed to fill it. Olmstead was a graduate of the Military Academy who had entered civil life, becoming finally chairman of the board of an insurance

[54] History of China Theater, Ch. III, pp. 12–13.

TABLE 3—U.S. TROOP STRENGTHS, CHINA THEATER: 1945

Month	Air forces	Ground forces	Other	Total
January	23,960	8,779	217	32,956
February	25,190	8,030	306	33,526
March	27,600	8,960	381	37,941
April	31,324	11,148	705	43,177
May	31,278	19,249	1,135	51,662
June	33,221	24,299	1,455	58,975
July	29,209	26,063	1,960	57,232
15 August	34,726	22,151	5,492	60,369

Source: Tabulation of G-1, China Theater, Reports in Folder, "Supply, China Theater, 1945." OCMH.

company; his combination of military background and commercial experience seemed an appropriate one.

Initially, G-5 had 4 branches: (1) Requirements and Assignment Branch (later, Lend-Lease Branch); (2) Procurement Branch; (3) Production, Planning, and Policy Branch; (4) Liaison Branch.

Division of responsibility between G-5 and SOS was clarified by the decision that G-5 would be the planning, policy-making, and supervisory agency, while SOS would be the executive body. As the quantity of lend-lease entering China grew with the steady improvement in deliveries over the Hump, the lend-lease responsibilities of G-5 grew with it. Areas of responsibility between the several staff sections in regard to lend-lease were defined anew: G-3 drafted tables of organization and equipment; G-4, together with G-4, India–Burma Theater, called forward supplies; G-5 obtained War Department approval of lend-lease requisitions, supervised accounting and storekeeping, and also supervised the lend-lease activities of such quasi-autonomous agencies as OSS and Navy Group, China.[55]

Wedemeyer's concern for the semi-independent intelligence agencies in China Theater has been noted before,[56] and since these agencies dealt extensively with Chinese civil authority and were dependent on lend-lease, G-5, rather than G-2, was employed as the staff agency for their control. On 1 March 1945, G-5 assumed control of clandestine warfare activity within China Theater. Theater headquarters told Olmstead to co-ordinate and control clandestine and quasi-military activity to ensure the greatest possible effectiveness in furtherance of the aims of the Chinese National Government and the Chinese-American military effort. The motive behind the reference

[55] History of China Theater, Ch. III, pp. 26–28.
[56] See Ch. V, above.

to limiting support to the Chinese National Government was to avoid participation in Chinese domestic politics.

In the day-to-day exercise of its duties G–5 evolved certain policies for control of clandestine warfare, which it applied to all agencies, American or Allied, through Wedemeyer's position as chief of staff to the Generalissimo. Anything suggested was appraised in terms of its demand on Hump tonnage, and approved only if it would add to the success of the theater's basic war plans, ALPHA and BETA. G–5 maintained close liaison with the American, Chinese, British, and French agencies. It kept in touch with the Chinese by periodic visits with the Chinese Board of Military Operations, and by discus-sions between Olmstead and his Chinese opposite number, General Cheng Kai-ming, at meetings of the Combined Staff. The General Officer Com-manding, British Troops, China, Maj. Gen. E. C. Hayes, kept in contact with Olmstead. The French worked with the OSS in China, so the link with the French agency, *Direction Generale des Etudes et des Réchèrches,* was through OSS. U.S. agencies maintained liaison officers at theater headquarters.[57]

The Problem of French Indochina

Hardly had Wedemeyer begun to grapple with the problem of forming the several Allied agencies in China into a harmonious team before Japanese activity in Indochina created a major problem of Allied co-operation both within and without China Theater. Fearing that the United States might be planning an amphibious assault on Indochina, *Imperial General Headquarters* on 28 February 1945 ordered its forces there to occupy the centers of ad-ministrative and military power, where the French had preserved an uneasy autonomy since 1941, in order to eliminate any chance of Franco-American co-operation.[58] Such an order had been anticipated by the Allies, for on 2 February the French military attaché at Chungking had said that the Japanese were insisting that the French disband and disarm, and Wedemeyer had promptly relayed the news to Washington.[59]

The Japanese demand gave the United States some awkward moments. The French fought back, and asked for help. If the U.S. forces in China responded, it would be a diversion from their meager resources. More to the point, the War Department's response to reports of fighting in Indochina showed that the United States Government was most reluctant to engage in activity that might result in its being associated with or supporting French

---

[57] Maj Martin F. Sullivan, G–5 Sec, USFCT, History of the Clandestine Branch, 15 Nov 45. OCMH.
[58] Japanese Study No. 45, pp. 183–84.
[59] Rad, CFB 32319, Wedemeyer to OPD, 2 Feb. 45. Item 335, Bks 1 and 2, ACW Personal File.

colonialism.   At the Yalta Conference, 4 February 1945, Roosevelt told the JCS he favored anything that was against the Japanese so long as the United States was not aligned with the French.[60]

One weapon that could intervene to support the 5,000 or so French and colonial troops who soon began fighting their way northward was the Fourteenth Air Force.   Chennault did his best by strafing Japanese columns. Current directives from the War Department appeared to permit operations against the Japanese directly or through support of forces resisting Japan, which would seem to include the French.[61]   Presumably the French requested help of the British no less than of the Americans, for in late March American pilots over Indochina observed British aircraft making airdrops to the French troops.   Shortly after, China Theater reported that the British were delivering infantry weapons in the area.[62]

However welcome this may have been to the French, who were trying to keep a foothold in one of their principal overseas possessions, it disturbed Wedemeyer, who believed that Indochina was part of the Generalissimo's China Theater, and that British forces could not operate there without prior permission from the Generalissimo.   The matter was presented to the Joint Chiefs of Staff.   Wedemeyer reported that he found British clandestine organizations most active both in French Indochina and in Thailand, that Mountbatten justified their presence there on the ground of a gentleman's agreement with the Generalissimo that permitted him to operate in those countries.   From the Joint Chiefs of Staff the matter went still higher, where Churchill argued that Wedemeyer and Mountbatten had an agreement that permitted the latter to conduct pre-occupation clandestine activities in French Indochina.[63]

The resolution of the difficulty over theater boundaries was agreement between Roosevelt and Churchill that Mountbatten would operate in the Generalissimo's theater only by prearrangement with him.[64]   Meanwhile, the luckless French were slowly trudging into Yunnan.   Their reception was mixed for there were incidents with the Chinese.   Having long memories,

---

[60] (1) Ltr, Hull to Wheeler, 22 Feb 45.   TS Reg No. 4945, Hq USF IBT Files, Folder 73, KCRC.   (2) Min, Mtg of President with Advisers, 4 Feb 45.   *Foreign Relations of the United States: Diplomatic Papers,* Dept State Pub 6199, *The Conferences at Malta and Yalta, 1945* (Washington, 1955).

[61] (1) Rad, CFB 34998, Gross to Chennault, 31 Mar 45.   Item 546, Bks 3 and 4, ACW Personal File.   (2) Chennault, *Way of a Fighter,* p. 342.

[62] (1) Rad, CFB 34921, Gross to Wedemeyer, 29 Mar 45.   Item 540, Bks 3 and 4, ACW Personal File.   (2) Rad, CFB 35143, Gross to Timberman, 3 Apr 45.   Item 553, Bks 3 and 4, ACW Personal File.

[63] (1) Rad, CFB 35759, Wedemeyer to Marshall, 15 Apr 45.   Item 588, Bks 3 and 4, ACW Personal File.   (2) Rad, WAR 66655, Hull to Wedemeyer, 12 Apr 45.   Item 572, Bks 3 and 4, ACW Personal File.

[64] Rad, WAR 68666, Marshall to Wedemeyer, 16 Apr 45.   Item 595, Bks 3 and 4, ACW Personal File.

some of the Chinese remembered the initial Japanese occupation of Indo-china in 1941, and suggested that then would have been the time to fight and to ask Chinese and American assistance.   On being evacuated, those French who needed hospital care were flown to Assam where the British assumed responsibility for them.   The others, after a rest period, were re-organized with the aim of using them for internal security.[65]

By late February or early March of 1945, Wedemeyer's China Theater was organized to provide a co-operative Allied effort in China.   Wedemeyer's addition to the liaison system, the device of passing disagreement up the chain of command, might well be the vital ingredient whose earlier absence had impeded the conduct of operations along the Salween and in north Burma.   Wedemeyer was also trying to weld the several Allied powers oper-ating in China Theater into a team, and his efforts in this regard had just met their first test in Indochina.

[65] (1) Ltr, Wedemeyer to Marshall, 13 Jun 45.   (2) Min, Combined Staff Mtgs 52, 67, CCC and Chinese Supreme Hq, 11 Jun, 20 Jul 45.   AG (CCC) 337.1, KCRC.

CHAPTER IX

Meeting the First Test in China

Arrangements to train, arm, feed, and co-ordinate the Chinese were carefully made and reflected several years' experience. But they were, after all, only so many attempts to solve known or anticipated problems. The Chinese Combat Command, the Chinese Training Command, the emerging Chinese SOS, all had to take the field and put the new machinery into operation. Whether it would produce results was the question, and provides the next chapter in the unfolding story.

The Thirty-six Divisions Take Form

The Logan Ration and the student volunteers would, if Wedemeyer's views prevailed, lead to an over-all improvement in the ALPHA divisions. But because the ration and student projects, the suggestion for reducing the size of the Chinese Army, and the suggestions for different command procedures touched so many sensitive aspects of the Nationalist regime, it was over these that China Theater met with the greatest difficulties. With the thirty-six divisions Wedemeyer had more success, and it is there, in retrospect, that Sino-American co-operation appears at its brightest. As noted above,[1] the CCC offered a means of remedying some of the obvious deficiencies of the Chinese Army. It set up a chain of communication from higher headquarters through intermediate headquarters down to divisions. (*Chart 5*) It supervised reorganization and amalgamation within the six area commands. It provided Chinese commanders with competent American general and special staff assistance in operations, intelligence, and logistics. It provided technical assistance for the Chinese in handling artillery and communications. It placed competent medical personnel among Chinese who had been trained primarily by experience. In co-operation with the newly organized Chinese Services of Supply, it organized and supervised a measure of logistical support. It conducted service schools and unit train-

---

[1] Ch. V.

CHART 5—SINO-AMERICAN LIAISON SYSTEM (SCHEMATIC)

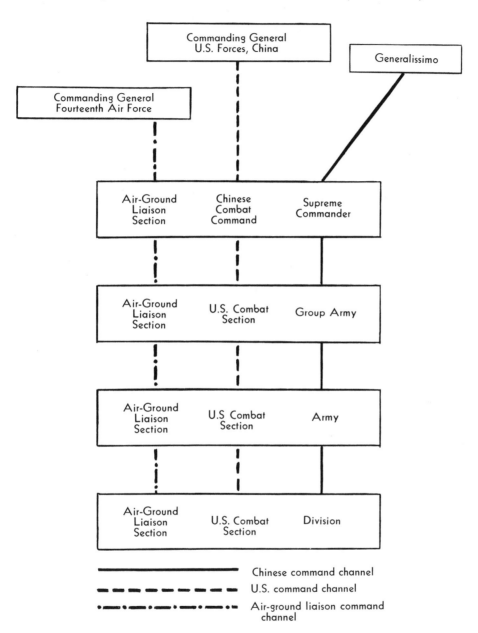

ing. In brief, technical assistance, professional training, and logistical support were offered to thirty-six selected Chinese divisions guarding Kunming.

The divisions the Chinese were willing to assign to the ALPHA plan were divided among six area commands. The essential Kunming supply installations were in the Reserve Command. North and east of Kunming was the Central Command, which included the vital road center of Kweiyang from which roads lead to Kunming and Chungking. Still farther east and north was Eastern Command, which included the Chihchiang airstrips, from which Chennault's airmen were currently operating, and the lost east China fields. Southeast of the Reserve and Central Commands lay the Kwangsi Command, whose farther border was the sea in the area of Luichow Peninsula and the then-obscure harbor of Fort Bayard. Directly south of Reserve Command, on the Indochina border, was the Southern Command, and to the west, on the Salween front, the Western Command. The Chungking area and the remaining 85 percent of the Chinese Army did not have a place in these area commands.

Of the six, the Reserve and Eastern Commands had the greatest initial importance—the first, because of the major role it played in training one third of the U.S.-sponsored divisions; the latter, because it lay between the Japanese and one of Chennault's most vital fields, Chihchiang. The task of reorganization facing Colonel Bowman and General Chang Fa-kwei in the Kwangsi Command was especially difficult. While a portion of the Chinese defenders of the Kweilin–Liuchow area fell back northwest toward Kweiyang, General Chang's forces had moved southwest to Poseh near the Indochina border. When Bowman opened his headquarters 27 December 1944 he found Chang with the remnants of six armies, which had "lost practically all their equipment. Their supply and medical systems had broken down. Their morale was broken." Bowman thought they could not stop a Japanese regiment. And they were in a food deficit area which meant that unless the Americans could bring in food, Chang's armies would have to desert in order to eat. So Bowman began to set up a line of communications, by airlift to Poseh and water transport forward. McClure greatly aided him by assigning a small group of liaison aircraft, which provided evacuation and courier service.[2]

McClure also sought to obtain rice for Chang's men. On 11 April he radioed Wedemeyer from the field that the SOS was operating in only an advisory capacity in Chang's vital area, and that food was scarce there. Chang had assured McClure that if he was given the money he could buy food from within the Japanese lines. Passing through them was easy in the Nanning

---

[2] (1) GO 7, Hq CCC USFCT, 29 Jan 45. (2) History, Kwangsi Command, CCC, Jan–Mar 45. CCC Files, KCRC. (3) Bowman comments on draft MS.

COL. EMERICK KUTSCHKO *is present at a demonstration of a tactical problem by Chinese 14th Division troops for an officer candidate class.*

area and done every day; the farmers would deliver rice to Chang as required. So McClure suggested that Chang be given funds to buy rice from Japanese-held Kwangsi areas, for there would be no rice available outside them after 1 May.[3]

The Reserve Command, whose Chinese troops were under General Tu Yu-ming, and which was commanded by Col. Emerick Kutschko, was primarily a training command.[4]   No combat took place under its authority. Its importance lies rather in its work of training and equipping Chinese divisions in China.[5]

As the basic plan prescribed, Colonel Kutschko organized his staff along the familiar general and special staff lines so that staff officers might deal with their Chinese opposite numbers, and attached a U.S. combat section to each Chinese army headquarters.   These sections in turn sent liaison sections to Chinese divisions, and by cutting personnel requirements to a fine point the Americans succeeded in finding at least one U.S. liaison officer for each Chinese regiment or artillery battalion.   Kutschko had the 35th and 60th U.S. Portable Surgical Hospitals and two veterinary detachments, which were used to strengthen the Chinese medical and sanitary services.

Commissioned and enlisted instructors for service schools were also available.   Signal Corps men to set up and operate a communications net linking the U.S. liaison sections and detachments completed Kutschko's modest force. As of 25 March 1945 it totaled 185 officers and 401 enlisted men.

Taking up their new stations, the Americans in February found that General Tu had four armies, the 5th, New 6th, 8th, and 54th.   The Americans estimated their strength at 96,316, divided among twelve divisions.   Of these divisions four had fought on the Salween and were far understrength, while the 14th and 22d were veterans of north Burma.   Kutschko reported that the Honorable 1st and 103d Divisions, 8th Army, "were in a deplorable state of malnutrition," and that 90 percent of the 166th Division had scabies. Transport was so scarce that central supervision of the training program was extremely difficult, to say nothing of the ration and equipment issue.

With its first directive, CCC had presented two thirteen-week training programs as guides for the American staffs of the several commands.   The goal was to have each unit capable of fighting effectively three months after beginning its training.   This program, plus specialist training in troop schools, was the foundation of the American program for the Reserve Command.   In the first 13-week cycle Chinese Combat Command focused attention on

---

[3] Rad CYF 13495, McClure to Wedemeyer, 11 Apr 44.   AG 311.23, CCC Files, KCRC.
[4] For General Tu's background, see *Stilwell's Mission to China,* Chapters III and IV.
[5] Save as otherwise indicated, data on the Reserve Command may be found in two historical reports, sent by letters.   Ltrs, Capt George E. McLaughlin, Actg AG, Hq Reserve Comd, CCC (Prov), USFCT, to CG CCC (Prov), 30 Aug 45, 7 Sep 45.   OCMH.

weapons training, for which were suggested 144 hours of the first 13-week cycle, and small unit problems, which received 116 hours, while marches and bivouacs plus sanitation were to receive 32 hours, and patrolling, 36.   In the second 13-week cycle, drill in the handling of weapons received less time (78 hours) while their tactical use moved up to 60 hours.   Tactics to include the battalion were to have 174 hours.   Plainly then, training was to be progressive; the soldier was to learn the use of his weapon and then be fitted into the team.

In proposing these training cycles, CCC directed its subordinates to inculcate the offensive spirit.   It reminded them that Chinese armies had been so long on the defensive that Chinese officers found it hard to think in aggressive terms.   The Americans were cautioned not to bypass the Chinese officers in training, but rather to teach them to train their men, then to supervise the finished product.   Unit training was to be practical.   "No organiza - tion ever had too much training in weapons."   In accord with the spirit of these instructions, McClure's headquarters limited defensive tactical exercises to security measures and protection of a captured point against counterattack.

Kutschko and his aides found that the training problem varied from one division to another.   The New 6th Army's 14th and 22d Divisions were in excellent shape, thanks to training in India and combat in Burma.   However, the 207th Youth Division could not begin training until after it received infantry weapons, which arrived by 1 May.   The 5th Army divisions varied in quality.   The 45th Division was promptly reorganized on the June 1944 Table of Organization, and was ready to begin its 13-week training cycle on 1 April 1945.   As for the 96th Division, some of its officers had attended the old Y–Force Infantry Training Center; it was hoped they would be fairly well qualified.   It too was to begin 13-week training on 1 April, as was the last division, the veteran 200th.   The 5th Army's three battalions of 75-mm. pack artillery had had either recent combat on the Salween or American training.   Some of the engineer and communication troops had already received U.S. training and equipment.   For these service troops, technical schools were planned.

Two divisions of the 54th Army, 36th and 198th, spent most of the February–March period in reorganizing to conform to the newly adapted Table of Organization.   Combat on the Salween had taken a heavy toll; the absorption of replacements necessarily resulted in delaying the beginning of the training cycle.   The 8th Division, 54th Army, was regarded as being in good condition and well trained, with but one great lack, transport animals, of which it had none.   The last of the four armies, the 8th, was handicapped by an outbreak of relapsing fever, plus a number of cases of malnutrition, in its Honorable 1st Division.   Despite this, during February and March classes for officers and enlisted men were carried out in the school of the soldier, of the section, and in the heavy machine gun.   The 103d Division was training officer cadres and recruits.   Schools for signalmen and 60-mm. mortar crews were also conducted in the preliminary period.   The last division, the 166th, was moving into its assigned stations and so could not begin any training until 26 March.   On that date all units of the 8th Army, save two regiments acting as airfield guards, began their 13-week training.   Therefore, of the Reserve Command divisions that needed training all but two were ready to begin work on or about 1 April.

The equipment problem was complicated by the transport shortage which made it very hard to deliver arms to the divisions.   The American SOS made deliveries to army headquarters.   In order to get the weapons to divisions the American liaison personnel had to borrow Air Forces and SOS vehicles. The rate at which American equipment was being received can be estimated from a table showing the percentage of weapons, authorized by the Tables of Organization, which had been issued as of 25 May 1945: [6]

	Percent	
5th Army Troops	100	(less 100 submachine guns)
45th Division	80	
96th Division	100	
200th Division	0	(except for artillery battalion)
8th Army Troops	80	
Honorable 1st Division	100	
103d Division	100	
166th Divison	0	
54th Army Troops	80	
8th Division	85	
36th Division	70	
198th Division	40	
New 6th Army (less 14th and 22nd Divisions in Chihchiang area)		
207th Division	60	

In grappling with the actual training of the Reserve Command's divisions the Americans had to adjust their programs to a number of factors.   For example, it was manifestly impossible to train mortar crews before the weapons were at hand.   For another, because training was progressive, the American staff believed the Chinese should master one phase of the program before passing on to the next even though this called for spending many more weeks on a particularly troublesome phase than had been suggested by the Chinese Combat Command's training schedule.

There were also local problems arising from the combination of circumstances that brought the Reserve Command into being.   Because the 8th, 53d, and 54th Armies had been heavily engaged on the Salween front, they had lost a majority of their junior officers, who would under U.S. Army

[6] Ltr, Col Laurence B. Bixby, CofS Reserve Comd CCC (Prov), to McClure, 25 May 45, sub: Progress Rpt.   CCC and Asgd Units Hist Rpt, OCMH.

training methods have done a great deal of the instructing. These men had to be replaced in short order, which was done by promoting noncommissioned officers. Many of these were illiterate and had only the slenderest professional qualifications. This gap was plugged in part by special officers' training schools. Other difficulties arose because many Chinese general officers were absent from their commands and thus could not place the weight of their authority behind the American efforts to train their men. The American side of the effort was initially handicapped by the small number of U.S. troops that were in China and available for instructor duties. Transfer to Reserve Command of the 1st Battalion, 475th U.S. Infantry, in May 1945 helped meet this need. Kutschko's staff reported that the poor health of the Chinese soldiers, "particularly among recruits," in many instances reduced attendance at training to 50 percent. For a time, it seemed to General McClure, Commanding General, CCC, that the problem was primarily one of physical rehabilitation.[7]

The success of Reserve Command's efforts to carry out its mission depended on its ability to solve the problems described above. As April began, Kutschko and his 500-odd subordinates settled down to training the twelve divisions that formed one third of the total force scheduled to receive American instruction.

Eastern Command's Work Interrupted

Western Hunan Province, the area allotted to Eastern Command on 29 January 1945, is a rough, mountainous area, which was then practically roadless and depended for transport upon the coolies trudging from village to village and upon the streams that run generally north and east toward Tungting Lake. The local Chinese forces were the XXIV Group Army, General Wang Yao-wu, which included the 18th, 73d, 74th, and 100th Armies. General Wang's headquarters was at Sha-wan, a town just south of the main road, Chihchiang–Heng-yang, and there Eastern Command of Chinese Combat Command set up its own headquarters on 2 February. (See Map 1—inside back cover; Map 15) Its mission was to supervise the training and equipping of General Wang's troops.[8] General Wang's XXIV Group Army divisions varied in troop strength, and had but thirty-three pieces of light artillery, French, Russian, Japanese, and Dutch:[9]

---

[7] McClure comments on draft MS.

[8] Save as otherwise indicated, this section is based on MS, Formal Historical Record, for the Period 29 Jan 45–1 Sep 45, for Brig Gen Woods King, Hq IV Army Group Comd CCC USFCT, 1 Sep 45. OCMH.

[9] (1) 1st Ind, Lt Col Ivan W. Ward, Actg AG CCC, 14 Jan 45, to CG CT&CC. G–3 Rpts, AG (CCC) 319.1, KCRC. (2) Special G–1 Rpt, Hq Eastern Comd CCC, 22 Jul 45. Folder, Histories 1945, 74th Army Combat Section CCC Files, KCRC. (3) Combined Staff Mtg 36, 14 Apr 45. AG (CCC) 338.1, KCRC. (4) When Eastern Command was set up the strength of the 18th Army was not known. However, strength figures obtained later suggest the estimate given above as the army's strength before it became engaged with the enemy in mid-April.

Unit	Combat Troops	Noncombat Troops
73d Army Total..	12,046	15,426
Army Troops...	1,547	8,318
15th Division..	4,961	4,426
77th Division..	4,714	2,030
Temporary-5th Division	824	652
74th Army Total (minus 58th Division)........................	15,497	14,562
Army Troops...	3,628	6,638
51st Division	6,552	3,749
57th Division...	5,317	4,175
58th Division...	(a)	(a)
100th Army Total...	8,508	6,774
Army Troops...	924	910
19th Division...	3,697	2,648
63d Division	3,887	3,216
18th Army.... (estimated total strength, 2,331 officers, 29,030 enlisted men)		
11th Division...	(a)	(a)
18th Division..:	(a)	(a)
118th Division..	(a)	(a)

a Unknown.

Col. Woods King, commanding Eastern Command, began work with nineteen officers and thirty-four enlisted men. Following the basic CCC plan of creating an organization parallel to the Chinese staff and command structure, Colonel King organized his own headquarters with a chief of staff and the four general staff sections. Combat sections were organized to work with General Wang's three U.S.-sponsored armies: 18th Army Combat Section, Col. John P. Lake; 73d Army Combat Section, Col. Lester L. Lambert; 74th Army Combat Section, Col. Alexander H. Cummings. The 100th Army did not receive a liaison section until much later. As of 1 April, King had 109 officers and 270 enlisted men under his command.

Examining their problems, the Americans received the impression that General Wang's command had little if any interest in medical matters. "There was practically no medical personnel in the area at the time that this command was established. The existing hospital facilities were deplorable." The local Chinese also seemed indifferent to problems of supply and evacuation.

Colonel King concluded that if he was to supply his own personnel, let alone get on with his mission, he would have to organize boatheads and

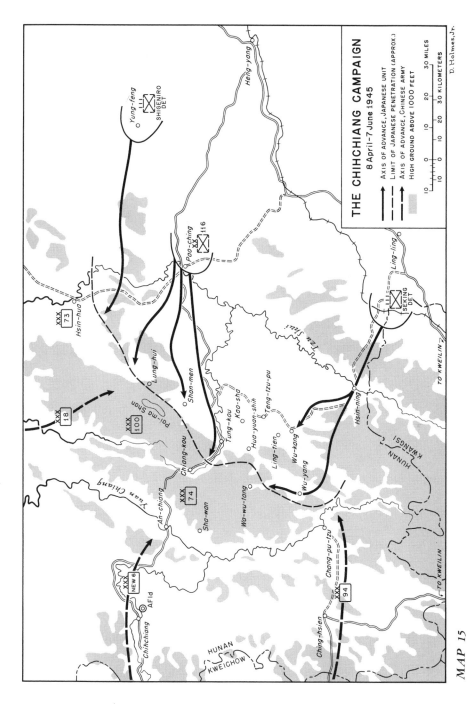

THE CHIHCHIANG CAMPAIGN
8 April–7 June 1945

Axis of advance, Japanese unit
Limit of Japanese penetration (approx.)
Axis of advance, Chinese army
High ground above 1000 feet

10   0   10   20   30 MILES
10   0   10   20   30 KILOMETERS

D. Holmes, Jr.

MAP 15

COL. WOODS KING

truckheads, operate and maintain ferry crossings, and arrange for barge traffic.
Since there was only a very limited American SOS operating in the area at
the time, King improvised a supply and evacuation system with his own
personnel. SOS began to establish itself and by April had four ferry crossings organized, river transport operating on three waterways, and boatheads
and truckloads at seven sites. There was still no Chinese SOS, only some
supply personnel. The medical problem was alleviated by the assignment
to Eastern Command of the 34th and 44th U.S. Portable Surgical Hospitals.[10]

Before launching the 13-week unit training program, Eastern Command
planned to create specialist schools for veterinary officers and technicians,
medical personnel, and radio and switchboard operators. At the command
headquarters, a school for senior Chinese officers was instituted. American
liaison personnel were sent out to Wang's four armies and twelve divisions
around 1 April to set up the training programs, both individual and unit.
In the case of the 74th Army, by mid-April plans were complete and build-

[10] Hist Rpt, CCC, Apr–Sep 45, p. 9. OCMH. (2) Min, SOS General Staff Conf, 5 Apr 45.
SOS China Theater Files, KCRC.

ings selected for signal technicians, while classes for veterinary and medical personnel were under way. Rifle, mortar, and machine gun ranges were largely completed by 16 April. Training aids were constructed and were ready for distribution.[11]

The team sent to the 57th Division, 74th Army, which may be taken as typical, comprised two liaison officers, one of field grade, a medical aid man, a radio team, and a Chinese major to interpret. The team had no transport and marched to its destination. Coolies helped carry its baggage. Included in the baggage were seven days' rations, later found "invaluable" as only rice and a little pork could be purchased.

On arriving at the town in which 57th Division headquarters was located the team opened for business in a school building some two miles from the Chinese headquarters, but linked by wire communication. Commanded by Lt. Col. Douglas C. Tomkies, the team spent the first two weeks of April trying to build training aids, training courses, and rifle ranges. In dealing with the Chinese the Americans at first found them reluctant to divulge information. The Chinese seemed to fear the Americans would promptly radio it to the rear and then in some way embarrass them. But gradually confidence was established, and only the barrier of language and custom slowed the flow of information.[12]

By mid-April, training areas and troop schools were ready in Eastern Command, specialist schools had gotten under way with their first classes, and the third classes for senior Chinese officers were in session.

While these Sino-American activities were in progress, the Japanese had been completing some preparations of their own. Early in 1945 *China Expeditionary Army* had directed *Sixth Area Army* to prepare two sets of plans, for a raid on Chungking and for operations against Lao-ho-kou (near Hsian in northwest China) and the American airfields at Chihchiang. This was in compliance with the 22 January 1945 order of *Imperial General Headquarters,* which emphasized strengthening the lower Yangtze valley and north China against possible American attack. "Prolonged and systematic raiding" of interior China was directed by small units only. Advanced American air bases were to be destroyed.[13]

References to raids in interior China represented a cherished project of *China Expeditionary Army,* which had long been anxious to take aggressive measures against Chungking. *Sixth Area Army* was less optimistic and ambitious in its outlook. As the Japanese planning got under way in Febru-

---

[11] Hist Data, LXXIV Army Hq, U.S. Combat Sec, Qtrly Rpt, 1 Apr–30 Jun 45, Sha-wan, Hunan Province. OCMH.

[12] Hist Data, Hq 57th Div, U.S. Combat Sec, Qtrly Rpt, 1 Apr–30 Jun 45, Yungkow, Hunan Province. OCMH.

[13] Japanese Study 129, pp. 70–74.

ary, *Sixth Area Army* decided that by April, the contemplated date of the operation against Chihchiang, it would be hard to accumulate sufficient strength for it.   Of the two divisions supposed to take part, the *116th* had been roughly handled at Heng-yang while the well-equipped and powerful *47th* was still in process of arrival from Japan.   *Sixth Area Army* was therefore inclined to think that the operation should aim only at reaching the Yuan Chiang, a stream which flows just west of the Eastern Command head- quarters at Sha-wan.   In the light of past experience it seemed to the Japanese that if they reached a point near the airfield the Americans would destroy it and withdraw.

Here entered the human factor.   Okamura, the Japanese commander in China, was visiting the headquarters of the Japanese *20th Army,* the organiza- tion scheduled to conduct the operation.   He found *20th Army* supremely confident, and so he decided to proceed with an operation directly against Chihchiang (which could serve as a base for the raiding operations that Okamura wanted) even though but one regiment of the *47th Division* would be on hand in time for the operation.   Therefore, with four regiments the *20th Army* prepared its drive on Chihchiang.   This left it two divisions with which to garrison the stretch of 200 miles of vital railway from Tung-ting Lake above Changsha down to the city of Ling-ling.[14]   In north China the Japanese prepared to take Lao-ho-kou as soon as possible.

Examining the China scene on 1 February, Wedemeyer listed a drive through Chihchiang on Kunming as being among several Japanese capabili- ties but did not see any indication of it.   He estimated that the Japanese would probably concentrate their forces on the coast and in the area of Changsha–Hankow–Peiping–Manchuria, an appraisal which was an almost entirely correct reading of the Japanese intentions.[15]   By 17 February Japa- nese intentions were more apparent, and Wedemeyer warned the General- issimo that the enemy might try to take the airfields at Hsian, Lao-ho-kou, and Chihchiang.[16]

As China Theater's staff estimated the situation, the major Japanese threat would be against Chihchiang; Japanese attacks on or toward Hsian and its neighboring airfields would be of lesser though still considerable importance. Therefore, since Wedemeyer's U.S. resources were strictly limited, the major defensive effort would have to be made around Chihchiang.   For the Hsian area, his staff carefully surveyed the situation and determined that the Chinese had some resources to supplement those in the I War Area at Hsian.   The Americans believed that the forces in the Hsian area were in poor shape,

---

[14] Japanese Study 130, Map 3, pp. 56–59, 74.
[15] Rad CFB 32476, Wedemeyer to MacArthur and Nimitz, info Marshall, 5 Feb 45.   Bk 2, ACW Personal File.
[16] Min, Mtg 40, Wedemeyer with Generalissimo, 17 Feb 45.   Bk 1, Generalissimo Minutes.

with no training program and very short of equipment. In making this appraisal, they eliminated without further description the twelve divisions they thought were watching the Chinese Communists. Their suggested solution was a liaison team to assist in a training program whose major impetus would have to come from the Chinese, and the distribution of projected Chinese arms production to the I War Area. The planners estimated this arms production for the six months March–August 1945 inclusive at:

Rifle, 7.92-mm.	50,400
Cartridge, 7.92-mm.	58,700,000
Machine gun, light	4,930
Machine gun, heavy	1,425
Trench mortar, 60-mm.	1,388
Trench mortar, 82-mm.	840
Shell, mortar, 60-mm.	385,000
Shell, mortar, 82-mm.	517,500
Gun, AT, 37-mm.	3
Shell, 37-mm. AT	5,000
Grenade	1,842,500
Mines	80,000

Having reached these conclusions, China Theater did not let itself be distracted by the opening of the Japanese northern offensive on Hsian and Lao-ho-kou on 22 March, with some twenty battalions of infantry, an armored task force, and a modest complement of pack howitzers with a few 150-mm. howitzers for siege work. To help Maj. Gen. Hu Tsung-nan's I War Area meet the drive, Wedemeyer sent a liaison team under Colonel Barrett to give training and technical advice, while Chennault sent air-ground liaison teams to direct the air support that his aircraft were soon giving under his personal leadership.[17]

In late March and early April, the forward movement of the Japanese toward their assembly areas in west Hunan Province began, giving an unmistakable indication of their intent to attack toward Chihchiang. Chinese Combat Command's G–2 estimated that 20,000 Japanese were massed in the area about Pao-ching (Shao-yang), a road junction west of Heng-yang, with another 5,000 to the southwest.[18]

On 8 April 1945, as the northern Japanese forces were entering Lao-ho-kou, strong enemy patrols probed the Chinese outposts just west of the stream Tzu Shui, which runs from south to north a mile west of Pao-ching. That same day a Japanese force estimated at 2,000 moved west out of Pao-

---

[17] (1) Japanese Study 78. (2) Min, Mtg 48, Wedemeyer with Generalissimo, 5 Apr 45; Mtg 40, 24 Apr 45. (3) Ltr, Col Barrett to Wedemeyer, 7 May 45, sub: Conf with CG First War Area. AG 337 Misc, Folder, Meetings from 1944 to 30 Aug 45, China Theater Files, KCRC. (4) Staff Study 11, Theater Planning Sec, 24 Mar 45. Register No. 06106–R, USFCT Files, DRB AGO.

[18] Ltr cited n. 6.

ching, and took up advanced positions, in the opinion of Eastern Command to cover the forthcoming offensive.[19]

The Japanese threat required immediate countermeasures. The Chinese forces that would have to meet it initially were substantially as they had been in previous campaigns. "Little American equipment" had been received for General Wang's troops, while the training program through sheer lack of time had not progressed beyond schools for specialists and officers.[20] However, Wedemeyer had made progress in the last few months, and there were assets present that were not at hand before. First, there seemed to have been no problems arising from Chinese domestic politics. Second, the American SOS helped supply food and ammunition on a systematic basis. Third, there was an American liaison net down to divisions so that there was usually timely information of Chinese movements and intentions. Fourth, Chennault's supply position was the best it had ever been. Last of all, there was what seems in retrospect an atmosphere of mutual co-operation between Chinese and Americans.

The American Share in the Chihchiang Campaign

As the Japanese were making their last-minute preparations, and as the Americans of Eastern Command were setting up their training program, the deployment of Wang's armies suggested that a Japanese drive on Chihchiang would trail its line of communications past the 73d Army at Hsin-hua, forty or so miles north of the Pao-ching–Chihchiang road, the 18th Army, at Chang-te, about 150 miles away to the north, and the 100th Army, forty-five miles northeast of Chihchiang. Only the 74th Army, deployed along the eastern edge of the hills that lie between Pao-ching and Chihchiang, was directly between the Japanese and their goal. The 58th Division of the 74th Army was forty miles south of the Chihchiang road at Hsin-ning, and well forward of the main Chinese positions. The 57th Division was at Hua-yuan-shih near Tung-kou, on the road, and the 51st was northeast of Tung-kou at Shan-men.

The first Japanese attacks on 8 April were estimated as made by two parallel columns of 2,000 men each, the northern moving west along the Chihchiang road and the southern toward Hsin-ning. The 74th Army thus faced a developing attack on a fifty-mile front. When it began, there were American liaison teams with the 51st and 57th Divisions, but the team for the 58th Division at Hsin-ning did not arrive until after that city had fallen.[21]

---

[19] (1) Ltr cited n. 6. (2) Japanese Study 78.
[20] Annex I to MS cited n. 8.
[21] (1) G–3 Per Rpt, Hq CCC, 11 Apr 45; Hist Rpt, IV Army Gp Comd (successor to Eastern Command). Folder, Histories 1945, 74th Army Combat Sec; CCC Files, KCRC. (2) Hist Data, Hq, 58th Div, U.S. Combat Sec, Qtrly Rpt, 1 Apr–30 Jun 45. OCMH.

EASTERN COMMAND HEADQUARTERS CONFERENCE *at Chihchiang. From left, General Sultan; Brig. Gen. William Barber, Chief of Staff, Chinese Combat Command; General McClure; Maj. Gen. Gilbert X. Cheves; and General Ho Ying-chin.*

As evidence of the weight of the Japanese thrust started coming in, the various headquarters began to react. By the 10th, Eastern Command was asking that movement of MARS personnel (instructors and demonstration teams) into the area be halted. Two days later General Wang asked that an army be sent to the Chihchiang area to act as mobile reserve. On 13 April the Japanese began a general advance.[22]

The CCC command and liaison system began to yield its first fruits on 14 April. A general conference, attended by Ho and McClure, their respective chiefs of staff, General Cheves of the SOS, and his staff, was convened. General Hsiao I-hsu, Ho's chief of staff, presented what became the basic plan of the campaign. Ho and McClure agreed to create troop concentrations on the north and south flanks of the Japanese drive. To the north three divisions from the VI War Area would be brought down to permit the 18th Army in turn to move to the east of Hsin-hua. To the south, General Tang En-po's 94th Army was to move to Ching-hsien, whence it could threaten the Japanese south flank or cover the road from Kweilin into Kweichow Province. Thus, the Chinese would be ready for a double envelopment. The center would be strengthened by moving in the elite 14th and 22d Divisions by air and truck, but only if the situation warranted. Every attempt would be made to hold the line Wu-kang–Hsin-hua, the forward edge of the hill mass mentioned above.[23]

The Generalissimo attempted to take an active part in the campaign, and Wedemeyer moved to forestall him. On 17 April Wedemeyer warned McClure that the Generalissimo was issuing orders to Ho and to General Wang's troops without referring them to the Sino-American combined staff. McClure was asked to see if Ho knew of such orders.[24]

While the Chinese regiments of the 74th and 100th Armies on the hills adjacent to the road to Chihchiang sought to stop or slow the Japanese advance, and the 73d Army, which the Japanese were bypassing, began to move south, the decisions of the 14 April conference began to take effect. Up north, at Chang-te, the American liaison team with the 18th Army, under Colonel Lake, had been setting up a line of communications by river from the Chihchiang area, in conformity with what they thought to be their basic mission, training and supply. Now that task was laid aside, and Colonel Lake with the Chinese army commander, General Hu Lien, spent several days around 23 April trying to learn just what the 18th Army's mission was to be. Colonel Lake's headquarters was shifted south and west from Tao-yuan near Chang-te to Yuan-ling, the American SOS headquarters for the area. Hu

[22] Rads, Eastern Comd to CCC, 10 Apr, 12 Apr 45. AG (CCC) 311.23, KCRC.
[23] (1) In Radiogram CYF 13528, McClure to Wedemeyer, 15 April 1945, McClure's language indicates the plan is basically American. (2) Combined Staff Mtg 36, 14 Apr 45. AG (CCC) 337.1, KCRC. (3) McClure comments on draft MS.
[24] Rad CFB 35833, Wedemeyer to McClure, 17 Apr 45. CCC Files, KCRC.

and Lake were first told that the 18th Army was to move to An-chiang, in the rear of the 74th. Forming a mobile command post group, Lake joined Hu's headquarters in the field and accompanied it during the rest of the campaign. Before the 18th reached An-chiang, the orders were changed. About twenty miles north of the road to Chihchiang, near Shan-men, the hills are big enough to be called a mountain, Pai-ma Shan. The 18th went there.[25]

To the south, the 94th Army, General Mou Ting-fang, was moving up to the scene of action. Troops of the 94th Army took orders from Tang En-po; that they should move from one war area to another to aid a neighboring commander was a major improvement over past practice. The 94th Army Combat Section, Col. George L. Goodridge, had joined them 6 February. He understood that his mission was to assist in training and, since he had had considerable past experience, he was authorized to prescribe his own program, to be completed 1 June. A series of movement orders made it impossible to get unit training under way, while only a few U.S. weapons were received. About 15 April the 94th Army was alerted; it received orders to move on the 16th, and got under way on the 25th. Colonel Goodridge, his G–2, and an intercepter "joined Mou's headquarters at his request and lived, ate, and moved with the general."[26]

On 15 April Colonel King of Eastern Command recommended that flying the 22d Division to Chihchiang begin at once, and the operation was code-named ROOSTER. The supply situation there, according to the SOS, would just support the 22d plus two battalions of field artillery. About 8,000 tons of Hump tonnage would be needed to support the move, it was estimated. The progress of the Japanese advance continued over the next few days, so on 21 April ROOSTER began. By the 25th one regiment of the 22d Division with a battery of pack howitzers and a company of 4.2-inch mortars was in Chihchiang. Soon the 14th Division too was under way in trucks manned by the U.S. 475th Infantry Regiment. By 29 April there were 15,624 men of the New Sixth Army at Chihchiang, with more scheduled to arrive every day. A few days later, 3,750 soldiers of the 14th arrived by truck at An-chiang. Since but five Japanese regiments were making the attack, unless the Japanese chose to make it a major operation their last chance of taking the field probably was gone by 29 April, whatever happened on its approaches.[27]

But though ROOSTER made Japanese success at Chihchiang most

[25] History of the American Combat Section [18th Army], 1 Jan 45–31 Mar 45, 1 Apr 45–30 Jun 45. CCC Files, KCRC.

[26] Rpt, 94th Army, American Liaison Team. Folder, History of III Group Command. CCC Files, KCRC.

[27] (1) Combined Staff Mtgs 38–46, 20 Apr–9 May 45. AG (CCC) 337.1, KCRC. (2) Ltr, Col Heavey to CG SOS, 28 May 45, sub: Rpt of Opns of Provisional Truck Organization. OCMH.

CHINESE NEW SIXTH ARMY TROOPS *and ammunition are being transported across the river to An-chiang, en route to the front.*

improbable, it had negative effects elsewhere in China; the gasoline require-ments of the move could only be met by cutting Chennault's operations to air defense and reconnaissance.[28]

At the front along the road to Chihchiang and in the immediate rear, where American medical and supply installations were establishing them-selves, American liaison teams were with the 58th Division, now between Hsin-ning and Wu-kang; the 57th, between Tung-kou and Chiang-kou (Ta-chiang-kou) on the road to Chihchiang; and the 51st, to the north of the main road.

The detachment with the 58th Division, a radio team and interpreter, was commanded by 1st Lt. Stan C. Hintze, a very junior officer for such a post, where he would perforce be advising a Chinese major general, but the short-age of personnel made it necessary. Lieutenant Hintze seems not to have tried to advise the commander on tactical matters but to have occupied him-self "aiding the division commander with the supply problem, air support,

[28] (1) Min, Mtg 50, Wedemeyer with Generalissimo, 24 Apr 45. Bk 1, Generalissimo Min-utes. (2) Rad CAK 10127, Chennault to Wedemeyer, 22 Apr 45. CCC Files, KCRC.

and keeping up on the tactical situation." On 25 April the Chinese commander began to fall back on the main Chinese forces to the northwest. He left a reinforced battalion to garrison Wu-kang, and withdrew his division westward. A U.S. air-ground liaison team joined Lieutenant Hintze on 29 April. Next day the Japanese *Sekine Detachment (217th Infantry Regiment plus two battalions, 58th Infantry Brigade)* opened its attack. Orders from higher authority directed the division to fall back again, this time to the Wa-wu-tang area, northwest and seventeen miles southwest of Tung-kou, to previously prepared positions.[29]

The 57th Division Combat Section was commanded by Colonel Tomkies. When the division received orders to move up on the road to Chihchiang, Tomkies learned of the move through the Chinese, and since his radio was not working he had to send couriers to the 74th Army Combat Section to inform them of the move. Once the 57th was in action against the main force of the *116th Division* on the Chihchiang road, Colonel Tomkies, assisted by two officers, kept in close touch with the tactical situation by having at least two U.S. officers at the front line every day. This was not easy, for the 57th was fighting on a wide front over hilly, almost roadless ground. When the staff of Tomkies' section opened their headquarters at Chiang-kou they found 130 wounded Chinese around the local bus station. There was no Chinese evacuation system; next morning thirty of the men were dead. Thereafter the Combat Section was alert to send wounded to the rear by any American vehicle that entered the area. When, on 28 April, Colonel King, commanding Eastern Command, and General Barber, CCC chief of staff, visited the 57th Division, the CCC party told the Chinese division commander that the present line had to be held until 11 May. At the meeting, the division commander remarked that the Americans had been very helpful in bringing up ammunition and evacuating wounded. Somewhat earlier, on 24 April, Tomkies took advantage of an inspection by the CCC G–2 to ask that automatic weapons be sent to the Chinese. Next day forty Bren guns arrived.[30]

The 51st Division had been the left (north) flank of the 74th Army, whose liaison officer was Colonel Cummings. By the third week in April it was apparent that the Japanese advance was being made by infiltration on the grand scale, with columns thrusting deep into the complex and jumbled hill mass and bypassing Chinese resistance. So when the 51st Division was moved to a point about fifteen miles northwest of Shan-men, probably to prevent any bypassing of the Chinese on the road to Chihchiang, it proved difficult to put the division into contact with the Japanese. The combat sec-

[29] (1) Hist Data, Hq, 58th Div, U.S. Combat Sec, Qtrly Rpt. 1 Apr–30 Jun 45, Wu-kang, Hunan Province. OCMH. (2) Japanese Study 78.
[30] Hist Data, Hq 57th Div, U.S. Combat Sec, Qtrly Rpt, 1 Apr–30 Jun 45, Tungkow, Hunan Province. OCMH.

tion commander, Col. Louis V. Jones, with another officer, a radio team, and an interpreter, learned from the Chinese division commander that the latter was moving out with two regiments on 14 April. The third was to follow later. Colonel Jones decided to follow in the wake of the division and with forty-four transport coolies began his hike on the 16th. The next day by inquiring he found that the Chinese commander and his two regiments had gone past the valley along which the Japanese, probably one of the three task forces into which the *116th* was now divided, were approaching from the east. That left the 151st Regiment alone to go into action against the Japanese that night, 17 April. Next day Colonel Jones was able to join the division commander and recommend a deployment for the division. Jones suggested bringing the 152d Regiment up into line on the left (north) of the 151st, to link with the 19th Division, 100th Army, to the north. To the south, there was no physical contact with the 57th Division, so the division held its six-mile front with its flank in the air.

An air-ground team and air support were requested on 19 April. The air support arrived, one plane on the 20th and four on the 21st. Then the rain closed in and no air support could be given. This was unfortunate, because the Japanese *116th Division* was now making considerable progress. The *133d Infantry Regiment* took Shan-men, which meant the Japanese now had a foothold in the hills. The rough terrain, which made a mile and a half an hour a good pace for hiking cross country, favored the defense, and the Chinese had held stoutly.[31]

Immediately to the north of the 74th Army, in the Pai-ma Shan area, the 100th Army held positions in a line that ended about ten miles northwest of Lung-hui. The troops were in contact with the Japanese *109th Infantry Regiment* all along their front, and were slowly withdrawing. Between the 100th Army and the 73d in the Hsin-hua area, thirty miles northwest of Lung-hui, was a considerable gap, into which the 18th Army was beginning to move. The 73d Army was in contact with a regiment of the *47th Division,* and was facing south. The 73d was holding well, and replying to every Japanese gain with counterattacks.[32]

Behind the lines on which the Chinese were holding well in the center and moving forward on the flanks, American and Chinese logistical support of every variety was building up. When the campaign opened, saving only the two portable surgical hospitals, the nearest SOS units had been those of the Kweiyang Area Command, a good 200 miles away.[33] The Chinese supply arrangements had seemed to Colonel King to be of the most inadequate

---

[31] (1) Hist Data, 74th Army, U.S. Combat Sec. CCC Files, KCRC. (2) Hist Data, Hq, 51st Div, U.S. Combat Sec, Qtrly Rpt, 1 Apr–Jun 45. OCMH.
[32] (1) Per Rpt, G–3 Hq CCC, 2 May 45 (for 21–28 Apr 45). CCC Files, KCRC. (2) Japanese Study 78.
[33] Tab 22, G–4, China Theater, Per Rpt, 1st Qtr 1945. CCC and CT Records, KCRC.

sort. Then the Japanese drive began, and more of China Theater's meager resources were deployed in that direction. On 4 June the old Communications Zone, China Theater, was subdivided into five base sections, four of which stretched out like a column of soldiers from Kunming to Chihchiang. Chihchiang became Base Section No. 4. In it by the end of the month were a base general depot, two platoons of the 21st Field Hospital, veterinary and malaria detachments, the 3447th Ordnance Medium Automotive Maintenance Company, and signal troops.[34]

The Chihchiang base supported forward truckheads and riverheads at eight different points, from An-chiang to Tung-kou on the east, and Hsin-hua to the northeast. The SOS delivered supplies to these points, where Eastern Command personnel took the responsibility of delivery by truck or sampan.

When the campaign began there had been two portable surgical hospitals in the area, the 34th and 44th. Ultimately, the 32d and 35th joined, together with the 3d Platoon, 21st Field Hospital. The American personnel strength of Eastern Command went up proportionately, to 230 officers and 1,326 enlisted men as of 1 May 1945, and to 264 and 1,509 respectively a month later.[35]

Though in looking back on the campaign Colonel King had been very critical of the Chinese medical arrangements as he saw them and though one American observer could not find much of an evacuation system, still the Chinese must have made a very real effort to meet the needs of their troops. As of mid-July there were eight Chinese base hospitals and six evacuation hospitals in the Eastern Command, together with a number of medical detachments. The Chinese were operating a base depot at Chihchiang as of mid-July, four intermediate depots, and eighteen forward depots. Ammunition was issued from eight ammunition supply points. The base at Chihchiang had seventeen days of supply for U.S.-sponsored divisions, and sixteen days for the Chinese. Four more points had five days of supply for U.S.-sponsored and Chinese units each, and two more had two days of supply. Rice was bought in the Tung-ting Lake area, carried south by junk and sampan, then transferred to trucks.[36]

---

[34] See map opposite p. 227, G-4, China Theater, Per Rpt, 2d Qtr 1945. CCC and CT Records, KCRC. (2) GO 45, Hq SOS USFCT, 4 Jun 45.

[35] (1) Special G-1 Rpt, Hq Eastern Comd, 22 Jul 45. CCC Files, KCRC. (2) MS cited n. 8.

[36] (1) Special G-4 Rpt, Eastern Comd, Hq CCC, 21 Jul 45. CCC Files, KCRC. (2) A day of supply in terms of rounds per weapon per day was prescribed by the War Department for each weapon. As of 31 March 1945, days of supply for certain important weapons in China Theater were: rifle, 3 rounds; machine gun, Bren, Maxim, Browning, 70 rounds; 37-mm. antitank, 5 rounds; 75-mm. howitzer, 25 rounds; 81-mm. mortar, 8 rounds. Cir 36, Rear echelon, Hq USFCT, 19 Mar 45. Reproduced as Tab 4, G-4 Per Rpt, 1st Qtr 1945. CCC and CT Records, KCRC. (3) Ltr, Heavy to CG SOS cited n. 27(2) says the 475th's trucks were used as ambulances on one occasion. The accompanying Chinese arrangements seemed to him inadequate.

CHINESE BOATMEN *aboard small sampan pour beans into sacks before unloading at the SOS warehouse.*

Over all this, the Fourteenth Air Force kept the skies. An occasional Japanese aircraft would be seen by liaison team members on what they took to be a reconnaissance mission, but the Japanese air force in China could no longer support the Emperior's soldiers in their last campaigns. The Chinese were supported in the Chihchiang campaign by the U.S. 5th Fighter Group with fifty-six fighters, and two squadrons of medium bombers. Eight air-ground liaison teams worked with the Chinese. Initially, the air-ground teams sent their requests for air support to a central control station at An-chiang, where the stream Yuan Chiang crosses the road to Chihchiang. Later, requests went directly to 5th Group headquarters. There the requests were accepted or rejected and, if accepted, given priorities. Fighters were then assigned as available, and armed with the weight and type of missile most suitable to the target.

During the two-month campaign, the fighter group used .50-caliber ammunition at the rate of 1,800,000 rounds a month, and flew 3,101 sorties.

Napalm was introduced to the war in eastern China. The six medium bombers flew 183 sorties.[37]

The Test Successfully Passed

As April began drawing into May, the Japanese advances became ever more localized. The Chinese held ever more strongly on the flanks, and Japanese advances were confined to the Chihchiang road sector. The Japanese took Tung-kou, but the Chinese were not disheartened, and a "stubborn swapping" of hills ensued. The front line, from south to north, was an arc along the points Wu-kang–Wawutang–Tung-kou–Shan-men–Hsin hau.[38]

From the south, the 94th Army (5th, 43d, 121st Divisions) was moving up toward the Japanese left flank and rear. The 43d Division was kept in army reserve; most of the fighting fell to the 5th Division. At 94th Army headquarters, the American liaison officer, Colonel Goodridge, his G–2, and an interpreter were in daily contact with the Army commander, General Mou Ting-fang. "Whenever the situation changed, the general called the liaison officer to the map and after explaining the situation, asked for his opinion. Usually a discussion of the merits of the plan followed with the general giving his reasons and ideas. In most cases the ensuing order followed along the lines of the plan suggested by the liaison officer."

The 5th Division's officers and noncommissioned officers had completed two weeks of training, in tactics and weapons respectively, when orders to move east, to Tien-chu, arrived. The march was halted for one day while the division was under way for it to receive summer uniforms, medical supplies, and a second issue of lend-lease ordnance, submachine guns, 60-mm. mortars, and Bren guns. By 29 April the division was at Chang-pu-tzu, forty-five miles southwest of Tung-kou, and on a road that led to the Japanese left flank. Here the Chinese turned north.

The 121st Division had also completed half of the noncommissioned and officer courses when it received orders to move. Some U.S. weapons were received, but lacked such accessories as rifle clips, bayonets, and slings. Like the 5th, the 121st received Bren guns and submachine guns while on the march. In its move eastward it took a course parallel to that of the 5th, but continued on to the next valley east of the one up which the 5th was now advancing. The 121st thus proceeded to the Wu-kang area, then moved north to Lung-tien.

The 5th Division met the Japanese on 2 May at the entrance to the Wu-yang valley. Next day a conference with liaison personnel resulted in a decision to attempt an envelopment. Completed over the 5th and 6th, the

---

[37] *The Army Air Forces*, V, Ch. IX.

[38] Summary, G–3 Rpts, Hq IV Army Group (Eastern) Comd USFCT. Folder, Histories, 1945, 74 Army Combat Sec, CCC Files, KCRC.

operation was a complete success, and yielded a fair amount of Japanese equipment including artillery, some documents, and six prisoners. On 7 May the division began moving northeast into the adjacent valley where the 121st was operating On the afternoon of the 11th it was in the area of Teng-tzu-pu, sixteen miles south of the Chihchiang–Pao-ching road, which was the main Japanese line of communications, and well east of Tung-kou.

Meanwhile, the 121st Division had been moving steadily north up the Wu-kang valley, so that in effect the 5th Division crossed its line of march. The Japanese were repeatedly outflanked, and hustled north. The night of 11 May the Japanese were observed to be burning the village of Kao-sha near the Chihchiang–Pao-ching road. The 94th Army had successfully turned the Japanese left flank.

Reviewing the performance of the 121st Division, the liaison officer, Col. William M. Jackson, noted the beneficial effect of the American ration scheme, and the effectiveness of the 60-mm. mortar and submachine gun. He praised the agressive spirit of the Chinese commanders, and the bravery of the men. The division commander discussed matters with liaison personnel and his staff, then made his decision. Airdropping of ammunition and supplies was most effective, and helped greatly to raise morale. In the liability column, he noted that small units were reluctant to envelop, and when they did left open an escape route for the enemy, a criticism also advanced by Colonel Goodridge for the 94th as a whole. There was not sufficient training in American weapons. Reconnaissance was usually poor. As a rule, unit commanders stayed in their command posts and operated with map and telephone.[39]

From the north, the 18th and 100th Armies were swinging down behind the Japanese even as the 94th Army was coming up from the south. The 19th and 51st Divisions, 100th Army, had borne the brunt of the Japanese attempts to move west through the Pai-ma Shan area. On 11 May the 63d Division began to move, forcing the Japanese back toward Shan-men. These being flank positions, the Japanese held them stubbornly to allow their forward elements time to withdraw toward Pao-ching. But there were not enough Japanese present for them to guard every avenue of Chinese approach, and on 11 May the 11th Division, Chinese 18th Army, which had been out to the north and east, swung back west to retake Shan-men. That same day the 118th Division, 18th Army, moved troops on to the Chihchiang–Pao-ching road. During these operations the 18th Army took Japanese supply dumps and captured 500 head of horses. At this moment a Japanese disaster might have seemed inevitable, but higher Chinese head-

---

[39] Report by 94th Army American Liaison Team, from which the quotation was taken; A History of 5th Div, 94th Army, 2 Sep 45; A History of 121st Div, 94th Army, 2 Sep 45. Folder, History of III Gp Comd, AG (CCC) 314.7, KCRC.

quarters intervened and ordered the 118th to move back off the road and let the Japanese retreat.

The local Japanese headquarters, *20th Army,* wanted to throw in the better part of two fresh divisions to retrieve the situation, but was overruled by *6th Area Army* because the Japanese forces in China were now engaged in carrying out orders of *Imperial General Headquarters* for a redeployment of the greatest magnitude for operations of corresponding importance. Chihchiang airfield was not worth interfering with that. So the Japanese withdrew.[40]

The Generalissimo bypassed Wedemeyer and the Chinese Combat Command, and on 6 May ordered Ho to seize Heng-yang, an action that would involve a major advance into Japanese-held territory. Learning of the order, Wedemeyer at once protested to the Generalissimo. As so often before, he pointed out that he as chief of staff could not co-ordinate Chinese and American activities if orders of which he was not informed were given to subordinate commands. He also argued that the Chinese were not ready for a major operation, and closed by stating that he did not challenge the Generalissimo's right to make decisions and would support them loyally once they were annouced.[41] The Generalissimo replied that the message to Ho was simply an opinion on his part, and that it had been issued as an order because of a misunderstanding by his staff.

From this point, the Chihchiang campaign is a story of Japanese retreat to the original line of departure at Pao-ching. The campaign ended 7 June 1945. The Chinese forces were not allowed to pursue the enemy farther because of logistical problems. Concentrating, arming, and supplying the Chinese in the Chihchiang campaign was a heavy drain on the air supply resources in China Theater. If the victory had been exploited, resources intended for BETA, the taking of the Canton–Hong Kong area, would have been consumed in a battle around Heng-yang and Changsha. If the Japanese had then been provoked into reinforcing the five regiments that had been so roughly handled, the outcome would have been unpredictable. So the pursuit halted, and Eastern Command was ordered on 29 May to guard against resources being drawn into a costly, premature advance by major units. On 22 June this injunction was reinforced by orders not to let the local Chinese commander, General Wang, engage in anything that might call for air supply. The Japanese were to be contained by diversionary action.[42]

[40] (1) Japanese Study 130, p. 69. (2) For a discussion of current Japanese strategy, see below Chapter XI.

[41] (1) Memo 562 and Incls, Wedemeyer for Generalissimo, 9 May 45. Item 37, Bk 9, ACW Corresp with Chinese. (2) Min, Mtg 54, Wedemeyer with Generalissimo, 8 May 45. Bk 1, Generalissimo Minutes.

[42] (1) Annex III to MS cited n. 8. (2) Missions, Eastern Command and Fourth Area Army, Annex to MS, Historical Data of Eastern Command, 16 Aug 45. Folder, Histories, 1945, 74 Army Combat Sec, CCC Files, KCRC.

WAITING AT CHANYI AIRFIELD. *Seasoned troops of the Chinese New Sixth Army are ready to emplane for the airlift to Chihchiang.*

Looking back on the Chihchiang campaign, the Japanese found they had suffered approximately 1,500 men killed, and 5,000 wounded. There was much of professional interest in their opponents' conduct of the campaign. "Most distinctive," to the Japanese, was the airlift of the New Sixth Army to Chihchiang. They did not notice anything of the "publicized modernization" of the Chinese forces except an increase in automatic rifles, presumably the submachine guns. The Chinese tactics in the Chihchiang campaign seemed to be a "great advance" over the past, and the Japanese were impressed by the work of the air-artillery-infantry team, accurate artillery fire, and concentration of fire on key points. In retrospect, some Japanese officers concluded that they failed because they did not take into account what their intelligence had warned them of—the improvement in the Chinese forces.[43]

[43] (1) Japanese Study 78 has the casualty figures. (2) Japanese Study 130, p. 68. (3) The thirty-six-division program was discussed in the Chinese press, much to U.S. displeasure. Memo 458, Gen Gross, Actg CofS, for Generalissimo, 22 Mar 45. Bk 16, ACW Corresp with Chinese. (4) Japanese Officers' comments on draft MS.

The successful defense of Chihchiang cost the Chinese heavy casualties. The 18th, 73d, 100th Armies, plus the 13th and Temporary-6th Divisions, lost 256 officers and 6,576 enlisted men killed, and 504 officers and 11,223 enlisted men wounded. To these figures must be added the unknown losses of the 94th and 18th Armies.[44]

Japanese operations in the Lao-ho-kou–Hsian area were more successful than those against Chihchiang, but only nominally, in that the Japanese did occupy the airfield at Lao-ho-kou.   Chennault had been able to commit the 311th and 81st Fighter Groups and the 426th Night Fighter Squadron of the AAF plus a fighter group and two bombardment squadrons of the Chinese-American Composite Wing, but by moving at night against slight Chinese resistance the Japanese had been able to occupy Lao-ho-kou.   So far events had followed a familiar pattern.   But at this point General Hu Tsung-nan's troops, whom the Japanese had rated as the best in China, counterattacked heavily.   The weak Japanese *110th Division* was soon in trouble and had to be reinforced with one artillery and two infantry battalions.   This was insufficient, and finally a total of seven Japanese battalions had to be added. The Japanese finally stabilized their lines and the fighting died down, but only after losses they called "tremendous" after the war.   While the fighting was under way, Colonel Barrett's liaison group worked to set up an infantry training center, whose doors opened 13 May.   The center opened too late to affect the fighting in any way, and honors went to the team formed by General Hu, his armies, and the Chinese and American airmen of General Chennault.[45]

The Chihchiang campaign demonstrated that Chinese troops whose commanders were determined to stand could successfully face the Japanese if they had sufficient numerical strength and a steady supply of food and ammunition.   In the Chihchiang campaign the Chinese used as many armies as the Japanese did regiments.   By aggressive maneuvering they were able to outflank the Japanese and force them to retreat.   The strong and weak points of Chinese commanders, staffs, and troops were fully displayed.

In the campaign, Wedemeyer's accomplishments to April 1945 were tested, and shown to be considerable.   Indeed, the test was the more severe in that his system was far from being in full operation.   The troops involved had not had unit training.   The officers and noncommissioned officers had received only brief schooling.   The Chinese soldiers had not received their full allowance of weapons, and had to get their familiarization training during march halts and between skirmishes.   Had the Chinese divisions received the

---

[44] (1) Special G–1 Rpt cited n. 35(1).   (2) The disparity between Chinese and Japanese casualty figures does not necessarily reflect on the accuracy of the latter.   As a rule, a force of higher professional quality than its opponent will inflict more casualties than it suffers itself.

[45] (1) Japanese Study 78.   (2) *The Army Air Forces,* V, 264.   (3) Hq Rpt, Hq I War Area Infantry Training Center to CO I War Area Liaison Team, 10 Jul 44, sub: Training Rpt.   OCMH.

contemplated twenty-six-week training, their performance would have been even better than it was.

Outweighing these handicaps were the achievements that Wedemeyer had effected: an over-all plan of campaign into which local plans might be properly fitted; a workable command system, both in the local Chinese forces and between the Allies; and a supply system which brought food and ammunition to the critical areas.   They were decisive to the campaign, and indicated that real progress was being made in China Theater.   That the Chinese adopted procedures which may have seemed to them contrary to their accepted practices reflected credit upon both their spirit of co-operation and the powers of persuasion of Wedemeyer, McClure, and their staffs.   However, a critique of this campaign shows that there were flaws which should have been eliminated if successful offensive operations were to be conducted.

The liaison system, through which the Chinese Combat Command was to have exercised virtual operational control of the Chinese, worked at a lower level than had been contemplated.   After-action reports do not suggest that the commanders of the combat sections commanded the Chinese armies. Rather, the impression given is that the more aggressive and experienced American officers forcefully advised their Chinese associates, and that those less capable simply acted as liaison officers, with reportorial and supply functions.   Several factors probably tended to make this so:

1. For logistic reasons, the American physical contribution to the campaign did not go beyond a modest level of air support, some heavy weapons and ammunition, and some medical aid.   Having largely to rely on their own resources, the Chinese tended to follow their own counsel.   Had the Americans paid more to the piper, they might have done more toward calling the tunes he played.

2. The system was meeting its first test.   None of the parties to it were quite certain of their roles.   Had time permitted, the workings of the liaison system might have conformed completely to Wedemeyer's intentions.   Therefore, on all levels of command Chinese officers did things, such as allowing surrounded Japanese units to escape, which were completely contrary to Western ideas of war.

The CCC's ingenious command and liaison arrangements took a long step forward toward a fully integrated Sino-American command structure during the Chihchiang campaign, but more months of training and campaigning would be needed before it could justly be said that CCC was functioning at full efficiency.[46]

---

[46] For a lengthy criticism of the campaign see Training Memo 8, Hq Eastern Comd, CCC, 12 Jul 45, Notes on Western Hunan Campaign.   Folder, Histories 1945, 74 Army Combat Sec, CCC Files, KCRC.

CHAPTER X

Role of the India–Burma Base

With the taking of Lashio on 6 March 1945, which meant the substantial accomplishment of India-Burma Theater's combat mission, theater head-quarters lost its immediate concern with combat. Its primary attention was now given to logistical support of China Theater and SEAC, which were still fighting. Logistical matters were the sphere of the SOS, but since India–Burma Theater headquarters had no longer to deal directly with combat, troop training, or strategy, the two headquarters, SOS and theater, were sharing common concerns.

Because the two were working on different but related aspects of the same problems, they both were concerned about finding men to fill the vacant spaces in Wedemeyer's theater organization, the supply and health of their own men, the best way to operate the new Ledo Road (or Stilwell Road as it came to be called), and deciding whether the Hump or the Stilwell Road should be expanded to meet the anticipated needs of China Theater. SOS for many months had primary concern in the routine but often absorbing tasks of operating its complex of ports, warehouses, pipelines, roads, and railroad at ever greater efficiency. (*See Maps 2 and 3.*) Operations neces-sarily involved two things, organizations and men to operate them.

A Unified Command Structure

When the CBI Theater was split in October 1944 the relationship of India–Burma Theater headquarters and SOS was still in process of evolution. During 1944 General Covell, the SOS commander, had advanced a number of suggestions, the trend of which lay toward giving SOS all operational responsibilities in the field of logistics. It appeared that theater headquarters was willing to have SOS organize a construction service and a transportation service, which would conduct those two major activities, but it was still reluctant to divest itself of signal functions and special staff sections such as ordnance, chaplain, chemical warfare, and judge advocate. There the matter stood when the theater was split.

P–51's Moving Through the Streets of Karachi. *Unloaded from Liberty ships in Karachi Harbor, these fighter planes are being hauled to Karachi Air Base.*

The operational structure of SOS after the split and during the winter of 1944–45 provided:

Base Section No. 1	Centering about the port of Karachi
Base Section No. 2	Centering about the port of Calcutta
Intermediate Section No. 2	Headquarters at Chabua
Advance Section No. 2	Headquarters at Ledo

Developments after the organization of India-Burma Theater were making the existing relationship between SOS and the theater obsolete, while the eastward course of SOS activities was forcing corresponding changes in its organization. In 1942 the Japanese had been such a threat to Calcutta that SOS activities had centered about Karachi, on the eastern side of India, and

shipping had been routed there.   By the end of 1943 Calcutta was the principal U.S. port in India, while Karachi was operating more or less on a stand-
by basis.   By 1945 hardly one ship a month was docking at Karachi for
India–Burma Theater.   Inactivation of Base Section No. 1 was in order, and
was accomplished on 15 May 1945.   Henceforth, base activities in India were
controlled by Headquarters, Base Section, at Calcutta.   Inactivation of the
port did not mean the end of SOS interest in the Karachi area, for Karachi
Air Base was the ATC's Indian port of entry and a major center of Air Forces
activity.   So, though the Air Forces assumed supply responsibility, there
remained in the Karachi area hospital and refrigeration facilities, such Quartermaster functions as malaria control and food inspection, the area engineer,
and a rail transportation office.

With the inactivation of Base Section No. 1, renaming the sections within
the SOS seemed in order, so Base Section No. 2 at Calcutta became simply
Base Section, Intermediate Section No. 2 at Chabua became Intermediate Section, and Advance Section No. 3 at Ledo became Advance Section.   Given
the concept that all of India–Burma Theater, or IBT, was the supply base
for China Theater, the Base Section thus became the port of debarkation for
incoming supplies and personnel.   Intermediate Section, in which lay the
Hump airfields and a general depot, was the port of embarkation for China.
The Advance Section now operated the ground line of communications to
China, which, with its Stilwell Road, pipelines, airfields, warehouses, ordnance
maintenance plants, and the like, was itself a major operation.

As for the theater headquarters—SOS division of responsibility and
personnel, the question of redistributing functions was raised again shortly
after the theater split.   The suggestion that the Commanding General, SOS,
become theater G–4 was weighed, but for the present rejected.   Finally, in
December 1944, the special staff sections of the two headquarters were
amalgamated.   The chief of each of the resulting sections then assumed a
dual responsibility, as theater chief of service and as head of the SOS section.
This arrangement meant that in one capacity he was technical adviser to the
theater commander, and in another he bore the operational responsibilities
proper to his branch of service as part of SOS.   Troops released by this step
were assigned to China Theater.

The actual amalgamation proceeded in a series.   Thus, the theater
engineer's office was consolidated with the SOS Construction Service by 11
January 1945.   SOS's provost marshal became the Deputy Provost Marshal,
IBT.   The two Information and Education Sections merged 23 April 1945.
With the special staff sections having completed amalgamation, and with the
end of combat for troops under IBT control meaning that logistics would
henceforth be the major theater concern, there seemed no reason to hesitate
longer in merging theater and SOS headquarters.   At 0001, 21 May, the

merger took effect.   SOS was formally inactivated.   Theater G–4 in effect was the successor of the SOS commander.

Merging the two headquarters did not bring about any conspicuous saving in manpower.   The SOS historian, Lt. Col. Harry L. Mayfield, considered that the greatest benefit lay in eliminating duplication of effort.   After 21 May events brought so many developments in the realm of logistics that it was fruitless to estimate whether the course of operations was better or worse than if the merger had not been effected.   One of the most conspicuous events to follow on the amalgamation was that General Covell was called back to the United States to take charge of a major activity in the Office of the Quartermaster General.[1]

Personnel Management Problems

Without men and women to make them a reality, organizations and projects are so much paper.   The personnel situation in India–Burma Theater, if not more difficult than in Europe or the Southwest Pacific, surely was the more colorful.   The Americans themselves were of course a fair cross-section of the United States, drawn from many races and creeds, but all of them Americans and most of them leaving the impression that they wanted nothing better than the speediest possible return to what they half jokingly, half fondly called "Uncle Sugar."[2]   As individuals, the 200,000-odd Americans in India and Burma, as in any theater, offered almost as many personal situations, but their superiors who had perforce to deal in large numbers found that certain general problems clearly emerged.   The most important was that of transferring men to China.   Then there were rotation and replacement, minority groups in the Army, and\medical problems.   And, since the War Department had a policy of keeping to a minimum the number of Americans shipped to India, Indian and Burmese civilians were hired in tens of thousands.

The most important personnel problem in India and Burma was that of finding men who could be spared to join Wedemeyer in China.   General Sultan, IBT commander, expressed his awareness and his policy clearly: "We must help China.   That is our job.   We must give, and give till it hurts." And again, "If there is a shortage we must both get on with less."[3]   IBT's problem in applying this policy was how not to give so much and such important manpower to China Theater as to impair its own ability to function.

Immediately after the theaters split, almost every section of theater and

---

[1] History of IBT, II, 208–16, 237–40.
[2] In the phonetic alphabet used in 1944–45, the letter *S* was rendered as *sugar,* so *U.S.* and *Uncle Sam* were quickly changed to *Uncle Sugar.*
[3] History of IBT, I, 49.

SOS headquarters yielded some officers and men for China duty.   As the process of amalgamation described above proceeded, surplus troops were offered to China.   Among them were the theater Engineer, Quartermaster, and Chemical Warfare Sections en bloc.   These transfers numbered 108 trained staff personnel.   All the American troops at Ramgarh Training Center were earmarked for China Theater, and were sent there as Ramgarh reduced its activity.   These were of course piecemeal transfers but every man helped.[4]

On 1 December 1944 China Theater called for 1,784 officers and 7,516 enlisted men.   The MARS Task Force, on completing its mission, was a logical source of men for the 6,800 that Wedemeyer wanted to put in the Chinese Combat Command.   For the SOS Wedemeyer wanted 2,000, and there, as SOS Headquarters combed its rosters, a clash developed between the desire to help China Theater and the necessity of keeping SOS operational. One immediate source of manpower was the seven quartermaster truck companies and one medium automotive maintenance company, organized as the LUX Convoy, which had arrived in India after an abortive attempt to deliver vehicles overland from Iran via the USSR to China.   Here were 1,000 officers and men, all qualified to cope with China Theater's perennial and crippling transport problem.   The rest of the desired 2,000 had to be found over the months ahead.   Inactivation of the Karachi base yielded 107 men.

While the search to fulfill China Theater's December request was under way, further requests continued to come in from that theater, one of them for "all key officer and enlisted personnel" at Calcutta.   Granting this request would have greatly hindered the port activities on which China Theater no less than IBT depended, so it could not be met.   Nonetheless, movement of personnel to China continued steadily.

Between October 1944 and May 1945, SOS was able to find 257 officers, 7 warrant officers, and 746 enlisted men from its several headquarters for service in China.   In addition, it transferred to China sixteen units totaling 3,762 men.   The greatest single category was four companies and one detachment of engineer petroleum distribution units.   In addition a medium automotive maintenance company, an ordnance ammunition company, a convalescent camp staff, a signal repair company, plus detachments of military police, quartermaster, engineer construction, and medical supply troops, were sent.[5]

While some soldiers were being sent from India to China, others were earning the right to be sent home to the United States, thus another set of problems was created.   Recognizing that long service in the tropics affects the health of men from temperate climes, the War Department announced a policy of rotating men back to the United States after two years overseas, provided a replacement was at hand.   This decision had hardly begun to take

[4] History of IBT, I, 50–56.
[5] SOS in IBT, I, 44–50.

effect, when the steadily increasing likelihood of Germany's defeat made it necessary to set up a system for releasing men from the armed services, a step toward demobilization.

The operation of these two policies, by May 1945, was producing a backlog of men eligible for return. Those who were eligible for rotation were not to go until replacements were at hand. These were slow in coming. As of February 1945 there were 4,586 troops eligible for rotation, against a monthly quota of 1,900 men. The biggest increases in troop strength in China–Burma–India had been from mid-1943 on; plainly, the number of eligibles was about to surpass the quota by far. The point system for repatriation and prospective demobilization produced another list of impatiently waiting men. As of 12 May 1945 there were 5,000 men in IBT who had 85 or more points and were therefore eligible, if no more than 5 percent of the unit strength was involved. Another 22,000 had more than 70 points. Many of them were airmen, who were given in effect a point for every mission flown.

Replacements for these men capable of filling their posts were hard to find and slow to arrive. On arrival they sometimes proved to be untrained for the posts they were to fill, and had to be retrained in India. Nor was air travel space always available. So the backlog grew, even though, by 30 June 1945, 3,408 high-point men had been returned to the United States.

The following is an example of the maneuvering that might arise after the arrival of a replacement who did not quite fit the post for which he was desired: [6]

When the Adjutant, 330th Engineer Regiment, became eligible for rotation, the replacement furnished was a captain of the Adjutant Generals Department. Unfortunately, the current Table of Organization for an Engineer General Service Regiment did not permit assigning a Captain, AGD, to such a unit.

Meanwhile, in Headquarters, Advance Section, a Captain, AGD, was eligible for rotation. However, no requisition for a replacement had been submitted, possibly because his promotion to major had been recommended, and it may have been understood that he would stay on in India.

In the Intermediate Section, a captain in the Corps of Engineers was eligible for rotation, and was awaiting arrival of a replacement.

Last of all, there was a major, of the Adjutant General's Department, in Advance Section, who had been selected for rotation.

At the cost of considerable paper work, all four of these situations were combined to find a proper adjutant for the 330th Engineer Regiment. The key man in the resulting moves was the engineer captain in the Intermediate Section. Instead of being rotated, he agreed to go to the United States for 45 days rest and recovery, which meant that he would come back to duty in India. His replacement therefore went to the 330th. The Captain AGD who had been originally scheduled for the 330th as a replacement went to Advance Section, and the Captain, AGD, in that headquarters was approved for promotion

[6] Paraphrased from SOS in IBT, I, 50–51.

and rotation.   His promotion was charged against the vacancy left by the Major in Advance Section, who was also rotated.

Not every one of the men who went home caused so much rearrangement but, as the example suggests, the aggregate impact of the thousands of replacements was considerable.

The changes described, which have some of the aspects of a puzzle, show what can be done by G–1 when the individual's capacities and needs are rather standardized.   But there were many people in or working with the Army who could not be easily categorized, and they caused problems in housing, recreation, clothing, and diet.

Social Problems

In large measure, the Stilwell Road was a monument to the strength, skill, and endurance of the Negro soldier.[7]   About 60 percent of the U.S. troops who worked on the road were Negro engineers.   Their superiors considered that their morale was higher than that of the white soldiers working on the road, but that their efficiency was less.   The reason for this latter, the Advance Section thought, lay in a lack of previous training, a lack of responsibility, and a lack of pride in accomplishment.   If Advance Section was correct in its analysis, these traits were all remediable, and action was taken.   Schools in engineering and in operation of equipment were organized, and an orientation program was instituted.

The basically healthy racial situation in the Advance Section, where most of the Negro troops were, produced a "marked absence of those incidents normally associated with inter-racial conflicts."   All recreational facilities, from theaters to sports, were nondiscriminatory.   One troubled area was in relations between Negro troops and the local peoples.   Incidents between Negroes and Indians were out of proportion to the number of Negro troops. The explanation may be a simple one—that the Negro troops mingled more freely with the Indians than did their white comrades, and that if the numbers of contacts could be correlated, the incidents would fall into a truer proportion.

In the Calcutta base section, an error in judgment in locating recreational facilities for Negro troops at Howrah led to considerable criticism.   For whatever reason the base section commander placed the recreational facilities inside a section of Calcutta which he had already declared out of bounds. Moreover, they were used for rest and recreation by Negro soldiers from the Ledo area.   Troops, on leave from the Advance Section, found the facilities largely monopolized by Base Section men.   And, as should have been foreseen, locating the rest camp near the brothels of Calcutta meant that the

---

[7] This and the following paragraph based on SOS in IBT, App. 4.

venereal disease rate reached alarming proportions. The situation went through the course of official inquiry during the latter part of 1944. Finally, in February 1945, the rest camp was relocated in a more appropriate section of Calcutta. In the next two months the venereal disease rate dropped sharply, as did also the number of disciplinary incidents.[8]

The problem of finding suitable housing and recreational facilities for Negro troops, at a time when the U.S. Army still practiced racial segregation, was not unlike the problem of finding suitable living and recreational quarters for the members of the Army Nurse Corps and Women's Army Corps who were sent to India. They, too, were a minority in a system best adapted to the gregarious, easy-going young male. In the first quarter of 1945 there were 1,017 nurses and 256 Wacs in India. The nurses had been in India since 1942; the Wacs arrived in July 1944 for duty with the Tenth Air Force headquarters.[9]

Finding living quarters for the nurses that would allow them comfort, privacy, and security was a problem that took time to solve in India proper. In the forward areas, tents had been the rule and service a real hardship. The result, in the opinion of the Theater Surgeon General, was tension and fatigue. Finding cool, sturdy, comfortable, and attractive clothes in enough quantity to permit frequent changes was another problem, for experience revealed that the basic uniform allowances were inadequate.

Trying to profit by these earlier experiences, Tenth Air Force headquarters made elaborate preparations to receive the Wacs. But the preparations were of necessity made by men, and not every need was foreseen. Thus, no slacks were provided for evening wear during the mosquito season, nor did the clothing allowance provide enough changes. The local mosquitoes carried malaria, and the doctors insisted that the women wear slacks. Fortunately, the Wacs were near Calcutta, and the Indian tailor, with his ample store of light cottons and clever needle, soon had the girls smart and comfortable in Indian khaki.

By March 1945 the theater surgeon was ready to conclude that the two biggest problems connected with women serving in India had been the early lack of appropriate housing and the lack of co-ordinated administrative control. The second point probably reflects the fact that Army nurses were of necessity stationed about the theater in little groups, and might have been helped by a small central office co-ordinating personnel problems. The surgeon felt that women stood the physical strain of the Indian climate as well as men.

---

[8] SOS in IBT, I, 58–59.
[9] Bringing Wacs to India was against Stilwell's wishes. See Mattie E. Treadwell, *The Wom-en's Army Corps,* UNITED STATES ARMY IN WORLD WAR II (Washington, 1955), Ch XXIII.

Some of the problems facing servicewomen came from the theater's marriage policy. In 1942 Stilwell had directed attention to the fact that under War Department policy marriages had to receive his prior permission. His motive in making this announcement, he explained privately, was "to prevent the mixed calamities that would develop." At that time, U.S. immigration laws would not have permitted an Indian or Anglo-Indian bride to enter the United States; diplomatic repercussions were feared if Americans were allowed to wed only British girls. In March 1944 a new policy developed when an officer about to return home asked permission to wed a British girl. Permission was granted, thus informally establishing a new policy that marriage was permitted if either party was about to leave the CBI Theater, permanently, within thirty days. Marriage was also permitted in cases of pregnancy.

Such marriage policies met with severe criticism. It was argued that they encouraged clandestine weddings, and put a premium on illegitimate pregnancies. The problem was regarded as deserving serious study, and the opinions of the theater judge advocate, chaplains, nurses, and others were obtained.

As a result, General Sultan approved a new order, effective 19 April 1945, under which two U.S. citizens could wed any time after a three-month waiting period. U.S. citizens were permitted to wed other nationalities when either person was scheduled to leave the theater within three months after the wedding.[10]

That the marriage question reached so high a level of command was perhaps because the number of Indians employed by the U.S. Army was high in proportion to the number of Americans stationed in India,—roughly, one Indian to every three Americans. There was also the circumstance that the Americans were in a sense guests in the Indian home. Good relations with the Indians would be a matter for the continuing attention of the theater commander. As of June 1945, over 70,000 Indians and Burmese, many of them women, were employed by the U.S. Army. The resulting scene, in supply depots and headquarters, and out along the Stilwell Road, was a picturesque one.

In a base area, for example, one might see at the door of a building the jaunty little Gurkha watchman, with small, sturdy frame, Mongolian features, ready smile, broad-brimmed hat turned up at one side, and the deadly, broad-bladed knife of the Gurkha tribesman at his side. In the corridor the visitor was sure to see, squatting sadly and patiently, a black-skinned sweeper, descendant of India's first inhabitants. Behind the typewriters there would be slim Anglo-Indian girls, brown-skinned, large-eyed, often fiercely British

[10] (1) History of IBT, II, 269–88.   (2) SOS in IBT, pp. 44–66.   (3) Treadwell, *The Women's Army Corps*, Ch. XXIII.

in speech and custom.   The clerks were sophisticated young Hindus of the commercial castes and sects.   Sometimes college graduates, almost always great students of the cinema, fond of debating politics and religion, they could be seen in the morning cycling to work in swarms.   Among these people there moved the Americans, wearing khaki that was worn and faded at the hands of the Indian washerman, plagued by the minor complaints with which India afflicts the stranger, but bringing to their work a driving energy new to the subcontinent.   Meanwhile, in the streets and bazaars, the pageant of India continued, seemingly heedless of the Western visitors, but with many of the actors determined that when the war ended India would go her own way.

In the Advance Section, building the line of communications to China made it necessary to assemble a labor force varied in the extreme.   Units of the Indian Pioneer Corps worked in areas where Japanese might be encountered; elsewhere contract labor was used.   The contract workers had no common tongue (though many understood a few words of Hindustani, the lingua franca of India) and shared few customs, which meant it was necessary to serve a most varied diet.   These people included Mahrattas, Madrasis, Bengalis, Hindu and Moslem Punjabis, and from the tribal and hill folk, Chamars, Oryias, Bihari aborigines, Garos, Nepalis, and Gurkhas.   To paraphrase a famous epigram, the labor force on the Stilwell Road was an anthropologist's dream but a mess sergeant's nightmare.

To hire these people, Advance Section filed estimates of its future needs with Eastern Army, the Indian Army headquarters for the Assam section of India Command.   Eastern Army then undertook to have them on hand. Civilians for other than construction work were hired through local employment offices set up under Advance Section.   General Headquarters (India)—GHQ(I)—the highest echelon of the Indian Army, co-ordinated hiring to avoid competition between Allied agencies.   Pay and workmen's compensation were furnished by the Government of India under reciprocal aid.   The importance of local labor can be judged by the estimate that it supplied about 7,800,000 man-days for building the Ledo Road as against the 6,618,000 of the U.S. Army engineers and 735,000 of Chinese Army engineers.[11]

Employment of Indians was also an experiment in social adjustment. Admittedly, generalization is difficult in so great and complicated a sphere, but some observations may be acceptable.   The Indians who worked for the Americans were markedly loyal to their employers.   India had strong traditions of loyalty to the immediate superior, reflecting the medieval past which never seemed far behind in that country in the early 1940's.   It meant the

---

[11] (1) Data on man-days from History of IBT, I, 194–95.   (2) History of IBT, II, 279–81.

Indian largely identified himself with the Americans.   On the other hand, the tempo of Indian life was that of the slow-moving tropics, where people conserve energy, and so to the Americans the Indians sometimes seemed lethargic and their work slipshod.   The observer could also see that many of the lower-caste Indians who furnished common labor were under-nourished and weakened by fever.   Consequently labor gangs had to be larger than expected until steady work at good wages permitted a better diet and more energy.   But when all was said and done, the Americans in India could not have done their work without the help and friendship of India's people.

Relationships between the two groups were good.   Racial prejudice, to one observer at least, was not conspicuous.   Indians and Americans seemed to accept one another as individuals.   The easy-going social democracy of the Americans, their generosity with their resources, personal and official, may have had a greater impact on India than could be imagined at the time.   The willingness of the Americans to perform manual labor, their liking for and understanding of machinery, were suggestions that not every society insisted on rigid caste distinction, that the Americans, by Indian standards wealthy and powerful as so many lords, might have become so through their own effort and ingenuity.

Preventive Medicine

Figures on the troop strength of the theater and its subordinate commands have been given above.   They are deceptive, because the unsanitary environment in India produced a correspondingly high rate of malarial and intestinal infections.   On any given day many men were ill, and still more, though not sick enough to stop work, were not well enough to work at full efficiency, even within the limits imposed by the heat and damp of India and Burma.   Summer was the wort time for sickness.   Thus in the summer of 1943 and again in summer 1944, the admission rate for the old China–Burma–India Theater soared to about 1,500 admissions per 1,000 men per year.   Then, in winter, it dropped below the 1,000 mark.

Malaria control had been slow in getting under way in India and Burma. Atebrin suppressive therapy was not begun in forward areas until April 1944. Not until winter 1944–45 did large amounts of the effective insecticide, DDT, arrive.   Perhaps the most powerful single influence toward remedying a health situation that severely strained the theater's personnel resources was the establishment of a Preventive Medicine Section in the Theater Surgeon's Office, 22 August 1944.   Most of the theater's sicknesses came from intestinal disease and malaria, which were controllable by methods that were well understood at the time and whose rigid application was in great degree a command problem. The new section used the method of closely supervising the preventive measures of lower echelons. Vigorous letters, with the authority of the theater commander behind them, pointed out deficiencies and suggested remedies.

In fall 1944 responsibility for malaria control was placed on unit commanders. The Medical Corps relinquished many of the operational responsibilities it had perforce assumed. These went to the troops, with the Quartermaster and Engineer Corps taking over those phases of malaria control previously allotted them by the War Department. Air spraying with DDT was continued. The most thorough and vigorous application of both suppressive and preventive measures was enjoined by theater circulars in January 1945, and commanders were held responsible for their application.

The several forms of dysentery plus fevers of unknown origin were a problem little less serious than malaria. The known causes of such complaints were attacked with a great deal more vigor than before. Thus, Sanitary Corps engineers were attached to all but the smallest subsection headquarters, and given staff responsibility for water purification. Water purification specialists were assigned to subordinate units in all sections. Water pumps and chlorinators had been in short supply, but by May 1945 this shortage was ended. Fly control was sought by screening DDT, better garbage disposal, and proper latrine construction. The fly population could not be fully controlled, through lack of something to suppress fly breeding. Indian mess assistants were forbidden to handle foods, and ample hot water was provided, as well as a germicidal rinse for dishes. Since many troops were stationed near Indian cities, the out-of-bounds weapon was used against insanitary restaurants, while eating places that tried to meet proper medical standards were allowed to buy Quartermaster chlorine compounds.

Thanks to these steps, admission rates in India–Burma Theater dropped sharply beginning in fall 1944, the fall in the malaria rate from 320 per 1,000 to 20 per 1,000 being most dramatic. The improvement did not reflect any large withdrawal from the Assamese and Burmese jungle areas to more salubrious parts; troop strengths in those areas in August 1945 were substantially what they had been on 31 October 1944.

Preventive measures may also have averted a serious outbreak of smallpox. From October 1944 to June 1945 there were 6 cases and 4 deaths, as against 20 cases and 6 deaths in 1944. This did not seem a great number of cases, but it was quite out of line with the incidence for the U.S. Army. Attempts were made to improve clerical procedures so as to ensure accuracy in recording immunization reactions. Proper strength and uniform quality of vaccine were obtained by designating one Indian laboratory as the sole source of lymph.

The other great scourge of India, cholera, was no problem. Cholera vaccine was given to all troops, and those in the Calcutta area were given lectures on avoiding potential sources of infection, like Indian soft drinks. Cholera statistics in the Indian press taught their daily lesson.[12]

Reciprocal Aid and Lend-Lease to India

The men and women who made up India–Burma Theater were, as noted above, largely fed, and almost completely clothed, by the farms and factories of India.   In 1942 the War Department had proclaimed the policy of using local resources in order to conserve shipping.   India had co-operated whole-heartedly, and both the American forces in India and the American-trained Chinese divisions were fed and clothed, and the Chinese paid, by the Government of India.[13]

Two problems involving reciprocal aid confronted IBT between December 1944 and June 1945.   The first was the possibility that the volume of recip-rocal aid to the Chinese and U.S. forces in India and Burma might decrease; the second, the extent of the Indian commitment to supply Chinese divisions after they had left Burma for China.

When the China–Burma–India Theater split in October 1944, the U.S. staff in New Delhi feared that certain indications from the Government of India presaged a cutback in reciprocal aid.   SOS did not make the situation a major issue, but took the attitude of meeting problems as they arose in following months.   Late deliveries were promptly and politely protested, while IBT's new power of screening lend-lease bids by the Indian Army and SEAC gave a potent lever.   But as the months went by it became apparent that though the pronouncements of Indian officials might reveal a sense of economic strain the Government of India was actually increasing the dollar value of reciprocal aid.   The explanation probably lies in the fact that the amount of petroleum, oils, and lubricants supplied grew so rapidly as to off-set declines in construction, transportation, clothing, and subsistence, the categories causing the greatest burden to the civil economy.   The increase in fuel and oil supplied reflected the effect of the opening of the Stilwell Road and the pipeline to China, plus the steady increase in Hump operations.

A decline in construction followed the completion of the IBT building program, while the completed deployment for the North Burma Campaign ended major troop movements.   As for food and clothing, IBT stocks were now complete to the prescribed level, with reserves in hand.   The cutback in reciprocal aid, so feared in mid-1944, thus took place without disturbing U.S. Army operations in India, while the Government of India met every new need as it arose in 1945.[14]

----

[12] History of IBT, II, 298–300.
[13] (1) *Stilwell's Mission to China,* Chapter V, describes the early days of the reciprocal aid system.   (2) Chapter I, above, gives the reciprocal aid situation in October 1944.
[14] History of IBT, II, 216–20.

When in December 1944 the Chinese 14th and 22d Divisions were flown back to China, the question of their supply arose.   The War Department ruled that they would be placed in regular U.S. Army supply channels for ordnance supplies.   However, the Government of India had been supplying the food, pay, clothing, and some of the equipment of these units.   These divisions therefore had been maintained on a scale far above that enjoyed by the rest of the Chinese Army.   China Theater was not as yet prepared so to maintain them from its own resources, yet Wedemeyer wanted to do so lest their morale be injured and they be unable to play their key role in China. The same treatment was desired for the remaining three divisions when they returned.   So SOS IBT and China both proposed that the Government of India continue to maintain all five divisions of the Chinese Army in India under lend-lease until 31 December 1945.   The British policy was that India should give food and clothing only to the 14th and 22d Divisions, and these items only until 30 June 1945.

Further discussions followed, and the Government of India agreed to maintain the five Chinese divisions until ninety days after they had returned to China.   In June 1945 this stand was further modified in that India would provide for another ninety days any items which could not be obtained else-where.   SOS made appropriate changes in requisitions on India and attempted to fill some needs by requesting supplies from British authority in London. The British would accept only a limited responsibility for supply of Chinese forces from their sources east of Suez, and the United States had to fill what gaps resulted.[15]

To India–Burma Theater, the problem of lend-lease to India Command and SEAC was the delicate one of giving the War Department theater views on the bids of the two commands for lend-lease.   The sums involved were large, for between September 1944, when the process began, and June 1945 the U.S. authorities in New Delhi screened $277,947,252.00 of lend-lease bids. Savings to the U.S. taxpayers were of a comparable magnitude, for only 49.98 percent was recommended for approval.

Three attempts were made by British authorities to end screening of their lend-lease requisitions.   On one occasion they claimed the process wasted time.   To this, IBT replied that if there was delay, the trouble largely rose from reluctance or inability on the part of General Headquarters (India) to supply information justifying its requests.   SEAC's records seemed to be in better shape, for its commands supplied data more promptly.   On another occasion the British objected to having the scale at which they wanted to supply equipment to their men questioned by IBT.   In 1942 the U.S. Army had taken the same stand, so the precedents seemed clear.[16]   In this case, an

---

[15] History of IBT, I, 157–60.
[16] *Stilwell's Mission to China*, p. 210.

attempt was made to cast the problem in terms that would not appear provocative.   IBT took the position that it would limit itself to recommending what proportion of the equipment desired was to come from U.S. sources, a stand which did not challenge the right of the British to set their own scales.

In commenting on British requests, IBT had no desire to be obstructive and believed that in many cases it could speed procurement, for example, by pointing out on occasion that certain desired items were present in its own stocks.   Several steps were taken to speed the progress of requisitions and to make screening a truly Allied process, whose aim would be to use Allied resources to the best and most economical advantage.   In the beginning SEAC and GHQ(I) made their requests through British channels to the War Department, which sent them back to IBT.   In December 1944 the process was altered.   The British War Office in London began to study U.S. production figures with a view to estimating when a bid from India Command or SEAC might receive favorable attention.   If such seemed likely, India Command or SEAC was so informed.   British authorities in India then placed the matter before IBT, which sent its recommendations to the War Department together with the bid.

In the course of the screening process, IBT staff officers conferred with their opposite numbers in SEAC and GHQ(I) to secure appropriate data. Much was needed, on reserves on hand, estimated wastage, estimated consumption rates, transportation factors, and the like.   When occasions rose on which IBT could not offer at least a reasoned estimate to the War Department, it refused to recommend approval.   As a rule, SEAC and IBT were able to agree and present to the War Department a requisition that represented their combined judgment.   In the opinions of the IBT staff, problems sometimes could be traced to the sheer length of time involved in passing requisitions through the different echelons of command in the British forces.   In the meantime, the situation changed, and March's requistion was obsolete in August.

Given the political and organizational habits of the English-speaking peoples, there inevitably arose from these informal contacts a committee, the India Cooperation Committee, with representatives of SEAC, GHQ(I), and IBT.   The committee expedited IBT requests for supporting data, followed the progress of requistions, and checked on all delays.   It was of great help in dealing with the question of scales, for the earlier compromise had done no more than place the question on a different level, at which IBT was not obliged to comment directly on whether British requests were in line with what the Americans thought a reasonable level.   GHQ(I), no doubt, had its own tale to tell of some American ideas on what constituted a legitimate item of reciprocal aid.

On one occasion, which involved a request for 800 ¼-ton trucks, IBT noted that the request if filled would give the units involved about 150 percent more than their Tables of Equipment required. U.S. experience in India had demonstrated that a unit could operate with 12 percent reserves and 36 percent for replacements. Since the bid was fairly small, IBT recommended filling it, but recorded its objection so that no precedent would be set. On another occasion, SEAC wanted U.S. antigas ointment instead of the British issue. IBT would not concur, on the ground that the British issue, though concededly not as good, was still adequate. Moreover, they challenged the British scale of two ointment kits per man with a 50-percent reserve. The U. S. scale was one each, and 30 percent. The War Department upheld the IBT point of view.

In appraising the importance of reciprocal aid and lend-lease screening, the IBT staff estimated that in 1944 and 1945 the two combined saved the U.S. taxpayer $2,000,000 a day, $730,000,000 a year, in addition to economizing on shipping space, raw materials, and production capacity in the United States.[17]

Supply Policies for China Theater Projects

The principal reason U.S. troops were in India and after October 1944 Burma was to support China. Therefore, the men whose presence in India and whose assignments created the difficulties just discussed were principally concerned with various logistical problems. In dealing with these they had to work in close co-operation with China Theater, whose communications zone they were now operating. Inevitably, agreements had to be reached between the two theaters on the division of responsibilities between them. These agreements in turn were the policy framework within which India–Burma Theater conducted routine logistical operations.[18]

The agreements reached in December 1944 between the theaters covered three major areas: requisition of supplies on India–Burma Theater and the United States; operation of the line of communications; and handling of lend-lease. The agreement on requisitions procedure was an SOS IBT suggestion approved by China Theater. By stipulating that all routine requisitions, such as those falling within Table of Equipment allowances, would be made by China Theater directly on the Intermediate Section's General Depot in Assam, India, the agreement underscored that IBT and China Theater in many ways functioned almost as one theater. Emergency requisitions were to go direct to SOS IBT. Requisitions which had as yet no War Department authorization were to go direct to SOS IBT with a statement that approval had been requested. Nonroutine items approved by the War Department authorization were to have their requisitions accompanied by a copy

---

[17] History of IBT, II, 220–29.
[18] See Ch. I, above.

of the Department's order.   Finally, SOS in China Theater was to set its own levels of supply.[19]

Dividing the responsibility for operating the line of communications from Ledo to Kunming was more complicated.   Since IBT's resources were far greater than China Theater's, it was much easier for the impetus of maintenance and construction of the lines of communications to come from the direction of Ledo rather than that of Kunming.   But since part of that same artery was within China Theater, adjustment had to be made.   General Sultan's basic directive permitted Wedemeyer and himself to accept responsibility for operations and installations in each other's theaters as necessity arose, so there was no obstacle to mutual accommodation.

Negotiated in November and December 1944, a comprehensive agreement defined the responsibilities of the two theaters:

Construction and maintenance of roads: IBT was responsible for the construction and maintenance of the Stilwell Road up to the Burma–China border in the vicinity of Wanting.   The China Theater was charged with all construction and maintenance within China.

Construction, maintenance, and operation of pipelines: IBT was responsible for the construction, maintenance, and operation of pipelines to Kunming.   An amendment in March 1945 added to IBT's responsibility the construction of the pipeline network connecting Kunming with the airfields lying to the east.

Signal communications along roads and pipelines: IBT was responsible for the construction and maintenance of wire communications along the Stilwell Road to Kunming and along the pipelines.

Operation of the Road: IBT was responsible for motor transport operations on the Stilwell Road as far as Kunming.   The China Theater was responsible for supplementary motor transport.

Hump priority and allocation: China Theater was responsible for designating cargo for delivery to China and allocation of such cargo to users in China.

Security: IBT was to arrange with SEAC for the security of the Stilwell Road and the pipelines up to the Burma–China border.   The China Theater was to arrange for the security of roads, pipelines, and wire lines within China.[20]

Notably, only in the matter of allocating Hump tonnage did the authority of China Theater reach into India–Burma Theater.   Within the sphere of local initiative policies on Chinese lend-lease of the India–Burma and China Theaters were arrived at in December by discussions in Chungking between representatives of the two theaters plus War Department liaison personnel. Their conclusions become War Department policy in a directive of 23 January 1945.

Certain salient points emerged from the directive.   In conformity with recent practice in the theaters, Chinese lend-lease for the initial equipping for the thirty-divisions-plus-10-percent program was to be shipped from the United States on the same basis as U.S. supplies and on arrival in India

[19] History of IBT, I, 57–58.
[20] History of IBT, I, 45–46.

would go into U.S. stockpiles. Since both Wedemeyer's supplies and lend-lease to China would be shipped from those same stockpiles the U.S. forces and the Chinese in effect drew upon one common source under their respective programs as approved by the War Department and the Munitions Assignments Board of the CCS. In accordance with the policy of pooling stocks to simplify bookkeeping and give greater flexibility, maintenance for the U.S.-sponsored Chinese divisions was to be drawn by SOS requisitions on the Los Angeles Port of Embarkation. The rule that nothing could be requisitioned unless it could be delivered in six months was reaffirmed.

In addition to U.S. lend-lease for China there were other stores in India destined for China with diverse origins and legal status that reflected the improvisations of 1941–42. Some of them were of Canadian origin; some were procured by Chinese ministries with U.S. credits or their own funds; some were bought by Chinese governmental agencies incorporated under U.S. law. These classes of matériel could only be diverted to U.S. account after notifying the War Department and obtaining the consent of General Wedemeyer, which meant that of the Chinese Government.[21]

In accordance with his basic mission and inherent powers as a theater commander, Wedemeyer was to determine the amounts, types, and priorities of lend-lease shipments to China. He also was to make the policy decisions in accord with which IBT would bid for initial issues under the thirty-divisions-plus-10-percent program.[22] China Theater was charged with recording all transfers of supplies to the Chinese. General Sultan as Commanding General, IBT, was to control bids for and deliveries to the Chinese Army in India, and was to receive, store, and transport lend-lease within his theater and as otherwise agreed on between himself and Wedemeyer (reflecting the division of responsibility for the line of communications).[23]

As soon as the War Department's January directive was issued, China Theater pooled all China Defense Supplies, Inc., stocks that were intended for the Chinese Army with its own supplies. In effect, this meant that at the last depot before supplies were transported to China, IBT merged such matériel with U.S. stocks. The International Division of Army Service Forces in Washington was at once notified of each diversion so that the Chinese account in Washington could be credited accordingly. Wedemeyer's action meant that henceforth military supplies entering China became one single resource to be used by the U.S. theater commander as necessity might dictate.

---

[21] (1) *Stilwell's Mission to China*, Chapter I, gives the background of this effort to aid China with matériel. (2) *Stilwell's Command Problems*, Chapter VII, describes the origin of the 1944–45 lend-lease policies.

[22] This program did not include five divisions of the Chinese Army in India.

[23] History of IBT, I, 161–63.

India–Burma Theater delayed in pooling China Defense Supplies matériel because it had been asked by the War Department to re-examine its supply status. The point at issue was whether IBT should continue to receive supplies on the basis of semiautomatic requisitions initiated in the zone of the interior (known as Phase II supply) or whether it was now ready to requisition everything it might need. After conferences with China Theater representatives, IBT concluded it was ready to take the responsibility of planning and obtaining its own supply. The change became effective 1 May 1945. IBT then directed that all China Defense Supplies be absorbed into U.S. stockpiles, effective 15 June 1945, thus ending three years of double accounting and double handling. In retrospect, IBT concluded that "both from the supply and tactical viewpoint, the supply from two separate supply systems of two fighting forces, working toward a common goal and mutually dependent operationally, is too inflexible and cumbersome a procedure to permit efficient and integrated action." [24]

Ports, Pipelines, and Railroads

Once policies for requisitioning and handling supplies had been settled, the next step in the supply process was to move them to the depots and tank farms from which they would begin their trip to China. This step involved the ports that received stores in India and the railroads and pipelines that carried them from the ports to the depots in Assam. There, by air, road, or pipeline again, they would begin their journey to China.

In spring 1945 the port situation reflected the steady growth in the efficiency and capacity of Calcutta, the continuance of Karachi in the stand-by status, and the discontinuance of Bombay as a terminal for troop transports.

The U.S. port troops at Calcutta were the 497th and 508th Port Battalions and the 540th and 541st Port Companies. The Base Section commander, General Neyland, was regarded by the SOS commander, General Covell, as notably successful in raising the morale of his men. This factor, plus the fact that cargo delivered to Calcutta was usually crated and so easier to handle than bulk shipments, may explain the success of the port troops in making Calcutta first in discharge rates among all U.S. Army ports. Between 15 and 27 March 1945 about 114,000 tons were discharged; at the end of March only 889 tons remained in the transit sheds. Once port congestion had made Calcutta a major bottleneck in CBI, but now this port led the rest.[25]

---

[24] History of IBT, II, 233–34. Quotation from page 165.
[25] For a discussion of the port problem in 1943, see *Stilwell's Mission to China*, pp. 143, 148, 203, 206, 314, 383.

Karachi, as noted above, was placed in stand-by status on 15 May, thereafter unloading only an occasional vessel calling with Air Forces supplies for the great Karachi air base.

Because Calcutta's port facilities were regarded as limiting the types of ships that could make their way up the Hooghly River to dockside, Bombay on the west coast of India continued to be the port of call for transports. There were certain disadvantages. After landing, troops had to move by rail across India—a long, slow, tiring journey. As a rule, three days were required to unload transports and entrain the troops. Moreover, the British were expecting the arrival of substantial troop shipments in spring and summer 1945 to replace their veterans, many of whom had arrived in India in 1942, and to repatriate Indian troops, some of whom had seen their first action in 1940 on the Egyptian frontier. So the British had asked for sole use of Bombay's facilities.

By various negotiations, IBT postponed return of the port and replacement center facilities at Bombay. The theater staff believed that Calcutta could not receive troopships of the "General" class then engaged on the run to Bombay. But the British needed Bombay, and so the War Department in January 1945 undertook to test Calcutta by sending two C-4-class troopships to that port. The ships navigated the Hooghly in safety and were unloaded in nine hours. Plainly, IBT could no longer justify its stand. SOS accordingly ordered evacuation of U.S. port personnel from Bombay by 1 June 1945. In its last month of operation, the Bombay complement moved 15,235 men through the port. Inactivation yielded thirty-two men for China service. A forty-five-man detachment remained for minor transport, procurement, finance, and censorship duties.

By April 1945 Calcutta handled troop movements as a matter of routine. "In the latter part of the month, 5,762 troops debarked from two C-2 transports. The first special train left Princep's Ghat 2½ hours after the vessels had completed mooring and all baggage and cargo [were] completely offloaded within 18 hours." The men went to replacement depots at Kanchrapara and Camp Angus, both near Calcutta.

From the Calcutta area, railroads, pipelines, and a river barge line led north to the depots and road and air terminals of Assam. Together, they formed the Assam line of communications, as it was called in CBI. Thanks to the completion of the pipelines and the improvements in railroad operations of 1944, the Assam line of communications in 1945 could forward all cargo put down at Calcutta.[26] Of this cargo, petroleum products caused the most concern in 1945. Where motor fuels and lubricants were concerned, the major problem lay in keeping stocks at an adequate level. One minor

[26] (1) The transport problem of 1944 is discussed in *Stilwell's Command Problems*, Chapters I, VII. (2) Quotation from History of IBT, II, 402.

crisis came from the diversion of some tankers from India just at the time the opening of the Stilwell Road, the expansion of Hump operations, and the British drive to Mandalay were putting a severe strain on local gasoline reserves. The diversion of the tankers in January 1945 caused a drop in anticipated receipts of some 41,000,000 gallons. Between expanded operations and diminished receipts, stocks of 100-octane gasoline in Assam dropped below the ten-day level and in the Base Section to twenty days. SOS IBT hastily appealed to the War Department, and receipts after April rose to a point that corrected the shortfall.

As IBT was looking toward the end of this minor crisis, a fuel shortage of more serious dimensions, which threatened to reduce theater activities, was developing in north Burma, and became quite apparent from March to June. The movement of motor convoys to China and the institution of ATC Hump operations from Myitkyina bore heavily upon stocks in the forward area. Coincident with this, attempts to build up stocks in China were hindered by the lack of fuel and oil containers. These were inadequate in quantity, poorly made, and often roughly handled by Indian labor at train transshipment points. All these difficulties, arising in the same few months, made gas and oil a critical problem.

The ATC's Hump operations from Myitkyina were regarded as the only marginal activity in north Burma, so ATC was warned that it would have to take the heaviest cuts in fuel allotments. All commands were ordered to maintain strict economy.

Fortunately, the crisis could not be one of long duration, because the pipeline and container program was nearing completion even as commanders in the forward area were most worried over the fuel situation. ATC operations dropped about 5 percent from March to April, while they had risen 15 percent from February to March, but permanent relief was at hand. On 31 March the first deliveries through a new six-inch pipeline from the port of Chittagong reached the Tinsukia tank farm in Assam. By 31 May a six-inch line from Tinsukia to Myitkyina was coupled, though not yet in operation. The U.S. Army in March began making its own 55-gallon containers at Tezgaon, Assam. Handling of containers in shipment was more closely supervised. The Government of India undertook to improve containers on hand by sealing their seams with melted bronze, thus sharply cutting losses from leakage.

Improvement in the fuel situation first showed itself in Assam. In late April SOS reported that the Assam valley air terminals were "saturated" with gasoline. With heavy receipts in Assam, with the six-inch pipeline to Myitkyina almost complete, the fuel shortage in north Burma was plainly to end soon.[27]

[27] History of IBT, II, 403–13.

ARMY AIR FORCE FUEL DUMP AT ASSAM

Railway operations in the first six months of 1945 were a story of steady improvement rather than of dramatic change. The dramatic changes had come in March and April 1944 when the U.S. Military Railway Service took over the management of key sections of the Bengal and Assam Railway and began stressing movement of freight cars toward the Assam terminals; the former policy had been to balance the movement of cars up and down the line.[28] The improvements of 1945 were an extensive program of siding construction, freight car construction, added watering facilities, the equipping of cars with vacuum brakes, and establishment of a tracer system to keep track of lost or mishandled shipments.

Of these several projects, building sidings was perhaps the most important. The railway authorities of the Government of India had believed that to increase the physical capacity of the Bengal and Assam Railway it would be necessary to double-track 578 miles. This would be a slow process, and a drain on Indian steel production. U.S. railwaymen believed much the same results could be obtained by construction of long sidings, each capable of taking a 100-car train. Then, two-way operation would be

[28] *Stilwell's Command Problems,* Ch. VII.

permitted by sidetracking the train with the lower priority. Ultimately, double-tracking was reduced to 165 miles, for building a total of 47 miles of passing sidings at 94 different locations eliminated 360 miles of double-tracking.

Greater supplies of rolling stock were obtained by borrowing from other Indian railways, by construction in India, and by imports from the United States. By May 1945 the United States had sent 10,113 freight cars to the Bengal and Assam Railway, about 60 percent of the total increase. The motive power, by the same date, was also 60 percent American.

As a result of these improvements, the 735th Railway Operating Battalion, which operated the division with the heaviest traffic, moved 42,734 cars east in March 1945, as against 8,836 cars in February 1944, before the Military Railway Service took over. The construction of forty 125-car sidings in this one division partly explained the feat.

Operating the Line of Communications to China

Though the first full convoy from India reached Kunming, China, on 4 February 1945, its arrival signaled only that the road was open to traffic, not that it was a fully operational line of comunications to China. The extent to which its capacity would be developed necessarily reflected the planning that took place before it was opened. In 1942 and until May 1943 the Ledo Road had been seen as an expedient which would serve to give more ample support to U.S. projects in China until the prewar line of communications through Rangoon could be restored. After May 1943 operations in Burma could not be agreed on beyond a limited offensive to take north Burma. That fact elevated the Ledo Road and its accompanying pipeline to new importance. Meanwhile, the Hump air line had been growing in capacity. Many, like General Chennault, Mr. Churchill, and the British Chiefs of Staff, thought it a far better investment than the Ledo Road, but the War Department always objected to diversion of transports from the main effort in Europe, while Army Service Forces had been enthusiastic in supporting the road.

When the North Burma Campaign opened in October 1943 it was at least arguable that a simultaneous attack from both sides of Burma might clear the Japanese from the trace of the Ledo Road in a few months, and open the road to China before the Japanese could make a major move there. By April 1944 the slow pace of the North Burma Campaign forced General Stilwell, then CBI Theater commander, to conclude that his mission in north Burma was now primarily to take Myitkyina so that Hump tonnage might be increased. In August 1944 British success at Imphal and his own imminent victory at Myitkyina made him think the road might still be open in

time to play a worthwhile role.   All during these months, the U.S. Pacific
campaign had steadily progressed, and by August an American landing in the
Philippines and the opening of a Chinese port could be foreseen.   In the
light of these factors and of the months that had slipped past since Stilwell
first suggested retaking Burma in July 1942, the theater and the War Department in summer 1944 had to fix a role for the Ledo Road.[29]

In August 1944 the War Department directed that the Ledo Road be
completed as a two-lane highway to Myitkyina, and as a one-way road beyond Myitkyina, to Wanting, China.   Operations over it were to be limited
to one-way delivery of vehicles and field artillery.   The motive of the War
Department was to free resources for the forthcoming attack on the Philippines.[30]   For some months CBI Theater planning had followed similar lines
as to the immediate future of road operations.   Vehicles and artillery would
be of use in the crisis the Americans then faced in China; more ambitious
efforts might well be too late to be of help.   But one-way delivery of vehicles posed a problem.   Drivers had to be found for them.   If Americans
were used, they would have to be flown back to India.   It seemed much better to train and use Chinese drivers who would be available for further service in China.

So, in the spring of 1944, CBI Theater began training Chinese drivers at
Ramgarh Training Center.   The program did not go smoothly, for the desertion rate was high.   Center headquarters believed that Chinese newspapers
had made extravagant promises to Chinese volunteer recruits which had not
materialized.   Conscripts arrived in poor shape physically.   In August 1944
forty-four of them died after flying over the Hump.   Brig. Gen. Haydon L.
Boatner, then commanding the Rear Echelon of the Chinese Army in India,
believed a partial solution lay in converting four Chinese tank battalions
then at Ramgarh into truck units.   It was not likely they would get tanks.
CBI headquarters would not accept the proposal, preferring to assign added
U.S. instructors to Ramgarh.   In the light of these reinforcements, Ramgarh
hoped to train 2,700 drivers a month.

After the theaters split, India–Burma again urged that the tank battalions
be converted into truck units.   On 1 January 1945 the Generalissimo agreed.

India–Burma Theater's suggestion may have reflected reports from Ramgarh, for when the new Chinese drivers took the road in February it became
apparent that they were not qualified.   For instance, one Chinese-manned
convoy of 90 vehicles reached Pangsau Pass, 38 miles from Ledo, with only
66 operational vehicles left.   General Boatner thought the Chinese driver

---

[29] *Stilwell's Mission to China,* Chapters V, IX, and X, and *Stilwell's Command Problems,* Chapter X, give the War Department, Army Service Forces, and CBI Theater views on the Ledo Road.
(2) Min, 2d White House Mtg, 14 May 43.   Official TRIDENT Conf Bk.
[30] *Stilwell's Command Problems,* Ch. IX.

BRIG. GEN. HAYDON L. BOATNER, *commanding Rear Echelon, Chinese Army in India, stops to speak to a wounded Chinese soldier in Burma, January 1944.*

program a failure. He did not think it reflected inefficiency at Ramgarh, but rather the general impossibility of training raw Chinese to the necessary standards in four weeks. To increase the difficulty, the British were pressing for the return of Ramgarh for their redeployment program. Plainly, expedients were necessary to get the convoys rolling to China.

Expedients were used, while emergency efforts were made to salvage the Chinese driver program. The Chinese 6th Motor Regiment, of lengthy Burma experience, took vehicles to Kunming and was flown back. The U.S. 330th Engineer Regiment supplied volunteers for the third, fifth, and sixth convoys, who made the trip to Kunming for a diversion while they awaited rotation. Units awaiting transfer to China drove themselves there. Volunteers were recruited from U.S. troops in IBT. Thanks to these expedients, clearly recognized as such, IBT dispatched thirty convoys in February, twenty-two of which reached China during the month; convoys dispatched after 16 February did not arrive until March.

Meanwhile, strong measures to bolster the Chinese driver program were taken. Training at Ramgarh went on round the clock, to handle some 9,844 Chinese volunteers, many of them students, who passed through the center in the first four months of 1945. Those Chinese who had graduated and some of whom had done badly were given a postgraduate course at Ledo. The four tank battalions yielded about 3,000 officers and men for motor transport duty.

These measures were no more than palliatives and IBT began to look elsewhere for drivers. Since Chinese drivers could not be obtained in quantity, and U.S. drivers were not available, there remained but one source, Indian civilian drivers, such as were then being employed successfully at SOS installations in India. IBT began to explore that possibility, with appropriate urgency.

The expedient measures for initial road operations were conducted under the routine that would be followed when drivers were available on a permanent basis. On 24 February, Headquarters and Headquarters Company, Motor Transport Service, was activated and assigned to Advance Section, Ledo. Its mission was to operate the 1,079 miles of highways in Advance Section's area. Motor transport operations divided into three phases: Ledo base operations; supply of activities in north Burma; deliveries to China.

Ledo Base operations were handled by Intermediate Section troops, Indian civilian drivers, and Advance Section men, reflecting the movement of traffic to Ledo, around Ledo, and away from Ledo.

Supply operations in Burma, which averaged about 30,000 tons a month, were the sphere of Motor Transport Service. At first, 6 x 6 trucks were used exclusively. In April, 4 x 6 tractors and 10-ton semitrailers were introduced

TABLE 4—VEHICLE AND CARGO DELIVERIES TO CHINA AND BURMA BY MONTHS
(1945)

Month	China						Burma
	Convoys	Vehicles	Trailers	Gross Weight [a]	Vehicle and Trailer Weight [a]	Cargo Weight [a]	Cargo Weight [a]
Total.........	433	25,783	6,539	146,948	108,886	38,062	161,986
February...........	22	1,333	609	5,231	4,120	1,111	27,087
March..............	22	1,152	745	6,788	5,279	1,509	34,579
April...............	38	2,342	1,185	15,447	11,249	4,198	31,797
May...............	78	4,682	1,103	28,080	19,645	8,435	28,357
June...............	82	4,901	964	27,962	20,977	6,985	14,923
July...............	75	4,745	828	23,370	17,470	5,900	16,085
August.............	51	2,652	647	15,866	11,582	4,284	5,046
September..........	53	3,060	408	18,599	14,291	4,308	4,112
October............	12	916	50	5,605	4,273	1,332	....

[a] Short tons.

Source: History of IBT, I, Ch. 3, p. 147.

on the relatively level stretch from Shingbwiyang to Bhamo, cutting driver requirements for that section about 50 percent.

Convoy movements on the Burma Road were as highly organized as traffic on a railroad. There were two classes of convoys—units proceeding to China and freight convoys. Both were dispatched by the Hump Regulation Officer in accord with priorities set by the Hump Allocation Office in China. In the case of freight convoys, Intermediate Section delivered the vehicles to Makum Junction, between Chabua and Ledo, where Motor Transport drivers took the wheel. These drove to Margherita, near Ledo, bivouacked there, and next morning crossed the initial point at Ledo. All movement from Ledo was controlled by Advance Section through the Motor Transport Service.

If a unit was going to China, it was staged at Kanchrapara, near Calcutta, where it received as many extra vehicles as it could manage. The Hump Regulation Officer dispatched it from Calcutta by rail to Siliguri, or Bongaigaon in Assam, and thence by road to Chabua. Here the vehicles were inspected and repaired, and extra vehicles assigned if possible. Then the unit went to Margherita, where it bivouacked again, waiting for its final dispatch to China.

Once on the road, drivers found way stations at regular intervals. By June 1945 nine of these were operating and offered maintenance for vehicles,

TABLE 5—GASOLINE DELIVERIES BY PIPELINE TO CHINA

Month	100-octane		Motor gas		Total	
	Gallons	Tons	Gallons	Tons	Gallons	Tons
April...................	122,072	439	....	....	122,072	439
May....................	671,440	2,442	843,000	3,088	1,514,440	5,530
June...................	138,919	505	1,278,200	4,682	1,417,115	5,187
July....................	1,684,130	6,124	1,495,200	5,477	3,179,330	11,601
August.................	1,873,760	6,814	1,113,735	4,085	2,987,495	10,897

Source: History of IBT, II, 161.

and transient messes and bathing facilities for men. Military police detachments patrolled the road from some thirty stations. Ordnance maintenance detachments manned twenty-two repair points along the road.

Driving the road was a strain. Ten days was regarded as the ideal time for a trip from Ledo to Kunming, but twelve to fifteen was more usual. Drivers operating on the road day in and day out were affected by the many rough, dusty stretches. Increasing numbers of men with dust pneumonia, cysts, fatigue, and kidney ailments began to appear at sick call. Quartermaster truck companies were obliged to take many men off duty.

Deliveries were also affected by operating problems. A shortage of fuel along the Chinese section of the road made April deliveries fall short of the target by 800 vehicles. During the first five months of 1945 about 10 percent of vehicles dispatched were either lost by accidents en route or delayed along the way.

Despite the driver problem and operational difficulties, an increasing amount of vehicles and supplies moved along the road.[31] The question soon arose: should it carry more? Road deliveries to points within Burma and to China are shown in Table 4. Pipeline deliveries to China are shown in Table 5.

The Line of Communications Reappraised

At various times the concept of the ground line of communications across north Burma had been challenged by those who thought air transport cheaper and more economical. As the years went by after 1942 the whole

[31] (1) History of IBT, II, 359–76. (2) Joseph Bykofsky and Harold Larson, *The Transportation Corps: Operations Overseas,* UNITED STATES ARMY IN WORLD WAR II (Washington, 1957).

strategic and logistical background of the argument was revolutionized. Where in 1942 the War Department had told Stilwell to live off the land and the White House had felt obliged to shift a handful of bombers and transports from Stilwell to support the crumbling Allied position in the Middle East, by December 1944 the Allies were far more secure, with much greater resources. Even the current desperate German offensive in the Ardennes, though disturbing, could not be compared to the menace that existed when General Erwin Rommel and the *Afrika Korps* were a few score miles from Alexandria. The Allies had shipping by the million tons; they had air transport, efficient ports, and lines of communications—in short, everything that had been lacking or scarce in 1942.

Army Service Forces had long been enthusiastic in support of the Ledo Road. In December 1944 Lt. Gen. Brehon B. Somervell, its commander, summoned General Covell to Washington to help him prepare recommendations on the scale at which operations on the road were to be supported in 1945. It would appear that Army Service Forces did not yet agree with the August 1944 War Department directive limiting the Stilwell Road to one-way delivery of vehicles and artillery. Projected road operations had to be weighed against Wedemeyer's 1945 requirements, and he was asked to submit them. Received 13 January 1945, they included the requirements of the projects he had earlier outlined. For April and May 1945, China Theater wanted about 77,000 tons; for June and July, about 80,000; and for August, 87,000. Here was the support for Plan BETA, 36 divisions, and two U.S. Army air forces in China.

With the Wedemeyer estimates came IBT's report of its current planning, which showed that unless transport efforts were drastically increased, deliveries to China Theater would fall short of Wedemeyer's estimates by amounts varying from 12,000 to 23,000 tons. The overland line of communications would be delivering vehicles, about 12,000 tons of gasoline, and some 2,000 tons of cargo a month.

The two agencies concerned, the India–China Wing of the Air Transport Command and the SOS IBT, submitted their estimates. The ATC believed that it could deliver 80,000 tons a month if it was reinforced by about 150 more C–54's plus reserves, an additional 968 officers and 4,326 enlisted men, and 0.7 ton of fuel for every ton of cargo scheduled.

To deliver 60,000 net tons of cargo a month, the SOS wanted for two-way operations 5,759 more 5-ton tractor-trailers; 56,500 troops, including 137 more quartermaster truck companies; and 0.6 ton of fuel for every ton of cargo scheduled. An extra 15,000 tons of maintenance supplies for the road would have to be dispatched from Ledo every month. These figures were a strong argument against the expansion of Stilwell Road operations. Moreover, other phases of the ground line of communications were being depreciated by events.   In 1942 and 1943 Stilwell had urged reopening the prewar line of communications from Rangoon to Kunming, in the belief that it could be done without asking the War Department for resources that agency had said it could not spare.   Now, in 1945, IBT surveyed the same route, and dismissed it because its rehabilitation would require resources not at hand in the theater.

The pipeline project from India to China was also being reappraised in January and February.   Originally, one six-inch and two four-inch pipelines had been planned.   When the estimates submitted were studied by the several headquarters in IBT, China, and Washington, the feeling grew that the second four-inch line need not be completed to China.   Its role would have been to support road operations.   Since these were being valued on a lower scale, General Chennault suggested that the pipe and crews which would have completed the line to Kunming should instead build a line from Kunming to the Fourteenth Air Force fields.   The suggestion was accepted, and set a precedent for suspending the six-inch line at Myitkyina.   This left the trans-Burma pipeline project at one four-inch line to Kunming.

A decision as to the most effective and most economical use of the Hump-road-pipeline combination was needed.   IBT sent the deputy theater commander, Maj. Gen. Frank D. Merrill, to Washington in February 1945 with five possible plans for deliveries to China Theater in 1945, Cases I through V.   Cases I through IV would provide 64,000 tons in April 1945 and from 116,000 to 158,000 tons a month by January 1946.   Case V was on a lower scale.   The principal differences between the plans lay in the amount of deliveries they assigned to the ATC.   Cases I through III assumed completion of the six-inch pipeline to China, and some cargo delivery over the Stilwell Road, but Cases IV and V, developed at a conference in New Delhi between officers from China and India, limited the road to one-way vehicle delivery.

Discussions in Washington during March 1945 attended by Wedemeyer, who was there to present Plan BETA for operations against Canton, led to the final recommendation, Case VI.   Case VI's proposals took advantage of the imminent departure of the B–29's from their great air bases near Calcutta.

Case VI undertook to meet China Theater's needs by adding C–46's and C–54's to the Hump, by basing C–54's on the Bengal fields of the B–29's for flight to China over the lower terrain of central Burma, and by building four more airfields at Myitkyina.   The Stilwell Road was to be restricted to one-way delivery of vehicles.   The six-inch pipeline was not to be extended past Myitkyina.   In effect, therefore, the major part of deliveries to China was to be by air.   The ground line of communications would be largely devoted to supporting the Myitkyina area.   From Ledo to Myitkyina there would be a two-way, all-weather road paralleled by two pipelines.   From Myitkyina to Kunming there would be a one-lane highway and one four-inch pipeline.[32]

There was one major assumption implicit in Case VI which if not satisfied would imperil the whole project for sharply increasing deliveries to China.   Case VI assumed that C–54's would be obtainable in sufficient number.   If this was indeed so, all would go well, but if it was not, China Theater plans would be adversely affected.

Transferring Support from SEAC to China

Though supply of the U.S. effort in China was India–Burma Theater's major mission, Sultan's theater also had commitments in Burma.   While the Chinese divisions and the Tenth Air Force were in Burma, IBT had to support them.   Slim's Fourteenth Army was also heavily dependent on U.S. transport aircraft.   Since these Chinese and American resources were ultimately intended for support of China, to China they would have to go at some point in the Burma campaign.   The choice of that point and the phasing of the departure were matters of importance and delicacy.

By mid-March 1945 the Generalissimo, Mountbatten, Wedemeyer, and Sultan were agreed that the rest of the Chinese Army in India and MARS Task Force would be released to return to China, since the Chinese did not want to move farther south.[33]   Meanwhile, Slim's forces were heavily engaged between Mandalay and Meiktila.   The difficulty in making the transfer lay in the demands on air transport that would result.   The easiest, quickest, and cheapest way to move the 30th, 38th, and 50th Chinese Divisions to east China was by air.   Air transport was also the obvious way to move the ground echelons of the Tenth Air Force to China.   But SEAC's transports that might be needed for this movement were engaged in support of Slim's forces, and were now the major contribution of the India–Burma Theater to the Burma campaign.   Indeed, 80 percent of SEAC's transports were American.

In agreeing that the three remaining Chinese divisions and MARS could be released, SEAC believed it had come very close to the limit of the resources that it could spare for China.   All that remained were the transports. They and their crews were being worked hard to bring ammunition, gas, and food to Meiktila.   Therefore, the JCS suggestion of 16 March 1945 that the aircraft to fly MARS and the Chinese divisions to east China should come from the transports supporting NCAC as well as from China Theater's own

---

[32] (1) History of IBT, II, 377–83.   (2) History of SOS in IBT, pp. 218–24.
[33] See Ch. VII, above.

resources and the ATC was disturbing to Mountbatten.   The Joint Chiefs had softened this proposal by stating that the Chinese Army in India was not to leave Burma before Rangoon fell or 1 June, whichever was sooner, but since SEAC was already on record as anxious to have the army moved out of Burma as soon as possible to aid the supply situation, the phrasing of the JCS proposal seemed to Mountbatten to offer no solution to his problem.

China Theater, which was asking for the transfer of the Chinese divisions, did not believe it had resources to spare for the move or that it could anticipate any reinforcements from outside India and Burma.   China Theater's own transports were fully engaged within China, in the ALPHA troop movements, and so its planners pointed to the 148 transports which had been supporting NCAC.   Since these were NCAC troops that were coming to China, they argued, their logistical support could come with them.

Such arguments did not impress Mountbatten, who placed his case before the British Chiefs of Staff as he had in a similar instance several months before.   He urged two points on them, that the Chinese divisions should be moved from Burma as soon as possible, and that no transport should be withdrawn from SEAC to move them.   The British Chiefs fully endorsed Mountbatten's views.   They were powerfully supported by the Prime Minister, who on 30 March sent a message to General Marshall.   Churchill wrote: "As General Marshall will remember from our talks at OCTAGON [September 1944], we greatly disliked the prospect of a renewal of a large-scale campaign in the jungles of Burma and I have always had other ideas myself."   Churchill pointed out that the British had loyally thrown themselves into the Burma campaign.   Furthermore, the British had kept Indian divisions in Italy to permit Canadian troops to join combined operations in Germany.[34]

In the War Department, these representations were received in a manner to suggest that the local commanders had misunderstood the JCS 16 March message on the transfer of U.S. resources from Burma, though its phrasing did support the conclusions drawn.   Since the United States had promised that it would not unilaterally jeopardize approved Fourteenth Army operations, the War Department Operation Division (OPD) had expected that the 16 March message would be interpreted accordingly.   OPD expected that NCAC aircraft would be used to move MARS Task Force with its two regiments, a far smaller commitment than flying back three Chinese divisions.

General Marshall, therefore, on 3 April 1945 assured the British that the United States was in fullest accord with Churchill's desire to continue Mount-

---

[34] (1) History of IBT, II, 333–36.   (2) Mountbatten Report, Pt. B, pars. 459–64.   (3) Prime Minister to Field Marshal Sir Henry M. Wilson, British Joint Services Mission, 022058.   Folder 66, OPD Exec 10.   (4) See Ch. V, above.

batten's offensive on to the capture of Rangoon.   He relayed the JCS assurance that the transports would not be transferred before 1 June or Rangoon's capture, whichever came first.   JCS reserved the general right to transfer resources to China if Rangoon did not fall before the monsoon began.[35]   The Chinese divisions would therefore be returned by ATC and China Theater.

Consistent with JCS policy, China Theater's next proposals for moving IBT air resources to China did not suggest the transfer of any transport squadrons until June, when two were requested.   For July, China Theater wanted two fighter groups, a troop carrier group less one squadron, and miscellaneous service elements.   The rest of the Tenth Air Force, which would include the last of the transports, was to be moved in September.[36]

When China Theater's proposals arrived at SEAC, that headquarters was making a major change in strategy.   On 23 February SEAC's field commanders had been sure they could reach Rangoon overland before the monsoon broke.   By 22 March, the senior ground commander, General Leese, had to point out that the advance was behind schedule, and a few days later suggested an amphibious assault on Rangoon, using some of the forces that were intended for Malaya.   The monsoon's approach set a time limit; great efforts would be necessary to make an amphibious assault before then.   Mountbatten's land, sea, and air forces, with veteran staffs and veteran troops, were at a stage of training and experience that permitted maximum flexibility, and so the decision was made.   Rangoon was to be taken by amphibious and air assault, and by 5 May.   Slim's men were now past Mandalay, moving south, and they were to continue as fast as possible.   Their problem was logistical. They had to have air supply just to stay where they were, for their overland lines of communication had been improvised on the assumption that air supply would be available.   Once the monsoon began they would have to be supplied through Rangoon anyway, so the best solution for Slim's logistical problem was for him to reach the port at the earliest date.   These needs and the decision to take Rangoon by amphibious and air assault meant that SEAC would not want to spare one transport before Rangoon fell.[37]

Therefore, China Theater's initial proposals for deferring until June the movement of Tenth Air Force to China were welcome.   They had hardly been received when the Japanese drive on Chihchiang in China forced Wedemeyer to make an emergency appeal for one transport squadron.   He wanted to rush troops to defend the Chihchiang fields and felt that if he had the squadron by 25 April the Chinese could hold the area.   General Sultan con-

[35] Memo, Hull for Marshall, sub: Conf with Field Marshal Wilson on CCS 452/44; Memo, Marshall for Wilson, 3 Apr 45.   Cases 6/4, 6/5, OPD 452.1
[36] History of IBT, II, 335–36.
[37] Mountbatten Report, Pt. B, pars. 498–507.

curred, for he believed the squadron could be found from those currently engaged in supply NCAC.

Mountbatten was willing that the squadron should go, since it was not currently engaged in central or south Burma, but he stipulated it must be regarded as coming from the June quota for China. He also asked Sultan how it was that in late April Sultan could spare a squadron for China when on 20 March he could not find one to help Slim in the battle for Mandalay. Sultan explained that in the interim enough Chinese troops had been moved from central Burma to lessen the need for air supply there, and so the squadron could be released.[38]

With the withdrawal of the Chinese divisions from SEAC, and the imminence of the Tenth Air Force's departure, it was possible in mid-April to forecast that the United States would soon withdraw entirely from SEAC. One reason lay in the fact that U.S. resources in SEAC were there to support China. Once Burma was retaken, SEAC would be involved in Malayan operations, in which the United States had no strategic interest, since the liberation of the Philippines plus the attack on Okinawa had already cut the Japanese oceanic line of communications to southeast Asia and the oil of the Indies. Moreover, the United States wished to avoid being in the position of supporting the re-establishment of European colonialism in southeast Asia.[39]

General Hull, chief of the Operations Division, discussed U.S. withdrawal from SEAC with General Marshall in April 1945. They agreed that SEAC should remain a combined headquarters so long as U.S. forces were assigned to it. On 16 May General Wheeler, who was the senior U.S. officer in SEAC, and also Principal Administrative Officer of that command, raised the issue again in a private letter to General Hull. If the United States continued as an active partner but contributed no forces, Wheeler pointed out, U.S. influence on SEAC policy would be nil. He thought it better to withdraw if no American forces were to be assigned. The Asiatic Section, OPD, described his views as "in complete accord" with theirs. But Marshall did not take too rigid a view of the existing situation. He did not permit Hull to answer until 18 June.

Hull's answer described U.S. policy on remaining in SEAC during hostilities. Hull believed that Marshall did not at this time want to raise the question of formal U.S. withdrawal. To Hull, he seemed reluctant to suggest a change because he had been a strong sponsor of the original idea of American participation on an Allied basis. Therefore. no change in the

[38] History of IBT, II, 335–37.
[39] See History of IBT, II, 161.

U.S. status was likely unless the British proposed it or some significant change occurred in the meantime.[40]

If the British accepted Mountbatten's views they would not be apt to suggest U.S. withdrawal from SEAC. Throughout SEAC history Mountbatten had stressed the "Allied" note. He appeared to value this not merely for what additional strength the Americans might lend, but for the idea's sake as well. As the campaign in Burma drew nearer an end he suggested that SEAC remain at least formally an Anglo-American command, through the presence of some American officers at SEAC headquarters, even after all American combat forces were gone. Therefore, as the fighting drew nearer to Rangoon, and the end of the campaign, SEAC remained an Allied command in name, though the combat effort was now exerted by British, Indian, and Burmese troops, which received most of their air supply from American cargo planes, and the Royal Navy and the Royal Indian Navy.[41]

The Last Battles in Burma

After securing the Meiktila–Mandalay area, Slim regrouped his forces for the dash to Rangoon by putting the motorized 5th and 17th Indian Divisions plus the bulk of his armor on the road and rail line from Mandalay to Rangoon. (*See Map 14.*) The rest of the force was switched to the Irrawaddy valley. In effect Slim was bypassing two still formidable groups of Japanese, *28th Army* to the west above the Irrawaddy, and *56th Division* to the east in the Shan States. Initially, Japanese resistance was stubborn, but as each Japanese position was reduced or bypassed, the daily bounds of Slim's forces grew even longer. On 6 and 7 April the Japanese *33d Army* tried to hold north of Yamethin long enough to permit preparations for a major stand at Toungoo to the south. The 17th Indian Division broke up the attempt and the *33d's* commander, Lt. Gen. Masaki Honda, barely escaped with his life. General Honda extricated his force, and again tried to stand at Pyinmana, forty-five miles south, on 19 April. The 5th Indian Division summarily ended the attempt. When the morning of 20 April arrived, Honda and his staff, fighting as infantry, managed to break through the Indian lines, but their radio communications were destroyed and they were out of touch with their troops. Slim's men had broken the last brittle crust of Japanese resistance above Rangoon, and were fairly in the clear. By 25 April the 17th Indian Division was 144 miles from Rangoon. If the weather

---

[40] Ltr, Wheeler to Hull, 16 May 45; Memo for Record, 16 May 45; Ltr, Hull to Wheeler, 18 Jun 45. OPD 384 TS, Sec I (1–20).
[41] History of IBT, II, 340.

AMERICAN OFFICERS, OSS DETACHMENT 101, *are shown with General Sultan at an advanced ranger base in Burma, June 1945.*

held, it could hope to reach Rangoon before the amphibious attack, then set for 2 May.

While Slim's men were cleaning their guns and preparing their tanks and trucks for the advance on Rangoon, off the flank, on what had been the NCAC front south of Lashio, a miniature campaign under U.S. sponsorship was developing. The NCAC move southward had been screened and guided by Burmese irregulars recruited, trained, and led by the OSS. As the campaign progressed they had grown in strength, and by late March they were taking the field in battalions. In early April OSS sought and received permission to continue south from the area of Lashio with about 3,200 men, armed with small arms, rocket launchers, machine guns, and trench mortars. On 27 April their offensive began.

The mission of the U.S.-sponsored Burmese troops, OSS Detachment 101, was to clear the Japanese from the central Shan States to the Taunggyi road. Fortunately for them, since their only support was the 60th Fighter Squadron,

Tenth Air Force, the Japanese *56th Division* had orders to move south into the southern Shan States.   The OSS battalions—1st, 10th, 2d, and 3d—deployed on a 75-mile front from near Maymyo on the west to the area Ke-hsi Mansam on the east.   In the days that followed, they exchanged some sharp blows with the Japanese.   An aggressive Japanese commander read the 1st Battalion a lesson on concentration of effort by attacking first one half, then the other, of its forces, and pushing it away from two villages.   Generally, the Japanese rear guard garrisons were content to hold what they had and try to run their convoys past the OSS troops' ambushes.   When, as on 8 May, the Japanese sent out punitive expeditions, the guerrillas would let the Japanese have a taste of fighting up steep wooded hillsides into machine gun fire, then withdraw when the Japanese pressure grew too heavy.

From the west, the 64th Indian Infantry Brigade was preparing to attack toward Taunggyi from the area through which Slim's task force had passed in its drive toward Rangoon.   In late May and early June it met stiff resistance west of Taunggyi, where bypassed Japanese held strong defensive positions.   The 64th had to fight its way up from the central Burma plain into the hills of the Shan plateau.   Not until 16 June did the 64th take Heho, thirteen miles west of Taunggyi, in the area where the 1st Battalion had its setback a month before.   With British forces now operating in the area, it seemed well to yield control of operations to them, and this was done as of 1 July.   Not until 25 July was Taunggyi taken, by the 99th Indian Infantry Brigade, which suggests that Detachment 101 cannot claim to have cleared the area.[42]

In central Burma, signs of Japanese weakness were everywhere, such as railroad trains overrun in the station yards.   Reading the signs aright, the Japanese-trained Burmese Army went over to the British en masse.   Not only was this a most severe psycholological blow to the Japanese, but the Burmans harassed Japanese rear installations and killed Japanese stragglers and small parties.   On 29 April there was plain evidence that the Japanese defense of Rangoon was finally breaking.   A column of some 400 prisoners of war from Rangoon, released by the Japanese, entered the lines of the 17th Indian Division.   Some of them had been captured by the Japanese from the 17th in the 1942 defeat; the wheel had turned full circle.   But unhappily for the 17th's hopes of being first in Rangoon, that same day the monsoon rains opened with a crash in the Pegu area.   Tanks and trucks were now largely roadbound.   Rangoon's occupation was left to the Royal Navy.

Beginning 27 April the several task groups for the air and amphibious assaults on Rangoon began putting to sea.   Attacks on Rangoon's seaward

[42] (1) ALFSEA Record, pp. 118–19.   (2) History of IBT, II, 342–49.

LT. GEN. RAYMOND A. WHEELER *(right), new Commanding General, India-Burma
Theater, shakes hands with his predecessor, General Sultan, during departure ceremonies
for the latter at New Delhi, 23 June 1945.*

defenses, including a paratroop drop, began on 1 May, and the minesweepers
started up the Irrawaddy. One aerial observer reported a message painted on
the roof of the Rangoon jail that the Japanese were gone. It was ignored
and bombing continued, but word of the sign must have spread quickly.
Next day an RAF pilot and observer saw no signs of activity at Mingaladon
airfield, outside Rangoon, and decided to land there. The field was well
cratered with bombing, and the plane crashed. Undaunted, the pilot walked
into Rangoon, on to the jail. The Japanese were gone. Rangoon was
occupied the day after, 3 May.

  After Rangoon's fall, there was in effect a long cordon of British troops
stretching from Mandalay to Rangoon. West of it were the remnants of
the Japanese *28th Army,* the veterans of the Arakan campaign. Their attempts to break through the British lines in July with some 25,000 men,
assisted by the *33d Army* to the east, marked the last major action of the
campaign. British intelligence and reconnaissance brought clear indication

of the projected breakthrough. The 17th Indian Division sited strongpoints in the path of the breakthrough along the few practicable routes left by the monsoon floods. From these, the 17th's veterans exacted the final retribution for 1942, as the Japanese sought to make their way through heavy machine gun and artillery fire. By the time the fighting ended in August, the Japanese did get a large portion of their force between the 17th's strongpoints and across the Sittang River. Estimation of their casualties is difficult because of administrative changes and lost records, but on 20 September, the *28th Army* mustered only 7,949 men for duty, had 1,919 in the hospital, and carried 4,822 as missing but expected to return. In contrast, the British lost but 95 dead and 322 wounded between 20 July and 4 August.[43]

The liberation of Rangoon and victory in Burma were fittingly celebrated by a victory parade in that city. While the festivities were in course, the India–Burma Theater commander, General Sultan, was surprised to receive a radio from Washington calling him back to be Chief of Engineers. His tour of duty ended 23 June 1945. For his services in India and Burma he received the Oak Leaf Cluster to the Distinguished Service Medal, the Bronze Star, and the Chinese Order of the Cloud and Banner with Special Grand Cordon. His successor was General Wheeler. Wheeler had created the SOS in CBI back in 1942, when every day was a struggle to improvise and expedite. From SOS commander he had become Principal Administrative Officer, SEAC. On Stilwell's recall in 1944 he added the title of Deputy Supreme Allied Commander. Now, he was to finish his overseas career as U.S. India–Burma Theater commander.[44] The biggest task facing him was that of supporting Wedemeyer's operations against the Canton–Hong Kong area, Plan BETA.

---

[43] (1) Japanese Study 132. Strength tables facing pp. 77, 56. (2) Mountbatten Report, Pt B, pars. 542–48, 591–603.
[44] History of IBT, II, 420.

CHAPTER XI

Preparing a Drive to the China Coast

The requests for tonnage that Wedemeyer presented to India–Burma Theater and the ATC were the logistical requirements for operations to take the Canton–Hong Kong area and support the transfer of the Tenth Air Force from SEAC to China. As soon as plans and preparations for ALPHA were well under way, Wedemeyer had ordered his planners to outline an operation in which the U.S.-sponsored Chinese divisions of the ALPHA plan would take the offensive toward the seacoast. On 29 January 1945 the Generalissimo was advised of the trend of Wedemeyer's thinking, and in the days that followed Wedemeyer mentioned shifting the center of China Theater operations toward the east.[1] (*See Map 1—inside back cover.*)

Plan BETA

By informally writing to General Hull, Wedemeyer began laying the groundwork for War Department approval of his plans. He told Hull that he envisaged a strategic air force (the Fourteenth) and a tactical (the Tenth) in China, the two commanded by some officer like General Stratemeyer. This powerful new force would support the ALPHA divisions in taking a seaport in the fall. By so writing, Wedemeyer was accepting an organization proposed by the Tenth Air Force on 15 January 1945.[2]

Operations on the scale envisaged would require aid from neighboring theater commanders and the concurrence and support of the Joint Chiefs. On 5 February Wedemeyer outlined his intentions for the benefit of his colleagues and his superiors. He thought that the ALPHA troops could take the offensive in July or August, with the weather in southeast China favoring their operations. By then, fifteen to twenty-five divisions should be ready. "We have considered an attack from Kweiyang eastward to acquire air bases and to cut enemy communications lines in area Heng-yang–Ling-

---

[1] Min, Mtg 34, Wedemeyer with Generalissimo, 29 Jan 45. Bk 1, Generalissimo Minutes.
[2] (1) Ltr, Wedemeyer to Hull, 29 Jan 45. Case 37, OPD 381 (TS), Sec II. (2) *The Army Air Forces in World War II,* V, 268.

MEETING AT YALTA, *in the Crimea, attended by President Roosevelt, Prime Minister Churchill, and Marshal Joseph Stalin.*

ling.   This would be feasible only if enemy materially reduces forces south of Yangtze.   An air and ground outline plan is being prepared for drive on Liuchow–Nanning area thence east against Canton–Hong Kong." [3]

While this radio was being studied by the staffs to whom it was addressed, President Roosevelt, Prime Minister Churchill, and Marshal Stalin were meeting on Russian soil, at the Crimean resort town of Yalta.   One of the topics of discussion was China.   Probably it was in preparation for Yalta that Marshall on 26 January asked Wedemeyer to report on the situation in China, which Wedemeyer did on 5 February.   "In event" the Russians entered the war in Asia, Wedemeyer thought they could do so four months after the German defeat (estimated as late spring) and that they could add thirty divisions to the thirty he credited the Soviets with having in

[3] Rad CFB 32476, Wedemeyer to MacArthur *et al.,* info Marshall and King, 5 Feb 45.   Wedemeyer Data Book.

the Far East. If this estimated timing proved correct, winter might restrict Russian operations in the Far East. Wedemeyer did not suggest that anything be done to obtain Soviet entrance into the Pacific war. His comments on the future course of Chinese operations suggest that as of 5 February he thought the Chinese armies carrying out the operations he now contemplated could "destroy the Japanese on the Asiatic mainland" and make impossible any large-scale Japanese redeployment from the Asiatic mainland to Japan in time to meet an American invasion.

> It will probably be the first of July at the earliest before effective ground operations can be undertaken. China Theater is striving to undertake coordinated ground and air operations against the Japanese from the west in time to disrupt their planned redeployment to meet possible U.S. advances from the Pacific and to prevent the withdrawal of forces from Asia into Japan proper. It is believed that if our operations can be initiated in July they will catch the Japanese off-balance and probably preclude planned redistribution of their forces. In the event they are preparing to withdraw bulk of forces to the north of the Yangtze these operations will probably hasten that withdrawal. In any event, our operations, if successful, would give the Chinese army much needed combat experience and confidence and could result in opening port of Canton-Hong Kong. When sea communications are reestablished, it will be possible to dispense with the prodigious effort required to supply China via India. Further, the increased flow of supplies in conjunction with victorious battle experience may inspire confidence and create conditions that will enable the Chinese forces to destroy the Japanese on the Asiatic mainland without large-scale American ground participation.[4]

At Yalta, President Roosevelt was willing to pay a high price for timely Soviet entry into the war against Japan. The three Powers agreed that the United States would obtain Chinese concurrence to the conference protocol's listing of Soviet aspirations in Manchuria as a *quid pro quo* for prompt Soviet intervention against Japan, and further guaranteed fulfillment of these Soviet claims. The Generalissimo was not to be informed of this agreement until the Soviet deployment was largely complete. During these conversations, Premier Stalin observed that he recognized "the need for a united China under Chiang Kai-shek's leadership." However, in the formal statement of accord between the three Great Powers at Yalta, the Soviet intent was modestly defined as "readiness" to conclude a pact with Nationalist China "for the purpose of liberating China from the Japanese yoke." [5]

The probable sphere of Soviet military action, Manchuria, Inner Mongolia, and north China, was far removed from the area of projected Sino-American

---

[4] *Ibid.*

[5] (1) Conversations Regarding Entry of USSR into War Against Japan, 10 Feb 45. *Foreign Relations of the United States: Diplomatic Papers*, Dept State Pub 6199, *The Conferences at Malta and Yalta, 1945* (Washington, 1955). (2) Robert E. Sherwood, *Roosevelt and Hopkins: An Intimate History* (New York: Harper & Brothers, 1948), pp. 866–68. (3) Quotations from Statement of W. Averell Harriman, 13 July 1951, to the Committees on Armed Services and Foreign Relations of the United States Senate, 82d Congress. Hearings on the Military Situation in the Far East, Pt. 5, App. and Index, pp. 3,333–34.

operations in China, the Canton–Hong Kong area, but if the Japanese concentrated their forces in north China to meet the Soviet threat, as Okamura had been warned was likely, then opportunities in southeast China would open for Wedemeyer and the Generalissimo. That, in retrospect, seems to have been the extent of the connection between U.S. theater headquarters in China and the implementation of the Yalta agreements.

The plan drafted by Wedemeyer's staff for an offensive in southeast China was an ambitious one. On 14 February, formulated as Plan BETA, it was formally presented to the Generalissimo at a gathering in Wedemeyer's headquarters. Present as distinguished American guests were Ambassador Hurley and Rear Adm. Charles M. Cooke, the latter just back from Yalta. Among the Chinese delegation was General Chen Cheng, Minister of War.[6]

BETA assumed that the war in Europe would end 15 May 1945; that Allied Pacific operations would continue as planned and force the Japanese armies in China to redeploy north and east to meet actual or projected U.S. landings in China; and that the Japanese would steadily weaken in 1945. As for logistical support, it was assumed that a four-inch pipeline would be complete to Kunming 15 July, and that the Hump and the Stilwell Road together would deliver 60,000 tons a month.

BETA's objectives, as listed by the theater planners, were fourfold: (1) to make effective use of the anticipated increase in supply deliveries to China; (2) to improve the local military situation and contribute to Pacific operations; (3) to improve the morale and efficiency of the Chinese Army; (4) to open a seaport, and help prepare China Theater to begin the preliminaries involved in destroying the Japanese armed forces on the continent of Asia.

Moving southeast to capture the Liuchow–Nanning area was Phase I. Kunming's present defenders, now in the Kweiyang area, could move on those cities by the target date of 1 May without disturbing their current dispositions or training schedules. Air and ground lines of communications to Liuchow could be set up to support further operations eastward. The Japanese seemed overextended and taking the area would cut their lines of communications to the south. Phase II was consolidation of the Liuchow–Nanning area. At this time, any soft spots which might reveal themselves, particularly toward the sea south of this area, would be exploited. Phase III would be the preparatory period for the actual attack on Canton and Hong Kong. The planners believed that one indication of completion of this phase would be successfully cutting off the Japanese to the south. At its conclusion the assault forces would be concentrated, fully equipped, at full strength, with their line of communications and supply dumps all in order.

The China Theater planners, under Col. Paul W. Caraway, realized there

---

[6] Min, Mtg 39, Wedemeyer with Generalissimo, 14 Feb 45. Bk 1, Generalissimo Minutes.

might be a very vigorous Japanese reaction, so they had an alternative course at hand. This was to open a coastal base in the vicinity of Luichow Peninsula, so that supplies brought in from the Pacific could give added weight to the attack on Canton and Hong Kong.

Phase IV of BETA was the actual attack on the two great seaports, to open an oceanic line of communications to a major Chinese port early in 1946. Such a port would be a great base from which to support later offensives, would permit a tighter air and sea blockade of Japan, and would facilitate cleaning up Japanese garrisons in Formosa, south China, and Hainan.

To assist this main effort diversions were contemplated all the way from Hanoi to Hsian. Ground patrols, reconnaissances in force, limited objective attacks, all were to distract the Japanese and keep them off balance. Wedemeyer's staff believed that some 208 Chinese divisions, with 1,700,000 men, could help in this, though it was thought shortages of small arms and ammunition would make it unsafe to plan on receiving help from more than 10 to 15 percent of these forces.

The time schedule for training and equipping divisions to take part in BETA was:

1 May 1945:	10 Chinese divisions for the main effort
15 May 1945:	5 Chinese divisions to menace Hanoi; 3 to threaten Heng-yang
15 July 1945:	7 Chinese divisions to complete the build-up in the Liuchow area
1 September to 1 November 1945:	11 Chinese divisions plus all that could be trained, equipped, and supported under this plan
1 November 1945:	36 Chinese divisions, numbering about 500,000 men at full strength

Twenty specially trained commando units, numbering 200 men each, were also to be created to be used as soon as possible before 1 May 1945.

The air forces were to have a major role in BETA, for they were to attempt the isolation of the Japanese defenders from their sources of supply in north and central China. To do this, the American air forces in China were to subordinate everything but maintenance of local air superiority to carrying out their share in BETA. The planners believed that Japanese lines of communication from north China and the homeland converged in the Hankow area. Thence, southward, the Japanese sent supplies by rail and river to Changsha, and from there by rail and road to Kweilin, Liuchow, and Nanning. BETA contemplated continuing interdiction of these routes by medium bombers and fighters and, in the latter phases, interdiction of local roads and rail lines in the objective area. Tactical air support was to be made available throughout. In the final phase, there was to be heavy bombing of the Japanese defenses in the Canton–Hong Kong area.

Air supply was to play a major part in moving the Chinese forces eastward. Heavy reinforcements of transport aircraft were expected after Germany's defeat. These were to help provide air supply to the forward areas. Once Liuchow was taken, then an airline from Luzon to Liuchow was to be organized. The planners thought this would be a potent means of accumulating supplies. The heavy dependence on air transport reflected awareness of the difficulties of moving arms and men in China. Though trucks were coming in over the Stilwell Road in increasing numbers, bad roads, poor drivers, scarcity of fuel, spares, and maintenance facilities all made it desirable, if the means were at hand, simply to fly over the hampering road net. Additional airfields would be needed, the planners concluded, and they wanted U.S. aviation engineer battalions to build them.

After weighing the pros of the operation, such as the tremendous impetus to U.S. activities in China that would come from opening a port, and the cons, such as the circumstance that much of BETA would have to be carried out during the season of low clouds and heavy rains, the fact emerged that internal distribution of supplies was the key to effective logistical support for BETA. Wedemeyer's staff hoped that bringing enough supplies into China to support two air forces and equip thirty-six Chinese divisions, then moving this tonnage many hundreds of miles east from Kunming, could be done by the contemplated increased Hump tonnage and by opening the airline from Luzon. Within China, every means of transport was to be utilized—truck, sampan, coolie, and aircraft.

The supply requirements for BETA, in terms of tonnage, reflected the planning of all the major theater agencies. If any erred in its estimates, activities all over China in 1945 would be affected. Tonnage requirements for BETA were estimated as follows: [7]

Agency	Jan	Feb	Mar	Apr	May	Jun	Jul	Aug
AAF	24,470	29,560	26,000	31,000	39,356	41,711	42,097	42,883
SOS	8,500	8,500	8,800	9,300	9,600	9,900	10,200	10,500
CCC–CTC	1,500	1,500	1,700	1,900	2,100	2,300	2,300	2,500

This, then, was BETA, a four-stage operation to open a seaport, and on the afternoon of 14 February it received the Generalissimo's approval. For the first time since China and the United States became Allies, the Generalissimo agreed to a major offensive effort within the historic provinces of

---

[7] Plan BETA, Tab D, App E. OCMH. The same plan gives the 1945 tonnage requirements for all China Theater activities, by month, as:

Jan	Feb	Mar	Apr	May	Jun	Jul	Aug
43,089	40,900	43,000	53,500	62,000	62,000	62,000	62,000

China proper.[8]   It was now necessary to obtain the approval and support of the U.S. Government.

Wedemeyer's Visit to Washington

From the War Department Wedemeyer received permission to return to the United States to present BETA to the JCS, together with his comments on the organizational changes he would like to make in China Theater to knit his command more firmly together.   Ambassador Hurley elected to return with Wedemeyer.   Some years after the war Hurley recalled that he had heard rumors of extensive concessions to the Soviets at China's expense, and that, since any such development would greatly affect his mission to China, he was anxious to be informed.[9]

Wedemeyer's presentation of BETA was effective.   The Joint War Plans Committee presented the view that U.S. operations against Okinawa would lead the Japanese to thin out their forces in south China and so make BETA possible by September.   On 20 April the JCS approved BETA.   On the vital question of logistical support, Wedemeyer and his party left Washington with the distinct impression that the C–54 transports required to support BETA and the displacement of the Tenth Air Force to China on the schedule desired by Wedemeyer would be forthcoming.   For its part, the War Department understood that it had approved sending Stratemeyer and his headquarters to command in China, to be followed by the Tenth as support became available.   So as they parted, Wedemeyer and his staff expected to hear that C–54's were coming to India, while the War Department expected to learn of Stratemeyer's move to China.[10]

In the field of high policy, the War Department was able to present Wedemeyer, together with MacArthur, Sultan, and Wheeler (the latter at SEAC), with a statement of U.S. policy toward China.   Explicitly desiring guidance for its staff and for Wedemeyer, the War Department had asked the State Department to furnish it.   The State Department responded, Secretary of War Stimson described the paper as "OK," and the War Department passed it to Wedemeyer with appropriate cautions: ". . . This policy should be made known only to key American staff officers who require the knowledge in the discharge of their duties . . . it represents the current State Department position and is subject to revision in the light of later development."   Wedemeyer was further told that the paper was for his "guidance."   Such a statement of policy regarding China was something of

---

[8] (1) BETA is described in History of China Theater, Ch. IX, pp. 1–14.   (2) Min, Mtg 39A, Wedemeyer with Generalissimo, 14 Feb 45.   Bk 1, Generalissimo Minutes.

[9] (1) Rad CFB 32477, Wedemeyer to Marshall, 5 Feb 45.   Item 346, Bks 1 and 2, ACW Personal File.   (2) Interv with Hurley, Jun 49.   The Yalta meeting lasted from 4 to 11 February 1945.   Hurley left soon after.

[10] Memo, Capt E. D. Graves, USN, Dep Secy JCS, for ACofS OPD and Aide to COMINCH, 20 Apr 45, sub: Priority of Resources for Operation RASHNESS.   ABC 384 China (15 Dec 43), Sec 1–B.

a novelty, for Stilwell had complained several times that he could not find out what was U.S. policy toward China.[11]

The paper stated that the short-term objective of the United States was to unify all China's resources for war against Japan. The long-term objective was to help develop "a united, democratically progressive, and cooperative China." The State Department believed that Wedemeyer should focus on the short-term objective, and the letter of transmittal put the stamp of War Department approval on the advice. Some rearmament of Chinese forces would result, but measures "now" to arm China so as to make her a strong power did not, according to the view stated in the paper, appear practicable. The State Department would have liked to see the arming of all Chinese willing to fight Japan. Currently, it was impolitic to arm the Chinese Communists. If the United States was to undertake operations on the China coast, commanders should be prepared to arm the Communists. The paper observed that interest in unifying China did not necessarily mean that China should be united under the Generalissimo. It closed by stating that a degree of flexibility should be maintained, which would, in turn, leave open the question of a specific postwar rearmament program.

The first impact of the attempt to state U.S. policy in China would appear to have been on Ambassador Hurley's efforts to mediate between the Nationalist and Communist forces, for he came to believe that the Chinese Communists, having obtained a copy of the statement of policy, were thereby encouraged to resist his efforts at mediation. For, if the United States was prepared to concede that unifying China did not necessarily mean that China should be united under the leadership of the Generalissimo, Chiang Kai-shek, then the Chinese Communists had a powerful incentive to maintain their identity and resist the Generalissimo's terms.[12]

---

[11] (1) Ltr with Incl, Hull to Wedemeyer *et al.,* 27 Feb 45, sub: U. S. Short and Long Range Objectives in China. (2) The paper is described as a "statement of policy" in a memorandum, Col. Harrison A. Gerhardt, Executive to Mr. John J. McCloy, Assistant Secretary of War, to General Handy, 26 February 1945. Gerhardt explained further that McCloy obtained the paper from the Under Secretary of State, Mr. Joseph C. Grew. (3) McCloy told Stimson: "As you recall, this report was requested by the War Department for the guidance of the staff and General Wedemeyer." Memorandum, McCloy to Stimson, 17 February 1945, with penned note from Stimson: "So far as it goes I think is OK—and I don't see how we can go much further in formulating policy until we are in the Jap homeland—and also know what Russia is going to do. H.L.S." All above in ABC 336 China (26 Jan 42), Sec 1–B. (4) *Stilwell's Command Problems.* Ch. XIII.

[12] (1) Hurley, in 1949, told the authors that a contact of his among the Chinese Communists gave him his first knowledge of the 27 February policy statement by using it to clinch the Communist argument that Hurley's statements to the Yenan regime did not represent current U.S. policy. There is no mention in the supporting papers to the 27 February statement of China policy that a copy of it was being sent to the U.S. Ambassador to China. (2) Ltr, Hurley to Stephens, 15 Dec 56. OCMH. (3) Memo, Somervell for Marshall, 15 May 45, sub: Overland LOC to China. WDCSA 091 China. This memorandum discusses the BETA operation (called RASHNESS for security reasons) from the ASF point of view. (4) Lt. Col. Gustav E. Johnson, The Deployment of the AAF to China From India and Events After August, 1945, 7 May 1956. Research Studies Institute, Air University, Maxwell Air Force Base, Ala. Hereafter, Johnson MS. (5) JCS 1238, 30 January 1945, approved an offensive in China. (6) JPS 609/1, 27 Feb 45.

In a sphere less august but still one where Wedemeyer had feared embarrassment, that of clandestine activity in China, he was able to have his wishes satisfied.   Navy Group, China, including its activities as part of SACO under General Tai Li of the Chinese secret police, was put under his control. Slightly earlier, OSS, China, had also been brought into the fold.[13]

While in Washington, Wedemeyer, Hurley, and Commodore Miles of Navy Group, China, offered their observations on the scene in China.   They spoke against a background of China Theater's effort to create thirty-six U.S.-sponsored Chinese divisions, well fed, well led, fully equipped, and trained, supported by an efficient services of supply and a revitalized air force, and thoroughly blooded by driving the Japanese out of south and central China. Their appraisals of China's future implicitly assumed the existence of such a force.

In his memoirs, Admiral William D. Leahy recalled that on 27 March Wedemeyer and his associates told the Joint Chiefs that "the rebellion in China could be put down by comparatively small assistance to Chiang's central government.   Wedemeyer seemed to believe then that further serious advances of the Japanese in China could be prevented, but he was encountering difficulties in controlling the Chinese war lords and political officers as well as having trouble with the British officials in Asia and with some of his own temperamental general officers."   A low estimate of the future military capabilities of the Chinese Communists and concern for British activities in China were expressed several times by Wedemeyer in April and May 1945 and by Hurley often in the first six months of 1945 and are part of the background against which they shaped their policies.[14]

Hurley left Washington 3 April 1945, to return to his post at Chungking via London and Moscow.   Having gone to Washington from China because he was disturbed by the versions of the Yalta agreement circulating in Chungking, he went to the White House to clarify the matter, and in a rather belligerent mood.   But finding the President looking worn, he approached the matter tactfully and quietly.   Over the next few days Roosevelt and Hurley had several discussions of the Yalta agreement, in which Hurley made plain his impression that the territorial integrity and political independence of China had been affected by the Yalta accord.   Initially, the President denied this,

---

[13] (1) CM–OUT 34942, Marshall to Wedemeyer, 7 Feb 45.   (2) Memorandum for Record by General Hull of OPD, 29 March 1945, WDCSA 091, China, covers Navy Group, China.

[14] (1) Fleet Admiral William D. Leahy, *I Was There: The Personal Story of the Chief of Staff to Presidents Roosevelt and Truman Based on His Notes and Diaries Made at the Time* (New York: Whittlesey House, McGraw Hill Book Company, Inc., 1950), p. 337.   (2) See Memorandum of Conversation between Generalissimo and Hurley, 16 February 1945, in which Hurley told the Generalissimo that when the war was over his well-equipped divisions would have a walkover if he fought the Communists.   Item 35, Bk 2, Hurley Papers.   (3) Rad, Hurley to Truman, 20 May 45.   Item 98, Bk 2, Hurley Papers.   (4) Rad CFB 38387, Wedemeyer to Marshall, 31 May 45.   Item 787, Bks 3 and 4, ACW Personal File.

but when Hurley reinforced his arguments by citations of the text of the agreement—after he had finally broken the elaborate security barrier and obtained a copy—the President agreed that something should be done, in Hurley's later phrase, to "ameliorate" the Yalta accord.

Hurley's reports of 13 and 17 April, written a few weeks after these interviews, give the instructions of the President as:

> . . . to obtain cooperation from the British and Soviet Governments for the American policy to support the National Government in China; to unite the military forces of China to bring the war with Japan to a speedy end and to support all reasonable efforts of Chinese leaders for the purpose of creating a free, united, democratic China. . . . [13 April 1945]

> . . . to confer with Prime Minister Churchill on unification of the armed forces of China and endorsement of China's aspirations to establish a free, united, democratic government of China. . . . To promote the foregoing program it had been decided to support the National Government of China under the leadership of Chiang Kai-shek. [17 April 1945]

Hurley's interviews with Churchill and Stalin on such large questions of policy were no casual matter, but a major diplomatic effort, undertaken on behalf of the President because Roosevelt had had long second thoughts on the Yalta agreement. Repair of the weaknesses in the Yalta accord could not be accomplished overnight; the first step was to persuade the other parties to agree firmly to support U.S. policy in China. Once that was obtained, then the Yalta accord would have to be interpreted in the light of the later Soviet and British commitments.

These interviews with Churchill and Stalin seemed to Hurley to have been eminently successful, and he so reported to the State Department, and to President Harry S. Truman, who at this delicate juncture in American foreign policy development had just succeeded President Roosevelt. In Hurley's report of 17 April he told the State Department: "We obtained from Prime Minister Churchill and Foreign Secretary Eden complete concurrence in the policy. . . . Stalin stated emphatically that the Soviet Government would support the policy. He added that he would be glad to cooperate with the U.S. and Britain in achieving unification of the military forces in China." [15]

On returning to Chungking, Hurley discussed the provisions of the Yalta

---

[15] (1) Intervs with Hurley, 1949. (2) Hearings Before the Committee on Armed Services and the Committee on Foreign Relations, United States Senate, 82d Congress, Part 4, pp. 2884–87. (3) Memorandum by Edward Page, Second Secretary of Embassy, Moscow, on Meeting 15 April 1945 Between Harriman, Hurley, Stalin, and Molotov. Item 69, Hurley Bk 2. Oddly enough, although Hurley began his interview by discussing with Stalin the question of unifying the armed forces of China, he said that the main purpose of his visit to Moscow had been to discuss the next question brought up by Stalin: When was Chiang to learn of the Yalta accord? When the unification issue was apparently settled, almost as soon as it was raised, by Stalin's ready acquiescence, Hurley may have thought it tactful to attach major importance to a point Stalin raised. (4) Rad, Hurley to Truman, 13 Apr 45. Items 66, 67, Hurley Bk 2. (5) Rad, Hurley to Secy State, 17 Apr 45. Item 73, Hurley Bk 2. In this radio, drafted by Hurley, the emphasis is on Stalin's agreement to support U. S. policy.

agreement with Chiang Kai-shek, but without identifying them as such. Thanks to this device, on 10 May 1945 he was able to give Chinese reactions as: "I am convinced that he will agree to every one of the requirements but will take exceptions to the use of two words 'preeminent' and 'lease.' These words have bad connotations in China. They have been involved in the controversies over extraterritoriality. These two words seem to impinge on the principles of the territorial integrity and independent sovereignty of China." Hurley, therefore, advised the President that the Chinese objected to the Soviets' having pre-eminent interests in the port of Dairen, to the lease of Port Arthur as a Soviet naval base, and to the pre-eminent interests of the Soviet Union in the Manchurian rail system. All that China would willingly have agreed to in the Yalta accord were those provisions relating to Japanese territory and to Outer Mongolia—neither of which was apt to pass under Chinese control. In his message Hurley suggested that Stalin's assent to telling Chiang Kai-shek formally of the Yalta accord be obtained as soon as possible. In acknowledging Hurley's report Truman confined himself to the question of notifying the Chinese of the Yalta agreement. He did not think the time appropriate.[16]

Logistical Obstacles to BETA

Even as Wedemeyer was presenting BETA to the Joint Chiefs, his staff and principal subordinates in China were beginning to find the logistical problems of BETA assuming a steadily graver aspect. As presented to the JCS, BETA set very definite and rather modest tonnages for the SOS and Chinese Combat Command. For the SOS, monthly tonnages were to rise slowly from 8,500 in January to 10,500 in July. The CCC was to have 1,500 tons in January and 2,300 in July. However, a rather considerable number of Americans were flown in to China in early 1945 to increase theater strength. The most conspicuous example was the project of bringing in the men who had formed MARS Task Force. As a result of these increases, the SOS jumped in strength from about 4,000 men in January 1945 to 10,000 in June 1945. The Chinese Combat Command went from about 4,000 men to 7,000.[17]

---

[16] (1) Rad, Hurley to President, 10 May 45; Rad, President to Hurley, 13 May 45. Items 88, 89, Hurley Bk 2. (2) Supporting the impression of second thoughts in regard to Yalta that is left by the Hurley papers are two documents in ABC 336 Russia (22 Aug 43) Sec 3. On 12 May 1945, the State Department asked Stimson for War Department comment on the diplomatic issues arising from the expected Soviet entry into the Pacific War, and said it thought the United States should receive safeguarding commitments and clarifications to the Yalta accords before carrying out its part of them. Ltr, Joseph C. Grew, Actg Secy of State, to Stimson, 12 May 45. Tab 2. The War Department replied that the USSR had the power to take what it wanted in the Far East. Because of this the War Department felt something other than military means was needed to obtain the desired commitments, which it agreed would be helpful. Ltr, Stimson to Grew, 21 May 45, Tab 5.
[17] Rpt, Col Roger A. Flood, Pres, Boards of Investigation on Strength, Distribution, and Organization of American Personnel in China Theater, 10 Oct 45, Tabs J, K, L. CT 41, Dr 1, KCRC.

SOLDIERS ON A TROOP TRAIN *en route from Kunming to Chanyi, 27 March 1945.*
These men are MARS Task Force veterans of the North Burma Campaign.

Since the SOS estimated that every American soldier brought to China required delivery of .62 tons of supplies every month, these increases meant
that approximately 3,600 more tons were needed in June to supply the SOS
than in January, while 1,800 tons more were needed for CCC.   Therefore,
even as the plan for an offensive against the Canton–Hong Kong area was
being discussed, the logistic underpinnings were being taken away by a
growth of the U.S. forces themselves which far outstripped that anticipated.
So marked was the trend toward devoting an ever greater share of the Hump
effort to support of the Americans themselves that whereas in January 1945
only 48 percent of the Hump's capacity had been so used, by August Americans used 73 percent.[18]

Moreover, estimates varied sharply as to the usefulness of these Americans
once they had arrived.   For example, the MARS soldiers were two representa-

---

[18] Memo, Cols Edward H. Young, Albert S. Johnson, John W. Childs, for Actg CofS China
Theater, 7 Jan 45, sub: Recommendations Pertaining to Reconsideration of Rpt on Strength, Distribution, and Organization of American Personnel in China Theater, Tab 16, CT 41, Dr
1, KCRC.

tive regiments of U.S. infantry, who in combat had done all their superiors asked of them, and done it well. On arrival in China they were expected to act as liaison personnel and instructors for Chinese troops. But many of the MARS personnel did not have either the background or the temperament to act as teachers and advisers. The G–3, Central Command, later testified that only 17 or 18 percent of the 900 MARS men assigned to Central Command were usable in their new roles. The rest, he thought, were simply a burden.[19] Yet they needed about 500 tons of supplies every month, tonnage that would if converted to ammunition be enough to maintain a Chinese army for thirty days.[20]

The tonnage figures in the BETA plan given above refer to tonnage laid down at Kunming. From Kunming, supplies had to be moved east, and this effort to distribute Hump tonnage to the ultimate users in China was a major one. In drawing up BETA, the supply planners estimated that 14,000 tons of Hump tonnage would have to be used for intra-China supply movements. In actual practice it was found that for August 1945, for example, the ground forces would need 29,060 tons to distribute their share of the supplies received over the Hump.[21]

By 26 March these factors were making themselves apparent. One of the junior participants at a commanders' conference in Kunming on that date, at which Chennault presided in Wedemeyer's absence, spelled out their impact:

For the month of April, we have 52,615 tons available to us; the bids are for 72,314. In May, 55,590 tons available to us; bids are for 76,707; in June, we have 56,650 tons available to us; the bids are for 86,877 tons; in July, we have 64,400 tons available to us; the bids are for 88,965 tons. . . .We are faced with a great deficit unless we get [Hump] augmentation, or the plans are changed and bids changed accordingly.[22]

These remarks, accepted by the other conferees, showed that arrival of the C–54's was needed to give added capacity over and above that originally given as the cost of BETA.

In April came a further blow—the Chihchiang campaign, with its demands for Hump tonnage to move Chinese troops to that area.

After completing his mission to Washington, Wedemeyer returned to China via Calcutta. There on 9 April 1945 he met with the senior officers of the Tenth Air Force and the India–Burma Theater to discuss what now appeared to him to be settled policy, early movement of the Tenth Air Force to China. In the course of the conference Wedemeyer remarked that since no U.S. divisions would be available for operations in China, Chinese troops would have to open a seaport. General Stratemeyer's chief of staff, Brig.

---

[19] Testimony, Col David A. Craig, Tab 8 of Memo cited n. 18.
[20] Maintenance factors for Chinese units are given on page 75 of the Plan BETA. OCMH.
[21] (1) Plan BETA, p. 35. OCMH. (2) Folder: Supply, China Theater—1945. By Service Forces for Air and Ground Forces. OCMH. Table, "Cost of Distributing Hump Tonnage in China." The Johnson manuscript states that CCC and SOS greatly underestimated their needs.
[22] Min, CT Conf, 26 Mar 45. OCMH.

Gen. Charles B. Stone, III, continuing the discussion, said that supply tonnage would be available to move the Tenth Air Force to China. On its arrival, the Tenth would become the tactical air force of the theater, while the Fourteenth, with the mission of interdicting Japanese lines of communications to southeast China, would be the strategic. General Stone added that Marshall and Arnold had approved bringing the Tenth to China. When Wedemeyer and his party returned to China, China Theater headquarters sent IBT its suggested schedule for transferring the Tenth.[23]

On his return, Wedemeyer had another task to perform, that of telling Chennault that the Fourteenth Air Force would be subordinate to another air headquarters, and that Stratemeyer would become the senior air officer in China. Chennault was not pleased by the prospect. On other occasions during this period he argued that moving the Tenth to China would not actually increase U.S. combat strength, because the Fourteenth was not receiving enough supplies to operate at capacity. The Fourteenth Air Force minutes of the 19 April conference between the two men record:

General Chennault stated that BETA Plan was dependent on gas and that SOS had completely fallen down on delivery of aviation supplies. General Wedemeyer said, "In fairness to Cheves, don't say that,"—"logistic supplies have made a difference; the Chinese are making inroads into these. If I had 30 or 50 well-equipped divisions in this Theater, I could go places. So far the effort has not been concentrated."

Gen. Chennault asked—"Do you supply these people?" [Chinese]

Gen. Wedemeyer stated that he wanted to cannibalize certain divisions and organize labor battalions under semi-military control.

Gen Chennault stated, "To illustrate what we mean about the tonnage deliveries—last year we received 6,500 tons; this year the figure is 1,000 over the Kweiyang highway by truck."

Gen. Wedemeyer stated [to Col. Caughey] "Make a note of that."—"We apparently haven't improved the situation in China at all. The figures should be just the opposite."

*   *   *   *   *   *   *

Gen. Chennault then summarized all the foregoing discussions in the statement that we have enough airplanes to do the job in mind but have not been able to operate them due to logistical status.

Gen. Wedemeyer stated that if Gen. Chennault were theater commander he would do the same as he is doing. Had no ground forces worthy of the name when I arrived and the ground effort is now nil, but I have got to increase it.

Gen. Chennault stated he was not questioning the above, but merely pointing out that we have enough air units in China now and that logistic matters will be even worse with additional units.

Gen. Wedemeyer stated we will have to move them in to prevent their going South.[24]

*   *   *   *   *   *   *

[23] (1) Johnson MS. (2) See Chapter IX, above, on the timing of the Tenth's move and the Burma campaign.

[24] Ltr with Incl, Col Fred C. Milner, AG Hq Fourteenth AF, to Wedemeyer, 28 Apr 45, sub: Transmittal of "Notes on Conference." AG 337 Misc, Folder, Meetings from 1944 to 30 Aug 45, Box BA 51513, KCRC.

MAJ. GEN. HOWARD C. DAVIDSON, *Commanding General, Tenth Air Force.*

In another interview with Wedemeyer, Chennault said that he would stay in China as long as his health permitted. Chennault commented freely on his long feud with Stilwell, and told Wedemeyer of his having corresponded directly with Roosevelt. But he assured Wedemeyer that he had no intention of circumventing Stilwell or the War Department.[25]

Then a misunderstanding over the commitments made at Washington began to appear, with an announcement of 25 April from Washington that because of the redeployment program from the European theater there would be no great influx of C–54's. The ATC would, however, be able to deliver to China at Kunming 49,400 tons in May, 50,400 in June, 51,400 in July, and 53,400 in August (so-called "short-haul" tonnage). Ten thousand tons more would be flown in from Myitkyina. This approximated previous estimates. On 1 May Wedemeyer issued a general order naming Stratemeyer as

---

[25] (1) Min, Conf at Fourteenth AF Hq, 19 Apr 45. OCMH. (2) Ltr, Wedemeyer to Marshall, 13 Apr 45. Case 45, OPD 319.1 Sec I.

Commanding General, Army Air Forces, China Theater, with the Tenth and Fourteenth as subordinate forces.[26]

But when Sultan's and Stratemeyer's staffs had time to study the 25 April message from the War Department, they concluded that it implied China Theater would receive 25,000 tons a month less than was now known to be needed.[27]

Seeking to adjust his organizational plans to the lesser amount of support available, Wedemeyer asked Stratemeyer if he would be willing to come to China as commander of a smaller air force, with Chennault at Cheng-tu having a strategic mission and General Davidson of the Tenth at Lu-liang, a city east of Kunming, with a tactical mission. Wedemeyer explained that there appeared to be no alternative and that "I personally am interested in obtaining the service of officers like you and Davidson whom I know in my heart and mind would be loyal members of our team. I can not be confident of team play under any other possible arrangement."[28] Stratemeyer declined. Since in Wedemeyer's opinion the War Department had not implemented the ATC plan to the extent promised, his hands were tied. Stratemeyer did not think Wedemeyer would want him to step down to a command so small as the one contemplated. Instead, he suggested that what he called "the three old men," Chennault, Stratemeyer, and Davidson, all be sent back to the United States. However, if after noting Stratemeyer's views Wedemeyer wanted him, Stratemeyer would gladly go to China.[29]

Thus matters stood when Wedemeyer held a staff conference 7 May to study the question of moving the Tenth Air Force to China. He was aware that the whole of the Tenth could not go to China, but was still interested in bringing in Stratemeyer to command there.[30] Representatives of the Fourteenth Air Force attended the meeting. After the war Chennault believed that they had demonstrated that moving the Tenth to China would actually reduce the air effort through that air force's demands on Hump tonnage. Apparently, Wedemeyer accepted their arguments, for he decided that the Tenth as such could not be moved to China. He contemplated a rather elaborate air command structure, with Headquarters, AAF, China Theater, in Chungking next to his headquarters, a tactical air headquarters in the field adjacent to the tactical headquarters directing the drive to the coast, and a strategic headquarters at Cheng-tu. For the present, he reserved decision as

[26] (1) CM–OUT 72735, Marshall to Wedemeyer, 25 Apr 45. (2) GO 59, Hq USFCT, 1 May 45.

[27] (1) Rad CFB 37059, Wedemeyer to Sultan, 9 May 45. (2) For example, in March, 89,000 tons were bid for July, but the 25 April radio indicated only 61,400 would be received.

[28] Rad CFB 36860, Wedemeyer to Stratemeyer (prepared by Wedemeyer personally), 5 May 45. Item 647, Bks 3 and 4, ACW Personal File.

[29] Rad CAB 5754, ACG, Stratemeyer to Wedemeyer, 6 May 45. Bks 3 and 4, ACW Personal File.

[30] Item 833. Bks 3 and 4, ACW Personal File.

to the identity of the senior air officer in China. To the War Department, he reported 11 May that China Theater's plans to augment its air strength were being restudied. He also observed that the Japanese drive on Chih-chiang had been stemmed only at heavy cost in Hump tonnage. This fact had further affected plans to open a seacoast port, so that it was necessary to restudy these plans as well. Wedemeyer then told Stratemeyer he had advised the War Department that the Tenth Air Force could not be absorbed in China for several months. Chennault was told that he would be the commander of the augmented China-based air forces after the Tenth arrived, and he and his staff began planning for the change.[31]

The developments and realizations described above registered their impact on the theater command. On 12 May Brig. Gen. Douglas L. Weart, commanding Rear Echelon headquarters, stated that General Wedemeyer did not want his officers to discuss the merits of theater plans with officers from out-side China Theater. The BETA plan (RASHNESS) might be beyond China Theater's present capabilities, Weart continued, but it did offer an approach toward the co-ordination of existing capabilities, and should be supported. Changes would be made as conditions developed. China Theater headquarters also decided that it would have to set 60,000 as the personnel ceiling for the year 1945—presumably till a seaport was somehow opened.[32]

The program for equipping Chinese divisions to take part in RASHNESS was affected by these influences. Though General McClure of the Chinese Combat Command could not agree with Wedemeyer's fears that Chinese divisions which had no place in RASHNESS were currently being equipped from U.S. stocks, he admitted that he found the equipment problem a puzzling one. As he put it: "Actually, Al, I have never known how many divisions could be equipped during 1945 or 1946, nor when any promised equipment would arrive in China. I do not know at present and there is no one I have met yet in the theater who can tell me. How in the Sam Hill can any of us plan on anything definite with such an indefinite L of C?" [33]

SOS Problems and China Operations

General Cheves, the SOS commander in China, faced a dilemma, that of coping with the transport problem without burdening the theater's resources. He was very much concerned with the transportation problem, to one phase

---

[31] (1) Chennault, *Way of a Fighter*, pp. 348–49. (2) Memo for Record, Gen Gross, Actg CofS, 8 May 45. AG 337, Folder, Conferences, Meetings, Etc. 1944–1945, Box BA 51513, KCRC. (3) Ltr, Wedemeyer to Marshall, 11 May 45. TS Reg 06106–M, DRB AGO. (4) Johnson MS.

[32] Min, Comdr's Mtgs, China Theater Hq, 12, 8 May 45. OCMH.

[33] Rad CFY 15688, McClure to Wedemeyer, info Weart, 5 May 45. Item 660, Bks 3 and 4, ACW Personal File

of which McClure alluded, and wrote on 20 March that transportation was and would continue to be his "bottleneck and headache." To solve the problem, to give the CCC the barest minimum of support, required men to drive and maintain the trucks, and to store and disburse supplies. Here General Cheves came up against his dilemma, for every man brought into China was a further drain on supplies, yet the SOS could hardly operate without more men. The shortage of spare parts, the shortage of trucks, the fact that soldiers cannot be made qualified truck drivers by an order, the primitive nature of the Chinese road net, all were further complications. So a week later Cheves told Stratemeyer, "I am accomplishing very little in the field." He had plans and money in abundance, but there was a sheer lack of men to do the SOS work, and so much of what he hoped to do had to stay on paper. Writing to an officer about to begin work with the Chinese SOS, Cheves observed: "I cannot give you any specific directive. All I can do is put you in the area, turn you loose, and tell you to see to it that the Chinese soldier gets a break in food, ammunition, and clothing and do not let technicalities stop you." [34]

Cheves attacked the transport problem in several of its aspects. Though the supply trucks were arriving steadily over the Stilwell Road, they were still relatively few, fewer even than drivers. So Cheves set up what he called the "block system." Under it, trucks were driven and maintained by men assigned to a section of the LOC, rather than to any one vehicle, and would, so Cheves hoped, operate for fifteen to twenty hours of the twenty-four. By 27 March the general staff sections of SOS began to feel that the block system was proving itself on those roads where it had been set up. [35]

The condition of the roads was disturbing. Even the best and newest of Detroit's products developed maintenance problems on China's washboard roads, while drivers grew tired and suffered various ailments. Roads and road repairs were under the Chinese Ministry of Communications. To approach its problem coherently, SOS concluded that it should assist the Chinese to repair those roads necessary to support the thirty-six-division program. This meant aiding the Chinese with U.S. earth-moving equipment and operators. The next difficulty lay in obtaining funds for the Ministry of Communications from the Chinese treasury, and then in persuading the Ministry to spend the money on projects not of its own devising. General Ho Ying-chin's field headquarters wanted General Cheves, as in effect commander of the Chinese SOS, to take over the whole project. Ho's chief of staff, General Hsiao I-hsu, thought the Ministry was reluctant to yield up such sizable sums and perhaps with it control of important public works. Untangling these prob-

---

[34] Ltr, Cheves to Brig Gen Edward C. Rose, 20 May 45; Ltr, Cheves to Stratemeyer, 27 Mar 45; Ltr, Cheves to CO American Sec, Chinese SOS, Kweiyang. AG 201 (SOS–Cheves), KCRC.
[35] Min, SOS Gen Staff Conf, 27 Mar 45. SOS USFCT Files, KCRC.

lems of administration and bureaucratic rivalry took time and during it the roads went unrepaired.[36]

In mid-April, Cheves observed that it was necessary to keep after the Chinese agencies. For the American part, he had not been able to bring in more than a negligible amount of heavy equipment, and on the matter of bridge material he was just beginning to get some encouragement.

The problem of finding adequate numbers of qualified service personnel was increased by the reluctance of the Chinese Government to permit Negro troops to move freely about China. Initially, the Chinese hesitated to admit Negro troops at all. General Wedemeyer protested, saying that a hard and fast rule would interfere with the war effort. Many of the American service troops in India were Negro, and would be needed in China as the war effort moved eastward. The Generalissimo then agreed that Negroes might enter China as far as Kunming. The Chinese leader felt that his people might be excited by the sudden arrival of the Negro troops, that they were just now becoming accustomed to the presence of white people.

By early February the Generalissimo was willing to let Negro troops go east of Kunming if required, but shared with Wedemeyer the understanding that they would be admitted to China in small numbers. Plainly, Cheves had to weigh more than administrative efficiency in deciding what units to requisition from India–Burma.[37]

On the question of obtaining drivers, the picture was beginning to brighten by mid-April. Discussions about starting a driver's school for the Chinese had been under way since the preceding November. Now, it was agreed that SOS would be responsible. Since the block system required numbers of drivers to make it work, recruitment was a vital point, but Cheves feared it was not appreciated by the Chinese, nor, he hinted, by Wedemeyer's headquarters. Surveying the whole of the SOS field, so profoundly affected by transportation problems, he felt that the SOS was not meeting Wedemeyer's requirements. To this view, Wedemeyer himself now inclined.[38]

Help that India–Burma Theater might give Cheves was rigidly limited by the slowly growing capacity of the line of communications to China. As early as 3 April, General Somervell of Army Service Forces doubted that India-Burma Theater could support China's projected operations. China Theater had, as noted above, decided to recommend suspension of the six-inch pipeline project in order to release personnel for service in China.[39]

---

[36] Min, Combined Staff (CCC and Chinese Supreme Hq) Mtg, 21 Feb 45. China Theater Files, KCRC.

[37] History of IBT, II, 283–84. (2) Min, Mtg 25, Wedemeyer with Generalissimo, 31 Dec 44; Mtg 38, 7 Feb 45. Bk 1, Generalissimo Minutes.

[38] (1) Ltr, Cheves to Wedemeyer, 17 Apr 45, sub: Opns of Chinese and American SOS's. OCMH. (2) Ltr, Wedemeyer to Marshall, 13 Apr 45. Case 45, OPD 319.1, Sec I.

[39] See Ch. VII, above.

This decision troubled Somervell, who thought the estimates of what might be flown in to China far too comprehensive. So he called the matter to the attention of India–Burma's deputy theater commander, General Merrill, who had accompanied Wedemeyer to Washington. Merrill replied that India–Burma felt it should not question Wedemeyer's decisions once their implications had been explained to him. Somervell said the answer puzzled him, and went on to add that he thought the air estimates were too large, and that if the road and pipeline projects were not continued at something near their original levels, then the projected campaign in China might suffer. Merrill replied there would be enough troops in India–Burma to maintain and operate the Stilwell Road and the four-inch pipeline. This did not satisfy Somervell: "You leave me with the gravest doubt that you will be able to support Wedemeyer's operations. Are you confident of your ability to do so?" Support of Wedemeyer depended on the ATC's doing as well as promised, Merrill thought, and if the ATC did, with the road and the pipeline, he could do the job.[40]

With the SOS in China finding its operations so hampered by the shortage of transport facilities, and with tight limitations on the number of Americans who could be brought to China for SOS work, it was plain that SOS in China could not of its own resources improvise anything to aid RASHNESS. And India–Burma Theater, through Merrill, made it plain that cutting back the road and pipeline in accord with the decision to concentrate on building up the Hump left it to the ATC to support the drive to take a seaport. That prospect seemed dim indeed in early May. Apparently China Theater could proceed with equipping the thirty-six divisions. The performance at Chihchiang showed that Chinese troops could stop anything short of a really major Japanese effort, but if China Theater was to advance beyond the planning stage and take the initiative, a major new development was needed.

The Japanese Save RASHNESS

In appraising RASHNESS for the JCS, the Joint War Plans Committee had ventured the opinion that by late summer or early fall of 1945 the Japanese might feel such pressure on Japan proper as to begin moving troops out of south China toward more vital areas in the north. This had been one of the suggested reasons for JCS approval of RASHNESS, so from the point of view of Washington, planning for RASHNESS had some of the aspects of a worthwhile speculation on anticipated Japanese weakness.

After the failure of the *SHO* Operation for a complex and powerful counteroffensive on the American drive into the western Pacific,[41] *Imperial General*

---

[40] Rad CRA 10316, Merrill to Sultan, info Wedemeyer, 3 Apr 45. Item 641, Bks 3 and 4, ACW Personal File.

[41] See Ch. II, above.

Headquarters in Tokyo during December and January had to plan a troop deployment for anticipated American exploitation of success in the Philippines. Surveying the Asiatic and Pacific theaters, *Imperial General Headquarters* feared it had to counter Soviet and U.S. thrusts into north China by land and sea, respectively; U.S. amphibious attacks on islands near Japan, such as Okinawa; U.S. amphibious attacks on south China; and even amphibious assaults on Japan itself. There seems to have been no thought among the Japanese leadership of retiring to some citadel area on the mainland of Asia and there fighting it out. Japan was their home. They would die there in defense of what they held sacred. They did not contemplate fleeing from their remembered shrines and pine-clad hills to die on the Manchurian plains. So the Japanese staff shaped all their deployments to guard Japan, in the hope that at last the Americans might tire of the war. If they reinforced north China, it would be to hold staging areas from which Japan might be attacked and factories and mines which could still arm the Japanese soldier.

Differences in point of view and responsibility produce very different outlooks, and Okamura's headquarters in China, *China Expeditionary Forces,* took a much less grave view of the situation during December and January, 1944–45. He and his staff wished to make a major effort to take Kweichow Province, whence roads branched to Kunming and Chungking, and to end the war in China. They were overruled. Higher authority in Tokyo believed that the Chinese saw victory inclining to the Allies, that they saw the end of the war approaching, and so Okamura's superiors did not think that even taking Kunming and Chungking would persuade the Generalissimo's government to make a separate peace. Instead of driving into the interior of China, Okamura was ordered on 25 January to turn his attention to the seacoast and to north China. These orders were an interim solution, and planning was still in progress.

Whatever the outcome of the planning might be, it would require troops, and *Imperial General Headquarters* set in train an ambitious mobilization that would strengthen the forces with which Wedemeyer would ultimately have to deal if he carried his campaigns to central China. To meet the feared invasion of Japan, *Imperial General Headquarters* activated sixteen coastal divisions in April, and eight fully mobile field divisions in May. To equip these forces, approximately one third of all the Japanese ammunition in Manchuria, about 30,000 tons, was sent to Japan. The Japanese thought this would supply thirteen divisions for three months. With it went as much of railroad matériel, bridging matériel, foodstuffs, and antitank munitions as the strained railroads and ferries could transport.

Okamura was to receive major reinforcements, and did in fact have his numerical strength increased 25 percent. *Imperial General Headquarters* wanted to secure air bases in China, maintain order in north China, defend southeast

China, and prepare a reserve for the Manchurian front.   So the Japanese set about increasing Okamura's force to 20 fully equipped divisions for operational duty; 20 more lightly equipped divisions for occupation duty; 6 more divisions for what was called guard duty; 17 independent mixed brigades; and 50 battalions to guard the railways.   This was no mere paper program; by April 1945 Okamura received 230,000 men.   From them he obtained a net gain of 1 division, 11 independent mixed brigades, and 13 independent guard units.   Save for 4,000 troops from Manchuria, and 12,500 reservists mobilized in China, these men came from Japan.   Thanks to them, by summer 1945 Okamura had 1,050,000 men south of the Great Wall, though their training, equipment, and supplies were not up to past standards.

Manchuria was the area whose resources seem to have made possible the Japanese deployments of 1944 to meet the American advance through the Pacific and of 1945 to defend the homeland and north China.   On the map Japanese-occupied Manchuria was an exposed salient jutting into Soviet-held territory.   Salients are hard to defend and the Japanese did not intend to try to defend this one.   They intended only to hold a line across its base.   So elite divisions came out of Manchuria to fight in the Pacific, and with them came supplies, plus cadres to activate new divisions.   In January 1943 the Japanese had 14 divisions in Manchuria.   Two years later, 10 divisions plus 50,000 men in smaller units had been shipped out.   Only 7 had been assigned to replace them, leaving a total of 6 well-trained divisions and 5 inferior ones.   Manchuria-wide mobilization began in February 1945.   To fill the gap left by loss of the good units and to create an appearance of strength, 8 divisions (*121st* to *128th*) were activated, whose cadres came from the *3d Cavalry Brigade* and border garrison units.   These were inferior units, to be regarded as part of a cover plan rather than as fighting strength.

On 19 February 1945 the U.S. Marines landed on Iwo Jima, a volcanic outcropping midway between the Mariana Islands and Tokyo.   Fighting was bitter, and at a pace which insured it would not be prolonged.   By 8 March U.S. fighter aircraft were operating off Iwo, and an alarmed *Imperial General Headquarters* issued orders 15 March recalling the 4 best divisions left in Manchuria to the homeland.   With them across the Korean straits came 3 new divisions and 6 tank brigades.

The American landing on Okinawa 1 April was another grave blow to the Japanese, for its loss would give the Americans staging areas close to Japan itself.   The beginning of operations on Okinawa coincided with the completion of *Imperial General Headquarters'* studies of a deployment to meet the grave danger to Japan.

The plan to defend Japan was called *KETSU*.   It embraced operations in both Japan and Asia.   To find the troops for *KETSU*, and to place the troops in Asia in position for their share in *KETSU*, the Japanese decided to shorten their lines in China and mass their troops, some around Hankow and Shang-hai in central China, and the rest in a great rectangle across north China, south Manchuria, and north Korea. The effects of this decision began to appear on 8 April in orders from Tokyo that sketched *KETSU* for the benefit of the field commands. At this same time, but coincidentally, a new pre-mier, Admiral Baron Kantaro Suzuki, took office. He and his cabinet repre-sented elements who wanted to make peace.

On the 14th *Imperial General Headquarters* sent a warning order to Oka-mura that four of his best divisions were to be moved to central and north China. Tokyo had earlier intimated willingness to evacuate Hunan Province, the great area where stood the contested cities of Changsha, Heng-yang, and Chihchiang. For its part, *China Expeditionary Army* did not want to give up Canton, Hankow, or the rail line between them, so in accord with Tokyo's and its own views, it prepared to take its troops off the Hunan–Kwangsi railroad. This line ran through Heng-Yang, Kweilin, Liuchow, and Nan-ning, and a branch forked off to Kweiyang. These were the cities of the east China airfields. In order that north China might be reinforced, the Japanese were willing to yield them. On 20 May the Japanese began to withdraw from Ho-chih, their garrison farthest west on the branch line to Kweiyang. On the 26th they evacuated Nanning, and thus broke land communications with Indochina. Deployment for *KETSU* was under way.[42]

As they assembled for *KETSU*, Japanese were harassed by OSS teams operating behind their lines. The Japanese were spread very thin over China, in a deployment very like that of an army of occupation, and there were many opportunities for guerrilla action. The OSS had five teams on or near the east-west truck railroad from Hsian to the coast. Four more teams operated near the rail line from Nanning to Heng-yang. A third group harried the Japanese engaged in the Chihchiang operation, and the remainder were near the coast. These teams guided U.S. aircraft to profitable targets, gathered intelligence, and reported that they blew up Japanese trains, shot individual Japanese, attacked small parties of Japanese, blew up warehouses and supply dumps, and sought generally to distract and gather information on the Japa-nese. That they exercised any influence on the course of events in China is not apparent from the Japanese studies; however the effort was still on a very modest scale, and the OSS was steadily gathering and training fairly large guerrilla forces behind the Japanese lines.[43]

The cities the Japanese now were yielding had been the targets of RASHNESS Phase I. To accomplish that phase, all the Chinese had to do was to follow

---

[42] (1) Japanese Study 45, pp. 160, 166–80, 183–94, 190–91, Chart 11, p. 197, 226–27, 231, 233–34. (2) Japanese Study 129, pp. 132, 133, 161, Chart 5, p. 81, 84, 82–86. (3) Ltr, Col Preston J. C. Murphy, FECOM Hist Sec, to Gen Ward, 18 Nov 52. OCMH. (4) Japanese Officers' comments on draft MS.

[43] OSS Weekly Opnl Rpts, AG (OSS) 322 Bk 1. TS Reg 06108–3–J, DRB AGO.

behind the Japanese. Any pressure they might apply would be all to the good. The implications of the Japanese withdrawal registered at once in Wedemeyer's headquarters, and a reaction was not delayed.

The Drive to the Sea Moves Off Dead Center

The War Department's announcement that ATC augmentation would not take place as rapidly as Wedemeyer had expected and the accumulating difficulties of supply and transport within China created a brief period, only a few days, when the drive to the sea hung on dead center. Then came the electrifying news that the Japanese were withdrawing. Wedemeyer appreciated the new situation, and wrote General Marshall in early June: "The recent Japanese withdrawals from the Nanning–Liuchow–Kweilin corridor, our occupation of Nanning and the anticipated capture of Liuchow and Kweilin has virtually eliminated Phase I of CARBONADO [new code name for the offensive]. As a result a revision of our plans has been directed to permit the early occupation, seizure, and development of the Nanning–Liuchow–Kweilin area as a base for an assault during the last quarter of 1945 against the Canton–Hong Kong area." [44]

As part of the Chinese Combat Command organization project of February 1945, the Central and Kwangsi Commands had been created opposite the area the Japanese were now evacuating. The Central Command included the Kweiyang area; the Chinese 94th Army from that command had distinguished itself in the Chihchiang campaign. The Kwangsi Command included that great province, and in it lay Ho-chih, Nanning, and Kweilin. The Central Command troops were under General Tang En-po's III Army Group Command, assisted by Brig. Gen. Frederic W. Boye. General Tang's forces included the 26th, 29th, 20th, 13th, and 71st Armies, totaling ten divisions. The II Army Group Command, General Chang Fa-kwei, included the 46th, 62d, 64th, and New 1st Armies, totaling eleven divisions. General Chang was assisted by Brig. Gen. Harwood C. Bowman. Of these twenty-one divisions, only those of the New 1st Army were ALPHA or U.S.-sponsored divisions. However, Generals Chang and Tang had co-operated in carrying out a considerable reorganization of their forces. Facing them were the Japanese *3d* and *58th Divisions*, and the *22d* and *88th Independent Mixed Brigades*.[45]

The food and medical situation had improved since February. General Chang had consolidated what had been six armies into three, launched a training program, and begun a systematic rebuilding of his forces.[46]

---

[44] Ltr, Wedemeyer to Marshall, with Incl, 13 Jun 45, sub: Activities and Developments, CT, May 45. TS Reg 06105-M, DRB AGO.

[45] (1) Japanese Study 129, map facing p. 86. (2) History of Chinese Combat Command, p. 11. OCMH.

[46] History, II Army Group Command, CCC (Prov), Apr–Jun 45. OCMH. (Hereafter, History, II Army Group Command.)

GENERAL TANG EN-PO, *Commander, III Army Group, China (center), and Brig. Gen. Frederic W. Boye (waving), former Commanding General, Central Command, Chinese Combat Command, drive along the Nanking Road in Shanghai. (Photograph taken 7 September 1945.)*

The original mission given Chang's troops under RASHNESS had been that of diversionary attacks. Preparations to that end were being carried on, but the armies themselves were still weak. The only offensive activity was that of a so-called Commando Battalion, which during April and May raided the hundred miles of Japanese-held road from Nanning to Chen-nan-kuan (Nam Quan) on the Indochinese border. The Chinese were not thought capable of moving across the road in force.

These Chinese "commandos" should not be confused with the rigidly trained, superbly equipped elite British units of the same name; rather they were Nationalist partisan detachments which had been given adequate food, training, and medical care, then assigned a mission within their capabilities. It was a long time since organized Chinese troops had shown the flag in that area; the Chinese civilians soon began bringing their surplus produce to the Chinese lines rather than the Japanese.[47]

In mid-May reports began to reach the Chinese that the Japanese were

[47] Bowman comments on draft MS.

contemplating withdrawal, and Chang began to redeploy so as to follow any evacuation. Over 19 and 20 May reports came that the Japanese were destroying the public utilities of Nanning. On 26 May the Chinese drove the small Japanese rear guard from Nanning. Bowman personally visited Nanning "to verify the capture," for the air forces had been skeptical. There were sixteen dead Japanese, and many Chinese casualties. There could be no further skepticism about the withdrawal.[48]

Theater headquarters at once began staff studies on how to exploit the Japanese move. Making a rapid advance to the Luichow Peninsula in order to gain access to the sea began to seem one possibility; with the U.S. forces now established in the Philippines, supplies could quickly be brought to the China coast from Manila. Wedemeyer requested the Generalissimo to order the local Chinese commanders to (1) keep close watch on all Japanese movements in the Canton–Hankow corridor, (2) keep pressure on the Japanese but avoid committing any large numbers of Chinese troops, (3) hold armies not in contact for reserves as the situation clarified, (4) continue to build up supplies for use by air and ground forces in forward areas, and (5) coordinate limited ground operations with U.S. air support. He wanted to avoid premature and large-scale commitment of forces that might be used in a drive for a seaport. That the Japanese would probably soon evacuate the Kweilin-Liuchow area offered help toward solution of the logistical problem of supporting the offensive, for supplies could be flown directly from India to east China and then distributed locally.

General Wedemeyer's revision of RASHNESS, called CARBONADO, was drawn up early in June. In preparing to take advantage of the Japanese concession of the objectives of what had been Phase I, the planners sought to change the existing plan as little as possible. The significant addition was giving a major role to the Kwangsi Command and Chang Fa-Kwei's troops. Where formerly these had been limited to diversionary attacks, now before CARBONADO was launched they were to seize the small seaport of Fort Bayard on the Luichow Peninsula about 250 miles southwest of Canton. Fort Bayard would then be a forward supply base to sustain CARBONADO.

CARBONADO itself now called for an attack on 1 September from the Kweilin–Liuchow area toward Canton, to take suitable forward concentration areas. From these the final assault would begin on 1 November. On 15 July there was to be a diversionary attack into French Indochina, to keep the Japanese too occupied for them to consider harassing the Kunming–Nanning line of communications. The air forces were to concentrate in the earlier phases on cutting Japanese communications, then switch to tactical support. The Philippine-based Far East Air Force would be asked to undertake strategic bombing of Chinese targets.

[48] (1) History, II Army Group Command.   (2) Bowman comments on draft MS.

In Wedemeyer's opinion, the biggest barrier to carrying out CARBONADO on schedule was the need to accumulate supplies in the forward area. Air transport would be relied on heavily. The fields around Liuchow were to be developed, together with one halfway between Liuchow and Canton, known as Tanchuk (Tan-chu). Supplies were to be flown direct from India–Burma to these fields, which were to be used for logistical support. Kweilin was to be reserved for combat. Roads to the forward area were to be repaired and their capacity increased.[49] These engineering projects would be a heavy burden on the Chinese SOS and governmental agencies.

New Commanders for CARBONADO

Execution of CARBONADO would be the task of new commanders and staffs, both air and ground. The most significant immediate change was that in the command of the Fourteenth Air Force. In his messages to the War Department after word was received that augmentation of the Hump airlift would be postponed Wedemeyer had pointed out that deployment of the Tenth Air Force to China would also be delayed. Apparently, he thought that this by implication covered the question of Stratemeyer's going to China. But the War Department did not take it so. On 16 May Wedemeyer was told by Lt. Gen. Ira C. Eaker, of AAF headquarters, that Chennault would be replaced in any event. A letter to Wedemeyer from General Hull of OPD suggested that there had been a basic misunderstanding when Wedemeyer and his party left Washington about the Hump airlift that was to be established. While Hull conceded that the War Department had not been able to meet the schedule of C–54 aircraft that Wedemeyer had presented, he did not believe that there had been any failure to meet any commitment made during Wedemeyer's visit. Since redeployment would not permit the C–54's to come to India, the War Department had agreed that the AAF in China should set its requirements in terms of tonnage delivered. rather than in numbers of aircraft assigned to the Hump. Hull also remarked that unless the Tenth Air Force could be supported in China a major part of it would have to be returned to the United States. Nothing was said about Stratemeyer, but since Hull believed the War Department was meeting all of its commitments to China Theater he may have felt that headquarters should proceed with the reorganization Wedemeyer had presented in Washington and to which the commitments were related.

These letters were exchanged against the backdrop of tremendous events elsewhere. On 12 April 1945 Franklin D. Roosevelt died, and was suceeded by the Vice President, Harry S. Truman. President Roosevelt had taken a keen personal interest in the conduct of American affairs in China, and had

---

[49] History of China Theater, Ch. IX, pp. 21–23.

kept many of the threads in his own hand.   From 1942 to the fall of 1944, he had sent several special emissaries to China, and kept in touch with the Generalissimo and his entourage through many informal channels.   Roosevelt had also been firm in his support of General Chennault in the disputes over strategy in China.[50]

About three weeks after Roosevelt's death the war ended in Europe.   The German chancellor, Adolf Hitler, died in the ruins of his shattered capital as the Russians took Berlin.   The German armed forces surrendered at Reims on 7 May.   The end of the fighting in Europe produced administrative and logistical problems as complex as those that followed on Pearl Harbor, though of a more agreeable nature.   With plans and orders succeeding one another in rapid fashion, it is not strange that the AAF plans should also have been in a state of flux, so that on 22 May Stratemeyer's headquarters heard that C-54's were on their way to India after all.   However, the letters from Washington with their indications, clear in retrospect, that the War Department believed reorganization of the China air force would proceed and the news of the impending move to India of the C-54's did not bring any reaction from China Theater headquarters.

Then came clear indication that higher authority in Washington wanted Stratemeyer to command the air force in China, for on 8 June General Marshall asked why the reorganization had not been carried through.

A detailed explanation was prepared by General Wedemeyer and held for several days in his files in case Marshall should want a fuller explanation than the brief one Wedemeyer sent him.   In it, Wedemeyer analyzed the Hump tonnage problem, then said his radios of May had not specifically referred to Stratemeyer because he still hoped to bring him to China.   He had wanted to discuss this arrangement with Arnold.   However, this had not been possible so he had decided to make Chennault Commanding General, China Air Force, and had so advised General Hull.   Wedemeyer's present relation to Chennault "rendered it difficult" summarily to relieve him, and replace him with Stratemeyer.   He therefore had to keep as his air officer a man who did not have Marshall's or Arnold's confidence (and the text of the detailed explanation showed that Wedemeyer briefly contemplated saying he himself agreed with Marshall and Arnold).   The explanation closed by saying that while it would be preferable to replace Chennault with Stratemeyer or someone else the impetus for that move had to come from Washington.

A week later, when Arnold was in Manila, he summoned Stratemeyer to confer with him.   At the conference, Arnold made it plain that he wanted

[50] (1) The Hopkins Papers in the Roosevelt Memorial Library, Hyde Park, N. Y., contain many interesting details of the President's interventions in military matters in China.   (2) *Stilwell's Mission to China*, Ch. IX.

THE GENERALISSIMO HONORS GENERAL CHENNAULT. *The retiring commander of the Fourteenth Air Force is guest of honor at a banquet given by Chiang Kai-shek. Facing forward, from left: Ambassador Hurley, the Generalissimo, General Chennault, Mr. Wing Shih-chih, and Mr. Ellis O. Briggs. General Wedemeyer is in profile at extreme right. General Chennault is wearing the medal presented by Chiang Kai-shek.*

Stratemeyer to command in China, that Stratemeyer had been promoted to lieutenant general for that purpose. Returning to China, Stratemeyer brought with him a letter from Arnold that suggested that Chennault be soon retired from the Air Forces, that the Tenth Air Force be brought to China, and that the Tenth and Fourteenth Air Forces be put under Stratemeyer. In compliance Wedemeyer replied that he was setting up such a structure, with Chennault as Commanding General, Fourteenth Air Force. About two months later Chennault retired. Headquarters, Tenth Air Force, opened at Kunming 23 July.[51]

By delaying immediate compliance with Arnold's letter, Wedemeyer let Chennault complete eight full years of duty in China, five with the Chinese Air Force and three with the American. In appreciation of his efforts for China, the Generalissimo presented him with the Order of the White Sun and Blue Sky, China's highest honor. His own government, on Wedemeyer's recommendation, gave him a second Oak Leaf Cluster to the Dis-

---

[51] (1) *The Army Air Forces in World War II,* V, 269–72. (2) Chennault, *Way of a Fighter,* pp. 345–52. (3) Wedemeyer's explanation is in Item 833, Bks 3 and 4, ACW Personal File. (4) Ltr, Hull to Wedemeyer, 15 May 45. By some quirk of the filing system this is in AG 014, Civil Affairs, TS Reg 06108–D, DRB AGO.

tinguished Service Cross. In leaving China, Chennault felt "anger and disappointment" because he had not been able to participate in the final victory, a victory to which he and his airmen had contributed in great measure with very small resources. If he could not complete his plans, in this he shared the frustration China inflicted on all the Americans in high command there, including both Stilwell and Wedemeyer. After the war a Japanese military historian concluded that until summer 1945 the Fourteenth Air Force had been the principal obstacle to Japanese operations in and troop movements from China.[52]

The conduct of ground operations was entrusted on 1 July to a newly activated Tactical Headquarters, and the former Rear Echelon at Kunming was scheduled for inactivation. The concept of a rear echelon headquarters had been criticized in the past on the ground that its activities duplicated those of Headquarters, SOS.

As originally conceived in April and May 1945, Tactical Headquarters was to be a forward command post of the theater commander, essentially an extension of theater headquarters. Thus, when General Wedemeyer took the field he would operate from Tactical Headquarters. So the deputy theater commander, Maj. Gen. Douglas L. Weart, had been made ex officio commander of Tactical Headquarters with the mission of co-ordinating the tactical plan and administrative operations of the SOS, the Chinese Combat Command, the Chinese Training Command, and the air forces. By 1 July, when Weart's headquarters opened, the basic concept had changed and Tactical Headquarters had become the headquarters of the China Theater's forces in the field. Weart and his staff were seen by the China Theater staff as a separate headquarters receiving orders from Headquarters, China Theater, through command channels, rather than as a part of theater headquarters which had moved forward.[53]

The relationship between the Chinese and American headquarters staffs took a long step forward in July. As originally conceived, when Wedemeyer began his work, the relationship was like that in the Anglo-American Combined Chiefs of Staff in that representatives of the two staffs met to form a conference, rather than an integrated staff. By 22 June the two staffs were ready to tell Wedemeyer: "It was concluded that the only desirable features of the [Combined] staff at the present time were the presentation of the

---

[52] (1) Chennault, *Way of a Fighter,* p. 355. (2) Col. Susumu Nishiura, in Japanese Officers' comments on draft MS.

[53] Compare the statement of China Theater's chief of staff, Maj. Gen. Ray Maddocks, who "reviewed the remarks of the various chiefs of section and stated that, although the original concept was to have the Tactical Headquarters staff a projection of the Theater staff, the present plan of operations is to consider the tactical headquarters a separate entity under Theater." AG 337, Folder, Conferences, Meetings, Etc. 1944–1945, has a "Summary of Discussions with Chiefs of Staff Sections, Theater Headquarters" on the several concepts of a tactical headquarters.

intelligence and operational summaries." This was perhaps too modest an appraisal, for meetings had always been followed by decisions and the choice of an appropriate executive agency. However, the Combined Staff now suggested, through its secretariat, that the "ultimate goal" be "joint planning on all phases of military operations." To accomplish this, the creation of Chinese-American G–2, G–3, and G–4 staffs was suggested. The Combined Staff suggested as well a transitional period of several months in which subjects of common interest would be discussed. Wedemeyer agreed, and told the Generalissimo that when the staffs had completed the transitional period the new Chinese-American staff sections would be ready for joint planning of intelligence, operations, and logistics. The Generalissimo's approval was given 10 July 1945; an experiment of great potential importance was about to begin.[54]

Preparations To Open a Seaport

In June 1945 active plans and preparations to open a seaport were under way in both India–Burma and China Theaters, and began to involve Admiral Nimitz' and General MacArthur's commands in the Pacific. The immediate goal on which attention was focused was taking Fort Bayard in August, but the training and construction programs in China for the thirty-six divisions, now further bolstered by the three returning from Burma, looked beyond Fort Bayard to carrying out CARBONADO operation, of which Fort Bayard was the overture. Opening Fort Bayard would be the task of Chang Fa-Kwei's divisions, most of which were not U.S.-sponsored. The modest preparations of Chang's men began with a visit by General McClure, 7 June, to Bowman's Kwangsi Command, to warn them of their new task.

General Bowman and his staff were complimented by McClure with the statement that they had done "more with less than any other group in China," a remark which reflected both their non-ALPHA status and their success in getting food and medical attention for Chang's men. The scarcity period was now to end. Chinese weapons to complete the Tables of Equipment would be expedited. Three ALPHA armies, 8th, 54th, and New 1st, would take their place with Chang's men. Adequate supplies were promised.

Meanwhile, two of the Kwangsi Command armies, the 46th and 64th, followed the withdrawing Japanese. Moving north, the 46th found itself slowed by the old bogy of Chinese forces, lack of food. The Chinese SOS had not set up a line of communications, and the countryside had no food

---

[54] (1) Memo 630–7, with Incls, Wedemeyer for Generalissimo, 4 Jul 45. AG 337 Misc Folder, Meetings from 1944 to 30 Aug 45, Box BA 51513, KCRC. (2) Memo 99, Gen Chien Ta-chun, Chief of First Dept, Generalissimo's Hq, for Wedemeyer, 10 Jul 45. Item 110, Bk 8, ACW Corresp with Chinese.

KWANGSI COMMAND HEADQUARTERS *in Nanning. Brig. Gen. Harwood C. Bow-man, Commanding General, Kwangsi Command, is visited by General McClure, 7 June 1945. From the left, unidentified Chinese officer, General McClure, General Ho Ying-chin, General Chang Fa-kwei, and General Bowman.*

to offer. The 46th had to halt, and in any event, since Liuchow, its goal, was in Tang En-po's area, General Ho wanted it to stop. Reluctantly Chang issued appropriate orders, but his 175th Division continued ahead, perhaps without his knowledge. To the south, the 64th Army occupied Nanning itself as the bulk of its Japanese garrison moved north. Kwangsi Command headquarters was established there. The 46th's difficulties showed what had to be done before Chang's men could take Fort Bayard; his forces had to be assembled well forward, and a ground line of communications had to be set up to feed them. Weather permitting, air supply could provide ammunition, but it could not feed whole armies of Chinese, such as CARBONADO would require. To provide a proper logistical base for the operation, of which Fort Bayard was the preliminary, preparations had to be made all the way from Calcutta to Kunming.[55]

[55] (1) History, II Army Group Command, pp. 11–16.   (2) Bowman comments on draft MS.

By 19 June China Theater was ready to set forth the detailed concept of Fort Bayard operations. The fort was to be taken 1 August 1945 by non-U.S.-sponsored Chinese troops at no appreciable cost to the main effort of CARBONADO. India–Burma and China Theaters were to support the project jointly, and develop it to the extent permitted by their resources, but hold construction to a minimum. Once Fort Bayard was taken, it was to be an auxiliary forward supply base, receiving supplies at a logistic cost far below that of Hump operations and distributing them to the Chinese troops in CARBONADO. These supplies were to be principally packaged gas and oil, vehicles, and ammunition. From an airstrip supplies would be flown to the airfields at Kweilin, Liuchow, and Tanchuk. The scale of the supply operation can be estimated from the provision that five Liberty ships a month were to bring supplies. China Theater was most enthusiastic over the project, believing that 25,000 tons a month laid down at Fort Bayard would permit delivery of 15,000 tons a month in the forward area, whereas the current line of communications required 60,000 tons a month at Calcutta to deliver 15,000 tons in east China. India–Burma's reception of the plan was affected by the belief that it could not find the troops for the project, that they would have to come from neighboring U.S. theaters in the Pacific. The planning problems were thus beginning to emerge, and the chain of conferences began. Nothing, of course, could be done without continued and effective operation of the line of communications from India, whose adequacy to support the projected operations in China had earlier been seriously questioned.[56]

In retrospect, India–Burma Theater headquarters believed its biggest operations problem in June and July 1945 was expanding theater facilities to support the incoming C–54's on which so much depended. Opening a Chinese port would mean that India–Burma could begin to close down, since the line of communications to China Theater would then run from the Philippines to the port. But for the present, receiving the new C–54's involved a number of expansions and improvements. Existing airfields had to be enlarged and new ones built. The fuel system serving the fields had to be enlarged to deliver the greater quantities of fuel and oil required. The turnaround time for Hump aircraft would have to be cut. More hands would be needed, which meant hiring more Indians. More supplies would have to be obtained to fill the cargo space in the new transports. This was not going to be easy, since India–Burma rarely had more than a ninety-day level, including supplies destined for China Theater. These added supplies would have to go on requisition in adequate quantity and of appropriate kind, be received in the ports (a further strain), and pass up to Assam over

---

[56] History of IBT, I, 6–8. OCMH.

railways now burdened with supplies for Mountbatten's forthcoming attack on Singapore.

So India–Burma engineers went to work. New fields were begun at Tezgaon (Bengal), and Shamshernagar (Assam), and the B–29 fields near Calcutta were converted to ATC use. A field near Bhamo in Burma was being rushed to completion to supplement the Myitkyina field. Also revived was the project to restore the prewar line of communications from Rangoon north, this time to the Myingyan area of Burma, forty miles southwest of Mandalay. Here more fields were contemplated, in the belief that 15,000 tons a month laid down at Rangoon might permit delivery of 8,000 tons of gas and oil to China. Not until the first week of August 1945 was the Myingyan project finally abandoned. At this same time construction elsewhere was proceeding steadily, some of it on the highest priority. Preliminary action was under way to provide storage space—1,000,000 square feet of closed and 7,000,000 of open—at Kharagpur, all to support the C–54's.[57]

Problems of the Ground Line of Communications

Operation of the ground line of communications to China brought some difficulties and embarrassments to India–Burma Theater in summer 1945. The difficulties arose over the division of control of the Stilwell Road and pipelines as between India–Burma Theater and China Theater. The original agreement between the theaters provided that India–Burma would operate the pipeline, motor transport to the China border, and signal communications to Kunming. In return, China Theater would support India–Burma personnel along the China part of the road, and maintain the road in China. After several months' trial, both parties were finding flaws in the arrangement. China Theater would not accept vehicles for delivery until India–Burma had overhauled them, yet the maintenance facilities it provided did not seem suitable to India–Burma personnel. India–Burma, for its part, had not made adequate provision to repair the trucks. India–Burma's Advance Section was dissatisfied with the rations given its drivers and mechanics as they arrived in China, and was bringing extra food to China by truck from Ledo. Maintenance of the Burma Road from Wanting to Kunming had been poor. In short, divided responsibility was not proving a solution. The question appeared to be whether the road should be put under one headquarters from beginning to end even if that entailed one headquarters operating in the area of another.

The several staff sections of India–Burma Theater considered the matter at some length, for proposing to operate one commander's line of communications in another commander's theater is a delicate matter. However,

[57] *Ibid,* pp. 69–76.

Wedemeyer's problems and limited resources were well known. India–Burma's mission was to support China Theater, and it was reasonable to assume that China Theater had done its best. So India–Burma Theater recommended that with a few minor exceptions it assume control of the road and pipeline operation all the way to Kunming.

On 5 August the two theaters agreed in Kunming that India–Burma would have all control, responsibility, and administrative functions for constructing, operating, maintaining, and guarding the line of communications from Ledo to the Kunming area. General Aurand, China Theater SOS commander, in turn agreed to conduct relations with the Chinese Government. China Theater would provide troops to guard installations in China and turn over to India–Burma all equipment and installations along the road, plus 10,000 Chinese laborers. To carry out its part of the task, Advance Section, SOS, India–Burma, was ordered to establish an Eastern Area Command including the Wanting–Kunming area.

The embarrassing aspects of road operation arose from the desire of the Government of India to make sure that the Stilwell Road was used only to support military operations. Of the five Chinese divisions in Burma, three returned to China by way of the Stilwell Road. The very large number of Chinese at Ramgarh also returned by road, in trucks under their control. Moreover, the Stilwell Road led from the bazaars of Assam to the shops of Kunming and Paoshan. These Chinese movements opened many opportunities to bring goods to China.

Shortly after the Stilwell Road opened the Government of India complained that Assam, which with the rest of India had inflationary problems, was being stripped of goods for Chinese account. These were leaving India without due regard to export formalities. So, between 7 March and 18 April, a combined investigation of the road, from Ledo to Kunming, was made by British Intelligence and the U.S. Criminal Investigation Department.

Completing their survey in May, the investigators called the Stilwell Road a "Chinese Army trade route" and stated:

> No complete estimate can be made of the tonnage of merchandise seen by the investigators along the Road still less of the volume of merchandise transported along the Road in any given period. The godowns of Namti and the Myitkyina area, the well-stocked Chinese bazaar at Bhamo, the overflowing bazaar at Paoshan, the innumerable displays in shops and stalls along the Road, to say nothing of the extremely well-stocked shops and stalls of Kunming, contain in the aggregate literally hundreds of truckloads.[58]

After the report was received, correspondence and conferences between the Government of India and U.S. authorities followed, in which the communications from India assumed a steadily stronger tone. Since the convoys were guarded by Chinese soldiers who did not hesitate to use force to keep

---

[58] Quotation in History of IBT, I, 29.

U.S. troops from checking them, it may be assumed India–Burma Theater hoped to avoid clashes with the Chinese until such time as the troop movements to China ended, thus limiting the smuggling to openly commercial ventures with which Indian and Burmese authorities could cope without international complications.[59]

By 20 July the Government of India felt constrained to observe "that when they agreed that control of traffic on this road should remain entirely American, they assumed that American control would be effective. At present it clearly is not and the Government of India therefore request that steps should be taken to make it as effective as possible. . . ." On 9 August, at which date but one more Chinese military convoy was expected, a conference at Ledo agreed to arrange an elaborate pass system for Stilwell Road traffic in Burma.[60]

The problems did not affect the performance of the line of communications by air and ground, which delivered a considerable quantity of supplies to China in July 1945, over and above the very considerable illicit traffic in consumer goods and post exchange supplies:

	Tons
Total	91,183
ATC	71,043
China National Aviation Corporation	2,639
Stilwell Road	[a] 5,900
Pipeline	11,601

[a] Net tons of goods carried, exclusive of vehicle deliveries.

The Stilwell Road also brought to China 4,745 motor vehicles, plus 828 trailers, and 53 troop units including 935 more vehicles.[61]

From late May 1945 until the end of the war, operation of the Ledo Road proceeded under monsoon conditions. There were a number of bridge failures in the Mogaung area, just as a year before there had been failures in the Hukawng area. In both cases, only the impact of the monsoon floods could reveal whether bridge structures could withstand the strain, and what remedial steps were necessary. These interruptions, plus the physical diffi-

[59] On 19 May Wedemeyer told the Generalissimo of an incident involving Ledo Road Convoy 120, of the Chinese 30th Division. The trucks, which were lend-lease equipment, were returning the 30th Division, with its lend-lease equipment, to China. When they were inspected on 14 May by U.S. troops near Pao-shan the latter discovered and seized certain unauthorized material being carried in the trucks. The Chinese convoy personnel then surrounded them and took the goods back at gunpoint. As a result orders were issued that U.S. troops were not to inspect convoys.

Wedemeyer pointed out to the Generalissimo that the sole purpose of the inspection was to be sure that all space was used for equipment that had been issued to the Chinese. To the extent that the Chinese used the space for commercial ventures, Hump tonnage would have to be used for replacement. Memo 578, Wedemeyer to Generalissimo, 19 May 45. Item 2, Bk 9, ACW Personal File.

[60] History of IBT, I, 31.

[61] Ibid., pp. 37, 74.

culty of road operations during the pouring monsoon rains retarded deliveries. What the Ledo Road might have delivered to China during the dry season of 1945–1946, under better driving conditions and with more efficient loading and operation of the vehicles, is a matter of conjecture.[62]

Logistical Problems of Fort Bayard

Tonnage entering China was now more than enough to support the drive to the coast, especially since Fort Bayard would be opened in August. The BETA plan had estimated that 62,000 tons would be needed for July 1945. The figure was later found to be about 14,000 tons too small because of underestimated costs of intra-China distribution. Thanks to the ATC, which overcame a 3,400-ton shortfall in pipeline deliveries by delivering 71,000 tons as against an anticipated 44,000, there would be enough.[63]

The logistical problems of Fort Bayard thus became the lesser one of being sure that the four Chinese divisions chosen to take the port had food and ammunition to carry them through the operation and the greater one of finding the troops and the supplies to put the port into operation, after the resources had been safely convoyed across the South China Sea from the Philippines. The difficulty was to find the resources without interfering with the initial invasion of Japan, now scheduled for 1 November 1945. Nimitz believed his forces could supply harbor defenses and naval escort for the operation, which he heartily endorsed, but he did not think that the landing craft so useful for putting ashore supplies in an underdeveloped port area could be found in his command. He envisaged resupply as being carried out by twenty landing ships (tank) but feared he could not spare them. As for MacArthur, in late June he promised "every practical assistance" and, turning the discussion at once to the highly practical, asked what air cover could be given to convoys as they entered Chinese waters.

The replies of China Theater's neighbors made it necessary for the War Department to co-ordinate the operation, find resources, and give local commanders assurance that they could release some of their resources. Shipping for the operation was located by 25 June—five Liberty ships, the first three of them to be loaded in the United States rather than in the Philippines. China Theater at once radioed to Army Service Forces its recommendations for the ships' cargoes, which principally comprised steel airstrip matting, sixty days' rations for 5,000 American troops, tentage, refueling equipment, gasoline, and ammunition.

India–Burma Theater's contention that supplying troops for Fort Bayard would reduce its ability to support China via the existing line of communi-

---

[62] Leslie Anders, a History of the Ledo Road, pp. 303–06, 328–31. Hist Div, Corps of Engineers.

[63] Table, Estimated Tonnage into China, Plan BETA, p. 101. OCMH.

cations was discarded; IBT undertook to supply 3,147 men, to China's 506. IBT's units ranged from a 40-mm. antiaircraft battery to a veterinary food inspection battalion, and included most of the units needed to operate a small port and supply center. Navy personnel to operate amphibious trucks and landing craft (medium) had arrived in India by 10 July, for Hump lift to China. Some of the units were to fly to east China from Bhamo and Myitkyina. However, no headquarters and headquarters company, port battalion, could be spared, nor could several Quartermaster units. In this case, the War Department undertook to fly Headquarters and Headquarters Company, 501st Port Battalion, from Europe to India.

Giving air cover was complicated by the fact that it was 470 air miles from the east China fields to Fort Bayard. Seizure of an advance airstrip appeared essential, yet might reveal the plan. Taking the island of Wei-chou, near Fort Bayard, was considered but rejected. The solution adopted was to have the convoys arrive near the China coast at dusk, make the run-in during the hours of darkness, and thus be an estimated 110 miles closer to shore when day broke and China Theater had to give air cover. The cover missions would be flown from Nanning. It was hoped that Tanchuk airfield, halfway to the coast, would be taken by Chinese troops en route to Fort Bayard and the distance to the convoys thus shortened.

Compared to operations in other theaters, the Fort Bayard operation was on a small scale, with five Liberty ships, improvised air cover from deep in China, and second-string Chinese troops. But it seemed essential if Wedemeyer's varsity was to succeed in its first big game. By late July plans and preparations for Fort Bayard were well advanced, awaiting only final coordination between Nimitz', MacArthur's, and Wedemeyer's theaters.[64]

To reach the stage where action was imminent, the project to open a seaport had had to survive many obstacles and setbacks. Having estimated his supply requirements, Wedemeyer had then presented the project to the Joint Chiefs. They had approved, and he had understood that the ATC expansion necessary to support his drive to the sea would be forthcoming and that he would also be able to improve the air support for the plan by moving the major part of the Tenth Air Force from India to China. Then further study had shown that the supply requirements had been seriously underestimated, while the end of the war in Europe seemed to preclude any immediate movement of transport aircraft to India to support China Theater. For a while the port project seemed to hang on dead center. Then the Japanese began to withdraw from the area of China that had been the objective of the first phase of the drive, and the transport situation greatly improved. Powerfully aided by these circumstances, the port project began moving steadily toward fulfillment as July passed into August 1945.

[64] (1) History of China Theater, Ch. II. (2) History of IBT, I, 3–15.

463995 O–59—25

CHAPTER XII

The End of Wedemeyer's Experiment

The Chinese Army, Summer 1945

The time was approaching for Chinese troops to open a Chinese seaport. The Americans had made substantial progress in preparing Chinese divisions, in training key Chinese personnel, and in supplying food, ammunition, and medical care to the U.S.-supported Chinese divisions. The heart of Wedemeyer's program had been the 36-division plan, now 39 (36 plus 3 from Burma). Beyond that, for specific missions in the CARBONADO operation, a few additional Chinese divisions, such as Chang Fa-kwei's, had been reorganized and given some added weapons from the Chinese supply.

As of the first week in August, the training program for the 39 divisions, which contemplated two thirteen-week cycles, had been carried to the following point: 3 divisions had been trained to U.S. standards in India; 2 divisions had been trained and had received combat experience in Burma; 11 divisions had completed thirteen weeks' training in China; 22 divisions were one-half to three-quarters through their thirteen weeks' training; and 1 division had not begun training.

As for the rearming of the 39 divisions, if one may take a slight liberty with chronology, by 23 August 1945 all of the 39 had enough ordnance to make them completely operable in combat with the principal exception of two items, one of which was 60-mm. mortars.[1]

The replacement problem was still unsolved. No machinery yet existed to give the Chinese divisions a steady flow of well-trained, physically fit replacements. Gravely concerned by this weakness, which if uncorrected would cause the new reorganized Chinese divisions to waste away in combat and would deter the commanders of the rest of the Chinese Army from committing it wholeheartedly to battle, Wedemeyer on 5 August sent to the Generalissimo a report that had been received in his headquarters:

Herewith memorandum which I feel contains information that should reach you. It

---

[1] Ltr, Col Edward C. Reber to Public Relations Officer, Hq CCC, USFCT, 23 Aug 45. AG (CCC) 314.7, KCRC.

has been carefully verified and I believe contains much factual data that will assist you and myself in our many intricate problems.

CONSCRIPTION

Conscription comes to the Chinese peasant like famine or flood, only more regularly—every year twice—and claims more victims. Famine, flood, and drought compare with conscription like chicken pox with plague. Every ravaging disease has its stages. These are the stages of the most ravaging disease that sweeps China.

FIRST STAGE

Seasonal conscription occurs in spring and autumn. Sometimes aggravated by an "emergency call" whereby the government decrees that until a certain date, half a million men are to be conscripted in a certain area and for a certain purpose. The specially urgent purpose in the spring of 1945 was partly the need to get soldiers for the American-led training centers in China.

The virus is spread over the Chinese country-side by the Pao-Chia system. One Chia consists of ten families. . . . Ten Chia form a Pao. . . . In practice it seems that [notwithstanding the regulations] the violent forms of onset are the more frequent ones and that only office, influence, and money keep conscription out of your house.

There is first the press gang.

For example, you are working in the field looking after your rice . . . [there come] a number of uniformed men who tie your hands behind your back and take you with them. . . . Hoe and plough rust in the field, the wife runs to the magistrate to cry and beg for her husband, the children starve.

*   *   *   *   *   *   *

This very rapid onset has many variations. Another way of being taken is arrest. If one man is wanted for conscription, the Hsienchang [county magistrate] arrests ten. Nine will be given a chance to buy their way out. The poorest stays in jail until the conscription officer takes him over.

. . . . The conscription officers make their money in collaboration with the officials and through their press gangs. They extort big sums of money from conscripts which have been turned over to them by the officials and replace them with captives.

Private dealers in conscripts have organized a trade. They are buying able-bodied men from starved families who need rice more urgently than sons, or, they buy them from the Hsienchangs who have a surplus or they pay a man who wants to sell himself because he finds life too difficult and doesn't know any better than to go into the Army. The dealers in conscription resell these men to conscription officers or Hsienchangs who have let off conscripts without being able to replace them through arrest or pressgang. The dealer might give $30,000 CN to the man who sells himself, or to the family or to the official. He sells the man for $50,000 CN to the Hsienchang or conscription official who had just let off a peasant's son for $100,000 CN. So everybody is happy except the conscript who soon will realize that he has been sold to something worse than death; to the slow approach of death, each stage leading up to the next and most miserable one, and death is but the end of misery.

THE SECOND STAGE

Having been segregated and herded together the conscripts are driven to the training camps. They are marched from Shensi to Szechuan and from Szechuan to Yunnan. Over endless roads they walk, billetting in small hamlets, carrying their rice and rations and nothing else. Many of those who run away run off during the first few days. Later

CHINESE ARMY REPLACEMENTS. *These soldiers await removal to a field hospital for rehabilitation before replacing troops on the battlefront. Kweiyang, May 1945.*

they are too weak to run away.   Those who are caught are cruelly beaten.   They will be carried along with broken limbs and with wounds in maimed flesh in which infection turns quickly into blood poisoning and blood poisoning into death.

As they march along they turn into skeletons; they develop signs of beriberi, their legs swell and their bellies protrude, their arms and thighs get thin.   Scabies and ulcers turn their skin into a shabby cover of an emaciated body which has no other value than to turn rice into dung and to register the sharp pains of an existence as a conscript in the Chinese Army.

In speaking of value we have to make a distinction between usefulness and market value.   "Useful" is anything that can be used for a practical purpose, such as, a copy of Sun Yat-sen's "Three Principles" or an officer's walking cane.   From this point of view most of the Chinese conscripts are entirely useless.   Anything which is in demand has market value, however useless it may seem. . . . From this point of view the conscripts' bodies have a great value, based on a far less romantic demand than that which makes people buy ornamental knickknacks or tiger bones.   A Chinese conscript's pay can be pocketed and his rations can be sold.   That makes him a valuable member of the Chinese Army and that is the basis of the demand for him.

Because of this demand, his journey has no end.   Being sick, he has to drag himself along. . . . Dysentery and typhoid are always with them.   They carry cholera from place to place.   Leaving behind them a wake of the sick and the dying, they are still fulfilling the most important function of a citizen of Free China! to be a source of income for officials.   During this second stage they are rapidly developing the full picture of the disease with which they are stricken.

If somebody dies his body is left behind.   His name on the list is carried along.   As long as his death is not reported he continues to be a source of income, increased by the

New Chinese Soldiers *of the 205th Division, 3d Army Command, were trained under the American 39-division plan. Kweiyang, August 1945.*

fact that he has ceased to consume. His rice and his pay become a long-lasting token of memory in the pocket of his commanding officer. His family will have to forget him.

*   *   *   *   *   *   *

The report went on to explain that those who arrived sick at the training centers, that is, too weak to stand, went to Chinese Army hospitals, which were described as similar to the German extermination camps at Buchenwald and in Poland. The U.S. Army had been obliged to leave hospital administration in the training centers to the Chinese. Only those conscripts able to walk received the better rations. Conditions in the hospitals were not entirely due to Chinese poverty. The Chinese general officer in charge of a conscript area that included an appalling hospital gave a visitor the bland explanation that the director of the hospital, who was leaving it, would naturally try to make the greatest possible profit from it. "The General had shown no embarrassment during the whole talk. He felt sure of his ground. These Chinese conscripts were purely a concern of the Chinese Central Government, which he represented."

The report closed:

. . . . Everybody in China, including the Government, knows that the Chinese Army is too big. To cut the Chinese Army in half and to distribute equipment, rations and training facilities to the stronger half and to discharge the weaker half is a measure which

TABLE 6—DIVISION TRAINING STATUS: 5 AUGUST 1945

Unit	Weeks in training	Unit	Weeks in training
New 1st Army		53d Army	
30th Div [a]	0	Hon 2d Div	9
38th Div [a]	0	116th Div [b]	7
50th Div [a]	0	130th Div [b]	7
New 6th Army		73d Army	
14th Div [a]	0	15th Div	3
22d Div [a]	0	77th Div	7
207th Div [c]	12	193d Div	5
5th Army		74th Army	
45th Div	13	51st Div	4
96th Div	13	57th Div	5
200th Div	13	58th Div	6
2d Army		71st Army	
9th Div [b]	0	87th Div [b]	6
2d Res Div [b]	0	88th Div [b]	5
76th Div [b]	0	91st Div	5
8th Army		94th Army	
Hon 1st Div [b]	13	5th Div	5
103d Div [b]	13	43d Div	6
166th Div [d]	6	121st Div	5
13th Army		18th Army	
4th Div	13	11th Div	4
54th Div	8	18th Div	3
89th Div	13	118th Div [e]	0
54th Army			
8th Div	13		
36th Div [b]	11		
198th Div [b]	10		

[a] Ramgarh-trained, veterans of Burma.
[b] Veterans of Salween front.
[c] Assigned when New 6th Army returned to China.
[d] Assigned when 8th Army returned to Kunming.
[e] Detached, fighting at the front.

Source: (1) Status Report, Eastern Comd, 22 July 45, Sec. V. (2) Ltr, Capt Eugene D. Hill to CG CCC, 26 Aug 45, sub: Brief History of 2d Army. AG (CCC) 314.7, KCRC.

had recommended itself for a long time to every military observer who came to this country. But as soldiers are primarily a source of income for officials and a source of political power and influence for generals, which general will allow himself to be robbed of his army? And as generals rarely stand alone but are part of a clique tied up with other cliques nobody who is wise would try to force a general; and everybody who is not a fool would hesitate to hurt a clique.

Armies are instruments to win wars. Does the Chinese Government not want to win the war? The answer is: Not unconditionally. Not at the price of entrusting Chinese concerns to the American Army. Not at the price of introducing democracy which might control the government and officials. Not at the price of collaborating with the Communists, with their exaggerated ideas of how to carry on a war of resistance, who wouldn't approve of the tactic of "waiting for victory." [2]

The Chinese Army as a whole was a long way from combat readiness. Sixteen of its divisions had had U.S. training through at least one thirteen-week cycle, had had better diet for some weeks, had all the weapons they needed to fight, while a beginning had been made in the systematic training of twenty-three more. (Table 6) The rest of the Chinese Army was as it had been. But, the training program for whole divisions was only part of what Wedemeyer was attempting. A comprehensive school system was in operation by summer 1945, while an American style services of supply for the thirty-nine divisions was being organized. If these two latter projects were long continued, the graduates of the one and the activities and example of the other might be a beneficial leaven in the Chinese Army.

The School System of the Chinese Training Center

While the Chinese divisions of the Wedemeyer program were receiving unit training from personnel of the Chinese Combat Command, individual students plus, in some cases, cadres of special units, were being trained by the Chinese Training Center.[3] Operation of service schools, preparation and distribution of training literature, and technical assistance to the Chinese Combat Command were the three missions of the center, Brig. Gen. John W. Middleton, commanding. Discipline and administration of the Chinese students was the task of a Chinese liaison officer, attached to each school with the title of assistant commandant, and assisted by a suitable staff and detachment.

Seven service schools and training centers were in operation, six of them

---

[2] Memo 678–7, Wedemeyer for Generalissimo, 5 Aug 45. Item 25, Bk 8, Wedemeyer Corresp with Chinese.

[3] Unless otherwise noted, this section is based on a letter and inclosures, Col Clinton I. McClure, CO, Chinese Training Center (Prov), to TAG, 1 Oct 45, sub: History, Chinese Training Center (Prov), 1 Jul 45–1 Oct 45, final rpt. OCMH.

around Kunming.[4]   Of these, the Field Artillery Training Center, commanded first by Col. Garrison B. Cloverdale and later by Col. Clinton I. McClure, was the largest.   At peak activity, some 1,000 Americans were training about 10,000 Chinese, some as individual aspirants for key posts in artillery units, others as members of battalions undergoing arming and unit training.   Emphasis was originally placed on the 75-mm. pack howitzer, but after the opening of the Burma Road and the graduation of units that had begun their work with the pack howitzer, emphasis shifted to the 105-mm. howitzer.   From October 1944 to fall 1945 the center armed and trained 11 75-mm. pack howitzer battalions and 3 truck-drawn 105-mm. battalions.   In addition, 9 105-mm. battalions were partially armed from Chinese lend-lease stocks.

In training the Chinese, the Americans had to combat their pupils' tendency to keep the bulk of their artillery safely in the rear, their habit of using pieces individually to save ammunition, and the physical weaknesses which malnutrition and lack of sanitation caused in the Chinese forces.   Instruction began with duties of the cannoneer and progressed to battalion massed fires.

Through the need to give students and training units weapons that would fire, the center had to develop shops that could repair existing Chinese ordnance.   Ultimately, these were capable of extensive and delicate repairs.[5] All together, 157 105-mm. howitzers, delivered to China by truck or aircraft, were prepared for service.   The 75-mm. pack howitzers which armed most of the center-trained battalions were thoroughly reconditioned before issue; a necessary step because of the rough treatment they received in being loaded and unloaded for air transport.[6]

The second class of the Command and General Staff School, Col. Elbert W. Martin, commanding, was in session when the China Theater was established in October 1944.   Ninety-three students, drawn from the Y–Force, were taking the three-month course.   The difficult problems of training aids, instructional material, and classroom techniques had been largely solved. The school's creation had been suggested by Brig. Gen. Theodore F. Wessels and Col. Norman McNeil to overcome the tendency of Chinese senior officers to resist the innovations American-trained junior officers were taking back to their units.

---

[4] With their dates of activation, or reactivation in the case of the Infantry Training Center, they were:
  Field Artillery Training Center, April 1943
  Command and General Staff School, May 1944
  Chinese Ordnance Training Center, October 1944
  Infantry Training Center, January 1945
  Interpreters' Pool, January 1945
  Heavy Mortar Training Center, February 1945
  Signal School, May 1945
[5] Of the type that the artilleryman knows as 5th echelon maintenance.
[6] Final Report of the Feld Artillery Training Center in China, 1943–1945.   OCMH.

In the daily operation of the school, the problem of interpretation was a major one, and affected the amount of instruction students received.   Since everything the American instructor said had to be translated to his students fully half of every hour was lost.   Only continuing rehearsal and practice could ensure that instructor and interpreter worked as a team.   The problem of relating instruction to the everyday workings of the Chinese staff system, then largely unknown to the Americans, was met by a systematic study of their procedures.[7]

When summer 1945 ended, 463 students had graduated from the school under the sponsorship of China Theater.   In addition, classes of the Chinese Army War College received fifteen-day courses in American weapons and staff procedures.   General Ho Ying-chin, supreme commander of the ALPHA divisions, sent about 130 members of his staff for a series of lectures, beginning 22 May, on staff organization, duties of the chief of staff and the several staff sections, and the co-ordination of their activities.   While this group of key officers was in attendance, the staff and faculty of the school were preparing a comprehensive plan for the reorganization of Ho's staff on lines the Americans thought more apt to be successful than the existing blend of Chinese, Japanese, and German practices.

An Infantry Training Center had been established in April 1943, then deactivated so that its plant might be used by the Command and General Staff School.   In January 1945 it was reactivated under Col. Mose Kent, to train battalion and regimental commanders.   Beginning initially with 18 Americans and a battalion of Chinese school troops, Kent saw the center grow until it had a staff of 233 and had graduated, by late summer, 288 students.

In preparing for the arrival of the first class in April 1945 the staff and faculty concluded that existing training literature was inadequate, and began an ambitious program of providing a manual for each of the infantry regiment's major components, plus seven more or general military topics.   The principal course of the school covered three major areas: infantry weapons, military subjects of a technical nature useful to infantry such as demolitions, and, lastly, tactical training of small infantry units.[8]

The Heavy Mortar Training Center, Lt. Col. Albert R. Volkmuth, commandant, received its first students at Na-chi, Szechwan, on 2 April 1945.

[7] That the Chinese staff system was largely unknown in fall 1944 may seem incredible, yet the language barrier alone would make it hard for an American officer to master the workings of a Chinese administrative system.   To teach staff officers, it was not enough to know that personnel matters, for example, were the concern of certain sections of the Chinese staff.   Forms, doctrines, filing systems, responsibilities, or their Chinese equivalents, would all have to be identified with precision and fitted into a system with accuracy.   Studies based on such researches would have to be reproduced and circulated.   The Americans under Stilwell began with the Chinese infantry regiment tables of organization and equipment; not until June 1944 were the problems of the higher staffs approached.

[8] Final Report, Hq, Infantry Training Center, Chinese Training Center (Prov), 1 Sep 45, OCMH.

DEMOLITIONS CLASS ON A BRIDGE. *Men of the Chinese 14th Division show members of an officer candidate class how to destroy a bridge with properly placed demolitions.*

Its mission was to retrain Chinese regiments as 4.2-inch mortar units. By late summer two regiments had attended the center, the latter being able to complete only one month of its unit training. The center's basic method was first to train the regimental cadre, then receive the rest of the personnel, fit them into their places, and train the whole unit.

In its daily course, the center met problems illustrative of the difficulties in teaching modern warfare to men from the simplest and most isolated of rural backgrounds. Some students had to be shown which way to turn a nut in order to tighten it. Some did not know how to use pliers or how to unfasten metal snaps. Others could not count from one to ten. On the other hand, the Chinese impressed the Americans as enthusiastic, curious, "extremely cooperative and worked exceedingly hard most of the time." Since the students wanted to learn, progress could be made by various expedients.

Thus, the men who found it hard to count were not asked to add or subtract, as they would have been had they been given fire commands of "Right (so much)," or "Left (so much); instead, they were given the complete sight setting for every change to right or left.[9]

To provide radio operators for the thirty-nine divisions, a Signal School, under Col. Willis R. Lansford, began operations 8 June 1945. By September it was ready to turn out 150 competent operators every month and had actually graduated 281. The school was organized by Colonel Lansford under conditions of great haste and difficulty. His 600 students were all at hand waiting instruction, while the thirty-nine divisions needed a supply of radio operators in time for the offensive against Canton. Housing was a problem, as it was with all the schools, but signal equipment was a major concern. The school had a low priority, signal equipment was scarce in China, and what did arrive at the school was often damaged in transit. Lansford and his men asked help of every American organization that might have equipment to give. Salvaged parts and assemblies were extensively used.

Many precautions ensured an acceptable student body. One of the newly organized student divisions[10] supplied students; almost every member of the division had the equivalent of a high school education plus some training in English. From this group 840 were selected by means of the standard Signal Corps aptitude test, its requirements slightly eased. From this group, 632 were found suitable. When it appeared that a 20 percent mortality through failure was probable a compensating number of students was added to the waiting list.[11]

The Chinese Ordnance Training Center, organized by Col. Kennedy Hassenzahl, trained ordnance maintenance detachments for the thirty-nine divisions, plus twelve ordnance weapons maintenance companies for more difficult repairs; trained arsenal instructors; and, lastly, set up a permanent ordnance replacement training center. Courses were given in the repair of small arms, optical instruments, artillery, and vehicles. The Chinese Training Center hoped this portion of the training program would show the Chinese how they themselves could create their own ordnance schools to service weapons of their own manufacture. When summer ended, the Ordnance Training Center had trained and fitted out twenty divisional maintenance detachments and one ordnance weapons maintenance company.

An Interpreters' Pool, activated 14 January 1945, tried to meet the need for interpreters, a need that grew with every expansion of the training program. Its members were graduates of the Chinese Government Interpreters'

[9] Final Report, Hq, Heavy Mortar Training Center, Chinese Training Center, 5 Oct 45. OCMH.
[10] See p. 249, above.
[11] Final Report, Signal School, Chinese Training Center, 8 Sep 45. OCMH.

School, and had honorary rank in the Chinese Army. Most had a working knowledge of English; all needed some background in military matters. In the course of their four weeks at the pool they were taught military terminology, translation, techniques of interpretation, general military subjects, physical training, and infantry drill. Eight classes, totaling 1,777, were graduated.

Helping the Chinese SOS

As noted before,[12] the first American attempts to assist the Chinese in setting up an SOS to support the thirty-nine divisions involved placing General Cheves in command, with the rank of lieutenant general in the Chinese Army, while another American, Col. Raymond R. Tourtillot, became chief of staff. Then Maj. Gen. Henry S. Aurand took over the China Theater SOS on 25 May. Aurand inherited Cheves's command status, but began to question its feasibility.[13]

As summer 1945 began, there were Americans present at many levels in the Chinese SOS. About 300 of them were at its headquarters. Each Chinese area command had as liaison officer the deputy commander of the corresponding American SOS command. In the field, 231 Americans manned a Chinese driver training school, and another 120 or so worked with various Chinese service elements.[14]

The structures of the Chinese SOS and American SOS were arranged on parallel lines, and in turn were fitted to the Chinese Combat Command. Thus, the American SOS Base Section 1 was divided into Districts A, B, and C, which in turn corresponded with Chinese area commands. The Chinese 1st Area plus District B of Base Section 1 supported the Southern Command of CCC; the Chinese 2d Area plus Base Section 2 supported the Kwangsi Command, and so on. In all, the Chinese had six numbered areas and one 1st Independent Branch. These areas in turn covered that section of China comprised in the Chinese Combat Command.[15]

At Chinese SOS headquarters, the distribution of the Americans suggests their estimate of the most pressing Chinese problems. Of the 300-odd present, 147 officers and enlisted men were in the Food Department, 84 in the Quartermaster, and the rest divided among Ordnance, Medical, Transportation and Signal, and Staff Departments.[16] The last, rather oddly named department, took its title from its mission of advising the Chinese on staff procedures.

[12] See p. 240. above.
[13] (1) GO 40, Hq USFCT, 1945. (2) Chinese Services of Supply, in Qrtrly Hist, SOS USFCT, Jul to Sep 45, 58.
[14] Rosters and Chart in Tab H of Hist cited n. 13(2).
[15] Chart cited n. 14.
[16] Rosters cited n. 14.

MAJ. GEN. HENRY S. AURAND, *Commanding General, U.S. Services of Supply, China Theater, arriving at Chihchiang in June 1945 for an inspection tour, is met by officials of the Chinese Services of Supply. From the left, General Pai Yun-shung, General Chang, General Aurand, and General Cheng.*

As its major activity, the Food Department sought and found some 1,400,000 bags of rice, plus an appropriate amount of salt, for the Chinese troops in CARBONADO. Quantities of rice had to be purchased in and transported from other provinces, after sacks for the movement had been procured by the Americans. The needs of the troops were estimated in tons, feeding stations were established, and SOS area commanders were told to issue rice through them to the troops as they moved east to concentration areas for CARBONADO. Another section of the Food Department co-ordinated the vegetable purchases of the Ration Purchasing Commissions with their distribution through the local Chinese supply depots. Looking toward the day of battle, another section within the department helped the Chinese to find suppliers of processed meat and dehydrated vegetable rations. The goal was a daily production capacity of 200,000 of each. By August, the one existing factory, a military establishment in Chungking, was preparing to produce 50,000 rations a day; plans had been drawn for two other factories with a combined production of 50,000; and plans had been prepared for a variety of processing plants. The problem of animal forage was attacked from several angles, for example, by flying in six hay balers from India.

The Medical Department began work on the reorganization and redeployment of the Chinese hospitals supporting CARBONADO. The department's head, Col. Harry G. Johnson, also served as Surgeon of the Chinese SOS. In his dual capacity, Colonel Johnson sought to improve the professional quality of Chinese medical services by providing six-week refresher courses for officers of the Chinese field hospitals, by printing tables of equipment for medical units, by building up stockpiles in medical depots, and by establishing reserves in the forward areas. The department also tried to end the Chinese practice of establishing hospitals in abandoned unsanitary temples by drawing plans for temporary hospital buildings. By August, funds to build some of these had been obtained. To provide for animal transport, a separate Veterinary Service was organized at General Ho's Supreme Headquarters, and was beginning to function.

The Ordnance Department reported that its chief accomplishment was the movement, in the face of grave transport problems, of 400 tons of Chinese ammunition to Nanning. After trying every other recourse, the men found they had to airlift the 400 tons. While working on this problem, they found that American ammunition was stored in fairly large quantities in Chinese depots in western Yunnan but because of the transport problem could not be moved to the front. The Transportation and Signal Department operated a Chinese driver training school which trained 2,000 drivers and 200 mechanics. Working with General Ho's Supreme Headquarters, the American SOS and various Chinese SOS agencies, the department arranged the movement of some 130,000 Chinese troops and 6,000 tons of cargo by truck, boat, and aircraft. It also established a signal net linking Kunming, Nanning, Kweiyang, Chihkiang, and Liuchow, some of it with equipment borrowed from the Chinese. Looking toward the future, the Quartermaster Department contracted for procurement of 540,000 winter uniforms, a major feat considering the handicraft nature of the Chinese economy.[17]

Thus, in the summer of 1945, 39 Chinese divisions were undergoing systematic training and rearming, service schools were instructing Chinese infantry, artillery, staff officers, and communications specialists, and some 600 Americans were beginning to create a Chinese SOS capable of supporting 39 modern divisions in combat. The effort was comprehensive, but it was just beginning to gather momentum. If the Chinese Government were to command the services of 39 first-rate battleworthy divisions, and be able to support them in battle for weeks on end, then time to complete the work in hand was needed. A considerable measure of Chinese co-operation and

[17] Chinese Services of Supply cited n. 13(2).

interest was now being given. Adequate American resources were at hand or in sight. If Japan fought on long enough, and well enough, that, paradoxically, might be the salvation of the Generalissimo's government.

The Communist Problem Emerges Again

Theater concern with the Communist issue in summer 1945 was linked with at least three antecedents—a desire to expand the CCC liaison system to Chinese units north of the Yellow River for operations against the Japanese in that area; dissatisfaction with the work of the American Observer Group in Yenan, the Communist headquarters; and the three-power Potsdam Conference of 17 July 1945. Expansion of the liaison system was related to Wedemeyer's continuing effort to persuade the Chinese to build an effective Army over and above the U.S.-sponsored divisions. On 8 May he told the Generalissimo that study had convinced him there were two deterrents to effective military effort in China: (1) dissipation of resources, and (2) piecemeal and premature commitment of troops. Wedemeyer believed the Chinese had originally had 327 divisions of which only the 5 of the Chinese Army in India were effective troops. There had been some response to his repeated pleas for a smaller Army; the Minister of War told him that 35 divisions had been inactivated. That left 253 divisions, not counting the 39 divisions in ALPHA, to be equipped and trained. Wedemeyer thought 45 would be ample for local security, over and above the U.S.-sponsored ones, and he suggested the Chinese might equip them from their own stocks. The remaining 208 divisions should be inactivated.[18]

A month later he reported to the Generalissimo that though the latter had ordered inactivation of divisions as a result of Wedemeyer's recommendations, the orders were being ignored. For example, Wedemeyer wrote, two armies (6 divisions) that the Ministry of War had reported as inactivated were still operating. Indeed, between 15 and 31 May the Chinese had added one army.[19]

Then China Theater headquarters received data from the U.S. War Production Mission which revealed that the capacities of the Chinese economy had been seriously underestimated. On the basis of the mission's conclusions, the Chinese could from their own current stocks and 1945 production equip and maintain 80 divisions. Wedemeyer accepted this view and suggested adding 40 U.S.-sponsored divisions for a total of 120.[20]

Operational control of 120 Chinese divisions, some of which would prob-

[18] Memo 560, Wedemeyer for Generalissimo, 8 May 45. Item 39, Bk 9, Wedemeyer Corresp with Chinese. ·
[19] (1) Memo 598, Wedemeyer for Generalissimo, 4 Jun 45. Item 125, Bk 8, Wedemeyer Corresp with Chinese. (2) For the Chinese Order of Battle at the end of the war, see Table 7.
[20] Memo 609, Wedemeyer for Generalissimo, 11 Jun 45, sub: Chinese War Production. Bk 8, Wedemeyer Corresp with Chinese.

TABLE 7—CHINESE ORDER OF BATTLE: 31 AUGUST 1945

Location	Number of divisions	Strength
Total	290	2,700,000
Supreme Headquarters (Ho Ying-chin)	70	790,000
I War Area (Hsian)[a]	36	280,000
II War Area (Shansi)	27	180,000
III War Area (Chekiang–Fukien)	21	220,000
V War Area (Northwest of Hankow)	10	90,000
VI War Area (I-chang Gorge area)	16	200,000
National Military Council (Szechwan)	26	220,000
VII War Area (Canton–Hong Kong)	7	90,000
VIII War Area (West Shensi, and west of Hsian)	24	200,000
IX War Area (Hsueh Yueh)	21	160,000
X War Area (Anhwei–Kiangsu)	14	130,000
XI War Area (Shantung)	6	55,000
XII War Area (Chahar)	12	85,000

[a] Twelve of these divisions were in a position to blockade the Chinese Communists.

Source: Item 3, Tab B, Bk 6, Vol I, Wedemeyer Black Book, DRB AGO.   The estimate of 12 divisions blockading the Communists comes from TPS–11, G–4, USFCT.   TS Reg 06106–1r.   DRB AGO.

ably operate in north China, raised issues of command. For himself, Wedemeyer had no desire to be field commander in China. He was concerned with some points he thought Ambassador Hurley might have overlooked in suggesting such command status, among them that command of Chinese troops involved power to promote, demote, punish, reward, transfer, and assign senior Chinese officers. And, appointment of an American to command would mean the United States would be credited with political motives if such an officer followed the course, inevitable for logistic and military reasons alike, of giving the greater bulk of U.S. arms to the Nationalist divisions. Such an embarrassment, Wedemeyer thought, should be avoided. His views prevailed.[21]

In mid-June, Marshall offered Wedemeyer the services of some of the returning American generals who had distinguished themselves in Europe, together with their key staff officers. At first, though he thought he had room for one commander, Wedemeyer hesitated, for he feared that officers accustomed to the precise discipline and logistic support of European combat would find it hard to adjust to conditions in China. Then came the realization in China Theater that several officers with their staffs would be a very welcome addition to the 120-division plan, and so the first of them, Lt. Gen. William H. Simpson, was invited to China to meet the Generalissimo.

[21] (1) Rad CFB 38387, Wedemeyer to Marshall, 31 May 45. Item 787, Bks 3 and 4, ACW Personal File. (2) In 1954 Hurley recalled that the technical points involved in Stilwell's command crisis had been his daily concern only a few months before and that he had not forgotten them.

Currently, Wedemeyer had two headquarters in China, his own in Chung-king, and a tactical headquarters to co-ordinate operations south of the Yangtze in the three provinces—Yunnan, Kwangsi, and Kweichow—where U.S. activities centered.   One of the two officers returning from Europe, General Simpson, would take command of Tactical Headquarters.   The other, Lt. Gen. Lucian K. Truscott, would command a new Chinese Combat Command (North), leaving McClure with what would become the Chinese Combat Command (South).   The dividing line would be the Yangtze. Simpson and the Generalissimo both endorsed this concept.[22]

Setting up a Chinese Combat Command north of the Yangtze brought two problems with it.   One was purely administrative, that of finding U.S. liaison personnel for the 80 divisions.   According to the practice in the 39 divisions, teams were to be sent to each division, army, and group army headquarters, totaling 1,461 officers and 2,429 enlisted men.   Truscott would be in operational control of the Chinese I, II, VIII, X, XI, and XII War Areas, when these were activated.[23]

The second problem, that of the Chinese Communists, was major and dramatic, for their territory lay north of the Yangtze.   If the new divisions were to begin fighting them instead of the Japanese the whole scheme would be endangered, while the larger consequences were unpredictable but obviously of the greatest importance.   So Wedemeyer sought to take appropriate action well in advance.   The solution he recommended to Nationalists and Communists alike was attachment of liaison teams to both sides, to provide him with factual data on any incident.   The background to this suggestion was Wedemeyer's belief that the Soviet Union, the British Commonwealth, and the United States should take strong measures to bring the two sides together.   Asked by Marshall for his opinions on the eve of the Potsdam Conference, Wedemeyer replied:

If Uncle Sugar, Russia, and Britain united strongly in their endeavor to bring about coalition of these two political parties in China by coercing both sides to make realistic concessions, serious post-war disturbance may be averted and timely effective military employment of all Chinese may be obtained against the Japanese.   I use the term coerce advisedly because it is my conviction that continued appeals to both sides couched in polite diplomatic terms will not accomplish unification.   There must be teeth in Big Three approach.[24]

[22] Rad WAR 17951, Marshall to Wedemeyer, 16 Jun 45; Rad CFB 39790, Maddocks to Marshall, 21 Jun 45; Rad CFB 1792, Wedemeyer to Marshall, 27 Jul 45.   Items 850, 868, 991, Bks 3 and 4, ACW Personal File.
[23] Memo 659-3, Brig Gen Ray Maddocks for Generalissimo, 25 Jul 45.   Bk 8, Wedemeyer Corresp with Chinese.
[24] (1) Rad CFB 526, Wedemeyer to Marshall, 9 Jul 45.   Item 924, ACW Personal File.   (2) Hearings Before the Subcommittee to Investigate the Administration of the Internal Security Act and other Internal Security Laws of the Committee of the Judiciary, United States Senate, 82d Congress.   First Session on Institute of Pacific Relations.   Part 3, p. 797.

The scheme for liaison teams to prevent Communist-Nationalist clashes was presented to the Generalissimo 30 July. He approved it, after suggesting that the Communist leader, Mao Tse-tung, be addressed as *Mister* rather than by his Communist title, *Chairman*.[25]

The avenue through which the proposal was made to the Chinese Communists was the American Army Observer Group at Yenan. The performance of this body had been a disappointment to Wedemeyer, who still felt, after the group had been almost a year in operation, that he acted in a vacuum as far as military intelligence on north China was concerned. One reason may have been that some of the group's personnel were preoccupied with political intelligence of the Chinese Communists, to the neglect of the military picture in north China. Another may have been that the Chinese Communists were unable to determine from the Americans' questions what was desired in the way of military intelligence. When the American order of battle expert was sent to Yenan, in September 1944, he found that he had to give his American colleagues a two months' training course to enable them to ask proper questions. In addition, Chinese Communist communications in north China were simple and overloaded, so that messages trickled into Yenan rather slowly. Last of all, and inevitably, the relations of the Americans in Yenan with the Chinese there fluctuated with the course of unification talks between Communists and Nationalists which Ambassador Hurley was conducting. The Communists were actively co-operative or merely polite as they were pleased or displeased with the progress of the negotiations. To them, military information was probably another bargaining tool, and in the Oriental fashion they proposed to use every bargaining asset they had.[26]

General Wedemeyer had also come to some conclusions about the quality of the advice and information current on the Chinese Communists. The political advisers who had been assigned to Stilwell's staff, then to his, and finally to Ambassador Hurley's, seemed to him to be primarily expert in Chinese culture, history, and language. He was not sure that this qualified them to speak with authority on political tendencies within the Chinese Communist Party, on the relationship of the several Communist parties to each other, and on other questions that might well affect the course of U.S. policy in China. So he sought for and obtained from G–2 in Washington the services of an expert on Soviet Communism and the Soviet Union, Col. Ivan D. Yeaton, to take command of the American Observer Group in Yenan.[27]

---

[25] Min, Mtg 68, Wedemeyer with Generalissimo, 30 Jul 45. Bk 1, Generalissimo Minutes.
[26] Capt. Robert L. Bodell, History of DIXIE Mission. OCMH.
[27] Interv with Col Yeaton, 3 Mar 52. Yeaton had been Chief, East European Section, G–2.

Yeaton presented Wedemeyer's letter to Mao about 30 July. In it Wedemeyer proposed that two American officers and five enlisted men, with a radio, be sent to each Nationalist and Communist division, in contact with or close to their Chinese opposites. These radio teams would render daily reports on unit movements down to and including companies. Wedemeyer pointed out here that there had been many conflicting reports of clashes between the Nationalists and Communists. Such a scheme would permit him to have a factual nonpartisan account to present to the United States. He told Mao Tse-tung that the Generalissimo had agreed, and urged Mao to do likewise, as a step toward averting civil war and achieving a united effort against Japan. But the march of events soon overtook this interesting suggestion.[28]

The progress of events also overtook what might have been a difficult situation for Wedemeyer, the use of American lend-lease arms by Chinese Nationalists to fight the Communists during hostilities against Japan. From time to time the Communists complained of such action by the Nationalists. Before late summer 1944, their complaints were almost certainly pure invention, intended to forestall any such diversion of lend-lease. But by late summer 1944, Navy Group, China, benefiting by the increased flow of tonnage over the Hump, began to receive several hundred tons a month of Hump tonnage. As noted above, Navy Group, China, worked closely with General Tai Li's secret police, and Wedemeyer believed they had issued supplies without accounting for them.

In June 1945 the Chinese Communists again complained about misuse of lend-lease by the Nationalist forces. Ambassador Hurley thought that the Communists were merely trying to stir up civil war. However, G–5 was concerned about the problem, and Wedemeyer took the complaints seriously enough to investigate the possibility that Navy Group, China, had joined in the emerging Chinese civil war. Wedemeyer appointed a board which included representatives of G–1, G–2, G–3, G–5, and Navy Group, China, with G–5 as chairman. On 22 August the board reported:

1. That no satisfactory evidence had been presented that Naval Group, China, personnel has been employed with Central Government or loyal patriotic troops against the Communists. However, the possibility exists, that they may be used in engagements if the Communists interfered with operations of the units against the Japanese.

2. That American equipment has been used at least defensively against the Communists.

3. That equipment has been furnished under other than lend-lease procedures; that no adequate records now exist of transfers made. . . .[29]

---

[28] Ltr, Wedemeyer to Mao, 29 Jul 45. Tab III, Item 5, History of DIXIE Mission.
[29] (1) Maj Martin F. Sullivan, G–5 Sec, USFCT, History of the Clandestine Branch, 15 Nov 45. OCMH. (2) Rad, Hurley to Secy State, 12 Jun 45. Item 12, Bk 3, Hurley Files.

The Chinese Reoccupy Their Land

As the Japanese forces in China proceeded to concentrate in the north China plain, and yield their holdings in south and central China, the Chinese troops began to flow into the vacuum created by the Japanese withdrawal. In north-central China, toward Lao-ho-kou and Hsian, the Chinese of the I War Area found themselves on the edge of the zone the Japanese meant to hold. The city of Hsi Hsia K'ou was the center of activity as Chinese units under one of the more capable and aggressive commanders and Japanese who intended to stay feinted, sparred, and occassionally clashed all during June and into July. By then the American liaison teams sent to the area during the Japanese drive on Lao-ho-kou were ready with training programs. Activity stopped as both sides broke contact—the Chinese to reorganize and train four armies, the Japanese content to hold.[30]

In central China, the Chinese had ended the Chihchiang campaign in contact with Japanese forces along the precampaign line Pao-ching–Hsinning. During June there were skirmishes around obscure little villages, as the victorious Chinese, from regiments freed of training schedules, kept touch with the Japanese. The skirmishes were patrol actions, village fighting, outpost clashes, but that they were taking place with the Chinese attacking showed how much the quality of the XXIV Group Army had improved over that of previous years. In late July General Wang's men were ready to make the diversionary attacks called for by RASHNESS. Two regiments of the 58th Division supported by a battalion of artillery retook Hsin-ning on 5 August, killing and capturing 100 Japanese. In this area, since it shielded the railway route north out of Kwangsi and Kweichow, the Japanese were obliged to hold, and only began falling back as the first week of August ended.[31]

The most extensive Japanese troop movements came in south China as the divisions there moved up the railway line toward Hankow and on to north China. The American liaison troops with the Chinese of the II and III Group Army commands did not believe that Chinese pressure was forcing the Japanese to withdraw, though they noted that Chinese communiqués spoke of heavy fighting and Chinese victories after pitched battles. The historian of the Chinese Combat Command called it:

. . . in no sense a combat operation similar to the Chihchiang defensive. It can better be understood as a Japanese troop movement, largely unopposed. Having decided to withdraw, the Japanese forces did withdraw in a leisurely and ordered manner. Chinese forces, unwilling to engage in, and unable to see any reason for, costly combat operations, followed closely but carefully. What fighting did occur was largely a matter of

---

[30] History of China Theater, Ch. X, pp. 4–10.
[31] *Ibid.,* pp. 15–19.

rear-guard patrol action. There were cases of Japanese platoons holding up Chinese regiments or divisions for several days or longer.[32]

The Japanese withdrawals of June 1945 from south China funneled through Liuchow. From Ho-chih on the west and the island of Hainan on the east, Japanese brigades and divisions slowly moved north. The forces retreating from Ho-chih turned on their pursuers at I-shan, perhaps to give units to the east time to clear the Liuchow bottleneck area. After taking I-shan on 10 June the Chinese were driven out the next day. The Japanese held it three days, then began moving east again. The Chinese followed after.

From Nanning, the Japanese retreated to Ta-tang, twenty-five miles southwest of Liuchow. They had to hold Ta-tang so that Ho-chih units could clear the area, and hold they did until late June. To occupy the Liuchow area the Chinese used the 29th Army plus the 175th Division of the 46th. By 22 June American liaison men could report that the city was on fire, a sure sign of imminent evacuation. Japanese resistance was limited to activity by isolated riflemen. The Chinese moved cautiously through them onto the outskirts of the former American base, now important to support of RASHNESS. The airfield was taken on the 26th, and by 1 July the Chinese had complete possession of Liuchow. The Japanese had had ample time for demolitions; the city was 60 percent burned and the airfield had thirty to forty large craters in the runway.

The Japanese retreat over the ninety miles to Kweilin paralleled that to Liuchow. Rear guards held off the Chinese while transport troops moved out equipment and demolition squads made ready to destroy utilities and bridges. North of Kweilin, however, the picture was different in that General Tang En-po's III Army Group command during July tried to cut the Japanese avenue of retreat to Heng-yang. One division from each of four armies was used. The Japanese defenses seem to have been on the reverse crests of the hills and ridges to the west of the route north. The Chinese attacked along a line all the way from I-ning just west of Kweilin to Chai-hsu, fifty miles north. The Japanese held stubbornly. The road net was notably poor, and lack of ammunition forced the Chinese 26th Division to fall back on one occasion.

By 26 July more Chinese from General Tang's army were up to the battle area, and an attack on Kweilin was possible. The CCC did not think that the Japanese would make a stand for Kweilin. Two Japanese divisions plus two brigades were believed to have cleared the area by the 26th. Next day, I-ning fell, and shortly after, Yung-fu, thirty miles south of Kweilin. Three days later the Chinese had taken Yung-fu, had covered the thirty miles, and were in Kweilin's southern suburbs. Soon after, the Japanese

[32] History of Chinese Combat Command, p. 11. OCMH.

LIUCHOW AIRSTRIP *as it looked when Chinese troops recaptured the airfield. Note large craters in runway.*

rear guards were pushed out of Kweilin, and as August began, the city was Chinese again. Except for Canton and Hong Kong, the biggest Japanese bases in south China had been relinquished by the Japanese. It was time to take Fort Bayard.[33]

What Are the Problems of a Sudden Peace?

Hints that events in the Pacific might be outstripping the course of the experiment in Sino-American co-operation to build a better Chinese Army, an experiment that had been under way intermittently since October 1941 when the American Military Mission to China began work, appeared in July. There were peace rumors. In distorted form, they possibly reflected happenings within Japan, where on 20 June the Emperor Hirohito moved to cut through the tangle of Japanese politics and personalities by inquiring about plans to end the war. The B–29's were devastating great areas of Japan's large cities, and her air defenses could not cope with these attacks. Japan's Navy was now grounded, camouflaged hulks, suitable for antiaircraft

---

[33] History of China Theater, Ch. X, pp. 32–34.

RETURNING TO LIUCHOW *1 July 1945, Chinese troops find the city virtually destroyed by the Japanese.*

batteries only.   The Americans firmly gripped Okinawa and Iwo Jima, close to Japan's shores.   The merchant navy was reduced to a few hundred thousand tons, and the specter of economic paralysis loomed.   The Japanese Army was intact, however, and many of its leaders pinned their hopes on one great and bloody battle on Japanese soil after which the Americans might offer terms.

The Emperor's intervention was a plain indication of the Imperial will, which under the Japanese constitution could at times have decisive power. Then came the conference at Potsdam in July 1945 between the Soviet Union, the British Commonwealth, and the United States, as a result of which there came what in effect were terms to the Japanese, with a threat of grievous harm if they were not accepted.   The United States understood that the Japanese declined them.   However, the highest military authorities in the United States now believed that Japanese surrender might not be long delayed.   On 30 July Marshall for the Joint Chiefs told Wedemeyer, MacArthur, and Nimitz that co-ordination of plans to be followed in event of Japanese surrender was a pressing necessity.   The Joint Chiefs thought it highly desirable to occupy key ports in Asia in this priority: Shanghai, Pusan, Chefoo, and Chin-huang-tao.   The radio went on: "The Joint Chiefs of Staff do not desire to become involved in the campaign in China on the mainland other than by air, but it is considered highly desirable to seize the ports in order better to facilitate the reoccupation of the country by Chinese forces." [34]

Wedemeyer had no illusions about the impact of a sudden peace on events in China. Not only were there the big problems of China, but there were also disturbing minor discords. There had been an increasing number of incidents between Americans and Chinese. These had been called to the Generalissimo's attention, with a note saying that there had been a steady growth in Chinese depredations on U.S. installations in China, and that local Chinese military and civil authorities had been most un-co-operative. Shootings, stabbings, affrays had occurred. Two U.S. soldiers had been killed by troops of the 30th Division. Moreover, there were morale problems among the Americans. Col. B. J. Birk, CCC surgeon, wrote to McClure on 24 July that morale in the CCC was "very low." He listed five reasons, ranging from prolonged service overseas to a "general feeling by the personnel that their efforts are futile." Across the letter McClure wrote: "C/S See if we can raise morale. R B McC." [35]

So, concluding a very long survey of the current picture for General Marshall, Wedemeyer wrote on 1 August:

We are striving to prepare for any eventuality reference Japanese capitulation—early and sudden peace, fighting for the next few months, and even an extended period of war. Frankly, if peace should come within the next few weeks we will be woefully unprepared in China. On the American side we could handle our own unilateral personnel and property interests but many of our activities are inextricably tied in with the Chinese, and, if peace comes suddenly, it is reasonable to expect widespread confusion and disorder. The Chinese have no plan for rehabilitation, prevention of epidemics, restoration of utilities, establishment of balanced economy and redisposition of millions of refugees. On the China Theater staff we have one U.S. military government officer, a Lieutenant Colonel Dobson, who at present is conducting a school in Chungking, teaching selected Chinese civilian officials the functions of civil affairs. This school has been established one week. I have emphasized to the Generalissimo the necessity for advanced planning in connection with the problems and he has issued instructions to his ministries. However, I am not optimistic about the results to be attained, if my experience with the military officials can be taken as a criterion. When in Washington last February I was informed that the United States would not become involved in the operation of civil affairs in China subsequent to Japanese surrender. We may be unavoidably drawn in as advisors to Chinese officials in a status analogous to that of Americans at present with Chinese military

---

[34] (1) USSBS, *Japan's Struggle To End the War* (Washington, 1946). (2) Rad WAR 40831, Marshall to MacArthur and Nimitz for action, info Wedemeyer, 30 Jul 45. Item 1000A, Bk 5, ACW Personal File.

[35] (1) Memo 640–19, Wedemeyer to Generalissimo, 15 Jul 45. Bk 8, Wedemeyer Corresp with Chinese. (2) Memorandum 651–7, Maddocks to Generalissimo, 20 July 1945, in the same file, summarizes a number of these incidents. (3) Min, Combined Staff Mtg 73, CCC and Chinese Supreme Hq, 3 Aug 45. China Theater Files, KCRC. (4) Ltr, Col Birk to McClure, 24 Jul 45. OCMH. This is the original.

forces. I am sure that you will agree that we should assist the Chinese in that manner to reestablish a modicum of order and normalcy.[36]

In accord with the JCS views on assisting Nationalist reoccupation of Japanese-held China, and with another request from Marshall for data on the Chinese attitude, Wedemeyer spent 31 July conferring with the Generalissimo and Soong. In the course of these discussions the Generalissimo made it clear that if American troops from the Pacific landed in China they must not be commanded by Stilwell. This was a major point to Soong and the Generalissimo, who stated their objections strongly, basing them on a clash of personalities and the need for a commander who had what they called "unity of spirit" with the Chinese. The Generalissimo agreed with the JCS that Pusan in Korea should be second only to Shanghai in priority of occupation, for in his opinion this would facilitate Chinese control of Korea before the Russians could establish themselves, and would forestall a Communist Korean Government. As for Chinese ports, the Generalissimo wanted U.S. troops landed there at once to hold them until Central Government forces could be flown in.

For his part, Wedemeyer warned the Generalissimo that lend-lease from the United States would stop. He had authority from the War Department to equip thirty-nine divisions, of which twenty now had 80 percent of their full Tables of Equipment. He did not list a Korean port among those to be occupied, nor did he, if the minutes are correct, react to the Generalissimo's suggestion that China occupy Korea. Wedemeyer agreed to do his best to fly in the Central Government forces, and hoped that occupation of a port would improve his capabilities. So far as possible, U.S. forces would not collaborate with the Communists. When the Generalissimo suggested that reluctant Japanese might be a problem requiring more lend-lease, Wedemeyer agreed and said he did not think there would be difficulty over lend-lease. He cautioned the Chinese to pay attention to the problems of civil affairs in reoccupied territory, for he did not think they were seriously aware of them. When the discussion ended, Wedemeyer agreed with the Generalisimo that ports should be occupied in this priority: Shanghai, Pusan, Taku, Canton, and Tsingtao.[37]

Reporting on this meeting, Wedemeyer said that the Generalissimo's comments on Stilwell were the first suggestion he had heard that the Chinese Army and people did not like Stilwell. Wedemeyer recommended that any U.S. forces landing in China be placed under his own command, that they seize ports to facilitate Nationalist redeployment, and that they avoid col-laboration with any forces opposing the Central Government. The Chinese

---

[36] Ltr, Wedemeyer to Marshall, 1 Aug 45. Case 61, OPD 319.1, Sec II.

[37] Min, Mtg 68A, Wedemeyer with Generalissimo, Soong, and Hurley, 31 Jul 45. Bk 1, Generalissimo Minutes.

needed help in redeployment, and were worried about internal problems. He closed with the warning: "Unless and until Central Government troops are [disposed] so that they can control communications, ports, financial and food centers it would be unsound to plan upon realistic Chinese assistance in the disarmament, demobilization, and deportation of Japanese forces on the Asiatic mainland." [38]

Events in the Pacific Overtake CARBONADO

Meanwhile, in the field and at the planners' desks, final preparations were being made to take Fort Bayard. Last-minute co-ordination on the inter-theater level was achieved through a conference at Guam on 6 August between representatives of China Theater, the Pacific theaters, and the War Department. General Simpson and General Boatner, of the CCC, plus key staff officers of Wedemeyer's headquarters, were present for China Theater. Obtaining naval service elements such as a barge pool and a construction battalion (stevedore) was discussed. Convoy lists were set up and naval protection by escort carriers and destroyer escorts arranged. The hydrographic features of Fort Bayard were analyzed. These were the quiet, unspectacular, earnest discussions of technical matters that must precede an amphibious operation. The conference adjourned; co-ordination was effected.

Within China, the final operational planning was done between the CCC, Tactical Headquarters, and theater G-3. Examining reports from the field, these agencies concluded that the Japanese had reduced their garrison on Liuchow Peninsula, at whose base was Fort Bayard, to some 6,500 men. Offshore, on Hainan, were 8,000 more. Three Japanese divisions and one independent mixed brigade in Indochina could intervene but this did not appear likely. However, these were formidable Japanese forces to oppose Chang's men. The risk was accepted in the belief that the Japanese supply situation did not permit the enemy to offer sustained resistance or to reinforce heavily. According to the Japanese postwar studies, the area garrison, far from being 6,500 strong, consisted of two battalions that were engaged in withdrawing on Canton.[39]

Prepared in June, the initial plans for the advance on Fort Bayard called for the drive to be made by the Chinese 46th Army after it had occupied Liuchow. General Wedemeyer could not approve the plan because the War Department planned to have three Liberty ships arrive at Fort Bayard 15 August; planning had to be based on that. Because this target date had to be met, Wedemeyer made a significant modification in the original concept of the operation by permitting use of the ALPHA divisions, among them

---

[38] Rad CFB 2305, Wedemeyer to Marshall, 1 Aug 45. Item 1001, Bk 5, ACW Personal File.
[39] Japanese Study 129, Map 6.

the elite New 1st Army. Given these resources, McClure estimated that on the basis of Chinese capabilities 1 September could be D Day. This was unacceptable, and theater headquarters suggested that elements of the 46th Army be sent toward Fort Bayard without waiting for the completion of operations around Liuchow. That city fell 1 July, releasing troops for the drive on Fort Bayard.

Perhaps as a result of these difficulties responsibility for making the operational plans was taken from CCC and given to General Weart's Tactical Headquarters on 17 July. Weart's later plans accepted the idea of an advance on Fort Bayard prior to Liuchow's fall, and events moved accordingly. In mid-July units of the 46th Army began moving toward the coast. The New 1st Army, being flown back to China, was to land at Nanning in east China rather than at Chanyi. By 26 July the 38th Division and army headquarters had landed at Nanning, about 200 miles west of Fort Bayard. Meanwhile, to help provide air cover for the Bayard operation, the 13th Army was en route to seize the Tanchuk airstrip, halfway between Liuchow and the coast. OSS groups had taken high ground overlooking the airfield on 3 July but lost it to a Japanese counterattack. In the next attempt, on or about 26 July, a regiment of the 89th Division took the heights and followed that success next day by taking the field. The town itself was occupied 5 August, and so that part of the Fort Bayard operation was successfully completed.

From Liuchow the 46th Army advanced steadily eastward. Not till 3 August did it meet the Japanese near Sui-chi, about twenty miles west of Fort Bayard. The Japanese reacted aggressively, attacking the right flank of the New 19th Division. The Chinese were present in too great strength, for the 175th and 188th Divisions came up and simply bypassed this Japanese concentration. The weather turned bad, hampering air supply, and the pace of the Chinese advance slowed. Then came the stunning news on 6 August that an atomic bomb had been dropped on Japan. Two days later the Soviet Union announced that it was entering the war on 9 August. These developments suggested to theater planners that the war might be ending, and the attack on Fort Bayard was halted to await developments. They were not long in coming.[40]

At 1845 Washington time, on 10 August, the State Department acknowledged receipt of a Japanese offer to accept the Potsdam terms, without prejudice to the Emperor's position. On that same day Wedemeyer received his first postwar directive, written in terms that confronted him with a dilemma he quickly recognized. The directive's architects prefaced its operative paragraphs by telling Wedemeyer that the directive "supplements" the 24 Oc-

---

[40] (1) History of China Theater, Ch. II.   (2) Bowman comments on draft MS.

tober 1944 directive, thus leaving intact his mission of advising and assisting the Generalissimo, then added a warning: "b. All of its provisions apply insofar as action in accordance therewith does not prejudice the basic U.S. principle that the United States will not support the Central Government of China in fratricidal war." [41]

Wedemeyer was told that help from MacArthur and Nimitz would be given to obtain control of key ports and communication centers in China, though there was no intent of involving U.S. troops in any major land campaign in China. When these supporting troops entered China, they would come under his command, and it would be his task to co-ordinate operations with the Generalissimo. The Generalissimo would have jurisdiction over the process of Japanese surrender in China, "except for any points such as Hong Kong, of which the status is in question. . . ." If through military necessity any Japanese forces surrendered to the Americans they would be turned over to the Central Government subject to assurance of satisfactory treatment from the Chinese. Wedemeyer would assist the Central Government in rapidly moving its forces to key areas in China, and would continue the necessary support which had become a normal adjunct to his mission.[42]

To Wedemeyer, completely cognizant of the menacing and complex problems emerging in the wake of war in China, this directive must have seemed a not very helpful guide, for in the second week of August he sought to persuade his superiors to transfer at least some of their attention from Japan to China. His radios to General Marshall give unmistakable expression to a fear that the United States would lose the rewards of victory if it did not take vigorous action in China. The background to his warnings was his recognition that the U.S.-sponsored divisions were not yet ready to maintain public order in China, that the Nationalists could not stand alone. Many years had passed before rebuilding the Chinese forces within China received first priority from the Chinese and American governments; the lost years were now exacting their price in the unreadiness of the Central Government to re-establish its authority in its own country.

On China's part, the Generalissimo through Wedemeyer told the United States that he was anxious to obtain American aid in disarming and demobilizing the Japanese forces in China. He envisioned three occupational areas, centering on Nanking, Peiping, and Canton, with Americans as chiefs of staff to the Chinese area commanders. Five American divisions were requested, two for the Taku area of north China, two for Shanghai, and one for Canton. He also remarked that at Cairo in December 1943 President Roosevelt had promised to equip ninety Chinese Divisions.

---

[41] Rad, WARX 47513, JCS to Wedemeyer, info MacArthur, Nimitz, Spaatz, and Wheeler, 10 Aug 45. ACW Personal File.
    [42] *Ibid.*

Wedemeyer underscored the Generalissimo's appeal with the blunt caution that the U.S. Government might be failing to appreciate "the explosive and portentous possibilities in China when Japan surrenders." He saw little possibility of trouble in Japan proper, but two major dangers on the mainland, that the Chinese Communists might begin civil war and that the Japanese forces might refuse to surrender. He urged that two U.S. divisions be sent to Shanghai, one to Taku, and a regiment to Canton, that high priority be given to occupation of Chinese seaports, and that the Japanese be instructed to surrender only to the Chinese Nationalists, never to the Communists (who now asserted that right).[43]

The War Department's initial responses to Wedemeyer's warnings and questions indicate that the United States had not settled on what was to be its postwar role in China. The messages came in piecemeal fashion, answering now one and now another of his operational queries but remaining silent on the great problems of Asia which he raised so urgently. His initial directive was a contradiction in terms, for it told him to continue his support of the Chinese Nationalists, then ordered him not to support them if they engaged in civil war. To this, Wedemeyer replied that on 19 August he was engaged in transporting Chinese troops to the key areas of China that they might be secured and the Japanese disarmed. This support could be construed as a deceptive maneuver, to give the Nationalists an advantage over the Communists, and the foreign correspondents were beginning to press him hard on just that line.

In its other messages, of 7 and 14 August, the Department warned him that he would receive only two divisions, and these would arrive in sections as shipping became available. He was directed as his first task to secure the key areas of China—the order so difficult to square with one part of his directive, however well it matched the other—and further told that when the situation firmed he should discuss this mission with General MacArthur. A personal "eyes alone" radio from General Marshall suggested that the Chief of Staff did not share Wedemeyer's fears in regard to Asia for it dealt only with Marshall's fears that the Japanese might be so afraid of both Chinese vengeance and administrative ineptitude that they would not yield.

Immediately after Wedemeyer's warnings China Theater took a step which foreshadowed a serious and self-imposed limitation on what the Americans might do in China, for on 22 August 1945 all training under American supervision was "suspended," probably because the units concerned had to take part in reoccupying Japanese-held China. This meant the dismantling of the elaborate apparatus of liaison and operational control, advice, and assistance that Wedemeyer had erected on the foundation laid by Stilwell.

---

[43] (1) Rad CFB 4317, Wedemeyer to Marshall, 11 Aug 45, Item 1047, Bk 5; (2) Rad CFBX 4352, Wedemeyer to Marshall, 12 Aug 45, Item 1045. ACW Personal File.

Thenceforth, the armies of the Central Government were increasingly on their own, though they had not been brought to the standard Wedemeyer contemplated.[44]

In the midst of these exchanges, the drive on Fort Bayard was halted 12 August by the War Department, to await developments, and active hostilities ended 14 August 1945. The soldiers who ran cheering into the streets, the Chinese civilians who offered incense and set off firecrackers, the Americans at home who shouted and wept and danced and prayed were all spared foreknowledge that in the future the day they celebrated would mark not the end of the twentieth century drama of conflict between Pacific powers but the end only of an act. The curtain was to rise again.

[44] (1) Formal Historical Record, for the Period 29 Jan 45–1 Sep 45, Prep for Gen King, Hq IV Gp Army Comd CCC USFCT, 1 Sep 45. OCMH. (2) Rad, CFB 4082, Wedemeyer to Marshall, 9 Aug 45, Item 1034, Bk 5; (3) Rad, WARX 47945, JCS to Wedemeyer, 11 Aug 45, Item 1044; (4) Rad, CFBX 4352, Wedemeyer to Marshall, 12 Aug 45, Item 1045; (5) Rad, WAR 48661, Marshall to Wedemeyer, 12 Aug 45, Item 1064; (6) Rad, WAR 49574, Marshall to Wedemeyer, 14 Aug 45, Item 1075; (7) Rad, WAR 49550, Marshall to Wedemeyer, 14 Aug 45, Item 1080. All in ACW Personal File.

Bibliographical Note

The manuscript of this volume was basically completed in 1954 and its content reflects sources available at that time. These sources fall in three categories: official records, collections of private papers, and published works.

Official Records

Official records are the principal source of information for this volume.*

(1) The major U.S. Army documentary sources used in the writing of this volume are to be found in two of The Adjutant General's records depositories—one in Alexandria, Virginia (the Special Records Branch), and the other in Kansas City, Missouri (the Kansas City Records Center). Between them these two depositories have those minutes, correspondence, and staff studies of the Combined and Joint Chiefs of Staff that are contained in the records of the War Department General Staff (mainly, the Office of the Chief of Staff and the War Plans Division/Operations Division); the war diaries of the Southeast Asia Command; and the records of the United States Forces in the China Theater (including the General Joseph Stilwell's Radio File, 1942–44) and the United States Forces in the India–Burma Theater and their subordinate commands. Of particular value were the Wedemeyer Files among the records of the United States Forces in the China Theater, including messages for the period 1944–45 and minutes of General Wedemeyer's conferences with the Generalissimo, a collection of Wedemeyer correspondence located with the records of the China Service Command, files of the Northern Combat Area Command containing documentation on the fighting in North Burma, and records of the Chinese Combat Command and Y–Force, subordinate commands of the United States Forces in the China Theater.

(2) U.S. Army radiograms will be found either in the Staff Communications Office, Office of the Chief of Staff, Department of the Army, or in files of India–Burma and China Theaters and their subordinate commands. Location of the latter radios is shown in the footnotes. Messages sent and received through Staff Communications are identified according to their local reference numbers and date, or by the CM–IN and CM–OUT numbers. Messages sent and received through theater agencies are identified by the call

---

*The date of each document is determined by the time zone at the point of origin; the exception is classified messages, which are dated upon receipt in Washington.

letters of their several headquarters, for example, CAK, CRA, CFB, and CHC.

(3) A variety of miscellaneous records was collected by the Historical Sections of India–Burma and China Theaters. Among records is a collection of papers on the DIXIE Mission, the U.S. Observer Group in Yenan. These are cited as History of DIXIE Mission and are located in the Office of the Chief of Military History.

(4) An account of Japanese operations and strategy, prepared by former Japanese officers, is found in the monographs cited as Japanese Studies in World War II. These monographs were prepared under the auspices of the G–2 Historical Section, U.S. Far Eastern Command, and translated by the Allied Translation and Interrogation Section (ATIS), Headquarters, Supreme Commander for the Allied Powers. Most of the directives and orders issued by Japanese *Imperial General Headquarters* are in volumes entitled *Imperial General Headquarters Army Directives or Orders.* They were compiled by the Military Historical Division, Military Intelligence Section, General Headquarters, Far East Command. Copies of the Japanese records are in the possession of OCMH.

The SEATIC Bulletins, prepared by the Southeast Asia Translation and Interrogation Center of SEAC, are based on interrogation of senior officers and staff members of *Burma Area Army* and its principal subordinate headquarters.

Thanks to Col. Preston J. C. Murphy, Chief, Military History Section, Special Staff, Far East Command, it was possible to obtain the comments of a number of former Japanese officers and their responses to inquiries framed by the authors. These recollections, which are on file in OCMH, offer interesting material on Sino-Japanese relations, 1944–45, and the war in China. Col. Susumu Nishiura, Chief Historian, Japanese Self-defense Forces, commented at length on the manuscript.

(5) Manuscript histories, prepared during or after the war, were drawn on extensively in preparation of this volume, far more so than in the case of the two earlier volumes in the CBI subseries. By the summer of 1945, India–Burma Theater and China Theater headquarters had fully staffed Historical Sections, which attempted to write narrative histories according to professional standards of research and documentation. Col. Harry L. Mayfield, of the India–Burma Theater, was responsible for the successful completion of manuscript histories of the Services of Supply in India–Burma, 1944–45, of the India–Burma Theater 1944–45 (two volumes), of the India–Burma Theater 1945–46 (three volumes), of the History of Combat in India–Burma Theater, and of the Northern Combat Area Command (three volumes). The volumes are extensively documented and are a rich source of material on the India–Burma Theater in its last eighteen months. Those portions of the

present volume which cover the India–Burma Theater are in a sense the final product of Colonel Mayfield's section, of which Riley Sunderland was a member. Copies of these manuscripts are currently in the possession of OCMH. In China Theater, Capt. Fenton Keyes, Chief, Historical Section, aided by a small staff, wrote a manuscript history of the China Theater. Much of the portions of the present volume dealing with China Theater is based on this staff's work, supplemented by the Wedemeyer material which was not then available to it.

The History of Northern Area Combat Command was begun by Capt. Edward Fisher while he was an officer of the NCAC staff and was completed by him at theater headquarters in New Delhi. Like all the wartime manuscripts, it is a first draft but is of great importance as a source on the North Burma Campaign. It included a great number of appendixes, many with original material. The Operational Record of Eleventh Army Group and ALFSEA, November 1943–August 1945, distributed by the British War Office, is a terse but comprehensive account of the fighting in Burma.

Information on collateral activities can be found in the manuscript U.S. Army Medical Service in Combat in India and Burma, 1942–1945, by Dr. James H. Stone; History of the Ramgarh Training Center, 30 June 1942–15 May 1945; History of the First Provisional Tank Group; U.S. Army Transportation in China, Burma, India during World War II, by Joseph Bykofsky. These manuscripts are in the possession of OCMH. Background information on the state of the Chinese economy in 1944 can be found in Economic Conditions in Free China and Their Effect on Army Procurement, January 1945, which is Inclosure 4, Appendix E, to the manuscript, History of Advance Section No. 1 (SOS in China), History of the Services of Supply in China–Burma–India, 1942–1944, in OCMH.

Air Force operations are described in Despatch on Air Operations in Eastern Air Command (SEA) Covering the Period 15 December 1943 to 1 June 1945, a record prepared for Lt. Gen. George E. Stratemeyer; Fourteenth Air Force Annual Summary, 1944; Growth, Development, and Operating Procedures of Air Supply and Evacuation System, NCAC Front, Burma Campaign, 1943–1945, prepared by the Military Observer Group, New Delhi, India. With the exception of the Fourteenth Air Force Annual Summary, 1944, which is now in the U.S. Air Force Historical Division, Air University Library, Maxwell Air Force Base, Alabama, the above manuscript histories are in the custody of OCMH.

Collections of Private Papers

To a lesser degree than in Volumes I and II of this subseries, this volume has drawn on private papers. These include: (1) collections of personal papers; (2) diaries; (3) letters and inclosures.

Personal Papers.   Information on the CBI Theater before Wedemeyer and Sultan assumed command is to be found in the records of General Joseph W. Stilwell, in the Hoover Library, Palo Alto, California, described at length in the biblographical notes to the earlier volumes of this subseries.

The personal papers of Maj. Gen. Patrick J. Hurley, U.S.A., Ret., are a rich source of information on the higher-level military and diplomatic aspects of China Theater from October 1944 to the spring of 1946.   General Hurley was most systematic in preserving his papers, and the greater part of them is bound in folders (referred to as books in the footnotes), with individual items numbered within the folder.   Currently the papers are in General Hurley's custody.   Extensive notes on the Hurley papers, taken by Romanus and Sunderland, are in OCMH.

Diaries.   The notebook kept by Brig. Gen. Earnest F. Easterbrook to record official matters that came to his attention as regimental commander is like a diary, though completely impersonal.   General Easterbrook also permitted use of his situation maps.

Letters.   The Office of the Chief of Military History has a number of letters from participants in events in India–Burma and China Theaters.   They contain comment and criticism on draft manuscripts of the volumes in this subseries that are a valuable source of retrospective information.   Of greatest interest is the file marked HIS 330.14, 1947–1957.

Published Works

Leahy, William D. *I Was There: The Personal Story of the Chief of Staff to Presidents Roosevelt and Truman Based on His Notes and Diaries Made at the Time.* New York: Whittlesey House, 1950.

Sherwood, Robert E. *Roosevelt and Hopkins: An Intimate History.* New York: Harper & Brothers, 1948.

Stimson, Henry L., and McGeorge Bundy. *On Active Service in Peace and War.* New York: Harper & Brothers, 1948.

United States Congress. Hearings of the Committee on Armed Services and the Committee on Foreign Relations, United States Senate, on the Military Situation in the Far East. Washington: U.S. Government Printing Office, 1951.

United States Department of State. *Foreign Relations of the United States: Diplomatic Papers,* Department of State Publication 6199, *The Conferences at Malta and Yalta, 1945,* Parts I and II. Washington: U.S. Government Printing Office, 1955.

———. *United States Relations with China: With Special Reference to the Period 1944–1949.* Washington: U.S. Government Printing Office, 1949.

Background on the Chinese Army in Burma, Chinese political thinking, and philosophy may be found in:

Ho Yung-chi. *The Big Circle.* New York: The Exposition Press, 1948.

On more strictly military matters are:

Field, James A. Jr. *The Japanese at Leyte Gulf, the SHO Operation.* Princeton: Princeton University Press, 1947.

Military History Section, Special Staff, General Headquarters, Far East Command. *The Imperial Japanese Navy in World War II*, 1952.

Ramgarh: Now It Can Be Told. Ranchi, India, 1945.

Roberts, Brig. M. R., DSO. *Golden Arrow* (Aldershot, 1952).

Report and Supplement for Combined Chiefs of Staff by the Supreme Allied Commander, South-East Asia, 1943–1946, Vice-Admiral Viscount Mountbatten of Burma. New Delhi, India, July 30, 1947.

Romanus, Charles F., and Riley Sunderland. *Stilwell's Mission to China* and *Stilwell's Command Problems*. UNITED STATES ARMY IN WORLD WAR II. Washington: U.S. Government Printing Office, 1953 and 1956.

Craven, Wesley Frank, and James Lea Cate, eds., *The Army Air Forces in World War II: IV, The Pacific: Guadalcanal to Saipan, August 1942 to July 1944.* Chicago: The University of Chicago Press, 1950.

———. *The Army Air Forces in World War II: V, The Pacific: MATTERHORN to Nagasaki. June 1944 to August 1945.* Chicago: The University of Chicago Press, 1953.

Treadwell, Mattie E. *The Women's Army Corps.* UNITED STATES ARMY IN WORLD WAR II. Washington: U.S. Government Printing Office, 1954.

United States Strategic Bombing Survey. *Air Operations in China, Burma, India.* Washington: U.S. Government Printing Office, 1947.

Woodward, C. Vann. *The Battle for Leyte Gulf.* New York: The Macmillan Company, 1947.

Glossary

AAF	Army Air Forces
Actg CofS	Acting Chief of Staff
ADMS	Assistant Director of Medical Service (British)
AF	Air Force
AGO	Adjutant General's Office
ALFSEA	Allied Land Forces, Southeast Asia
ALPHA	Plan to defend Kunming and Chungking
ASF	Army Service Forces
Asgd	Assigned
AT	Antitank
ATC	Air Transport Command
BAN	Japanese *Burma Area Army* plan to defend the Mandalay area
BETA	Plan to take the Canton–Hong Kong Area
Bk	Book
BROADWAY	British airstrip, twenty-seven miles southeast of Hopin, Burma
CACW	Chinese-American Composite Wing
CAI	Chinese Army in India
CAPITAL	Plan to take north Burma, originally Phases I and II of Plan Y, which were very similar to Plan X
CARBONADO	Revised BETA
CBI	China–Burma–India
CCC	Chinese Combat Command
CCS	Combined Chiefs of Staff
CG	Commanding General
CM–IN	Classified Message sent into Pentagon
CM–OUT	Classified Message sent out of Pentagon
CO	Commanding Officer
Comd	Command
Conf	Conference
Corresp	Correspondence
CT	China Theater
CT&CC	Chinese Training and Combat Command
CTC	Chinese Training Command
DAN	Japanese *Burma Area Army* plan to keep China blockaded
DCofS	Deputy Chief of Staff
Div	Division
DRB	Departmental Records Branch
DRACULA	Sea-air assault on Rangoon; originally Plan Z
EAC	Eastern Air Command
ELOC	Eastern line of communications
	Field Artillery

FEA	Foreign Economic Administration
FECOM	Far East Command
G–1	Personnel section of divisional or higher staff
G–2	Intelligence section
G–3	Operations section
G–4	Supply section
G–5	Civil affairs/military government section
GALAHAD	5307th Composite Unit (Provisional), known colloquially as "Merrill's Marauders"
GHQ(I)	General Headquarters (India)
Gmo	Generalissimo Chiang Kai-shek
GO	General Order
Gp	Group
Hist	Historical
Hq	Headquarters
HRB	Historical Records Branch
HUMPALCO	Hump Tonnage Allocation and Control Office
IBT	India–Burma Theater
ICD	India-China Division, Air Transport Command
ICHIGO	Japanese operation to take the East China airfields
JCS	Joint Chiefs of Staff
KAN	Japanese *Burma Area Army* plan to defend the Burma coast
KCRC	Kansas City Records Center, Adjutant General's Office
KETSU	Japanese plan to defend the homeland
LUX Convoy	A convoy of vehicles organized in the Persian Gulf Command which entered China via the Ledo/Burma Road
MARS Task Force	5332d Brigade (Provisional)
Mins	Minutes
Mtg	Meeting
NCAC	Northern Combat Area Command
OCTAGON	Quebec Conference, September 1944
OCMH	Office, Chief of Military History
OSS	Office of Strategic Services
OPD	Operations Division, War Department General Staff
Opnl Dir	Operational directive
Opns Jnl	Operations journal
Plan X	Plan to occupy North Burma down to Kalewa–Lashio
Plan Y	Plan to drive on Central Burma
Plan Z	Plan for direct assault by sea and air on Rangoon
QM	Quartermaster
RAF	Royal Air Force
RASHNESS	Revised CARBONADO
ROOSTER	Flying the 22d Division (Chinese) to Chihchiang
RPC	Ration Purchasing Commission (American)
Rpt	Report
Rr Ech	Rear Echelon
S–3	A battalion or regimental operations section
SACO	Sino-American Special Technical Cooperative Organization
SACSEA	Supreme Allied Command, Southeast Asia

SEAC	Southeast Asia Command
SEATIC	Southeast Asia Translation and Interrogation Center
Sec	Section
SHO	Japanese operational plan to counterattack U.S. forces attempting to penetrate the Western Pacific area
SOS	Services of Supply
Sv	Service
USAF	United States Army Forces; United States Air Force
USFCT	United States Forces, China Theater
WDGS	War Department General Staff
Y–Force	30 U.S.-sponsored Chinese divisions in Yunnan
Y–FOS	Y–Force Operations Staff (American)
Z–Force	30 Chinese divisions the United States once hoped to reorganize in East China
Z–FOS	Z–Force Operations Staff (American)

Basic Military Map Symbols*

Symbols within a rectangle indicate a military unit, within a triangle an observation post, and within a circle a supply point.

Military Units—Identification

Antiaircraft Artillery . . . .

Armored Command . . . .

Army Air Forces . . . .

Artillery, except Antiaircraft and Coast Artillery . . . .

Cavalry, Horse . . . .

Cavalry, Mechanized . . . .

Chemical Warfare Service . . . .

Coast Artillery . . . .

Engineers . . . .

Infantry . . . .

Medical Corps . . . .

Ordnance Department . . . .

Quartermaster Corps . . . .

Signal Corps . . . .

Tank Destroyer . . . .

Transportation Corps . . . .

Veterinary Corps . . . .

Airborne units are designated by combining a gull wing symbol with the arm or service symbol:

Airborne Artillery . . . .

Airborne Infantry . . . .

*For complete listing of symbols in use during the World War II period, see FM 21–30, dated October 1943, from which these are taken.

Size Symbols

The following symbols placed either in boundary lines or above the rectangle, triangle, or circle inclosing the identifying arm or service symbol indicate the size of military organization:

Squad . . . .   ●

Section . . . .   ● ●

Platoon . . . .   ● ● ●

Company, troop, battery, Air Force flight   I

Battalion, cavalry squadron, or Air Force squadron . . . .   I I

Regiment or group; combat team (with abbreviation CT following identifying numeral) . . . .   I I I

Brigade, Combat Command of Armored Division, or Air Force Wing   X

Division or Command of an Air Force   XX

Corps or Air Force   XXX

Army   XXXX

Group of Armies   XXXXX

EXAMPLES

The letter or number to the left of the symbol indicates the unit designation; that to the right, the designation of the parent unit to which it belongs. Letters or numbers above or below boundary lines designate the units separated by the lines:

Company A, 137th Infantry . . . .   A⊠137

8th Field Artillery Battalion . . . .   ▫•▫8

Combat Command A, 1st Armored Division . . . .   A⬭I

Observation Post, 23d Infantry . . . .   △23

Command Post, 5th Infantry Division . . . .   ⊠5

Boundary between 137th and 138th Infantry . . . .   —137 III 138—

Weapons

Machine gun . . . .   ●→

Gun . . . .   ●

Gun battery . . . .   ⊔⊔⊔

Howitzer or Mortar . . . .   ◆

Tank . . . .   ◇

Self-propelled gun . . . .   ⬡●

United States Army in World War II

The multivolume series, UNITED STATES ARMY IN WORLD WAR II, consists of a number of subseries which are tentatively planned as follows: The War Department, The Army Air Forces, The Army Ground Forces, The Army Service Forces, Defense of the Western Hemisphere, The War in the Pacific, European Theater of Operations, Mediterranean Theater of Operations, The Middle East Theater, The China–Burma–India Theater, The Technical Services, Special Studies, and Pictorial Record.

The following volumes have been published or are in press: *

The War Department
> *Chief of Staff: Prewar Plans and Preparation*
> *Washington Command Post: The Operations Division*
> *Strategic Planning for Coalition Warfare: 1941–1942*
> *Strategic Planning for Coalition Warfare: 1943–1944*
> *Global Logistics and Strategy: 1940–1943*
> *The Army and Economic Mobilization*
> *The Army and Industrial Manpower*

The Army Ground Forces
> *The Organization of Ground Combat Troops*
> *The Procurement and Training of Ground Combat Troops*

The Army Service Forces
> *The Organization and Role of the Army Service Forces*

Defense of the Western Hemisphere
> *The Framework of Hemisphere Defense*

The War in the Pacific
> *Okinawa: The Last Battle*
> *Guadalcanal: The First Offensive*
> *The Approach to the Philippines*
> *The Fall of the Philippines*
> *Leyte: Return to the Philippines*
> *Seizure of the Gilberts and Marshalls*
> *Victory in Papua*
> *CARTWHEEL: The Reduction of Rabaul*

*The volumes on the Army Air Forces, published by the University of Chicago Press, are not included in this list.

European Theater of Operations
> *The Lorraine Campaign*
> *Cross-Channel Attack*
> *Logistical Support of the Armies, Volume I*
> *Logistical Support of the Armies, Volume II*
> *The Supreme Command*

Mediterranean Theater of Operations
> *Northwest Africa: Seizing the Initiative in the West*

The Middle East Theater
> *The Persian Corridor and Aid to Russia*

The China–Burma–India Theater
> *Stilwell's Mission to China*
> *Stilwell's Command Problems*
> *Time Runs Out in CBI*

The Technical Services
> *The Transportation Corps: Responsibilities, Organization and Operations*
> *The Transportation Corps: Movements, Training, and Supply*
> *The Transportation Corps: Operations Overseas*
> *The Quartermaster Corps: Organization, Supply, and Services, Volume I*
> *The Quartermaster Corps: Organization, Supply, and Services, Volume II*
> *The Quartermaster Corps, Operations in the War Against Japan*
> *The Ordnance Department: Planning Munitions for War*
> *The Signal Corps: The Emergency*
> *The Signal Corps: The Test*
> *The Medical Department: Hospitalization and Evacuation, Zone of Interior*
> *The Corps of Engineers: Troops and Equipment*
> *The Chemical Corps: Organizing for War*

Special Studies
> *Three Battles: Arnaville, Altuzzo, and Schmidt*
> *The Women's Army Corps*
> *Rearming the French*
> *Chronology: 1941–1945*
> *Military Relations Between the United States and Canada: 1939–1945*

Pictorial Record
> *The War Against Germany and Italy: Mediterranean and Adjacent Areas*
> *The War Against Germany: Europe and Adjacent Areas*
> *The War Against Japan*

Index

U.S. GOVERNMENT PRINTING OFFICE: 1959 OF—463995